Six Years That Shook The World

W.R.
KOSS

SIX YEARS THAT SHOOK THE WORLD

The Story of the Internet, Telecom
and Optical Market Revolutions

2006

Six Years That Shook The World

CONTENTS

ACKNOWLEDGEMENTS

This manuscript would not have been possible without a long career in the networking and technology industry and for the many friendships, colleagues and mentors I was fortunate to be blessed with during that time. The content of this book is as I remember from first person experience, from research, or retold to me by friends and colleagues who were there. As for the final manuscript, I would like to extend a personal acknowledgement of appreciation and gratitude to the following people who played important roles in helping form the content of the manuscript: Gregory Koss, Larry Samberg, Steve Waszak, Bill Janeway, Bart Stuck and Anura Guruge. A final note of thanks to my wife Francesca for her patience during the development of the manuscript as her support was beyond measure.

FOUNDATIONS

Lost, yesterday, somewhere between Sunrise and Sunset, two golden hours, each set with sixty diamond minutes. No reward is offered, for they are gone forever. - Horace Mann

The revolution, spawned by the internet, fiber optics, computers and telecom deregulation has not ended. This revolution continues to be a driver of globalization by accelerating the pace of economic and social interaction as well as a dependency on and adoption of technology. We have only glimpsed the beginning of what this great revolution will yield – yet the economic and financial trauma of the past several years has left many with a negative judgment of this revolution. We must not forget that we are witnessing the affects of a significant cycle of change and not the end of a great revolution. Perhaps in the time of our children, or our children's children, will the effects of this revolution be calculable. Revolutions are not simple affairs that are easily concluded. They are long, traumatic affairs that tear apart societies and inflict change on a scale unanticipated in the time leading up to the revolution. America has been a declared, sovereign nation-state for two hundred and thirty years come 2006. By global standards, the United States is still a young nation-state. Could our founding fathers have envisioned the results of their actions in the 1700s, only a few years into their revolution? In the same perspective, the total impact wrought by the internet, telecom privatization, and fiber optic revolutions of the 1990s cannot be declared at such a young age. These revolutions are still evolving and their impact will be played out over many decades and calculable only in time when the mantle of leadership has been passed to a new generation. In 1994, Al Gore, then Vice President of the United States declared, *"I have a vision for a planetary information network, the mother of all networks. A vast web of electronic pathways that will put enormous amounts of valuable information at the fingertips of everyone,"* [see Al Gore, *Inside the White House*, Red Herring, August 1994]. The significance of this statement is that the internet, even in its earliest days, was in the fore of public thought leadership and a driver of significant regulatory and innovative technological change.

During the five-hundred and eighteen days from August 2001 to January 2003 the world changed significantly from the last years of the prior millennium. The attacks in New York and Washington on September 11, 2001 were the beginning of a series of global geo-political events that changed our perception of the world. Terrorism had come to America and in a macro view the events of 9/11 were a result of the perception that America was the leading force behind globalization, which was a distinct product of the 1990s and the end to the Cold War. 9/11 was a violent reaction to the declaration of the Second American Renaissance that followed the end of the Cold War. There are distinct linkages between the first American Renaissance, which was promoted by Henry R. Luce, began with the victories of the Second World War and the adoption of the Chicago School of economic thought by Ronald Reagan, and closed with the ending of the Cold War. The Second American Renaissance began with the collapse of the Soviet Union in 1991 and the emergence of America as the only global military, economic, and social super power. *"The rest of the world may improve their public policies through accelerated deregulation and prudent fiscal policy. They may reform their closed and opaque financial systems; they many embrace more fully the technological and logistical revolutions sweeping the business world; they may send their sons and daughters to business school; they may strive to open up their more parochial business and national cultures. But America will not be standing still. If anything, American business should widen its lead over the rest of the world. France had the seventeenth century, Britain the nineteenth, and America the twentieth. It will also have the twenty-first,"* [see *A Second American Century*, Foreign Affairs, May/June 1998, Mortimer B. Zuckerman, page 31]. The 1990s were a confluence of events that drove a powerful social undercurrent that economically separated nation-states, facilitated social interaction on a global scale and became a unifying and procreating driver for anti-American forces.

For the people involved in the technology industries in the 1990s, the boom period of the 1990s was an unprecedented event that rivaled the gold, steel, railroad, and oil rushes from prior centuries. *"We have reached the next big moment of opportunity in the history of technology. As Sun Microsystems' co-founder Bill Joy predicted in his 1990 Churchill Club address, 1995 would be the cusp for new huge opportunities, and I think he was right on! Look at some of the basic indices to support this argument. In 1995, there were more PCs sold in the United States than TVs. By 1997, this will be the case around the world. In 1995, there were more e-mail messages sent {95 billion} than postal messages {85 billion}. I read that in THE HERRING! Must be true, right?"* George Gilder made this statement in the February 1996 edition of Red Herring and he was not alone. Many intellectuals who provide thought leadership believed that the end of the Cold War, the emergence of the United States as the only global superpower, and the adoption of the internet as a unifying force based on mathematics was the dawn of a new era for mankind. Even the CEOs of leading technology companies were consumed by the perception of the limitless potential of their industry *"{The Internet will be a}...major traveler of change into the next millennium, everyone will be connected to everyone and everything,"* John Chambers, CEO of Cisco Systems, 1999 CES Show.

Post the 9/11 attacks and throughout 2002, technology markets in the U.S. and abroad entered into a market ecosystem recession that negatively impacted global financial markets. The devastation within the telecom services and technology equipment industries in the Untied States was unparalleled. Thousands of people were unemployed and hundreds of companies were forced into bankruptcy. In a little more than twenty-eight months, more than a half a million people were unemployed. By historical comparisons, the rapid collapse of the American based telecom industry was far faster and affected far more people than the collapse of the American automotive industry in the late 1970s and into the early 1980s – yet no one has made a movie about this collapse. There has been no *"Bernie and Me"* or *"Armstrong and Me"* or *"Rich McGinn and Me"* or *"John Roth and Me"* movies made. The insular industry of telecom services and technology equipment were not main stream industries that generated awareness beyond the specific business media that covered the telecom industry.

Within the technology industry, there were weekly terrifying stories of layoffs and downsizing. Rumors posted on various web sites, providing leading indicators of recession that was taking hold. Everyone heard about the collapse of the real estate market in Silicon Valley and how hundreds of companies were trying to negotiate out of extraordinary high building leases. It seemed that there was a well-funded technology startup closing every day. How could it all go wrong? What had changed to enable an entire industry to collapse faster than the boom and bust cycles of the oil business, the railroads in the 19th century and the tulip bubble in the Netherlands? The list of technology startups shut down was shocking. Below is a partial list of some of the well-funded companies closed in the networking equipment vertical:

Company	Founded	Closed	Capital ($Ms)	Company	Founded	Closed	Capital ($Ms)
Tachion	1996	2001	$85	Cinta Networks	1999	2002	$75
Chairo Networks	1996	2006	$234	Equipe	1999	2004	$103
Krestrel Solutions	1997	2002	$187	Gotham Networks	1999	2002	$33
Pluris	1997	2002	$215	Geyser Networks	1999	2002	$64.50
Ironbridge	1997	2001	$85	Accelight	1999	2003	$78
Ennovate	1997	2001	$81.50	Centerpoint	1999	2002	$200
Luminous Networks	1998	2005	$183	Celox Networks	1999	2002	$155
Brightlink	1998	2002	$121	Crescent Networks	1999	2003	$66
Village Networks	1998	2002	$50	Coriolis	1999	2004	$84
Cereva	1998	2002	$157	Appian Networks	1999	2004	$80
Corona	1998	2003	$78	Polaris Networks	2000	2003	$77
Mayan Networks	1998	2001	$90	Metera	2000	2001	$30
Innovance	1998	2003	$130	Allegro Networks	2000	2003	$89
Airfiber	1998	2003	$92	Tiburon Networks	2000	2002	$33
Tenor Networks	1998	2003	$120	Photuris Networks	2000	2004	$107
Alidian Networks	1998	2003	$100	Cratos	2000	2001	$16
Mahi Networks	1999	2005	$255	Sedona Networks	2000	2001	$22
OptiMight	1999	2002	$57.50	Maple Optical	2000	2003	$100
Metro-Optix	1999	2003	$155	Latus Networks	2000	2001	$28.10
PhotonEx	1999	2003	$178	Ceyba	2000	2003	$93
Network Photonics	1999	2003	$106.50	Coree	2000	2002	$30
Gluon Networks	1999	2004	$76	Opthos	2000	2002	$36.50
Jasmine Networks	1999	2002	$72	Axiowave	2000	2004	$130.00

Figure 1: Startup Shutdown (Source: Author's Research)

The total value invested in the companies from the above table is $4.639 billion dollars. The $4.639 billion from this list is real cash lost on bad investments – not paper profits and losses. The money invested in these companies is gone. It is spent. In comparison, when Long Term Capital Management collapsed in 1998, it required a $3.65 billion investment from a syndicate of banks to keep solvent [see, *When Genius Failed*, Roger Lowenstein, 2000]. It might be easy for the government of the United States to make a three billion dollar error and recover, but it is unlikely that university educated professionals who are entrusted with making significant returns on capital can make a $4.639 billion dollar error without being held accountable. From a historical perspective, the amount of capital invested in failed companies, in a single technology vertical market called networking equipment suppliers, is more than the total amount of venture capital committed in 1980 across all market segments in the United States. There is no comparable event in the history of venture capital to weigh against what has happened between January 2001 and December 2005. An error of this size has a dramatic affect on the private capital market as well as the surviving companies and venture capital firms. There had to be a set of reasons or an explanation to the headlines that went by each week about Enron, Worldcom, Global Crossing, Lucent, Nortel, and others. The go-go nineties were very much a decade for personal achievement. The social undercurrents within America anecdotally supported a thesis of irrational exuberance, consumerism and social achievement based on wealth. Consumer consummation for self-indulgence and status awareness outwardly appeared to be accelerating towards the new millennium. We applauded the successful technology entrepreneurs who sold their companies for vast sums and then purchased basketball teams, vineyards, private jets, second homes in posh locations and mega yachts. At some point it became respectable to pay outrageous prices for bottles of wine, multi-million dollar homes and expensive cars. If the 1980s were a decade of indulgence – the 1990s ended as a decade of indulgence an order of magnitude larger than the 1980s. During the years *"...1996-2000, the high-yield market raised $502 billion, of which $240 billion was for telecom and media. To put this in perspective, throughout the 1980s, it raised only $160 billion. A key difference is that the companies that raised money using junk bonds in the 1980s were industrial companies with hard assets that generated positive cash flow and had products,"* [see Ravi Suria, interview with Thestreet.com, March 28, 2001].

Embedded in this culture were the companies and intellectuals who championed the Second American Renaissance. *"WorldCom is at the intersection of everything we like – no carrier in the world can offer the integrated set of facilities that it does. The company has nothing to lose and everything to gain,"* said Jack Grubman in the November 1997 issue of *Red Herring*. *"The achievements of business in America grew out of a culture that has long valued individualism, entrepreneurialism, pragmatism, and novelty. American culture nourishes its mavericks, cherishes its young, welcomes newcomers, and dramatically opens to energy and talent rising from the bottom up. In the nineteenth century, men like Carnegie, Frick, Rockefeller, and Morgan seized the chances. Today, their heirs are Bill Gates, Ted Turner, Larry Ellison, Craig McCaw and the many others who vie for the top of the Forbes' list of the 400 richest people in America,"* [see *A Second American Century*, Foreign Affairs, May/June 1998, Mortimer B. Zuckerman, page 22]. New metrics were adopted to assess value as we entered the new era of the new economy *"As with all Internet stocks, a valuation is clearly more art than science,"* was the opinion of Henry Blodget in December 1998. The mid nineteen nineties were a period of a revolution in technology, telecom, and in the stock markets. People referred to the internet, telecom and optical markets (i.e. ITO) as revolutions. The stock markets soared to new heights, the Cold War was won; we declared an end to big government and connected computers to the internet. It seemed as if it was a magical time. *"As technologies and industries converge, what is emerging is a new 'global information industry.' The new marketplace will no longer be divided along current sectoral lines. There may not be cable companies or phone companies or computer companies, as such... There will be information conduits, information providers, and information appliances and information consumers,"* Al Gore, Vice President of the United States.

A sleepy industry, called telecom, exploded on America and the world. A digital revolution was upon us. Do you remember the Qwest commercial that showed a man checking into a hotel in the desert and asking about the services only to receive a reply that the hotel did not have any services – but it did have every movie and television show ever created available at any time? Grand sweeping declarations were made about the revolution that was swirling around the world in 1996. *"Industry is being driven by two exponentials. The first is the Law of the Microcosm, which states that computer processing power and value double every 18 months. This law has really been the driving force behind world economic growth over the last 20 years. The huge new opportunity that is emerging derives from the Law of the Telecosm, which declares that when you take any n computers, and connect them on networks, you get n2 performance and value. And it's not just an increase in the number of computers, but also an increase in the power of each computer. So the steady increase in the power of the computer is imparted by Law of the Microcosm, and compounded by the increase in the value of the system imparted by Law of the Telecosm. These two compounding exponentials explain the explosive rise of the Internet and all the technologies associated with it. Now things will really start popping,"* George Gilder, February 1996. The digital revolution of the late 1990s did create unimaginable wealth and unequalled failures in six summers. Clear, dramatic statements outlining the stakes of the proposition were made. *"I'll say it once again, the companies that do not develop an Internet strategy will not be competitive,"* John Doerr, Partner, Kleiner Perkins Caufield & Byers.

Despite the viewpoint of the internet's relevance to future competitiveness of business, in seventy-two months a giant industry was born and torn down. How could this happen? How could trillions of dollars in value be created and eliminated in the time that it takes a child to go from conception to the first grade? Following 9/11, it became increasingly plausible that globalization on social, economic and technical levels was affecting geo-political balances – but the effects were far reaching and deeper than first accepted. This realization created a new set of questions. Is there a linkage between financial markets, technology, social undercurrents, nationalism, religious fundamentalism, and a variety of geo-political drivers under the macro term of globalization? Are new methods required to determine the creation and destruction of markets? Can a new method of understanding technology markets be applied to measuring value? Does this measurement or understanding of markets help predict the future? These were the questions that began to come into focus post 9/11. This discourse endeavors to understand how regulated markets interact with technology and financial markets and how they relate to change and human nature.

The emergence of the commercial internet in the early1990s and the passage of the Telecom Reform Act of 1996 laid the foundation for the rapid growth of three markets that were fundamentally linked. In turn, these markets play an important role in the evolution of globalization. The internet, telecom and optical markets were called revolutionary by market analysts, industry consultants, financial professionals, and industry sycophants. The *"new economy is the internet,"* said John Chambers, CEO of Cisco Systems in 1999. The foundation of the internet was the personal computer, networking technology and optics. In the spring of 1994 Amazon.com founder and CEO Jeff Bezos came across the statistic that the number of bits traveling across the internet was increasing by 2,300 percent per year. Anything growing at that rate was viewed as an indication that something important and special was occurring.

Reflecting upon the quotes by various intellectuals on the internet, new economy and its impact on our lives, leads to an unimpressive conclusion. The scope and magnitude of the comments are amusing now – but at the time, there was sufficient evidence to support these perspectives. These are not quotes from people on the lunatic fringe of society – these are quotes from accomplished, educated intellectuals who are regarded as thought leaders within society. They have reached their positions within our society because they have distinguished themselves and have a record of accomplishment. They are respected and their opinions are sought after. Even in early 2000, there were few people who were offering cautionary remarks such as *"A lot of the thinking these days is much too oriented toward money and cashing out rather than building a strong organization with good people, good products, and a defensible strategy. It's really important for all of you entrepreneurs out there to remember this, because it's what ultimately will bring all this crashing down,"* [see, Richard Burnes, Partner, Charles River Ventures, January 2000]. Knowing the credibility of these people, it leads to the question; how was the environment that supported such exuberance created? What was so convincing that it was the driver of a trillion dollar investment? What was the foundation and causes of this revolution? How did we arrive at a point that where we were convinced that we were creating a new economy that was revolutionary and unlike anything before?

Hypothesis: The internet and telecom boom of the 1990s and its crash post-2000 were the product of a cycle of regulation and deregulation that will, in time, result in the change of the regulatory controls on the service provider industry. These are the same controls that were changed in 1934 and 1996 that fostered a massive economic investment in technology and telecom services. For more than seventy years, the regulation of telecom services has been the purview of the Federal Communication Commission. In order to guarantee the investment required to provide universal service, the telecom industry of the United States became a regulated industry in 1934; thus protected from market forces. In return for protection from market forces, AT&T accepted the mandate of universal service. Over time, the affect of regulation, protection, and universal service created an artificial cost for services that restricted innovation and the deployment of new services. The breakup of AT&T in 1984, and the deregulation of the telecom industry in 1996, was championed in the belief that this would result in a rich set of new services delivered within a competitive market by a variety of companies at lower costs to the end consumers. The result of deregulation of the telecom industry was the (a) release of the inherent market value that had been building and contained by regulation, (b) over investment in the telecom market post deregulation that was seeking to extract the inherent value, (c) the deployment of enough infrastructure to create the genesis of a pull economic model, (d) but not enough infrastructure to deliver on the promises of a digital revolution or a new economy and (e) the concentration of market share within a few service providers that do not have healthy business models to support the capital investments required to deliver on a broadband universal service. The end-result of deregulation of the telecom industry in 1996 is that further deregulation is required to create a free market as well as the imposition of a service or usage fee that will be directed towards capital investments for technology infrastructure. Investment in the communication infrastructure is mandatory to enable the United States to be a leader in the emerging pull economic structure. The proceeds of this service fee will be overseen by state or local public commissions. If the government chooses to impose new regulations to protect the companies in the market, as it did in the first great cycle of regulation in 1934-1996 and the second cycle 1996 to the present day, the result will be the creation of a protected market in which inherent value will be artificially created, contained and a few large companies will dominate and the communications infrastructure of the United States will suffer. Future thought leaders will then argue for the deregulation of the industry structure in order to garner the inherent market value contained in the artificial market structure as well as to foster competition, innovation, and reach to marginal cost for services. The effect of this cycle can be anticipated and applied to a variety of industries and markets. If the government chooses to completely deregulate, unprotect companies from competitors and market forces, this will create a free market, but it must include a mechanism to ensure that all geographic markets receive infrastructure investment – this would ensure the establishment of a real and complete technology infrastructure for a new economy in the United States.

The model developed from studying the telecom industry is based on an assessment of market share. Building a market model around the concept of market share enables the evaluation of markets, and companies as markets evolve through a change event (e.g. regulatory or technological). When a change event or revolution occurs, market share that was static becomes fluid. Static markets contain some amount of inherent value. As market share becomes fluid, inherent value is released from a stable, static market structure. The potential release of inherent value is the driver of financial capital to be invested with the objective of capturing the previously static inherent value in the new fluid market structure. This is the course of events post the Telecom Act of 1996. A previously regulated and static market structure became fluid. Investment capital flowed into companies throughout the ecosystem of companies that composed the telecom and technology markets. The acquisition of market share by companies can be understood by analyzing the structure of regulation of the markets and the flow of capital within the market ecosystem. This model can be applied to most industries in which a regulatory or technology events change the structures which drive the ebb and flow of market share.

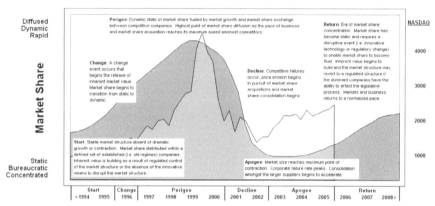

Figure 3: G3 Market Model for ITO Revolution with Superimposed NASDAQ Composite Index

The market model above is called the Generation 3 Market Model or G3MM. Throughout this discourse we will use the G3MM to analyze the internet, telecom, and optical markets of the 1990s. The G3MM has six distinct phases that will analyze the context of the subject markets in the proceeding chapters. The model is constructed on the X axis of time and the distribution of market share amongst competing companies on the Y axis. Both of the X and Y measurements are variable, therefore there can be an infinite number of competitive companies and the period of time can be months, quarters, or years. As a general introduction, the G3MM is designed to reflect the evolution of a stable market or the creation of no market once a significant competitive or unnatural change event occurs. In the case of the internet, telecom, and optical markets of the 1990s, we use the deregulation of the internet as well as the deregulation of the telecom service market in the U.S. as the significant change event. Additionally, it is possible to use the G3MM to reflect the introduction of new technologies as a corollary to Moore's Law.

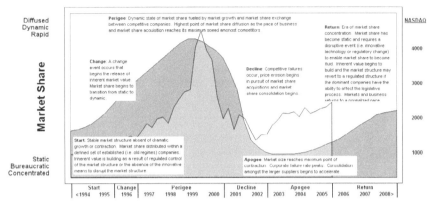

Figure 3: G3 Market Model for ITO Revolution with Superimposed NASDAQ Composite Index

In the supporting essays beyond the overview of the G3MM within the internet, telecom and optical revolution of the 1990s, we will overlay the G3MM with a social model for sociopolitical change. Joseph Schumpeter wrote in *The Theory of Economic Development*, *"Social facts are, at least immediately, results of human conduct, economic facts results of economic conduct. And the latter may be defined as conduct directed towards the acquisition of goods. In this sense, we also speak of an economic motive to action, of economic forces in social an economic like, and so forth. However, since we are concerned only with that economic conduct which is directed towards the acquisition of goods through exchange or production, we shall restrict the concept of it to these types of acquisition, while we shall leave that wider compass to the concept of economic motive and economic force, because we need both of them outside the narrow field within which we shall speak of economic conduct."* Wherein Schumpeter declined to include social forces and outside forces in his circular flow of economic life, we will endeavor to include the affect of these forces on market development. We will not consider an *"isolated community,"* but rather, examine a market and the affect of regulation and social forces on that market. In retrospect, we have learned that beliefs such as *"...technological paradigms are neither artificial nor arbitrary: they are the governing force that underlies human progress..."* are simply not true [see *Telecosm,* by George Gilder, 2000, page 59]. What I believe to be true is that our sociopolitical and market structures undergo a well-defined process of change and that this process of change can be modeled.

The underlying driver of human progress is the human condition. Schumpeter stated in *The Theory of Economic Development* that *"Economic activity may have any motive, even a spiritual one, but its meaning is always the satisfaction of wants."* The process of change and the political aspects of change are well understood. We have witnessed many revolutions in complex societies since the dawn of the European Enlightenment. The process in which humans invoke political and social change varies in subtleties, but the process of change and revolution can be modeled. Change can be anticipated, especially in artificial markets governed by regulation; therefore, we should be able to successfully apply a model for change to markets. Technology revolutions are not different from markets. The creation of markets is no different from the process of understanding business. Markets are created, suppliers are formed to acquire revenue from said markets and eventually the market becomes well defined amongst a number of suppliers until a change, or a revolution, affects the structure of the market. Aristotle concluded that Man is by definition a political animal, long before the invention of the internet.

PRICE, VALUE, AND RISK

It takes a national war to weld the parts together by giving individuals and groups memories of a struggle in common. Needless to add, nationalism can arise only when a nation in this full sense has come into being.

- Jacques Barzun

IBM introduced the mainframe computer, called the S/360 in 1965. With the availability of commercial computing power, businesses were given the capability to increase productivity and business planning through computational analysis. Computational analysis draws upon historical data created by business transactions to identify trends and develop models that are used to create and refine business practices. This is a process of analyzing lagging business indicators of ever increasing age. For the past forty years, this practice has been the model for businesses planning. As a result of the internet, telecom, and optical revolutions, a sufficient amount of technology infrastructure has been deployed to enable the evolution from the use of lagging business indicators to the use of near real time business indicators. This is a deep and profound change that affects the relationship between (a) technology, (b) financial markets, (c) the assessment of risk and (4) where and how value will be created. These four underlying elements were important drivers of the internet, telecom and optical revolutions that were a product of deregulation, available capital, and the perceived migration to a new economy. The collapse of the technology bubble was the product of unrealized, inferred expectations measured through a stochastic process on the basis of time. It was the element of time that was incorrectly perceived – not the expectation of the fundamental changes wrought by the internet, telecom, and optical revolutions.

The internet, telecom and optical (i.e. ITO) Revolution accelerated the impending assimilation of two disciplines, behavioral economics and computational (i.e. adaptive) economics, to quantify, assess, and measure risk in proportion to value to determine a state of expectation. The assimilation occurs due to the evolution from a push economic model to a pull economic model. The consideration of risk management and how underlying technology changes are affecting behavioral sciences was first brought to my attention by Bill Janeway, Vice Chairman of Warburg-Pincus, well after what I thought was the final draft of this manuscript. From his assertion of the importance of risk analysis as a critical component of economics and its linkage to information technology, I was able to find the links from quantitative economics, to behavior economics, to the political theories of Crane Brinton, to the contributions made by the intellectuals who shaped military strategies at the RAND Corporation in the 1950-1970s, to John Boyd, and finally to the amalgamation of these disciplines today in the result of the internet, telecom, and optical revolutions. Interestingly, in a time of computational and near real time business acceleration, the regulatory policies of the United States are focused on controlling information and slowing the ability of corporations to utilize emerging information tools to manage and deploy risk as a business tool. This is primarily being accomplished through fair disclosure regulation and Sarbanes-Oxley Section 404 compliance.

Forming an Opinion

The theory of rational expectations finds its roots in the development of computational economics that began in the U.S. after the Second World War and accelerated through the work of John Muth in the early 1960s. The core meaning of rational expectations is the belief that people form judgments, or best guesses, or expected models of the future using all available information. If the same set of information is available to all people, the conclusions by separate people and groups will be the same or similar. Unexpected events, termed shocks by many economists, cannot be anticipated by everyone and therefore, everyone's conclusion will be equally affected. Robert Lucas advanced the rational expectations hypothesis and for his work he was awarded the Nobel Prize in Economics in 1995. The contribution that Lucas made was in promoting a theory that became known as the Lucas Critique. The Lucas Critique states that prediction of the future using historical variables and the rational expectations theory would be false if an event alters the relationship between the variables (i.e. actors). Lucas went further and concluded that the market had only one equilibrium point and it was from this point that participants in the market will begin to form opinions and judgments. This was important because of the rise of adaptive expectations.

The concept of adaptive expectations implies that people will form judgments about the future, based on what has happened in the past. If a series of shocks occur, the models using historical data will lead people to believe that this is the norm, which is a departure from the long term past, and thus begin to anticipate further shocks as their prediction of the future. Hence, the use of adaptive expectations increases the level of endogenous risk in the models or opinions of the future if the data used to build conclusions does not remain stationary. The process becomes self-fulfilling because the use of historical (i.e. lagging) indicators to develop models or expected results becomes driven by assumed future changes, events, or shocks. For example, economists and analysts often anticipate interest rate changes from central banks before these changes are actually announced and implemented by central banks. Financial models are then fine tuned, based upon the actual information, when it is made available to all people. When the new data is entered into the models with the historical data, a revised future prediction is created, by the models using the historical data with the newest data points added. Before a central bank changes interest rates, the financial markets are already trading on models that have been built using the presumed equilibrium point of the market, post the interest rate change.

Drawing upon historical data, economists and stock analysts build models that reflect their expectations for the future, based on assumed risks and the potential to create value. As the future is non-quantifiable, these models are based on assumptions. *"If people were rational then their rationality would cause them to figure out predicable patterns from the past and adapt, so that past patterns would be completely useless for predicting the future,"* [see *Fooled by Randomness*, Nassim Nicholas Taleb, 2001, page 98]. The assumptions used to model future expectations may or may not have some historical basis as a foundation. If we were building a five year future model of General Motor's ability to sell cars, we have a massive amount of historical data to draw upon. If we were building a five year model of a new company called X that was just created, we have no historical data upon which to predict revenues. Both models are highly speculative with a varying degree of risk. In the early 1990s as telecom deregulation neared and the internet began to permeate society, the investment in the technology sector was driven by market models that predicted a shift in productivity, thus creating new value in new sectors of the economy. The concept of building an information based economy was a central theme to the Telecom Act of 1996. Thought leadership injected into society by economists, visionaries, analysts, venture capitalists, consultants and business leaders who created business cases based upon future projections of market development, market sizes, technology life-cycles, and the ability of companies to capture market share (i.e. revenues) and generate earnings. As identified in the succeeding essays, historical statistical trends were used to project the future of the internet, telecom, optical, and technology markets such as the adoption rate of televisions, telephones, internet traffic growth rates, and capital expenditure rates. *"Practitioners of these methods measure risks, using a tool of past history as an indication of the future. We will jut say at this point that the mere possibility of the distributions not being stationary makes the entire concept seem like a costly (perhaps very costly) mistake,"* [see Taleb, page 98].

An important leveling event that occurred during the ITO Revolution was adoption of Regulation FD on September 23, 2000. This law required corporations to equitably disclose material information. Before the adoption of the regulation, corporations had the ability to selectively release material information to industry analysts. Investment firms where able to use the research generated by analysts from selective disclosure events to upgrade or downgrade stocks, based upon the results of the financial models that had been updated with the early release of material information. This essentially provided a class division of who had updated information and who had increasingly lagging information that was material to assessment of corporate and market performance.

Keynes and the State of Long Term Expectations

In 1936, John Maynard Keynes published his manuscript for economists entitled *The General Theory of Employment, Interest, and Money*. Throughout the following essays we will continually find evidence that the retreat from economic policies labeled "Keynesian," that began in the late 1970s in Britain, to economic policies of free markets or the Chicago School of economics was a macro enabler of the ITO Revolution [see page 48-49]. Although the retreat from state ownership of the commanding heights of the economy through privatization and deregulation would become an important driver of technology and telecom investment in the 1990s, there is another Keynes contribution that is often overlooked and that is the state of long term expectation. This contribution is applicable from a historical perspective to the ITO Revolution and the capital invested in the new economy, but it is the potential influence that this Keynes thesis will have in union with the information revolution, which is being enabled by technology and the successful proofs from the ITO Revolution that is of interest over the long term.

Keynes defines the state of long term expectation as the basis upon which decisions are made. The level of confidence in the forecast or model of long term expectations for a company is how the value of the company is derived. *"The state of long-term expectation, upon which our decisions are based, does not solely depend, therefore, on the most probable forecast we can make. It also depends on the confidence with which we make this forecast — on how highly we rate the likelihood of our best forecast turning out quite wrong. If we expect large changes but are very uncertain as to what precise form these changes will take, then our confidence will be weak. The state of confidence, as they term it, is a matter to which practical men always pay the closest and most anxious attention,"* [see Keynes, page 148]. The level of confidence in the long-term expectation for a company is derived from assessing all the knowledge that concerns the company, including the macro state of the market or markets in which the company is involved. *"We are assuming, in effect, that the existing market valuation, however arrived at, is uniquely correct in relation to our existing knowledge of the facts which will influence the yield of the investment, and that it will only change in proportion to changes in this knowledge; though, philosophically speaking, it cannot be uniquely correct, since our existing knowledge does not provide a sufficient basis for a calculated mathematical expectation,"* [see Keynes, page 152].

Complicating the determination of value based upon long term expectations is the fleeting nature of the facts and data points used to determine valuation. Data is rarely current or real time. It is best classified as lagging indicators that are historical in nature. If companies take weeks or months to report quarterly results, how is that an indication of how their present day business is succeeding? Most leadership teams within public companies are worried about meeting objectives in the current quarter – not reviewing the past. Predicting the future is not a precise function. In stable market conditions in which companies possess market share that has minimal fluctuation due to competitive forces, we would expect fewer dynamic changes to the conventional valuation of company. In conditions in which market share is dynamic, we would expect the state of long term expectations to change frequently; which is why corporate leaders are often reluctant to provide forward looking guidance. *"A conventional valuation which is established as the outcome of the mass psychology of a large number of ignorant individuals is liable to change violently as the result of a sudden fluctuation of opinion due to factors which do not really make much difference to the prospective yield; since there will be no strong roots of conviction to hold it steady,"* [see Keynes, page 154].

Keynes adds another important element to his thesis which was derived from his observation of markets and investing. He made the assertion that a stock market is equivalent to a casino and he reached this conclusion after observing the stock market in the U.S. and determining that the brightest minds were not concerned with building long-term value, building companies, or assessing the state of long term expectations – but rather with making money. This is where he defined a conflict of interest between various parties investing capital in a financial market. *"It happens, however that the energies and skill of the professional investor and speculator are mainly occupied otherwise. For most of these persons are, in fact, largely concerned, not with making superior long-term forecasts of the probable yield of an investment over its whole life, but with foreseeing changes in the conventional basis of valuation a short time ahead of the general public. They are concerned, not with what an investment is really worth to a man who buys it 'for keeps', but with what the market will value it at, under the influence of mass psychology, three months or a year hence,"* [see Keynes, page 155]. If price is not derived from the state of long term expectations, then it must be valued by some other set of metrics. Keynes described this metric as the assessment of price based upon the determination of average opinion of all investors using all available information and anticipating change. *"Thus the professional investor if forced to concern himself with the anticipation of impending changes, in the news of or in the atmosphere, of the kind by which experience shows that the mass psychology of the market is most influenced,"* [see Keynes, page 155].

Keynes went further in his essay and provided a metaphor to describe how markets determine price. In hindsight to the ITO Revolution and the run up of the stock markets in late 1990s, this metaphor seems accurate. *"Or, to change the metaphor slightly, professional investment may be likened to those newspaper competitions in which the competitors have to pick out the six prettiest faces from a hundred photographs, the prize being awarded to the competitor whose choice most nearly corresponds to the average preferences of the competitors as a whole; so that each competitor has to pick, not those faces which he himself finds prettiest, but those which he thinks likeliest to catch the fancy of the other competitors, all of whom are looking at the problem from the same point of view. It is not a case of choosing those which, to the best of one's judgment, are really the prettiest, nor even those which average opinion genuinely thinks the prettiest. We have reached the third degree where we devote our intelligences to anticipating what average opinion expects the average opinion to be. And there are some, I believe, who practise the fourth, fifth and higher degrees,"* [see Keynes, page 156]. If we think through the IPO process that thousands technology and telecom companies engaged in during the 1990s, we see the function of pricing the initial public offering as a function of average opinion. Facts, projections, models, trends et hoc genus omne were a function of creating opinion and driving the determination of the average opinion of the mass of investors, higher.

In the final essay of this manuscript, the linkage between Keynes and Boyd will be explored. Both of these thought leaders reached the similar conclusions from different application backgrounds. Keynes looked at how perception and judgments are formed (i.e. price is determined) within financial markets and Boyd looked at how perception and judgments are formed within the context of warfare. Both concluded that risk and the ability to succeed are inherent within the context of the market or theater of operations. Boyd determined that strategy is the process of forming judgments about the judgments of others and anticipating the ability to form judgments, hence disrupting their decision making process. As we will see with the ITO Revolution, the winning companies clearly anticipated the strategy of companies that lost. Within the financial markets, the expectations used to promote and price companies, were in direct conflict with the strategies employed by companies to acquire and control market share. In the endeavors of war, business and financial markets, only your appointment can decide when others are defeated and in this respect, Keynes and Boyd clearly accepted that victory is determined in the mind of others.

The Two Sides to Risk

When determining the state of expectations, there are two types of risks that affect the average opinion of the price of a company. The first form of risk is called exogenous. Exogenous risks are risks that exist outside of the markets – outside of the category of rationally considered risks to a company. Exogenous risks are often termed "shocks." Example of exogenous risks, or shocks, include 9/11, Hurricane Katrina, and the Iraq invasion of Kuwait in 1990. These risks are difficult to model and difficult to anticipate and quantify – hence most people believe that these events affect all investors in the market equally since few, if any, anticipated their occurrence in absence of trending data.

The second type of risk that exists is called endogenous risk. Endogenous risk originates from within the market and increases by internal growth. Endogenous risks are the product of the market itself. If Keynes is correct and price is a function of the average of the determination of the average opinion of all investors, using all available information, then risk to price becomes a problem of stationarity. *"We take past history as a single homogeneous sample and believe that we have considerably increased our knowledge of the future from the observation of the sample of the past...in other words, what if things have changed?"* [see Taleb, page 97]. This is the point at which the output of the ITO Revolution will have an impact on price within financial markets and the value of companies with business markets. Two examples of endogenous risk from the ITO Revolution can be illustrated by the herding nature of venture capital investments and the belief that internet traffic was doubling every 100 days.

In terms of venture capital investing in technology companies, a herding pattering was clearly visible. How many internet search engines or web portal sites were required? How many pet supply or grocery delivery services were needed? If the U.S. required two or three additional long-haul companies, speculative capital provided us with ten. If one DSLAM company was founded, venture capitalists were quick to give us five more. This is the herding nature based on stationary extrapolation of historical data to determine a speculative future. In respect to the internet doubling every 100 days, as late as August 2000, this belief was being speculated upon by mainstream media as a proof of the new economy.

Amos Tversky and Daniel Kahneman were pioneers in the study of cognitive science – how humans handle risk and the manner in which cognitive powers can be applied to economics. Together, they developed what became known as the prospect theory. In short, the prospect theory suggests that people are more motivated by losses than by gains. They developed a model which showed that the way in which an investment is framed affects the choice that people will make. The term "frame" is being used in the economic context. A foundation of behavioral economics is that framing biases affect how investment and lending decisions are made. Investors are more likely to be motivated by losses, than by rational choices. Within the concept of endogenous risk, the contributions of Tversky, Kahneman, and Shiller begin to harmonize and provide five behavioral attributes that can be identified in the ITO Revolution. Robert J. Shiller helped popularize the perspective that information has negative value and can force completely rational people to participate in a herd behavior produced by an information cascade [see, *Irrational Exuberance*, Robert Shiller, 2000, page 151].

- **Need for Thought Anchors**: The process of making decisions is most comfortable when we can associate the decision to that which is familiar. We tend to justify a decision by saying, "this is just like when we made the decision to do X last year." We begin with what is familiar and try to associate future with the past. John G. Stoessinger described this action as image transfer because "*…policy makers often transfer an image automatically from one place to another or from one time to another without careful empirical comparison,*" [see *Nations in Darkness*, John G. Stoessinger, 1971, page 279]. Dr. David D. Burns described this behavior as "*all-or-nothing thinking*" or "*labeling*" behavior [see *The Feeling Good Book*, David D. Burns, 1989, page 8-11]. It is much easier for humans to use thought anchors to build their decision making process around – rather than pursue unfamiliar thought positions.

- **Power of Story and Legends**: Decision making based on story and legend often motivates more than facts and research. Humans are emotionally driven people. That is why revolutions are emotionally draining events. The power of story and legends is a basing of decisions based on simple reasons and not investigating and understanding the complexities of the decision criteria.

- **Overconfidence and Ignorance**: There is a tendency for humans to be overly confident on subject matters on which they are enormously ignorant.

- **Herding Behavior**: The power of the crowd. The power of revolution. In the absence of facts, or when facing a daunting amount of work to justify a decision, it is easier to follow the crowd.

- **Denial – Failure to Accept Mistakes**: Humans rarely admit, or learn from, their mistakes. Mistakes are a natural byproduct of being human. Admitting and learning from mistakes is an unnatural human activity.

Assessing exogenous or endogenous risks necessitates an assessment of value. In business markets and technology markets, value is created by controlling market share. Value is the derivative of the size of the market, the profitability potential of the market and a company's control of market share within the market. The quality of a market is a product of the size of the market and the ability of companies to generate profits in a specific market or set of markets. The U.S. telecom market had for many years existed as a (a) large market and (b) highly profitable market because it was regulated by the government and therefore possessed artificial price points that protected the companies who controlled market share from price erosion due to competitive, technological, and market forces. The size of a market may expand and contract, which affects value, but a company's value is still a product of the quality of the market (i.e. ability to generate profits) in which they operate, the market share they control, and the assessment of risks to these two variables, which can be termed "the state of long term expectations." The risks of changes in the quality of the market, positively or negatively, and risks to a company's ability to control market share are the basis of upon which value is determined – but this is not how value is priced in the market.

Keynes states that financial markets price companies on the assessment of the average opinion of investors in the market, which is derived from the state of long term expectations. Companies are not priced on the value they will posses over the long term, but rather on what the consensus of opinion of the price will be amongst the investors in the market at a given moment. Value is a judgment of a company's ability to execute and the long term worth of the quality of their market or markets. Price is a judgment of what the investors think the average opinion of a price should be for a company. Price may not have any relation to value. Value may not have any relation to price. If price and value are different measurements, then the risks to price and value are separate functions.

- <u>Value</u>: Value is the determination of the quality of the market and a company's capacity to execute within the market. The quality of a market is a product of the size of the market and the ability for companies to generate profits in the market. Capacity is a measurement of a company's ability to control market share and generate profits.

- **Price**: Price is as defined by Keynes. It is the function of the average opinion as to what the average price of a stock will be in the market.

Value and price are both subject to endogenous and exogenous risks. A popular conclusion has been that the technology and telecom bubble of the late 1990s was a one time occurrence similar to the tulip bubble in the Netherlands. Clearly there was an overspend and belief in unreasonable business assumptions, but what if the bubble was a perfect storm created by a repetitious cycle that may not result in a bubble of similar size again, but the pace, cadence, and economic ecosystem developed will remain as a permanent structure albeit in a smaller market size? The hypothesis has been advanced that a pull based economy is emerging from the traditional push economic structure. The emergence of this new economic ecosystem is the product of the technology and telecom bubble that peaked with the dawn of the new millennium. The full aspect of this economic structure will be explored in the final essay, but if it is true, then it will have an affect on risk and value assessments.

Game Theory and RAND

In 1928, John van Neumann, a brilliant mathematician, devised a theory that would affect economic and military thought for many years to come. The theory that Neumann developed was based upon several observations he made during a game of poker. The first observation that he made was that wining and losing was the interdependent upon all players. A wining strategy was not solely based upon a single player's strategy – but rather the product of all the player's strategies. In order to devise a winning strategy, Neumann had to account for other player's strategies, assuming that their objective was to win the game. From these observations Neumann developed what became known as game theory and he applied the theory to economic markets. Previous economic models used traditional neoclassical economic assumptions that a seller and buyer acted solely on the mission to maximize their gains. A seller is looking to maximize profit and a buyer wants the maximum value for capital spent. The contribution that Neumann made was to define a seller and buyer as a transactional unit that was dependent upon each other, but not necessarily driven to maximize profits and value for capital.

Game theory became a sensation in 1944 when Neumann and Oskar Morgenstern co-wrote *The Theory of Games and Economic Behavior*. This book is a 642 page tour de force on game theory and its application to economic models. To be of value, the models, derived from using Neumann's game theory require precise mathematical values. If the values are subjective, it can lead to false results. In terms of economic models, applying game theory to markets in which social behavior must be quantified requires an understanding of utility. Utility is a measurement of satisfaction. People's actions are governed either by the drive to increase utility or the satisfaction of their condition in the context of all information. Aristotle called this the pursuit of leisure time. Beaumarchais measured utility in the motivating power of the eternal Figaro. It has been argued that utility is an inaccurate value, as people tend to compartmentalize decisions, or pass on decisions that promote the long term state in favor of the short term gain. A component of the measurement of utility is diminishing marginal utility, which states that the more one has, the less difference an additional unit of utility will make. In terms of market share, if a company has 83% market share and they gain two or three points of market share, it has marginal utility value on the company. Conversely if a company had one percentage point of market share and they gain three or four points of market share, it has significant utility value to the company.

The end of the Second World War was heralded as a triumph for science and technology. The power of the atom had been demonstrated and the industrial power of America was crowned the Arsenal of Democracy. After America entered the war in 1941, a group thought leaders were recruited from the Harvard Business School (HBS) to the Pentagon to form a new organization. This group was called the Statistical Control Office of the Army Air Corps and it is important because it was the beginning of the fusion of new age business strategy, neoclassical economics and the strategy of war. The Stat Control Office as it became known was established with the mission of the Stat Control Office to apply the management techniques and quantitative economic theories developed at HBS to war effort. The objective of the team was to find methods to improve the overall efficiency of the war effort through analysis of production, logistics and warfare. The group helped coordinate the collection of statistics, the interpretation of statistics and the development of models that revealed methods to improve productivity of manufacturing, logistics and combat operations. They were especially skilled at improving the combat efficiency of U.S. strategic bomber commands. Strategic bombing entailed complex logistical supply chains and the coordination of aircraft and analysis of results. The mission of strategic bombing was to destroy the production capacity of a nation-state to wage war. It was assumed that business people who have an understanding of logistics and the means of production would be of value to strategic bombing. The emergence of the atomic age post the war, was intellectually focused on atomic bombs, reasons for their use, means of delivery and impact on the battle field. There was a natural fusion between the old Stat Control Office methods, the RAND Corporation and the military strategy adopted by the U.S. for the first fifteen years after the end of the Second World War. One of the major contributions that the Stat Control Office created during the war was a methodology called *operational analysis* which defined the state of best expected return given a set of conditions. This is a military term for framing. Financial people frame investments, military people provide operational analysis of the state of expected return.

After the war, during the late 1940s and into the in the 1950s, game theory became a driving force in place called the RAND Corporation [see, *The Wizards of Armageddon*, by Fred Kaplan, 1983]. Originally funded by the Air Force, the RAND Corporation played a prominent role in thought leadership in defense related strategies post the Second World War. RAND figured prominently in the development of America's cold war strategies and game theory became a basis for many of their early studies on various strategies and their outcome. In 1947, Albert Wohlsetter and his wife Roberta published an internal RAND paper that included an application of Neumann's game theory was well as adaptation of operation analysis by Edwin Paxson called *systems analysis*. At RAND, systems analysis exploded across the organization and became a fundamental element of the thought leadership provided by RAND across all intellectual domains to which the organization contributed. Systems analysis answered the question of given the mission, what are the characteristics required by something or someone to accomplish the objective of the mission. In an organization dominated by mathematicians, systems analysis was broadly accepted as true science.

The weakness of systems analysis is the broad assumption of theoretical facts. In real life, outcomes are usually different then those projected by models and conjecture. In the early 1940s, the collision between systems analysis and operational analysis was plainly visible. The projected affect of weapon systems created by RAND was not in line with the operational analysis from data collected during the Second World War. Paxson and others eventually concluded that people do not always act in accordance with the mission – they are not always logical. People make decisions based on other criteria and often the decision making criteria is occurring in real time. It is at this point that we begin to pick up the elements of behavioral economics. People who subscribe to behavioral economics attempt to augment future projections by compensating for human behavior. The theory is that people are prone to cognitive dissonance, irrational behavior and anchor behavior.

The system analysts of the Pentagon took two paths post the Second World War. A group of them soon found their way into the fabric of corporate America and most notably the Ford Motor Company. This group included Charles (Tex) Thornton, Arjay Miller and Robert McNamara [see, *The Whiz Kids*, John Byrne, 1993]. Those who remained in the service of the defense industry of America soon found they had plenty of work ahead. As the Cold War intensified, it became an assemblage of ideological, scientific and economic warfare. The RAND Corporation played an important role in shaping the defense related strategies of U.S. In their history we can find many examples of the problem of inference, survivorship bias and applications of game theory, counterforce, systems analysis, mutually assured destruction and the Nash equilibrium. It is not the purpose of this manuscript to detail the history of the thought leaders at RAND, but rather to highlight three broad trends that emerged from the thought leaders at RAND. The intellectual environment at RAND helped establish a position of thought leadership that (a) set forth a predominance of reliance upon system analysis and mathematics, (b) which was countered by the use of game theory to inject elements of social behavior into intellectual thinking and (c) these disciplines created as part of national defense found their way into private sector through the use by economists and business leaders.

There is a cyclical wave between the social sciences and the hard sciences. At times one is in favor and the other is out of favor. The decades after the First World War and before the Second World War were dominated by social sciences. The Second World War hastened the rise of science and mathematics and the decline of the social sciences. This rise is due to the process, operational analysis and hard science investments (e.g. B-29 Program, Manhattan Project) that emerged from the war and was promoted by thought leaders at RAND. What started from the working levels of government and the private sector eventually gained positions of leadership by the 1960s. At RAND, for a time the social sciences were viewed as inferior by the hard science leaders. Mathematics was the only hard proof that utilized concise logical to draw precise conclusions about the past and enabled a prediction of the future. Game theory played a prominent role in the development of strategies for the military and drove assessment of the bomber gap, the missile gap and eventually collapsed inward as a result of endogenous risks created by the inferred conclusions. This was not the first time that pursuit of natural sciences was held in higher regard then the social sciences. During the 19th century, Auguste Comte promoted a view that societies operate according to the laws of nature, thus understanding the laws of nature then facilitates and understanding of societies and negates the need for the social sciences. This thought movement became known as positivism. It can be broadly defined as a scientific study contained to the facts and the relations between the facts present to derive a viable understanding and observation. Positivism is an early attempt at game theory, systems analysis and rational expectations.

As the thought leaders inside RAND played out various cold war game theories, a concept called *counterforce* was developed. Counterforce was originally pioneered by Bernard Brodie and inserted into the public domain in a January 1954 article in Foreign Affairs [see, *Nuclear Weapons: Strategic or Tactical*, January 1954]. John Kaufmann further developed the concept of counterforce as a strategy option to a Soviet invasion of Western Europe. The idea of counterforce was not to massively destroy the Soviet Union, but rather destroy the ability of the Soviet Union to wage atomic war by destroying their military forces. Until this time, U.S. military strategy was focused on the massive destruction of every aspect of the Soviet Union using atomic weapons. Counterforce did not have official adoption as a U.S. military strategy option until the election of John F. Kennedy as President and his selection of Robert S. McNamara as Secretary of Defense (i.e. SecDef).

When McNamara became SecDef in January, 1961, one of the key members of the Stat Control Office returned to the Pentagon and a position of intellectual leadership within the defense establishment of the U.S. This is important because McNamara had been honing his skills at the Ford Motor Company since the end of the war. Upon returning, he was trust into an intellectual battle between the branches of the armed services that wanted more weapons, more money and believed that any conflict with the Soviet Union would result in a massive atomic exchange and the analysts at RAND and other places who were advocating opposing views. When McNamara reviewed the Single Integrate Operational Plan (SIOP) for response to escalating tensions with the Soviet Union, he was terrified by the singularity of the plan and limited options. It assumed many worse case scenarios about the Soviet threat and provide a single war plan involving a massive atomic strike on the Soviet Union. When he was given the Kaufmann briefing on counterforce, McNamara found an intellectual solution to system wide problem. Counterforce provided options for the U.S. atomic strategy. It provided a means to control spending and moved the intellectual thinking away from absolutists such as Herman Kahn. This is important because much of the U.S. defense thought leadership had been about making atomic war winnable and survivable.

Counterforce was interesting because it altered the operating assumptions of the U.S. war plans that had been based on precise mathematical analysis of the blast radius and destructive force of atomic weapons. The analysts at RAND had studied the bomb damage assessment reports from the Second World War to infer and project the destructive capacities of atomic weapons. As part of the Gulf War One and Two, bomb damage assessment reports would go mainstream as part of the technology revolution and would play a prominent role in the media coverage of both wars. Vietnam became the ultimate showcase of counterforce strategy. The U.S. strategy was never to win the war, but rather to deter North Vietnam aggression and destroy their military forces without destroying the social infrastructure of nation-state. Counterforce failed because people do not act rationally. The North Vietnamese people were operating under a different set of principles. Counterforce was originally promoted as a game theory analysis of Soviet and U.S. war plans. It concluded that a strategy based upon destroying the military capacity of the Soviet Union to engage in an atomic war and generally avoiding destruction of their cities, would change their military strategy and force them to pursue a cessation of hostilities favorable to the U.S. The endogenous risk to strategies derived from game theories is that people do not act rationally.

Post the end Vietnam War and the entrance of America in the 1970s, it seemed we had lost our way. The mathematicians and hard science was again in decline and the philosophical and social sciences came to the fore. It would be in the 1990s, that hard science and mathematics would once again gain a dominant position in thought leadership. Out of the counterforce debacle in Vietnam and the dominance of defense and public policy by neoclassical theories, emerged John Boyd who developed a philosophy and process that formulates strategy based on all data and uses dynamic analytics to continuously evolve strategy to achieve objectives. This is not a game theory strategy that mathematically outlines various outcomes based on strategies employed. It is not a precise mathematical formula that defines risk. Boyd believed that strategy is an ever evolving and highly iterative process designed to achieve victory. It requires assumptions of risk with constant analytics of the operating environment. Boyd believed that the real target was your enemy's perception for it is enemy who decides when they are defeated – not you. Keynes would describe this as the participants in the financial market who decide when you have won or lost – it is the not the companies. In the business market it is the companies competing for market share who decide when they have lost.

It is Boyd's hypothesis that the enemy perception was the real target and it is in this belief we find the failure of counterforce. Counterforce assumed that by striking at the enemy's ability to wage war, they will be left with only one choice. This fallacy of this thinking is that we cannot predict human actions. Humans are irrational and often unpredictable. Humans make decisions based on facts and emotions that we may not even know they were considering. The thought leadership around defense strategies post the Second World War through the close of the Vietnam War was dominated by wining an atomic war. While a great deal of thought was going into military strategies, the real battle of the Cold War was happening on the economic and ideological front. Reagan was not playing to defeat the Soviet Union by military force – Reagan was playing a game that Keynes would know well. Reagan was speculating that the Soviet Union could not match his rate of investment and in turn would be forced to withdraw from the Cold War, thus providing a favorable change in the conventional basis of valuation and power. *"Even outside the field of finance,*

Americans are apt to be unduly interested in discovering what average opinion believes average opinion to be; and this national weakness finds its nemesis in the stock market. It is rare, one is told, for an American to invest, as many Englishmen still do, "for income"; and he will not readily purchase an investment except in the hope of capital appreciation. This is only another way of saying that, when he purchases an investment, the American is attaching his hopes, not so much to its prospective yield, as to a favourable change in the conventional basis of valuation, i.e. that he is, in the above sense, a speculator. Speculators may do no harm as bubbles on a steady stream of enterprise. But the position is serious when enterprise becomes the bubble on a whirlpool of speculation. When the capital development of a country becomes a by-product of the activities of a casino, the job is likely to be ill-done. The measure of success attained by Wall Street, regarded as an institution of which the proper social purpose is to direct new investment into the most profitable channels in terms of future yield, cannot be claimed as one of the outstanding triumphs of laissez-faire capitalism — which is not surprising, if I am right in thinking that the best brains of Wall Street have been in fact directed towards a different object," [see Keynes, page 159].

In the mid-1990s, the rise of technology and hard science again can to the fore of thought leadership in form of the internet, optical and telecom revolutions. A Princeton professor once remarked to me at a wedding reception that he was convinced that the internet generation was the emergence of binary world. There would be two types of social classes in the new economy world. The first estate would be those who understood mathematics and second class would be those who worked for those who understood mathematics. The emergence of a digital world based on technology and hard science presupposed a need to be fluent in mathematics. With the U.S. education community attention was suddenly focused on our lagging leadership in mathematics. If innovation and productivity is being driven from the hard sciences, then the millions children in China and India who had been given an earlier predisposition to mathematics in their education curriculum would have stronger mathematical skills and this in turn would relegate the U.S. to a service class society. Innovation and technology leadership would soon transfer to emerging nation-states in the pacific rim and the before the second American Century could take hold, the leadership position won after the end to the Cold War would transfer to new nation-states.

How the Internet, Telecom and Optical Revolution is Altering Value and Risk

The ITO Revolution was heralded as the dawn of the new economy and the creation of an information based society. Old economy companies were forced by perceived exogenous risks to their business models to adopt new business practices that leveraged the technology infrastructure that was being built through telecom deregulation, new technologies and end-user business practices shifting to a dependence on internet. The financial capital invested in technology markets, technology companies and technology infrastructure post 1994, was quantified by market models that used data points that showed an every increasing market that was becoming increasing pervasive in ever facet of society, business, government and culture. As this was occurring, the infrastructure required to build an information based economy was incomplete. Complex computing and networking problems had yet to be solved. The internet and the financial capital invested in technology infrastructure during the six years post the Telecom Act of 1996, did increase the availability of data – but it not create a pervasive economy based upon the internet as the underlying economic transaction and social mechanism.

The internet and the networks created through telecom deregulation and the optical revolution did increase access to and the availability of information. There are clear examples that the internet created an information revolution. The availability of information has manifested itself throughout society and government has become a driver of change – but it did not alter the economy, structure of business and society in the totality of the visions that dominated mainstream opinion in the mid to late 1990s. The reason why access to information did not fully alter the economic foundation is that information that was made available to businesses and consumers was predominately historical in nature. The ITO Revolution made it easier to access information and to connect to sources of information, but it did alter the state of information. The real promise of the ITO Revolution is to increase and improve productivity by creating the infrastructure to analyze, conceptualize, and act upon information as a leading function – not a trailing function.

The ITO Revolution has laid the foundation for a computational revolution that will begin to close the lagging window of time between (a) the collection of transactional data, (b) the analysis of the data and the (c) the implementation of business strategies based upon analytics. Conceptually, there is a fine point to understand within the function of acting on data points. If a corporation has the ability to collect data and process the data in near real time, then it has the ability to quickly respond to market data points. If a pull economic structure is emerging as an outgrowth from the infrastructure deployed by the ITO Revolution, then a hypothesis would be that the companies with the smallest time lag between the three points delineated above would have a competitive position in the market. The first great contribution of the ITO Revolution was improving access to information. The next phase is making information useful and timely to improve the costs of productivity. The companies that harness the infrastructure of the ITO Revolution to improve their competitive abilities will be the companies that separate themselves from the other market competitors. This will be the moment that separates old economy companies from new economy companies. The separation is already visible in the markets in which companies, such as Dell and Wal-Mart participate. Real time integration of economic transaction data with demographic data, supply-chain capacity, competitive pricing, and exogenous risks is the real revolution that is an outgrowth of the ITO Revolution. This was clearly visible during Hurricane Katrina. Wal-Mart was able to shift resources and modify their supply chain to minimize the impact on their global business and still drive specific supplies to affected areas.

Katrina also represents how exogenous risks affect the ecosystem of technology companies. The technology infrastructure destroyed by the hurricane resulted in a sudden influx of orders to technology suppliers. Since the collapse of the technology bubble, equipment suppliers had decreased capacities in their supply chains and outsourced manufacturing to reduce cost. The result was increased delivery times – yet service providers were requesting accelerated delivery schedules to replace the damaged infrastructure. The companies who had built adaptable supply chains were able to respond, while other companies missed a market opportunity that quickly developed from an exogenous risk. This can easily be dismissed as a rare event, but assume that the evolution to the pull economy is occurring. The definition of a pull economic structure implies that end-users, whether they are a business or a consumer are going to have shorter buying cycles that move closer to an on demand model. The companies that can realize where in the market economic transactions (a) can occur (b) will occur or (c) are occurring will be the companies that capture market share. Ownership of market share is how value is created.

If companies have the ability to react in near real time to market changes then, by definition they have the ability to assume more risk in deploying strategies against their competitors. If business leaders and can increase their company's level of risk, it provokes the question of the role of regulation in the determination of acceptable risk. The passage of Fair Disclosure regulation for public companies was a leveling function as a result of the ability of the ITO Revolution to provide access to information and perform this function in a reasonably equitable manner. The Sarbanes-Oxley law was aimed at minimizing risks by strengthening internal controls and reporting structures for public corporations. Neither of these laws altered the level of risk that the leaders of companies can assume.

The ITO Revolution imploded upon itself because it was driven to meet ever increasing expectations that were based on forward market projections created by the economic models used to measure the new economy. New economy companies and old economy companies transitioning to the new economy models had long term financial expectations that were highly difficult to meet. This is what drove spending, mergers and acquisitions, capacity swaps, and in some cases outright fraud. An executive at a telecom equipment supplier once told me a story of how a deal to procure equipment was completed during the bubble. A wireless supplier was purchasing equipment for their network, but their subscriber rate was trending behind the rate that financial analysts expected when the company was due to report results in a few weeks. To win the business and ensure the health of their customer, the equipment supplier purchased 30,000 subscriber contracts and included this cost in the contract back to the wireless provider. The net result was a win, win for all involved – but it further masked the failure of the market to develop as quickly as projected and in prolonged an ever increasing dependency upon lagging indicators to project forward developments.

The pressure to meet financial expectations was enormous. Worldcom fixed the books to meet the expectations that were set for the company by the stock market and the analysts who covered the company. This was done because of the tremendous amount of value dependent on success of this company from banking fees to equity ownership. The computational models used to assess risk and project value assumed that markets would continue to evolve based upon lagging market indicators. As the technology bubble increased, the pressure to meet expectations to secure stock value and financial capital eventually became too great for many companies to manage. The risks that collapsed the new economy were endogenous to the market. *"After the Bay acquisition, Roth asked a Wall Street institutional investor what he wanted from Nortel. The guy told him he wanted a nice, predictable company. 'With that kind of thinking, you'll be able to predict when I'll be bankrupt,' Roth protested. 'Right,' said the investor. 'But then I'll know when to sell,'"* [see, *The Industry Standard*, Sept 11, 2000, Jason Krause].

While there was a general promotion of the belief that ITO Revolution was a global unifying social force of equality, few of the companies operating in the ITO markets where naïve enough to base their business plans on social justice and building the information based economy. They were pleased to use these macro market visions to add credibility to their business plan – but they were not the foundations of a business plan. The foundation of the business plan was to achieve a return on capital invested in the business plan. Greed was far more pervasive than social justice and utopian objectives.

Most of the companies in the ITO Revolution and the leaders who led them were focused on making money, capturing market share and defeating their competitors. These were the real objectives of the companies in the ITO Revolution. Changing the world and bringing about world peace is beyond the scope of most technology companies. As telecom service providers continued to build networks, there was a belief that a wave of tremendous growth in new services would be created. The advancement in technology developed during the ITO Revolution was astounding – but the challenge turned out to be deploying enough of the new technology to make a difference in bringing about the visions of the new economy. These services would drive traffic onto the internet as new economy companies took market share from old economy companies. Capital flowed into the entire market ecosystem for technology companies from technology suppliers to service providers to end-users. Unfortunately for all the analysts who predicted the emergence of the new economy, the companies building the new economy did something they were expected to do; they tried to make more money by capturing market share. What most analysts did not anticipate was that most companies would attempt to capture market share by destroying the profitability of the market through ever increasing innovation and better cost points.

Companies in the ITO Revolution were not noble in nature; they did exactly what humans have been doing for thousands of years. This is the real reason why the technology bubble collapsed. Instead of working with hundreds of new competitors to upgrade the telecom infrastructure of the U.S. to deliver the panacea of digital revolution, the RBOCs decided to put their competitors out of business by slowing providing access to local loops and stifling profits through inter-state tariffs. Cisco Systems was not interested in having a host of alternative companies supplying routers and switches. They wanted it all and ruthlessly acquired competitors and forced others into restricted and declining business models. Microsoft responded to the Netscape threat by giving their browser away. What has happened to Microsoft's Internet Explorer since the demise of Netscape? The answer is; not much innovation. The reason Microsoft took so long to commit resources to building a better browser is because there is no threat to their business and no compelling reason to build a better browser. That is why Monzilla FireFox has found a market as an alternative to Microsoft's browser. When companies acquire dominant market share by destroying the price points in the market, it by definition changes the value of the market. The price of Monzilla's browser is zero dollars. The day Netscape went public it was worth $1.96 billion dollars and had but a single product, an internet browser. Deregulation, technology, and competition have a commoditizing affect on price within technology markets. The destruction of the internet browser market is not broad enough to justify imposing regulatory controls on the market. It is really a software product – not a market or industry which is strategic to the development and foundation of U.S. economy. In hindsight, we realize the tactical aspect of an internet browser, but in late 1996 the fate of Netscape was a closely watched event. *"That the contest caught even the President's {Clinton} eye underscores just how seminal it is: The battle is for nothing less than the soul of the Internet,"* [see, *Cyberspace Showdown*, BusinessWeek, October 7, 1996].

In hindsight, we now understand the endogenous risk of promoting a browser as the soul of the internet and the price set by the market for Netscape. What was missed, with the focus on the web browser, was that the real difficult problem to be solved was the broadband upgrade of America. The development of broadband infrastructure in the U.S. is of sufficient strategic value that some form of regulatory controls should be considered.

There are several prominent examples of endogenous risks that were missed during the ITO Revolution. The most prominent risk was the belief that the internet was doubling every one hundred days. This might have been true at one time, but the internet did not double in size every one hundred days – yet as late as the year 2000, this statistic was still being widely quoted by analysts. The reason why many people, who were part of the ITO Revolution, believed that the internet was doubling every one hundred days is because it justified their business plan and their investment choices or stock price. The internet doubling every one hundred days laid the foundation that justified the future year growth models for companies on internet time. The impact from the conclusions of these models was massive. Telecom deregulation produced hundreds of companies that spent billions upon billions of dollars building networks to attract customers. Why did this occur? It occurred because telecom and computing infrastructure was viewed as the foundation of the new economy. In turn, service providers and enterprises drove billions of dollars of capital into the companies that provide technology and equipment, dramatically increasing their value. The entire ecosystem from financial markets to service providers to technology companies to the end user was dependent on growth and migration to the new economy.

The risks to the financial markets driven by technology stocks and the private and public investments in technology companies were in the market. The expectations for new economy companies were a reflection of the consensus judgment of how the markets believed these companies would be priced. During the run up of the stock markets in the 1990s, technology companies were viewed and priced differently from other companies. This does not mean they had a higher value than old economy companies, but they clearly were priced by the market differently because the consensus judgment of the market based upon of the full weight the thought leadership that was occurring external to the financial market altered the perception of how these companies were priced. Why was technology companies priced higher than non-technology companies? Why did technology companies have access to capital that other companies did not? The pricing of companies in the ITO Revolution was a function of the market and the belief that a new economy was rapidly taking hold. When thoughtful, credible leaders across many social sectors speak passionately about revolutions, paradigm shifts, and global changes, even the average person begins to pay attention. When access to capital became nearly ubiquitous during the technology bubble of the 1990s, the desire to achieve quick profits began to trump the desire to build long-term value. This became a cyclical function that built upon itself until the markets collapsed in 2000. Keynes was a harbinger of this event some sixty-four years earlier. *"Investment based on genuine long-term expectation is so difficult to-day as to be scarcely practicable. He who attempts it must surely lead much more laborious days and run greater risks than he who tries to guess better than the crowd how the crowd will behave; and, given equal intelligence, he may make more disastrous mistakes. There is no clear evidence from experience that the investment policy which is socially advantageous coincides with that which is most profitable. It needs more intelligence to defeat the forces of time and our ignorance of the future than to beat the gun. Moreover, life is not long enough; — human nature desires quick results, there is a peculiar zest in making money quickly, and remoter gains are discounted by the average man at a very high rate. The game of professional investment is intolerably boring and over-exacting to anyone who is entirely exempt from the gambling instinct; whilst he who has it must pay to this propensity the appropriate toll. Furthermore, an investor who proposes to ignore near-term market fluctuations needs greater resources for safety and must not operate on so large a scale, if at all, with borrowed money — a further reason for the higher return from the pastime to a given stock of intelligence and resources,"* [see Keynes, page 157].

Why did the technology market and stocks markets driven by technology companies begin a sustained collapse in 2000? The answer is a two part function. There is difference between why digital revolution or new economy failed and why the stock market collapsed. Keynes guides that the manner by which financial markets price assets is different from the manner in which the non-financial market determines value. Hence, the decline in technology valuations from their peak in 2000 is a two-part function. The success of the ecosystem of technology companies, service providers, and financial services (i.e. venture capital, private equity, debt, investment banks) was dependent on the consumption of technology and technology related services by enterprises (i.e. businesses) and consumers. When the consumption rates began to stabilize, decline, or in some cases fail to materialize, a cataclysmic correction in price occurred in the financial markets. This does not mean the ITO Revolution was a failure, it means that the pricing of ITO Revolution companies and assets was ahead of leading indicators by an incorrect inference of the future value, based on lagging data. The failure of the digital revolution and the new economy to emerge in six years will be detailed in the proceeding essay.

Although the new economy did not supplant the old economy in six years, it does not mean that the evolution is not occurring. There is a digital revolution occurring in the ecosystem of technology companies and throughout the industries that consume and rely upon technology. The revolution is the emerging ability to conduct business (i.e. complete transactions) and modify business strategies in near real time. A real time model may never fully occur, but companies can close the gap between the collection of data, the analysis of data, and action based upon data. The adoption of a pull economic model affects the quality of information. If the first stage of the ITO Revolution improved access to information and improved the distribution of information, then the second stage of the ITO Revolution is acting upon that information in a productive manner. When consumers and business have access to information, it will create new buying patterns that emerge quickly and trail off quickly. Apple announced a video capable iPod on October 12th, 2005. The emergence of a video capable iPod enables a consumer base that will want access to video content. Creators of movies, television shows, and creative commercials now have an outlet to sell their content for $2.99 a view. If a broadcaster transmitted a premier of a hit show the night before, they can capitalize on interest in the show by offering an after market viewing downloadable to the iPod for a few dollars. This opportunity will quickly emerge and decline in time. This is the pull economy. Retails who offer merchandise based on movies and books have to respond to market demand and awareness. If the O.J Simpson saga or other high profile legal or news event occurred tomorrow, the time to access consumers of content is immediate and declines as we move further from the event. This will affect all businesses in time.

ESSAY ONE

A Short History of Telecom, the Personal Computer, and the Internet in the United States

CHAPTER ONE:
Genesis

War having been determined upon, the first point to be decided is whether it shall be offensive or defensive.

- Jomini

In January 2003, Cisco Systems possessed almost as much cash or cash equivalents (~$21 billion) then the total combined market capitalization of its four nearest rivals (i.e. Nortel, Lucent, Alcatel, and Juniper Networks). By comparison, in August of 2000, the combined market capitalization of Nortel ($276 billion), Lucent ($161 billion), Juniper Networks ($51 billion) and Alcatel ($89 billion) was $577 billion. Twenty-eight months later their combined market capitalization was less than $25 billion, a loss of more than $550 billion dollars in market capitalization terms. In stark comparison, Cisco Systems enjoyed a market capitalization of $110 billion in January 2003, no debt and a balance of $21 billion in cash on hand. *"You win in battles with the timing in the Void born of the timing of the cunning by knowing the enemies' timing and thus using a timing which the enemy does not expect,"* Miyamoto Musashi, *A Book of Five Rings, The Ground Boo.* Cisco's ability to time the market was perfect in comparison to its rivals. Cisco perfected the business model of making money – while its competitors became befuddled in a massive market correction that descended on the telecom, internet, and optical markets in 2001.

Understanding the evolution of the telecom and computing markets from the Bell System and IBM to the frenzied height of the technology bubble in 2000, requires three perspectives. (a) The first perspective is activity within the structure of specific markets. The G3 Market Model is the tool that will be used to analyze activity within markets. From a high level, markets will be defined as: consumer, enterprise, service provider and technology providers. (b) Above the market level is the ecosystem level. Markets form an ecosystem and activity within markets is affected by the interdependencies between markets (i.e. technology providers, service providers, consumers and businesses). Understanding the evolution of the telecom market within the U.S. requires a general knowledge of how and why capital flows between consumer, business, service provider, and technology provider markets. Within each of these markets we will look closely at why events occurred and how regulation and technology changed the structure of the market. It is clear that large investments were made based upon the assumption that capital would flow between these markets and that the overall size of all these markets would collectively increase. See **Chart 1: Market Ecosystem** in the Chart and Model section.

The (c) perspective is the technology level. (c) Technology evolves and the cycle of innovation drives a Darwinian ageing process. Some technology ages faster than other technology. A well known example of this process is Moore's Law. In 1965 Gordon Moore, co-founder of Intel, observed that the number of transistors per square inch on integrated circuits had doubled every year since the integrated circuit was invented. From this observation he hypothesized that the trend would continue for the foreseeable future. Although the pace has fluctuated, the density of data has double approximately every 18 months. The invention and subsequent adoption of technology clearly affects the overall market ecosystem. The high level market structure illustrated below represents the structure of the market ecosystem in 1965. See **Chart 2: 1965 Market Ecosystem** in the Chart and Model section.

The years 1964 and 1965 mark important milestones in the history of computing and telephony. In 1964 AT&T opened the first central office in the United States. This was the beginning of the migration from operators and five digit dialing, to a nation-wide deployment of circuit switching technology and ten digit dialing. In 1965, IBM introduced the S/360 mainframe computer. The 1965 Market Ecosystem is dominated by the service of voice. The mainframe computer was new; the telephone had been around for decades. The dominant provider of telephony services was AT&T or as it was then known, the Bell System. There were many other independent phone companies in the U.S. market, but AT&T was clearly the company serving the majority of the market with its regulatory mandate to provide universal service. The flow of capital in the 1965 Market Ecosystem begins with demand from consumers and enterprises for telephony services. AT&T required products and technologies to provide telephony services. The products and technologies used to deliver telephony services were developed by Bell Labs and manufactured by Western Electric, which were all members of the Bell System. Few independent, non-Bell System companies supplied telephony equipment to the Bell System in 1965. Within the 1965 Market Ecosystem model, the creation of capital from consumer and business end-users flows to the service provider (i.e. AT&T or Bell System Companies) in return for telephony service. The capital received by AT&T for delivery of telephony services is then invested in technology to build networks to provide services. In 1965, the primary inventor and supplier of telephony technology and products were the other divisions of the Bell System. Hence, within the 1965 Ecosystem Model the capital created for telephony services flowed uniquely into one entity which combined telephony services, technology product development, and manufacturing. To support this entity, telephony rates were regulated to ensure that profit levels remained high-enough to sustain the deployment and improvement of the telecom infrastructure of the United States. This mandate was called universal service and the bearer of this burden was AT&T

Land of the Giants

In 1980, the industry of computers was dominated by International Business Machines or IBM. Every major corporation had an IBM mainframe computer worth millions of dollars in their data center. The data center was typically referred to as the glass house, as it was a restricted facility, with special power, cooling, and glass windows that enabled the mere mortals of the corporation to walk around it, but not gain access. In 1974, IBM introduced a technology called Systems Network Architecture or SNA. SNA was one of the first major initiatives at developing networking technology to connect mainframes and mid-size computers using traditional telephony lines supplied by another giant corporation called American Telephony and Telegraph or AT&T. SNA enabled corporations with IBM computers to extend the reach of those computers to other users at remote locations around the world through a process called networking. Computers that were networked were able to communicate with other computers as well as allow users to access computers and information at distant locations. IBM has spent the last twenty-five years evolving, enhancing, and sustaining SNA as an important technology for its customers. By 1980, IBM was building multi-host (i.e. mainframe) networks with parallel paths, mesh architectures that could support multiple sessions (i.e. users). What had started as a solution to provide simple point-to-point network connections had begun to evolve towards sophisticated network designs that could route around failures and handle increased traffic loads. The simple need to connect two remote computers, evolved into what is generally referred to as a network of many computers and many paths. The importance of SNA was summarized by the well known SNA consultant Anura Guruge in January 2004, *"SNA's remarkable twenty year reign over IBM sector networking is now finally and unequivocally at an end. Most IBM mainframe 'shops', though still inescapably reliant on mission-critical SNA applications, are in the process of inexorably moving toward TCP/IP centric networks – in particular those that combine TCP/IP and Internet {ie. Web} technology to create what are now referred to as 'intranets' and 'extranets'. Mainframe resident SNA applications will, nonetheless, continue to play a crucial role in successfully sustaining worldwide commerce well into the next millennium, way past the Year 2000."*

The seminal achievement of SNA in the late 1970s to mid 1980s was to make minicomputers viable from an enterprise perspective. Enterprise computer networks were completely dependent on the mainframe computers supplied from IBM or one of the minor mainframe suppliers. SNA was a proprietary solution implemented by IBM, but it was an open source solution. This enabled the suppliers of mini computers such as DEC, Wang, Prime, Data General, Apollo, and others to use SNA technology to deploy their systems into the network. Open source meant that competitors as well as providers of non-competitive systems had access to the technical implementation of SNA and thus could use SNA to add their computers to an SNA network. The mini-computer vendors implemented a PU_Type 2 node capability on their computers, which enabled these machines to seamlessly interact with mainframe computers as well as each other. This was the genesis of distributed computing. It was a seminal moment that gave birth to the commercial network within the enterprise market and started the progression towards the client/server network. This occurrence may not have had the dramatic overtones of Roger Kildall flying his plane while IBM waited in his lobby to license CP/M for the personal computer – but it is significant because networking of computers started with IBM.

Just as powerful and dominant as IBM was in the world of computing, AT&T was the supreme ruler of the telecommunications industry in America. For most of the twentieth century, American Telephone and Telegraph (AT&T) Company held a virtual monopoly in the United States telecommunications industry for long distance and local telephony services. By the 1960s, 80% of the American population had a telephone and AT&T carried more than 90% of all domestic long distance calls. Consider this fact in relation to the home computer. It took sixty years for telephones to be accepted into 80% of all American homes. *"By way of comparison, since 1980 and the sale of the first PC – an initial base of zero – the PC industry has created more then $250 billion in net shareholder value. Now we are embarking on an industry just beginning to tap the base of 150 million PC users. In the first 15 years of what might be called the enhanced-communications industry, or whatever it ends up being called, we feel that over time the shareholder value created from developments in the internet (starting in 1994, for the sake of argument) could exceed that created in the first 15 years of the PC revolution,"* [see, *the Internet Report*, Mary Meeker and Chris DuPuy, February 1996, page 1-2,]. By 2003, more than 50% of the homes in America had a personal computer. The home computer market is just over twenty-five years old and it has secured more then 50% of the American market. It took AT&T and other small phone companies twice as long to reach the same levels of market penetration for the telephone.

AT&T, as a dominant market force, began before the dawn of the twentieth century. Until 1913, AT&T was financially controlled by J.P. Morgan.

To complement the only long distance network in the United States, Morgan instructed the leaders of AT&T to acquire as many small independent phone companies as possible. The local telephone companies gave AT&T control of what is called the local loop or local access line. The local loop is the phone line from the consumer or enterprise business to the local switching office, which is often referred to by the general phrase "central office" or CO. At the CO, each phone call is switched to its local destination or placed on the long distance network. AT&T owned the long distance network and by acquiring ownership of the local loops, AT&T would be the service provider for local calls as well as long distance calls beyond the reach of the local serving area.

AT&T used their advantage as the only long distance service provided, to coerce small telephone companies to join the Bell System at terms favorable to AT&T. The Bell System is a term used to describe the entire AT&T conglomerate, which included the long distance network, Bell Labs, Western Electric, and the twenty-three local telephone companies. Without AT&T's long distance network, local phone companies could not connect their customers beyond their local service territory. As the only provider of long distance service in America, AT&T was in a powerful position to coerce small companies to accept their terms for a buyout. The Interstate Commerce Commission (ICC) investigated AT&T's business practices and determined in 1913, the year of Morgan's death, that AT&T had used its leverage as the only provider of long distance service to broker preferred merger terms. The government forced AT&T to stop its predatory business practices and agree to refrain from purchasing any of the remaining independent phone companies. At the time of the agreement, there were about fifteen hundred independent local phone companies in America that became known as ILECs or Incumbent Local Exchange Carriers. AT&T also agreed to provide long distance service to all independent phone companies in an agreement called the Kingsbury Commitment.

The Communications Act of 1934 created the Federal Communications Commission (FCC) and gave it the power to regulate the telecommunications industry. The Act also set forth a policy that America should enjoy affordable and universally available phone service. AT&T was designated as a regulated monopoly with the mission of providing the United States with *universal service*. *Newton's Telecom Dictionary* defines universal service as *"Milton Mueller of Syracuse University observes that universal service has gone through two generations: 1. First generation (1907 – 1965), 2 Second generation (1965 to present). The first generation was about connecting competing networks into 'one system, on policy, universal service.' This was the Theodore Vail vision. Vail was the first president of AT&T. The second generation started after World War II. As a response to political pressures, regulators decided to keep local rates low using the surplus generated by long distance. This system of cross-subsides was threatened by the rise o f long distance competition in the 1960s and early 1970s. That was a shock to telephone monopolies because it meant that long distance rates were about to go down and therefore the subsidies were about to decline. Telephone companies tried to defend their monopoly privileges by claiming cross subsidies were essential to the preservation of widespread household telephone penetration. This way, the term "universal service" was dusted off by the monopolies and got a new meaning: a telephone in every home (universal service as we understand it today). Now for some history: The Communications Act of 1934 defined the nation's telecom goal as 'To make available, so far as possible, to all the people of the United States a rapid, efficient Nationwide, and worldwide wire and radio communication service with adequate facilities at reasonable charges.' The same act created the FCC (Federal Communications Commission), charging it with the responsibility to carry out this policy, as well to regulate the telecommunications industry, in general. Prior to the breakup of the Bell System sub early 1984, AT&T and the BOCs (Bell Operations Companies) administrated a fund through the "settlements" process, which essentially reimbursed the LECs (Local Exchange Carriers) for the use of their local networks in originating and terminating long distance calls. 'High Cost' (i.e. rural) LECs were compensated at very high levels, in recognition of the universal service policy. Since 1983, NECA (National Exchange Carrier Association) has been charged with this responsibility. The Telecommunications Act of 1996 considerably expanded the definition of 'universal services' to include "access to advanced telecommunications and information service...for similar services in urban areas." The Act goes on to provide for discounts to elementary and secondary schools and classrooms, health care providers, and libraries. The Telecommunications Act of 1996 also directed that a special universal service Joint Board comprised of federal and state regulators and a consumer advocate develop recommendations for the FCC identifying services that will be supported by a federal universal service funding mechanism. Relying heavily on the Joint Board's November 9, 1996 Recommended Decision, the FCC released a Report and Order that undertakes to modernize universal service policy in an increasingly competitive marketplace and to fundamentally expand its applicability."* [see *Newton's Telecom Dictionary, 18th Edition 2002*, Page 782].

For the following forty years, AT&T and the FCC would act together to preserve the Bell System under the premise that it was an important and strategic national asset mandated to provide universal service. In 1946, the FCC ruled that microwave communication systems would be limited to experimental projects and the commercialization of microwave technology in order to provide telephony services was prohibited. There was some concern that microwave technology was still unproven, but the main driver of this decision was that microwave systems could be used to build an alternative long distance network at cost points lower then AT&T. This alternative network could then be used to compete against AT&T. In short, microwave technology was a threat to the installed base of copper phone lines that were a critical asset of AT&T and foundation for universal service. This is an important point to remember, as it will be a reoccurring theme throughout the telecommunications revolution in America. Microwave transmission systems held the potential to enable competitors to enter the telephony market at operational costs points significantly lower than that of AT&T. It is the process of technical innovation that created microwave technology and thus enabled potential competitors to avoid the costly and complex construction of a nationwide network based on copper transmission lines. The potential entrance of new competitors into AT&T's market would be financially distressing towards the company. AT&T was one of the most important companies in America as well as a major player on the stock market. The governing mission of universal service was more important at a time when America was building her industrial infrastructure, than creating a competitive telephony services market.

The 1950s witnessed two important rulings against AT&T. The first was called the consent decree, which forced AT&T to divest its manufacturing facility, Western Electric, and to grant the use of non-exclusive patents to anyone. After a long process, the FCC ruled in 1959 to allow new carriers using microwave technology above 890 MHz into the U.S. market for private line services that were not open to the consumer market. AT&T responded to the opening of this market by substantially reducing prices on private line services. Private line services are dedicated circuits that can be used exclusively by an organization to connect multiple sites. AT&T's price adjustment for private line service became known as the Telpak Tariff. This new tariff raised many questions regarding whether or not AT&T was a monopoly and the cost elements that enabled AT&T to provide such reduced pricing since all tariffs were based on operating costs and the costs required for subsidizing local markets. After ten years of deliberations, the FCC ruled that the Telpak Tariff was illegal, for it priced AT&T services below the actual cost to carry the services and as such, was designed to keep private microwave networks out of the market. By attempting to erode the profitable price level of private line services, AT&T was attempting to create a market condition that limited the profitability of MCI's services, thus reducing the capital MCI had to invest in the network as well as their ability to raise capital by ruining the market conditions and their business plan. This would not be the last time that large incumbent service providers used the power of their diversified balance sheets to wage war for market share against new entrants and competitors.

In 1954, the FCC ruled that foreign attachments could be connected to AT&T's network. Before this ruling, the only products that could be attached to AT&T's network were products purchased from AT&T's manufacturing division, Western Electric. This included what we term today as handsets or telephones. For the next twelve years, AT&T fought many inventors of products that were designed for use by the consumer. This included speakerphones, privacy cups that fit over the mouthpiece, and a host of other telephony related inventions. AT&T not only threatened legal action against the inventors, but they warned customers not to use these products as they might disrupt telephone service as only products from AT&T were tested to work on the AT&T network. In 1967, the FCC ruled to allow devices developed outside of AT&T to be connected to AT&T's network. Think about the significance of this ruling the next time you use a modem or a hands free headset or a phone manufactured by any company other than AT&T.

The 1980 Market Ecosystem had significantly changed from the 1965 structure in three primary aspects. The first significant change was the continued deployment of computing power and the emergence of the need to network computers. With the deployment of computers came the need to network computers via data connections supplied primary by AT&T, the independent operating companies (IOCs) that were not part of the Bell System, and a few emerging service providers such as MCI and GTE. By 1980, AT&T was not the only supplier of telephony technology equipment. Northern Telecom was selling voice switches and companies such as DSC, Tellabs as well as foreign suppliers (i.e. Alcatel and Siemens) were acquiring market share selling technology – still the primary driving force within the U.S. telecom market was voice revenues. Computer networking was a niche market in 1980 and clearly not a driven of major profits for service providers. Credit card transactions, which we take for granted as automated today, were manual lookup processes for fraud and not automated at the point of purchase. In time, the emergence of electronic commerce would change the ecosystem – but for much the 1980s the telecom market in the United States would be focused on the breakup of AT&T. Additionally, the introduction of the personal computer in 1981 and the development of the client/server model throughout the 1980s would set the foundation for the growth of the enterprise market to be a major driver of data services. See **Chart 3: 1980 Market Ecosystem** in the Chart and Model section.

As a corporation, AT&T was a giant conglomerate of services, research, development, and supply. In 1980, AT&T owned the vast majority of the local loops in the major markets of the United States. When AT&T was broken up in 1984, the local telephone portion was divested from the long distance network, research, and supply divisions of the company. The break up of AT&T created nine regional telephone companies that were prevented by the FCC from offering long distance services. These nine companies were known as Regional Bell Operating Companies or RBOCs. *Newton's Telecom Dictionary* defined an RBOC as *"Regional Bell Operating Company, also called a Regional Holding Company (RHC). Here's the story on this soon-to-be-obsolete term: On January 8, 1982 AT&T signed a Consent Decree with the United States Department of Justice, stipulating that* *at midnight December 31, 1983, AT&T would divest itself of its 22 wholly-owned telephone operating companies. According to the terms of this Divestiture Agreement, also known as the Modified Final Judgment (MFJ), those 22 operating Bell telephone companies would be formed into seven RHCs of roughly equal size, with Federal Judge Harold H. Greene making the final determination as to the reorganization. The seven RHCs (and the operating companies that formed them) were Ameritech (Illinois Bell, Indiana Bell, Michigan Bell, Ohio Dell and Wisconsin Telephone), Bell Atlantic (Bell of Pennsylvania, Diamond State Telephone, The Chesapeake and Potomac Companies and New Jersey Bell), BellSouth (South Central Bell and Southern Bell), NYNEX (New England Telephone and New York Telephone), Pacific Telesis (Pacific Bell and Nevada Bell), Southwestern Bell (Southwestern Bell), and US West (Mountain Bell, Northwestern Bell and Pacific Northwest Bell). In October 1994, Southwestern Bell Corporation changed its name to SBC Communications Inc., for reasons we'll see in just a sentence or two. In April, 1996 Bell Atlantic acquired NYNEX for $22.1B. NYNEX lost its identity. Also in April, SBC Communications, Inc., bought Pacific Telesis for $16.7 billion, with Pacific Bell and Nevada Bell continuing to operate under these names. On October 9, 1999, Ameritech was acquired by SBC and lost its identity. On June 30, 2000, Bell Atlantic acquired GTE and changed the entire name of the company to Verizon. Also on June 30, 2000, US West was acquired by Qwest, an upstart long distance carrier and now operates as Qwest. Of the original seven RBOCs, only BellSouth has not yet been merged, acquired or otherwise morphed, at least not at the time of this writing. Continuing our little story, the terms of the MFJ also placed a number of business restrictions on AT&T and the RBOCs. These restrictions were threefold. The RBOCs weren't allowed into long distance, equipment manufacturing or information services. AT&T wasn't allowed into local telecommunications, so it couldn't compete with the newly formed RBOCs. But it was allowed to manufacture anything it wanted, including computers. (That was effectively a lifting of a prohibition on it by the earlier 1956 Consent Decree which had not allowed it to make computers.) The federal courts overseeing slowly relaxed the restrictions. The BOCs were allowed into information services, and AT&T into local services. Some of the RBOCs have been allowed to offer interLATA intrastate long distance service, but have yet to be allowed into the more lucrative interstate business. This is a continuing saga,"* [see *Newton's Telecom Dictionary, 18th Edition 2002,* Page 613]

The RBOCs were prevented from offering long distance services, as AT&T, who was the original parent company, retained the long distance network and services. The seven baby bells that emerged from the AT&T break up were: Pacific Bell (PacBell), Southwestern Bell (SBC), Nynex, Bell Atlantic, Ameritech, Bell South and US West. By August 2000, the seven baby bells had been reduced to four. Bell Atlantic purchased Nynex in 1994 for $22 billion and was renamed Verizon. US West was purchased by Qwest for $65 billion in 2000. SBC purchased Pacific Bell in 1996 for $16.5 billion and then purchased Ameritech for $62 billion in 1998. The four remaining companies that were part of the original Bell System were Verizon, Bell South, SBC, and Qwest. In August 2000, these four companies had a combined total market capitalization of approximately $381 billion dollars. In comparison, their former parent company, AT&T, had a market capitalization of less than $26 billion in August 2000. If you included the market capitalization of Lucent Technologies in August of 2000, another $178 billion respectively can be added to AT&T, bringing its theoretical market capitalization, including divested assets to $585 billion dollars or a half a trillion dollars. This is the inherent market value contained within AT&T if telecom services had remained a regulated market in the United States.

In America during the mid to late 1980s, the seeds of great revolution were being planted. The product of these seeds began to emerge when the personal computer was introduced to corporate America (i.e. enterprise market). This single achievement, primarily accomplished by IBM, set in motion a chain of events in 1981 that would last through the dawn of the new millennium. Consider that fact for a moment. The introduction of the personal computer was the fundamental element that spawned the creation of many new technology opportunities (i.e. markets), which in turn means financial opportunities. IBM introduced the personal computer to corporate America on August 12, 1981. The operating system called DOS was from a small company in Seattle named Microsoft. By the end of 1983, IBM had sold more than a half a million PCs. That is more than thirty thousand per month during that period. The PC was the foundation for what would become two major markets, the enterprise and consumer computing markets that, in turn, would drive the service provider market via the internet. *"There are two major market opportunities for internet usage: enterprise and consumer. A recent survey by Dataquest showed that 60% of 100 medium to large organizations in the U.S., all departments had some access to the Internet. Similarly, the rapid take-off of America Online shows that consumer adoption of online/Internet access, while still less than 8% of U.S. homes, is growing quickly. The enterprise market is dominated by access for information services (internal or external), while the consumer market will likely be dominated by online/Internet entertainment and information services,"* [see, *The Internet Report*, Mary Meeker and Chris DuPuy, page 1-2, February 1996]

When the personal computer debuted on the enterprise market desktop, it possessed a few compelling applications. Spreadsheets and word processing were the applications that formed the cornerstone of desktop productivity. These programs improved personal productivity, but they did not interface with traditional back office corporate computing systems such as informational databases for inventory management, supply chain operations, customer relations, billing systems, and other data intensive functions. The core business applications of the corporation were still housed on mainframes and mid-range computing platforms that were networked using SNA. Companies such as IBM, DEC, Apollo Domain, Stratus, and Tandem were the rulers of this market. At some point in the future, the PC would need to communicate with the traditional back office systems that were networked using SNA. The introduction of the personal computer into the workplace enabled the development of desktop productivity applications. It was from the desktop that the revolution of networking would be launched that would eventually change the structure of the telecommunications industry in America and the world. Helen of Troy may have been the face that launched a thousand ships – but it was the personal computer that launched thousands of technology companies in the 1980s and 1990s.

The next step in the evolution of the networked personal computer occurred with the introduction of the client/server network. The client/server architecture is the reason why Cisco Systems exists as a company today. The general population may think of Cisco in the context of the internet, but Cisco Systems was built by providing corporate America, and most of the industrialized world, with multi-protocol routers and switches that link client/server local area networks with back office mainframe and mid-range computing platforms. The introduction of the PC created the necessity for the creation of the server – which would drive the development of the client/server network. Cisco is the company that providing the routers to connect the computer networks of corporate America, but with this accomplishment it achieved a deeper position of strategic importance. By plan, accident, or both, Cisco's routers became the control plane for the enterprise network. This is a position of strategic importance and as the network evolves post-2006, the question is; what will be the control plane of the future?

A server is a more powerful computer that houses data and applications that PC users can access to store, retrieve, and process information. In the early days of the PC industry, computer hard drives and storage space were expensive. It was technically easier and financially superior to network PCs in the same way mainframe computers and terminals were networked. The server would act as a host (i.e. mainframe) and users (i.e. personal computers) would access applications and data on the server over the network. To create the local area network (i.e. LAN) of PCs and servers, networking technologies such as Ethernet, Token-Ring, and AppleTalk was deployed. Ethernet was developed at Xerox's Palo Alto Research Center (PARC). Token-Ring was developed and introduced by IBM. For much of the late 1980s and into the early 1990s, Token-Ring and Ethernet were the competing technologies for the deployment of LANs. Today, Ethernet runs more the 95% of the LANs in the world. It is the most widely deployed LAN technology and beginning to emerge as a technology for the Wide Area Network (WAN). Token-Ring has been relegated to legacy networks and within a few years will be resigned to history.

The development of applications to reside on servers by companies such as Novell enabled the desktop computer to access a central computer (i.e. server) that housed data and applications. To create a LAN, companies needed to provide connectivity from each desktop computer to the location of the client/server. The architecture for networking a client/server network came from the heritage of the SNA network. IBM deployed mainframe computers in a central location (i.e. glass house) and linked them to remote terminals (i.e. personal computers). The client/server LAN deployed servers in a central location, called a data center or wiring closet, and networked each personal computer to the server using Ethernet or Token-Ring. Suddenly, there was a market beyond the desktop computer and it began to spawn many new companies. In the early to mid-1980s the first networking companies began to emerge. The first explosive growth market for networking companies was not for routers or bridges – it was for hubs. Hubs were switching platforms that enabled corporations to rewire their office facilities and provide to each desktop computer access to central locations where the servers resided. The mass introduction of the PC into corporate America began in the early to mid 1980s. At the time, LANs were new. Buildings had to be wired to support the personal computer and products installed to provide connectivity. The two dominant companies to emerge in this market segment were Cabletron and Synoptics. The second tier players were Ungermann-Bass, Chipcom, Bytex, 3Com, DEC, and a host of minor players. The wiring of corporate America was the first great networking market to find its roots directly linked to the PC. Cabletron Systems, located in New Hampshire, would become a large company publicly listed on the New York Stock Exchange. By the late 1990s, the business of networking LANs had evolved into a mature market. Cabletron struggled as the market for hubs matured and in 2000, announced plans to split the company into four separate companies called Riverstone Networks which sells to service providers, Enterasys which makes enterprise LAN gear, Global Network Technology Services who sells professional IT services, and Aprisma Management Technologies which sells a network management platform called Spectrum.

Synoptics, located in San Jose, was the west coast archrival of Cabletron. In 1985, Synoptics was spun out of Xerox's Palo Alto Research Center (i.e. PARC). Synoptics' claim to fame was that it commercialized the standard for 10BaseT connection for Ethernet. Before 10BaseT, Ethernet networks consisted of large, bulky cables with a copper core. The revolution that Synoptics introduced was Ethernet over simple phone wiring called 10Base T. Suddenly, there was an inexpensive method of wiring a LAN. In 1994, Synoptics agreed to merge with Wellfleet Communications to form Bay Networks for $1.02 billion.

3Com Corporation was another successful networking company that could trace its roots to Xerox's PARC. Ethernet was invented at PARC and 3Com was formed to commercialize Ethernet technology by Bob Metcalf. In 1987, 3Com and Bridge Communications merged in what can be considered one of the first, if not the first important merger between networking companies. From that point forward, 3Com became a major player in the LAN networking market through a number of acquisitions. In 1995, 3Com acquired Chipcom for $775 million and in 1997, 3Com acquired US Robotics, a market leader in modems used by millions of people to connect to the internet, for $8.5 billion. It was after 1997 that 3Com began to experience difficulties as their markets matured and competitors such as Cisco and Bay Networks assumed greater market share. The remaining players in the HUB market such as Bytex, Ungermann Bass, known as UB, eventually faded away or merged as the market matured and began to decline.

With the development of the LAN, two networks began to exist within the corporate network. One network revolved around the client/server network and the other around the mainframe and mini-computers. These networks needed to communicate. They needed to exchange information, share data, and interact. Before the invention of the router, these networks rarely interacted. Corporate America could clearly see the value of having thousands of its workers with desktop PCs having access to the back office systems and data housed on its expensive mainframe computers. The need to network the many LANs with the legacy networks was the need that launched the next great revolution in networking.

The first companies to begin to address the market of networking the LANs with Wide Area Networks or WANs were bridge companies. These companies included Retix, CrossComm, ACC, Bridge Communications, Vitalink, IBM, and several smaller players. Bridge companies built layer-2 devices that connected the client/server LANs via circuits provided by the phone companies to other LANs and networks. A PC user could now access servers at other geographic locations as well as some of the legacy back office systems. The challenge with the solution from bridge companies was that their layer 2 solutions could not scale to adequately address the growing magnitude and complexity of enterprise networks. As the networks became larger, the layer 2 solutions would slow down due to network congestion. There was not enough bandwidth in the network to support large scale layer 2 networks. The solution to the problems presented by the ever increasing network sizes was the development and deployment of layer 3 products that were capable of intelligent processing of high-speed traffic flows. The early bridge networks could not efficiently support large-scale networks. The solution to this problem came from a product called a router. Routers were complex devices that made intelligent decisions regarding the processing of traffic at layer 3, which is called the network layer. Routers were able to translate between computer protocols (i.e. languages) across different types of network media (i.e. physical connections) and intelligently regulate and route – hence the term router – traffic flows.

Cisco Systems was founded in 1984 by Sandra Lerner and Leonard Bosack of Stanford University. The company was formed to develop and market a product called a router, created by Bosack and Lerner, to enable them to share email across different computer networks at Stanford. Cisco Systems was started by Lerner and Bosack in the classic form of a Silicon Valley startup – it was bootstrapped and funded by the savings accounts, credit cards, and mortgages of its early employees. Although Cisco Systems was twenty years old in 2004, it has already experienced three distinct evolutionary periods. The first period was the years 1984 through 1988. During this time, Cisco Systems was the classic startup. In the early days, it was run from Stanford University before it moved into the home of Bosack and Lerner. The small group of employees who were part of the Cisco team, lived for the company. They worked one hundred hour weeks and sold their product primarily to other educational institutions. Cisco was not a mature company, capable of growing into a dominant multi-national corporation. It was probably best described as an odd offshoot of the Silicon Valley lifestyle full of dedicated computer nerds. The company acquired a cult following. Amongst the university educated computer crowd, Cisco was a hot product. No one envisioned Cisco as the company that would empower the internet generation with Super Bowl ads.

Cisco's second development stage began in 1988 with the arrival of John Morgridge as Chief Executive Officer (i.e. CEO). John built the foundation of the Cisco Systems we know today, but not the company as we see it today. His first tasks were to begin to recruit a professional leadership team, formalize the company's operating procedures and infuse the company with the DNA it required to be successful. From 1988 to 1995, Morgridge's company successfully positioned itself to make quantum leaps beyond its competitors in a short period of time. To cross the chasm from a small company to that of a large company, Morgridge (a) transformed the leadership team, (b) imbued fiscal responsibility, (c) created a fanatical devotion to customers and (d) created the business plan to expand into multiple markets thus diversifying Cisco's customer base and revenue sources.

These four objectives were serendipitously timed with revolutions in the internet, telecom, and optical industries. Morgridge recruited into Cisco a professional business leadership team that was capable of managing growth and providing guidance. From Cisco's first phase, the leadership team developed a fanatical devotion to customers and customer support. This devotion utilized an early form of the internet to openly communicate with customers. There is no question that Cisco's early presence as a supplier of routers for the internet put Cisco first in line for the companies that would reap rich rewards from the internet explosion. The fourth component that Morgridge contributed to Cisco was a business plan to diversify its business within its defined market. On September 21, 1993, Cisco acquired Crescendo Communications for $89 million worth of Cisco stock. This was Cisco's first acquisition and it had a dramatic and lasting affect. The acquisition was driven by Cisco's customers, specifically Boeing and Ford Motor Company. Each of these customers told Cisco that they were planning to make sizable purchases of Crescendo products and they would prefer a relationship with between Cisco and Crescendo. Cisco's fanatical focus on its customers and the desire to diversify its product line beyond routers, but to stay within its market segment, was fulfilled by the Crescendo acquisition. In 2003, the Crescendo product line was still a part of Cisco's product catalog and has been responsible for more than $500 million in sales. What is of further interest is that many of the executives that were part of the Crescendo team are still part of Cisco and many are in senior positions. A quick look at the Cisco web page in 2003 revealed that Mario Mazzola, CEO of Crescendo and two of his top lieutenants Jayshree Ullah and Massimo Prati were still employed and active within the Cisco leadership team. All three were Crescendo alumni and more then ten years later they are all still at Cisco Systems. Within the ranks of Nortel Networks and Lucent Technologies, who were active acquirers of companies in the late 1990s, it is nearly impossible to find senior leaders who are still part of the company ten years after any acquisition.

John Morgridge was elevated to Chairman in 1995. His replacement as CEO was a man named John Chambers who had been at Cisco since 1991 as SVP of Operations. This extraordinary executive fused his career experiences from previous technology markets with the challenges of growing Cisco from a successful public technology company to a global networking power. To position Cisco as a leader in its field, Chambers accelerated and revolutionized the strategy of acquisitions while leveraging Cisco's strong internal technology development resources and market leading position in the router market. Before his arrival at Cisco, John Chambers had successful positions at two large technology companies: IBM and Wang. During his career stops at these two companies, he bore witness to the troubles that IBM experienced when DEC and other mini-computer suppliers successfully introduced SNA capable computers at a fraction of the cost of an IBM mainframe. When he joined the mini-computer and word processing powerhouse of WANG in 1983, he arrived just in time to bear witness to one of the most stunning collapses in technology history, as nine years later WANG would file for bankruptcy protection. Both of these career experiences provided hard lessons for Chambers, but would become foundations for his principles in leading Cisco. As will be identified, the lessons of IBM pre-Gerstner and WANG would not empower him to foretell the collapse of the technology markets post 2000 – but it would provide Chambers with the skills and strategies necessary to adroitly lead Cisco through a market that many companies would find perilous.

When Chambers took the helm at Cisco, he organized the company in somewhat decentralized structure that fostered internal entrepreneurialism. The objective was to enable the customer-focused technology teams, which had been the foundation of the company, to continue to innovate without the overhead of a centralized structure. This structure worked extremely well as the internet exploded in 1996 and Cisco found itself in an increasingly large and accelerating marketplace. Decentralization is typically a more wasteful corporate structure, but when markets are rapidly growing and time to market is the critical path, decentralized is the optimal structure as proven by IBM's PC development team. Within the decentralized structure the concept of internet time was developed. Internet time is a theory that companies that are competing in hot, rapidly growing, emerging markets must move faster than their competitors. Nine to five are standard working hours – but five to ten is more common when on internet time. Above all the companies to network computers, Cisco Systems personified the belief that the network was the enabling component of the internet and the fundamental driver of a new world. *"Networking is going to change everything. It's going to change the way we live, work, play and learn. Are you ready!?"* [see David Bunnell quoting John Chambers, CEO of Cisco Systems, *Making the Cisco Connection*, 2000, Page 45]

Under Chambers leadership, Cisco revolutionized the strategy of acquisition within the technology community. For the five year period from 1996 through the end of 2000, Cisco acquired 63 companies for a total of cost of approximately $33.4 billion. Post the year 2000, Cisco has made 38 acquisitions (as of March 2006) for a total approximate value of $11.8 billion. Although Nortel and Lucent were acquiring companies during this period of time, it was Cisco that refined the acquisition process started by 3Com and Bridge from a tactical customer driven process with Crescendo, to an internal growth strategy designed to foster external strategic growth in new technology vertical markets. This was unique to Cisco as compared to Nortel and Lucent; Cisco was a young upstart that was still forming its customer base, internal processes, and corporate DNA. Somewhere inside Cisco, there is a report that details the success or failure of each acquisition, as that information is not in the public domain. Not all of Cisco's acquisitions were successful, but they did not shy away from making decisions and moving quickly to alter their business and capture market share when opportunities developed. The following table outlines the external messaging that Cisco provides regarding their acquisitions from the web page circa mid 2005.

Year	Company Acquired	Transaction Value	Year	Company Acquired	Transaction Value
1993	Crescendo Communications	$94.5 Million	2000	PentaCom Ltd.	$118 Million
1994	Newport Systems	$94.9 Million		Seagull Semiconductor, Ltd.	$19 Million
	Kalpana Inc.	$203.8 Million		ArrowPoint Communications, Inc.	$5.7 Billion
	Lightstream Corporation	$120 Million		Qeyton Systems	$800 Million
1995	Combinet Inc	$114 Million		HyNEX, Ltd.	$127 Million
	Internet Junction	$55 Million		Netiverse, Ltd.	$210 Million
	Grand Junction	$348 Million		Komodo Technology, Inc.	$175 Million
	Network Translation	NA		NuSpeed Internet Systems, Inc.	$450 Million
1996	TGV Software, Inc.	$115 Million		IPmobile, Inc.	$425 Million
	Stratacom, Inc.	$4Billion		PixStream, Inc.	$369 Million
	Telebit's MICA Technologies	$200 Million		IPCell Tech and Vovida Networks, Inc.	$369 Million
	Nashoba Networks	$100Million		CAIS Software Solutions	$170Million
	Granite Systems	$220Million		Active Voice Corporation	$266 Million
	Netsys Technologies	$79 Million		Radiata, Inc.	$295 Million
	Metaplex, Inc.	NA		ExiO Communications, Inc.	$155 Million
1997	Telesend	NA	2001	AuroraNetics, Inc.	$150 Million
	SkyStone Systems	$89.1 Million		Allegro Systems, Inc.	$181 Million
	Global Internet Software, Group	$40.25 Million	2002	Hammerhead Networks , Inc.	$173 Million
	Ardent Communications Inc.	$156 Million		Navarro Networks, Inc.	$85 Million
	Dagaz	$108 Million		AYR Networks, Inc.	$113 Million
	LightSpeed International	$160 Million		Andiamo Systems, Inc.	$2.5 Billion
1998	WheelGroup Corporation	$124 Million		Psionic Software, Inc.	$12 Million
	NetSpeed Inc.	$236 Million	2003	Okena, Inc.	$154 Million
	Precept Software	$84 Million		SignalWorks, Inc.	$13.5 Million
	CLASS Data Systems	$50 Million		Linksys Group, Inc.	$500 Million
	Summa Four, Inc.	$116 Million		Latitude Communications, Inc.	$80 Million
	American Internet Corporation	$56 Million	2004	Twingo Systems, Inc.	$5 Million
	Clarity Wireless Corporation	$157 Million		Riverhead Networks, Inc.	$39 Million
	Selsius Systems, Inc.	$145 Million		Procket Network, Inc.	$89 Million
	Pipelinks Inc.	$126 Million		Actona Technologies, Inc.	$82 Million
1999	Fibex Systems and Sentient Networks	$445 Million		Parc Technologies, Ltd.	$9 Million
	GeoTel Communications Corp.	$2 Billion		P-Cube Inc.	$200 Million
	Amteva Technologies, Inc.	$170 Million		NetSolve, Inc.	$NA
	TransMedia Communications, Inc.	$407 Million		dynamicsoft Inc.	$55 Million
	StratumOne Communications, Inc.	$435 Million		Perfigo, Inc.	$74 Million
	Calista, Inc.	$55 Million		Jahi Networks, Inc.	$16 Million
	MaxComm Technologies, Inc.	$143 Million		BCN Systems, Inc.	$34 -122 Million
	Monterey Networks, Inc.	$500 Million		Protego Networks, Inc.	$65 Million
	Cerent Corporation	$7.4 Billion	2005	Airespace, Inc.	$450 Million
	Cocom A/S	$65.6 Million		Topspin Communications, Inc.	$250 Million
	WebLine Communications Corp.	$325 Million		Sipura Technology, Inc.Vihana, Inc.	$68 Million
	Tasmania Network Systems, Inc.	$25 Million		FineGround Networks, Inc.	$30 Million
	Aironet Wireless Communications, Inc.	$799 Million		Sipura Technology, Inc.	$70 Million
	V-Bits, Inc.	$128 Million		Vihana, Inc.	$30 Million
	Worldwide Data Systems, Inc .	$25.5 Million		FineGround Networks, Inc.	$70 Million
	Internet Engineering Group, LLC	$25 Million		M.I. Secure Corporation	$13 Million
	Pirelli Optical Systems	$2.15 Billion		NetSift, Inc.	$30 Million
2000	Compatible Sys. and Altiga Networks	$567 Million		KiSS Technology A/S	$61 Million
	Growth Networks, Inc.	$355 Million		Sheer Networks	$97 Million
	Atlantech Technologies Ltd.	$180 Million		Nemo Systems	$12.5 Million
	JetCell, Inc.	$200 Million		Scientific-Atlanta	$6.9 Billion
	infoGear Technology Corp.	$301 Million		Intellishield Alert Manager	$14 Million
	SightPath, Inc.	$800 Million	2006	SyPixx Networks	$51 Million

Figure 4: Cisco Acquisitions (Source: *Cisco Web Page*)

As Cisco Systems went through the internet revolution during 1996-1999, it provided the company with a unique opportunity. It is rare that markets collide, especially mature markets wherein there are a small number of large incumbent suppliers (i.e. old regimes). This is what happened to the networking and telephony markets in the mid to late 1990s. The internet was the force that drew together the traditional telecom equipment markets that were dominated by Nortel and Lucent and the enterprise data market that was being increasingly dominated by Cisco Systems. As these markets neared collision, it provided Cisco a crossover opportunity. As part of the acquisition strategy under Chambers, Cisco acquired companies that enabled them to compete in the telephony market, compete in larger deals, and compete against incumbents such as Nortel and Lucent. The creation of hundreds of telephony companies post the Telecom Act of 1996 was a great benefit to Cisco. Almost overnight, there was a large and growing market in which there were no incumbent suppliers. Cisco, Nortel, Lucent, and many other companies found a large green field market with few barriers to entry. The market was open to any company that could move fast and this certainly played to the strength of Cisco and Chambers' leadership focus.

As Cisco moved into the year 2000, revenues had grown to more than $4 billion per quarter. This is a remarkable achievement for a company that was modestly started only sixteen years earlier. Cisco was now the global leader for networking in the enterprise market and making progress towards becoming an important supplier in the telecom industry. Under Chambers, Cisco executed far better than any other company in the networking industry. Comparisons to Microsoft are respectable. Both Cisco and Microsoft have strong product margins, dominant market share, and strong cash balances. By the end of 2000, Chambers had led Cisco through a golden age of networking, wherein they were able to conquer new markets, provide resources to ensure the long-term survival of the company, and developed customer base in all developed nation-states in the world. The first five years during which Chambers led Cisco are not without fault, but the success far outweighs any failures.

When looking at the history of Nortel Networks, we can define five distinctive evolutionary phases from the history of the company that parallel the creation and evolution of AT&T. The first phase occurred during the years 1895 through 1914. The company known as Nortel Networks did not always go by this name. In 1895, Bell Canada spun off its telephone equipment manufacturing operations. The new company was named Northern Electric and Manufacturing Company. The primary source of revenue was telephone equipment manufactured under license from AT&T as well as non-telephone products such as phonograph machines and sleigh bells.

In 1914, the Northern Electric and Manufacturing Company was combined with the Imperial Wire and Cable Company to form Northern Electric Company Limited. This was the second historical phase of the company that would someday be known as Nortel Networks. Forty-four percent of the new company was owned by Western Electric and fifty percent was owned by Bell Canada with a small group of minority owners.

By 1929, 56.3% of Northern Electric Limited was owned by Bell Canada with another 43.6% owned by AT&T's Western Electric equipment division. This ownership arrangement enabled Northern Electric to share the technology discoveries of Bell Labs as well as manufacture under license the products developed by Bell Labs for the Canadian market. Northern Electric emerged from the Second World War with a strong manufacturing base and growing markets for the telephone, television and radio products that it manufactured. The technology licensing agreement with Western Electric continued until 1962. The changing structure of the telecommunications market in North America forced Northern Electric to modify their corporate strategy. These changes mark the transition from the second to third phases of the evolution of Nortel Networks.

The arrangement to license and share technology from Western Electric existed until 1962. The Consent Decree between AT&T and the United States Government in 1956 forced a number of changes at Northern Electric. The first change was the divestiture of Northern Electric from Western Electric. This change was mandated by the Consent Decree of 1956. The second change was the selling off of all non-telecommunications assets in 1957. Northern Electric was making the commitment to focus on telecommunications. The end of the relationship with Western Electric left Northern Electric without a technology research arm to develop products. Northern responded by creating Northern Electric Laboratories in 1959 and by becoming a wholly owned subsidiary of Bell Canada that mirrored the model of AT&T in the U.S., wherein AT&T owned the long distance network, many of the local telephone companies and the research (i.e. Bell Labs) and manufacturing operations (i.e. Western Electric) that supplied products to the long distance and local telephone divisions.

By 1970, the company was changing again as the impact of the Carterfone decision against AT&T opened the U.S. market to Northern Electric. Nineteen seventy also bore witness to a major organizational change in the structure of Northern Electric. Northern Electric Laboratories, created in 1959, became Bell-Northern Research (BNR). It was jointly owned by Bell Canada and Northern Electric. Northern Telecom Incorporated was created to be the sales and distribution arm of the company in the United States. By 1976, Northern Electric changed its name to Northern Telecom and was the first telecommunications supplier to have a complete line of digital phone switches (i.e. DMS). What had started as a Canadian subsidiary of Western Electric, with a broad line of telecom and non-telecom products to cover the vicissitudes of the telecommunications market, was now a fully independent company with a research division capable of developing and manufacturing telephony switches to compete with the best switches from the AT&T Divisions of Western Electric and Bell Laboratories.

The years from 1970 to 1994 mark a period of growth and maturity as Northern Telecom emerged from Canada to become a global supplier of telephone switches and the archrival of its former owner, AT&T. The history of these twenty-four years is the story of the evolution of the telecom market in the United States and abroad. Northern Telecom's focus during these years helped form the DNA of the company. A number of leaders in the company focused its research resources on developing products that were ahead of the technology adoption curve. Northern delivered a full line of digital switching products before AT&T (i.e. Lucent). The discussions regarding the breakup of AT&T in the early 1980s opened the door for Northern to secure business from AT&T in 1982. Northern rapidly expanded into Europe and Japan when it secured the first foreign supply agreement with NTT of Japan in 1983 for its DMS product. The breakup of AT&T opened the U.S. local telephony market to Northern. By the mid-1980s, Northern was supplying switches to many of the U.S. RBOCs as well as emerging European carriers, such as Mercury, in the UK.

The late 1980s and early 1990s are the time that defined and formed the fifth stage of Northern's evolution. The digital phone switch business was maturing and Northern was clearly a major player in this global market. Within the telecom industry, some people viewed other technologies as the future of the industry. How many more telephone companies needed phone switches? Within the industrialized world, telephone adoption within populations of certain nation-states had reached the upper ninetieth percentile. In 1989, Northern revealed its future when it announced FiberWorld. FiberWorld was Northern's entrance into and commitment to the world of fiber optic communications. There was initial success, but the program did not meet the company's expectations through the early nineties. While FiberWorld was in its formative stages, Northern was breaking into the China market in 1993 and beginning to become a major supplier of switching equipment for wireless networks. As Northern Telecom approached its one-hundredth year in 1995, it had emerged as a multinational corporation, providing technically advanced solutions the world over.

From 1980 to 1990, the structure of the market ecosystem had significantly changed. Mobile phone providers and paging companies were a hot market on the enterprise side of the model as few consumers could afford mobile phones in 1990. Vast sums of money were being spent to wire and network enterprise facilities around the world because of the proliferation of the personal computer and servers. The large corporations that had made substantial investments in mainframe and mini-computers found themselves with two parallel networks in 1990. One network was mainframe centric and the other network was client/server centric. Both networks required wide area network (i.e. WAN) connectivity and companies were emerging to supply networking equipment to the enterprise as well as the service provider to support the increase in data connectivity. Despite the growth of data connectivity, it was still a small percentage of the overall service provider revenue mix. Voice was the service that generated the majority of top line revenues and bottom line profits for service providers. In the 1990 Market Ecosystem model technologies such as ATM and Frame Relay were emerging as potential technologies that would impact the services and the flow of revenue in the future. Internet access was based on dial-up lines, with a limited number of companies, universities, and government agencies having high-speed dedicated lines. It should be noted that in 2005 we measure high-speed access to the consumer market in terms of megabits. In 1990, high-speed internet access was measured in kilobits per second or a fraction of a megabit. What was soon to change was an explosion of service providers offering telephony services, bandwidth options, and internet access. See **Chart 4: 1990 Market Ecosystem** in the Chart and Model section.

Through the Looking Glass

In 1992, only a small number of technically perceptive people had heard of the internet. These people were technology specialists in universities, governments, or obscure computer companies. If one looks back at the 1994 Annual Report from AT&T, the following passage can be found from the world's largest telecommunications company: *"Think back just three years ago. Unless you were an academic or a computer hacker, chances are you had never heard of the worldwide computer network known as the Internet. And you weren't tired of references to the Information Superhighway because no one was talking about that either. A lot has happened. More trans-Atlantic telecommunications circuits were added in the past three years than in all previous history. The Internet now connects some 25 million people worldwide. Electronic mail, voice mail and portable phones have become everyday staples for many. At the same time, half the world is still waiting to make its first phone call, and the waiting period for a phone line in some countries is 10 years. The good news is that many of them may not be waiting much longer. Developing countries now recognize the indisputable links between communications capability and economic development. What does all this mean to the shareowners and employees of AT&T? In a word ,opportunity. As technologies and industries converge to meet expanding demand for everything from portable communications to information services to interactive entertainment, what is emerging is a new 'global information industry.' What has so* *many people excited is that this new industry is worth well over $1 trillion today and it's growing 8 to 10 percent annually."*

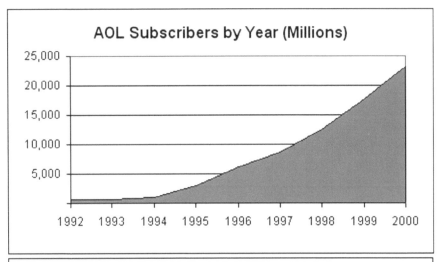

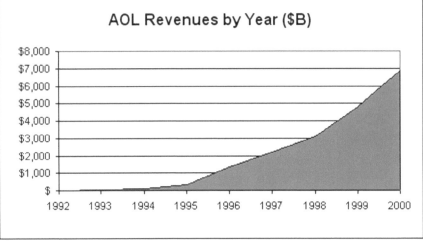

Figure 5: AOL Subscriber and Revenue Growth
(Source: Author's Research from AOL SEC Filings)

The internet, as we know it today, did not exist in early 1994. When we think of the leading brands of the internet, we think of eBay, Amazon.com, Yahoo, Netscape, AOL, Napster, Priceline, Google, and many other companies. In 1994 only one of these companies existed, America Online. AOL had one million subscribers by late 1994, but by mid-2002 it had exceeded 35 million subscribers. Their customer base had grown 35 times in seven years. For a business that was twelve years old to experience customer growth of 35 times in seven years, is an indication that sometime unusual or revolutionary was happening. AOL was not always known as AOL. It was founded in 1982 as Control Video Corporation or CVC, targeting on line services for the Commodore 64 home computer. In 1985, CVC changed its name to Quantum Computer Services. They had ten thousand subscribers for their service. By 1987, the evolving computer market forced a change of focus from the Commodore computer to the Macintosh computer. A new service was launched in conjunction with Apple called AppleLink. In 1989, AppleLink was renamed America Online, but the company was still known as Quantum. For the first twelve years of the company, subscribers grew from a few thousand to one million in 1994 and then five million in 1996. From 1996 to 2002, the company grew their subscriber base seven times more than the entire customer base achieved in the first fourteen years. Revenues grew 70 times from $98 million in 1994 to $6.8 billion in 2000. This is highly unusual. Companies that have been in existence for more than a decade do not often grow revenues from sub one hundred million to $1.3 billion in two years or ten times revenue growth in eight quarters. In 1996, if you were looking for evidence of a revolution or a new economy, you had to look no further than AOL to find the evidence you needed to make an investment decision. While AOL was twelve years old in 1994, other soon-to-be-famous dotcom companies were in their formative stages hoping to capitalize on the same revolution as AOL.

eBay would be incorporated in September 1995. Amazon.com opened its virtual doors in July of 1995. A company called Mosaic Communications was founded on April 11, 1994. It would eventually be renamed Netscape Communications in late 1994 and go public in August 1995. Yahoo was founded in 1995 and Google would not be incorporated until September 1998. The impact that these companies had on the established companies cannot be underestimated. Understanding the scope and significance of this revolution is a multipart process. It is part technical, part financial, part social, and definitely global in nature. Before exploring the key elements of this revolution, we must return to the analysis of Cisco Systems, Nortel Networks, Lucent Technologies, and AT&T.

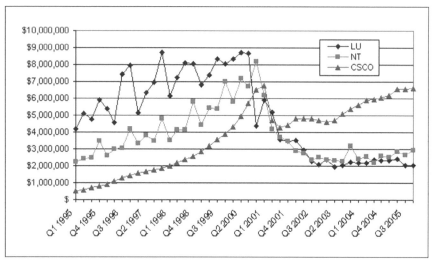

Figure 5: Lucent, Nortel and Cisco Quarterly Revenues ($Billions)

Nortel and Lucent were born as children of the Bell System. They are products of the fundamental growth of global telephony services. Both companies can trace their roots to the 19th century. From a revenue perspective, Lucent only started reporting revenues separate from AT&T in 1994. For discussion purposes, we will assume that Lucent had its first quarter with revenues exceeding four billion dollars in 1995, which was the first quarter they reported revenues separate from AT&T. During that same quarter, Nortel reported revenues of $2.2 billion and Cisco reported revenues of $515 million. Lucent was twice the size of Nortel and eight times the size of Cisco. Five years later, Lucent reported revenues of $8.3 billion, Nortel $5.8 billion, and Cisco $4.3 billion. It took Lucent and Nortel nearly one hundred years to reach the level of $4 billion in quarterly revenues. Cisco achieved the $4 billion in quarterly revenue milestone in sixteen years.

For a company to grow at that rate in an adjacent market segment that was becoming increasingly overlapping, something unusual had to be occurring. If we look forward another seven quarters, we find Cisco consistently achieving quarters in excess of $4 billion, while Nortel and Lucent were reverting to quarterly revenue levels from the early 1990s. This is one of the important drivers of the revolution we are seeking to understand. Cisco Systems grew from a small group of computer geeks to a company that could challenge the state sponsored incumbent suppliers of telephony equipment in a fraction of their lifetime. This is the power of revolution. Revolutions have the ability to disrupt the economic order that had existed for decades. What was once a sleepy, government regulated business that could be accused of being a closed duopoly, suddenly changed and enabled what had long been impossible. Again, this is the power of revolutions. They can change what had seemed for a long time to be impossible to change. Revolutions provide hope, where there was no hope, and fear where there had been no fear. A revolution can make the impossible seem possible. For those companies and people caught in the impending revolution, many fundamental beliefs that had remained unchanged for years would be shattered during the late nineteen nineties and into the new millennium.

CHAPTER TWO:
A Coming Revolution in a Regulated Market

War in its ensemble is not a science, but an art. - Jomini

The history of technology, telecom, and computers in the United States is the story of creation and destruction. With each new significant technology an adjacent or new market vertical was created to the existing market structure. New companies rose to prominence and successfully moved into new markets or suffered the fate of fleeting glory as their markets declined over time and new companies with new technologies and solutions rose to power. Independent of market vertical, this cycle of creation and destruction can be identified over a long period of time over many inter-related technology markets.

	Mainframes	Mini-Computer	PC/Workstation	Client/Server	Databases	Internet	Storage	PC	Web Services	Grid Computing
Computing	IBM CA EDS Amdahl	DEC DG Tamdem Wang Stratus	Microsoft Intel Compaq SUN	Novell Lotus	Oracle	Yahoo Netscape Amazon eBay	EMC Network Appl. Sun	Dell	IBM Microsoft BEA HP	IBM Google MSFT
Networking	**Voice Switches** AT&T (Lucent) Northern Telecom	**CrossConnects** Tellabs DSC	**HUBs** Synoptics Cabletron 3Com Chipcom	**Bridging/Routing** Cisco Wellfleet Vitalink Crosscomm Bridge Retix	**Switching** Cresendo Kalpana Grand Junction Synernetics Xylan	**FR/ATM** Cascade Stratacom Ascend Newbridge Fore	**SONET** Fuji Cerent Nortel	**GigE** Extreme Foundry	**Optical** Nortel Ciena	**Apps & Security** Games? Intel? ?
SP	**Monopoly** AT&T	**AT&T Breakup** RBOCs MCI Sprint GTE Sprint	**Cellular/Paging** McCaw SkyTel	**Digital Cellular** NextTel	**Broadband & PCS** Omnipoint Voicestream Worldcom	**Wireless** Sprint PCS Verizon Cingular	**Deregulation** Verizon SBC Qwest	**ISP** AOL	**Consolidation** Comcast Verizon at&t(SBC)	**Content** Apple Disney ESPN NFL? ?
	1980	1984	1985	1987	1990	1995	1997	1998	2000	2006+

Figure 7: Technology/Innovation Cycle of Creation and Destruction

The above chart outlines at a very high level, the evolution of the service provider market, networking technology, and computing technology with companies that can be considered the winners or extremists in each stage. The computing segment is a data centric market and the service provider market is a voice centric market. The networking segment is the bridge between the two markets, over time the distinctive trend is towards a convergence of the telecom and computing markets. Computing and the service provider market become increasingly integrated with each other via the networking segment. An interesting observation is that the winners in each market segment are typically not repeat winners in other market segments. Over time, winners are acquired, eliminated, or left to decline.

In the previous chapter the history and the impact that the introduction of the personal computer and networking technology had on the corporation was summarized. On its own, the introduction of the personal computer into the fortune 10,000 market is a revolution – but this is really a revolution within a revolution. It is true that the PC changed the manner in which corporations deployed computer technology and the productivity methods of the employee, but the revolution we are going to examine occurred post 1994. What fuelled the growth of the PC market and the computer industry was the ability to network computers. The PC, an IBM mainframe or mini-computer from DEC, WANG, or Data General is interesting as a standalone tool, but it becomes a powerful workplace tool when it is networked, wherein it can exchange information and foster productivity in multiple locations. People working on networked computers, in multiple locations, sharing information, collaborating, and interacting is far more useful than one user on one computer. The story of the *Six Years that Shook the World* is in part the story of the PC, but in large part it is the story of the network. The internet is just a name for a network. It is true that the internet is the largest global public network, but it should be viewed as a network that contains many sub-networks. The ubiquitous proliferation of computer networks interacting through the internet is the fundamental change that launched the internet, telecom, and optical (ITO) revolution of the 1990s.

To fully provide a framework with which to understand the ITO Revolution, we will use the G3 Market Model. The G3MM provides a framework for understanding the exchange of market share. To put the G3 Market Model into context with the ITO Revolution, let us focus on the U.S. telecom market pre and post 1996, which are outlined in this chapter. In this chapter we are focusing on the non-shaded portion of the G3MM, which is the first phase of the model:

Start: A stable market condition typically regulated or one in which there is a minimal exchange of market share. This condition is not an emerging market, but rather a mature market typically dominated by large corporations. Within this market, the regulatory constrains placed on it have provided for a stable market in which an undetermined quantity of inherent value has been accumulated. See **Chart 8: G3MM Start Stage for ITO Revolution** in the Chart and Model section.

A Viewpoint from 1994: The Old Regimes of Telecom and Networking

1994 was the last below average year for technology stocks before 2000 - 2001. There was a market correction for internet stocks in 1997, but it had little long term affect on the leaders of the ITO Revolution. 1997 was merely a pause in the ITO Revolution. Many weak dotcom companies were chased from the market, while the strong companies continued to gain market share and strength from the public equity markets. Companies such as Cisco, Nortel, Amazon.com and Yahoo all peaked in market value in early to mid 2000. eBay seems to be the exception to this group as it has continued to appreciate in value well into 2004. The intervening years between 1995 and 2001 are the *Six Years that Shook the World*. These are the years that would give rise to Global Crossing, WorldCom, Enron, @hOME, Yahoo, Netscape, US Robotics, Redback Networks, Cascade, Ascend, Lucent, and AOL/Time-Warner; who culminated the period with the largest merger in the history of business at $156 billion in January 2000 – which would be only a few months before the peak of the ITO bubble. These companies were created in the hot fires of a great revolution at a time when the old regimes (i.e. companies) were under great stress to adapt to rapid changes, real or perceived in their markets, in their customer base, and in their methods of business.

In 1995, the U.S. telecom markets were on the verge of a great change. The change had not yet occurred, but companies were already positioning themselves to seize on what they perceived the future structure of the U.S. telecom market would be after it underwent radical changes. The old regimes of 1994 were giant corporations of the newly labeled old economy world; companies such as AT&T, MCI, Bell South, US West, Bell Atlantic, Nynex, Bell South, Ameritech, Pacific Bell, and a host of dominant technology suppliers such as DEC, IBM, Data General, Wang, Cray, Unisys, NCR, and others. Some of these companies would emerge post-2001, while most would be absorbed in the acquisition frenzy that dominated the late 1990s. The word acquisition is used rather than the word consolidation. Consolidation occurs under specific market conditions. The acquisition frenzy that dominated the late 1990s was more of a speculative action, than the natural evolution of the ITO markets.

The economic prosperity of the United States before the ITO Revolution is a critical element of support to validate the conditions for revolution. When we use the term "revolution" we are using this term interchangeably with the word "change." Revolution and change are not necessarily negative processes. They are a natural discourse in the evolution of a market, a society, a business, and life in general. At the end of 1994, we find that the old regimes, that were part of the old economy, are in crisis – not the markets. Companies were dealing with an immediate and substantial change in the methods in which they do business. Suddenly, everything was about the internet. The prevailing state of mind was that if you were not on the internet, you would not be in business in the future. This opinion stemmed from the emergence of e-commerce, which can be defined as a form of electronic commerce in which buying and selling occurs over the public internet, or private intranets, between companies and consumers. The e-commerce revolution forced a massive structural change for global markets and the companies that comprise these markets. Information exchange and the need for information storage exploded into a massive market. The internet created trillions of new pages of electronic content. Corporate leaders were led to believe that companies that conducted business through the postal system, fax machines, and telexes where incapable of functioning in the e-business world without a significant change to their operational procedures. Global reach would be made easier by the internet because it was breaking down traditional barriers between nation-states and cultures. This assumption implies the creation of a global market on an unprecedented scale.

The systematic change to the business infrastructure that the internet possessed was a direct threat to old businesses (i.e. regimes) as well as nation-states. The North American Free Trade Agreement (NAFTA) was signed on September 14, 1993. NAFTA was the prelude to internet and the belief that a global economy free from interference from individual nation-states was emerging. The European Union seemed on the verge of cooperation and the plan was being laid to create a single European currency called the Euro. The internet suddenly emerges onto the corporate landscape and a mechanism exists that fosters rapid commerce between businesses and consumers on a global scale. Within the United States, there was a prevailing belief that a new economy was emerging. The confluence of the 1993 Omnibus Budget Reconciliation Act, NAFTA, and technology developed within the computer and computer networking markets were the foundations of this premise. The new economy would be based on rapid business-to-business (B2B) and business-to-consumer (B2C) transactions. To facilitate these transactions, a new global network would be required to support the emerging global IT infrastructure, which was the underlying foundation of the new economy. In this new order, companies must be free to rapidly exchange information, engage in commerce, and enter and exit markets. To survive in this new world, new companies would need to be created and to create new companies, (i.e. revolutionaries) capital would be required.

As 1994 moved into 1995, the financial capital required to fund new companies was readily available. The economy of the United States was coming out of a recession, but this recession was not preventing access to private capital that fostered the creation of technology based startup companies. From an economic perspective, the economic conditions were equitable to those identified by Brinton in all four of his revolutions. The government was dealing with a fiscal crisis that included budget deficits, an opposition to bureaucracy, and social security funding – but the private markets where strong and private capital was poised to enter new markets when the government signaled their intention to deregulate. When governments deregulate or privatize industries and allow these industries to be competitive, entrepreneurial capital will be invested. The reason capital will be invested is because there is an opportunity for the creation of value and thus an opportunity for substantial financial gain. Concerning the ITO Revolution, the early stages of the revolution were funded by private capital, but the size and scope of the revolution would not have been possible without access to the public equity markets. No discussion of the ITO Revolution is complete without a discussion of the role that venture capital and initial public offerings played in creating and sustaining this revolution. Once the ITO Revolution began, access to the public markets would become open as the stock markets advanced in the mid to late 1990s and foundation of the great revolution took hold.

The wave of telecom privatizations that started in the 1980s and continued throughout the 1990s are part of the process of change from the state ownership of key economic assets to the theories of Hayak [see *The Commanding Heights*, by Daniel Yergin and Joseph Stanislaw]. The idea that the state should own key economic assets is often attributed to an economist named John Maynard Keynes, who was discussed in the introduction essay. John Maynard Keynes was English born economist who was an economic advisor on the British delegation to the Versailles Conference in 1919. He was convinced that the harsh economic terms dictated by the Allies would reap a terrible harvest in the future and as such resigned from the British delegation. Unfortunately for Europe, he accurately predicated the root causes of the Second World War. His primary contribution was *The General Theory of Employment, Interest and Money*, which was published in 1936. The ideas set forth in this work would have a profound affect on the global economies post the Second World War. Keynes's theories were rooted in the belief that the western economies were unstable and they would suffer extreme fluctuations driven by inadequate investment and savings, which are rooted in the psychology of personal uncertainty [see Yergin and Stanislaw, page 40]. The solution to the uncertainty produced by the private sector was to replace private investment with public ownership. Keynes believed that the government should make deliberate investments in public works for the public good and that these investments would serve to stabilize economic fluctuations. Keynes theories became the foundation for macroeconomics and they played a prominent role in world economics after the Second World War for two reasons. The first was the severity of the Great Depression in the United States and the success that President Roosevelt had in starting an economic recovery by making large public investments. In short, here was proof that public investment, public ownership, and government deficits were good. It was under Roosevelt that projects such as the Hoover Dam and TVA were started. These projects invested capital into the economy as well as provided infrastructure for the nation-state. The second contributing factor was that in the nation-states of Europe, wherein economic depression was not defeated such as Germany and Italy, totalitarian regimes took control. Keynes believed that his theories would encourage economic stabilization, provide hope, and offset totalitarianism that forms as a result of economic desperation. Post the Second World War, Keynes and his theories played an important role as the new world order set forth the economic policies of recovery. Keynes was a primary contributor at the Bretton Woods Conference, from which the World Bank and International Monetary Fund were developed. Interestingly, Keynes' role in creating the World Bank and IMF, placed Keynes on the side of globalization and these institutions had contributive roles to the ITO Revolution and the events of 9/11. His greatest contribution was the promotion of his theories of a managed economy and the near universal adoption of his policies in many economies of the world. Keynes provided the world with the economic blue print for a managed, welfare orientated economy. It would take nearly forty years for Keynesian theories to fall out of favor and the transition from state-ownership to private ownership was not only a part of the ITO Revolution, but a major driver of the revolutionary change.

Opposed to the ideas of Keynes, we find the economist, Friedrich von Hayek, and the Chicago School of Economics. The renowned professors at the Chicago School of Economics were believers in free markets. Markets that allowed for open competition produced the best results in quality of goods and services. The Chicago School argued against government intervention and ownership, for government intervention artificially affected the prices of goods and services. The real cost of goods and services are obtained in a free market wherein unsubsidized competitive forces are allowed to react to the ebb and flow of supply and demand [see Yergin and Stanislaw, page >144]. During his tenure at the University of Chicago, Friedrich von Hayek wrote *The Constitution of Liberty*, which was published in 1960. In this work, Hayek argues that free markets were not enough, but rather governments needed to play a role to ensure that laws and rules were enforced. Governments do not manage economic markets – but rather manage the institutions that maintain and ensure a fair and equitable market.

All of this brings us to the very early stages of the ITO Revolution. 1984 was the year that AT&T was broken up – but it was also the year that British Telecom (BT) was privatized. In the U.S. market, AT&T had existed with little meaningful competition until the formation of MCI. In the UK Market, British Telecom held unchallenged control of the stagnant market for telephony services. There was no competition in the UK telecom market and BT existed as a classic government managed bureaucracy in which its employees were more concerned with pensions and work hours than customers and services. As the Conservative Government of Margaret Thatcher took control, they began to mandate new fiscal policies and BT was the first government entity to be targeted for privatization. Prime Minister Thatcher infused competitive life into the UK telephony market by allowing for the creation of competitors to BT, such as Mercury, and then forced the privatization of BT. British Telecom was forced to stand on its own as a for profit company – with no government subsidies. Even at this earliest stage of the ITO Revolution, the shifting economic policies of the western nation-states from state ownership to privatization, set in motion the initial inertia that would culminate in a great revolution in the mid to late nineteen nineties. Revolutions take time and governments that are entrenched in market ownership do not easily relinquish control of economic assets. BT was not the only major telecom service provider to be privatized. From the early 1980s through the late 1990s, a wave of telecom privatization in excess of $154 billion dollars as well as market deregulation expanded throughout the industrialized world. Below is an incomplete list of some of the notable telecom privatization and deregulation projects:

Nation-State	Company	Amount Raised ($millions)	Year	Nation-State	Company	Amount Raised ($millions)	Year
UK	BT	$22,931	1984	Hungary	MATAV	$1,727	1993
Japan	NTT	$70,469	1986	Korea	Korea Telecom	$3,514	1993
Canada	Teleglobe	$467	1987	Singapore	Singapore Telecom	$4,336	1993
Chile	CTC	$35	1987	Latvia	Lattelkom	$160	1994
Belize	Belize Telecom	$52	1988	Pakistan	Pak-Telecom	$327	1994
Chile	ENTEL	$121	1988	Czec Republic	SPT Telecom	$1,450	1994
Gibraltar	Gibraltar Nynex Comm	$10	1989	Indonesia	PT Indosat	$119	1994
Guinea-Bissau	Guine Telecom	$3	1989	Denmark	TeleDanmark	$3,035	1994
Jamaica	TOJ	$84	1989	Netherlands	KPN	$3,791	1994
Israel	Bezeq	$178	1990	Peru	Telefonica del Peru	$3,202	1994
Argentina	Telecom Argentina	$1,779	1990	Bolivia	ENTEL	$610	1995
Argentina	Telecom Argentina	$1,499	1990	Cape Verde	Cabo Verde Telecom	$20	1995
Malaysia	Telekom Malaysia	$1,287	1990	Cuba	ETECSA	$323	1995
New Zealand	Telecom Corp of NZ	$2,500	1990	Mongolia	Mogolian Telecom Company	$11	1995
Mexico	Telmex	$7,769	1990	Indonesia	PT Telkom	$1,590	1995
Barbados	Barbados External Telecom	$22	1991	Portugal	Portugal Telecom	$1,925	1995
Barbados	Barbados Telephone Compan	$3	1991	Ghana	Ghana Telecom	$38	1996
Guyana	Guyana Telecom Corp	$17	1991	Greece	OTE	$530	1996
Australia	Optus	$1,200	1991	Guinea	SOTELGUI	$45	1996
Venezula	CANTV	$2,792	1991	Ireland	Telecom Eireann	$290	1996
Puerto Rico	Telefonica Larga Distancia	$142	1992	Beligum	Belgacom	$2,400	1996
Spain	Telefonica de Espana	$1,579	1992	Germany	DT	$13,360	1996
Estonia	Esti Telepfon	$25	1993				

Figure 8: Sampling of Telecom Privatiizations
Source: 1997 World Telecommunication Development Report, International Telecommunication Union

In the early 1990s, the internet, telecommunications, and optical markets were all on the verge of massive change that would unleash static inherent value. The internet was beginning a remarkable transformation from a government funded research program run by the National Science Foundation (NSF), to a commercially viable network managed by private industry. This may seem simplistic, but it is really the creation of new market. A massive market that would draw in billions of invested capital and create billions in wealth. In 1991, the NSF lifted its ban on the use of the internet for commercial traffic. This was the dawn of the age of e-commerce on a global scale. In 1992, the internet contained more than one million hosts, but it would not be until 1993 that first commercial browser called MOSIAC would be introduced. Most of the revolutionaries (i.e. companies) that would change the world and launch the ITO Revolution were not in existence in 1991.

In the early 1990s, the internet was still controlled as a government funded networking project devoted to university and defense related research. The entire telecom industry within the United States was a tightly regulated business. Open market competition and government deregulation would not be enacted until the mid-1990s, but the process was starting. Agents of change were providing thought leadership within society at many levels and thus forcing the government to consider deregulating the telecom industry. The push to commercialize the internet would force the government to privatize the internet and thought leaders promoted an almost natural connection between the internet and telecom deregulation. By 1994, these changes had yet to occur, but the structural weakness of the government's position was identifiable. The structural weakness of the government enabled the forces of change to use the political process to force a revolution in the telecom industry in the United States and abroad. It is not coincidental that this change occurred at a time when the internet was exploding on the world and the PC was moving from a functional tool in the workplace to an essential element of the home. *"We're right at the center of the true information revolution. As these information tools become pervasive in business, on the road, and in your home, the way we will live our lives and conduct commerce will be revolutionized. I think that the idea of information available at your finger tips and instant global communication is realizable. It will happen substantially over the next four or five years. As a result, we may end up suffering a little from information overload, or spend a little more time on the couch, but I see that as a symptom of our success. Everything we've been talking about is going to create incredible opportunities for software companies like Microsoft that are even larger than we can imagine. And, frankly, I'm very excited about it"* [see Bill Gates, *Red Herring*, October 1, 1993].

By 1995, the growth of the internet and its potential for business had exceeded the ability of the NSF to manage and the internet was transformed into a commercial entity. At this stage in its development, the internet was perceived to possess a vast commercial opportunity. Networks had always been the domain of governments or private corporations. The internet presented an opportunity to develop a global public network that would be used by all people in all nation-states. Sociologically and economically, this had the potential to change the way in which societies behaved as well as to potentially alter economic development. The structural weakness was the not the internet – but rather the old economy methods of business. When the NSF (i.e. government) relinquished management of the internet, it unleashed the forces of change. The internet and its potential to alter the economies and social structure of nation-states were the reasons for change. As 1995 dawned, all the elements for the ITO revolution were falling into place. There was a driver of change in the form of the internet. The government was signaling their weakness to govern by withdrawing from control of the internet and they were on the verge of deregulating the U.S. telecom market. The seeds of the revolution were sown, now it was time for the revolutionaries to seize the day.

Deregulating the U.S. Telecom Market

While the commercial foundations of the internet were being laid, massive changes were on the verge of occurring within the telecommunications industry in the United States. The primary driver of this change would be the Telecommunications Act of 1996. The significant fact to understand is that the telecommunications industry in America was a highly regulated industry before 1996. During the discussions to breakup AT&T in the early 1980s, many argued that the communications infrastructure of the United States was a national asset and therefore should be under the control and regulation of the government of the United States. As a regulated agent, AT&T was charged with the responsibility of building and maintaining the communications infrastructure of the Unties States. Casper Wineberger, then Secretary of Defense, and Arno Penzis, winner of the Noble Prize in physics for discovering background radiation, argued against the breakup of AT&T and against free market competition. Despite opposition by these intellectuals, the leaders of revolutionary forces were able to effect thought leadership to bring about change in the way the U.S. telecom market functioned. This change would not have occurred if there was not a structural weakness within the U.S. government and within the telecommunications market that compelled them to succumb to the forces of change. The breakup of AT&T in 1984 and the Telecom Act of 1996 were seminal moments that changed the fundamental way in which the telecommunications market would affect America and the world. *"The breakup of America's telephone system, acknowledged to be the most efficient in the world, will affect nearly every aspect of our society. How all this came to pass is a frightening example - at a time when America's industries are in a fight for survival against foreign competitors - of what can happen here to a company recognized as one of our major national, and national defense, assets. It is a company that grew by its own efforts and with its own resources to become the world's largest business, whose Bell Laboratories led us into the information age,"* [see, Walter H. Anneberg, 1983].

The structural weakness that existed in the telecommunications market, as well as with the internet, was the perception that the government was preventing economic growth, precluding competition, and denying choice and the government's regulation of these industries stifled innovation. The concept of competition and innovation are the key elements required to support a healthy market that provides a variety of higher quality services to consumers. By 1994, it was obvious to the leading industry revolutionaries who affect thought leadership in the market (i.e. researchers, entrepreneurs, visionaries) that deregulating the telecom market and privatizing the internet would create massive economic growth [see page >60]. Competition would lower the cost of services to the consumer, yet allow capital to be invested to broaden and improve services. *"As technologies and industries converge, what is emerging is a new 'global information industry.' The new marketplace will no longer be divided along current sectoral lines. There may not be cable companies or phone companies or computer companies, as such…There will be information conduits, information providers, and information appliances and information consumer…"* said Al Gore, Vice President of the United States.

In the early 1990s, the fiber optic equipment market was a relatively small market. The major telecommunications companies such as Sprint, MCI, and AT&T were building long distance fiber optic networks, but metropolitan (i.e. metro) builds of fiber networks were limited in scale and mainly confined to cable service providers. Do you remember the Sprint pin drop commercials? Important developments in fiber optic technology were being made at Bell Laboratories and Corning, but there was no significant driver of capacity usage to force telecom companies to upgrade their networks and deploy fiber optics on a massive scale. This would change with telecom deregulation and the commercialization of the internet. The structural weakness within the optical market in the early 1990s was the deficiency of growth drivers. There was no massive economic proposition that would drive the need to deploy large-scale fiber optic networks. Without the need to create fiber optic networks, there was no need for companies to build products to enable the deployment of fiber optic networks. Nortel Networks launched FiberWorld in 1990 and it was a failure. Fiberworld was an attempt but Nortel Networks, at the time Northern Telecom, to bring to market the industry's first line of SONET (Synchronous Optical Networks) based products. Nortel had beaten its competitors to the market by more than year. In reality, Nortel was early to the market and FiberWorld did not meet corporate expectations – but it did lay the foundation for optics expertise inside Nortel, which Nortel would use to dominate an important optical market in the mid to late 1990s.

At the end of 1994, the United States was experiencing important changes within the legislative branch of the federal government. President Bill Clinton was in his second year in office. The economy was growing – yet the Republicans won control of Congress. In a dramatic change of fortune for the Democrats, the Republicans swept to power by nationalizing local issues such as Clinton's policies for universal healthcare and big government. The popular sentiment in the country was that that government was in the way of progress. People and business were being held back by government regulation. The society of the United States was not in retrograde – the government was in retrograde. There were strong political fractures between liberals and conservatives and a general backlash towards the system was building was evident in the O.J. Simpson trial and subsequent riots. Despite these challenges, the country was strong economically. The government looked weak, but the country was strong. America was changing, but the overall economy was strong and there was a general *laissez faire* sentiment that if the government removed regulatory restrictions, the economy would grow, people would be successful. There was a definite feeling that people could be self-sufficient and it was the government that was preventing real growth.

Within the United States, the desire to reform the government came in the form of deregulation. Momentum in thought leadership was building and a policy shift by western nation-states from economic polices perceived to be routed in Keynes to the adoption of economic policies grounded in Hayak and the Chicago School had rescued the western world from the economic malaise of the 1970s – only to bring about opportunity for great success and great failure. Prime Minister Margaret Thatcher and President Ronald Reagan had started this process in the 1980s. By the 1990s, the energy and telecommunications industries were being deregulated or reformed, which opened previously closed markets to competition. There is no doubt that the reform of government policies played an critical part in laying the foundation for a massive investment in the ITO markets, that would explode over the next six years. Once the ITO markets were deregulated, the building mass of private capital [see *Essay One, Chapter Three*] would flow into these markets fueling growth. Revolutions occur when the engines of change are fueled. This would occur in the mid-1990s and create a near *Perfect Storm* in the form of the internet, telecommunications, and optical markets.

A Dawn like Thunder

In 1994, Lucent Technologies did not exist as a standalone company. It was better known as AT&T's Systems Division. In 1995, Lucent began trading as a separate company apart from AT&T. Overnight, a gigantic standalone corporation was unleashed in the market. In their first annual report, dated 1996, Lucent declared on page one, *"The Company is one of the world's leading designers, developers and manufacturers of telecommunications systems, software and products. The Company is a global market leader in the sale of public telecommunications systems, and is a supplier of systems or software to most of the world's largest network operators. The Company is also a global market leader in the sale of business communications systems and in the sale of microelectronic components for communications applications to manufacturers of communications systems and computers. Further, the Company is the largest supplier in the United States of telecommunications products for consumers. In addition, the Company has provided engineering, installation, maintenance or operations support services to over 250 network operators in 75 countries. The Company's research and development activities are conducted through Bell Laboratories ('Bell Labs'), which consists of approximately three-quarters of the total resources of AT&T's former Bell Laboratories division, one of the world's foremost industrial research and development organizations."*

To put into perspective the size of Lucent Technologies, in comparison to Cisco Systems and Nortel Networks, we only have to look at the revenue numbers. From 1995 through mid-2003, Lucent Technologies recorded over $194 billion in top line sales. During the same period, Nortel and Cisco recorded $137 billion and $102 billion is sales respectively. In short, Lucent had sales of more than $56 billion when compared to its nearest rival, Nortel Networks. In regard to global sales, Lucent reported in their 1996 report that its "*...competitors are Alcatel Alsthom, Northern Telecom Limited, Siemens AG and Telefonaktiebolaget LM Ericsson. In 1995, the Company and these four competitors collectively accounted for about 34% of the world's public network systems sales, of which the Company's sales of systems for network operators accounted for 9%.*" Lucent's sales in 1995 were $19.94 billion. If $19.94 billion is 9% of the market, then this is a $200 billion global market. It is noteworthy that Lucent does not reference Cisco Systems as a competitor. Why would AT&T divest a business unit of the company that is contributing nearly $20 billion in annual revenues? To understand this, we need to think about the conditions for revolution and change. In 1995, AT&T was suffering through a massive series of changes. Internally, they were structurally weak as forces inside and outside the company were winning the battle to force a restructuring of the company in order to realize the internal value that was contained and restrained within the company structure. There was a financial crisis in the form of AT&T's stock price and financial condition. The overall economy was stable, yet AT&T was being forced to address a perceived reduction in value. This was its own financial crisis, which highlighted its internal structural weakness and enabled the politics of change to take hold. In a historic move, AT&T's CEO, Robert Allen, announced on September 25, 1995 that AT&T would split into three publicly traded companies. With regard to Lucent, Allen said, "*Changes in customer needs, technology and public policy are radically transforming our industry. We now see this restructuring as the next logical turn in AT&T's journey since divestiture. It will make*

AT&T business more valuable to our shareowners, even more responsive to their customers, and better able to focus on the growth opportunities in their individual markets."

Lucent was not being cast off from AT&T without financial support and long term support obligations. Lucent inherited approximately 100,000 retirees who had worked for the business unit that AT&T was divesting. To support the pension, health care, and retirement obligations, AT&T transferred to Lucent a $28.9 billion pension fund and $3.7 billion trust fund. Few companies going through an IPO process have $33 billion in pension assets on their books and 100,000 retirees to support. The role that these pensioners play in the future evolution of the company and their ultimate fate would be symbolic of ITO Revolution and represent another linkage to historical revolutions within nation-states.

Lucent Technologies was not the only sleeping giant emerging to seize the day of the ITO Revolution. In 1998, Northern Telecom acquired Bay Networks, changed its name to Nortel Networks. *"With this transaction, Nortel and Bay Networks will effectively break out and redefine the center of the information industry – the unoccupied space where data and voice networks, driven by the Internet, are expected to converge,"* [see, John Roth, Nortel CEO, June 15, 1998]. The first major initiative to come out of the merger was called WebTone. WebTone was an attempt by Nortel to build on the familiar. For the previous one hundred years, Nortel had been a supplier of solutions for the dial tone. WebTone represented a transition attempt from the legacy market of the old regimes, to the emerging markets built around the internet or World Wide Web. Nortel was a leader in supplying digital voice switches to telecom providers as well as providing telephony equipment such as PBXs and handsets to enterprise customers. With WebTone, Nortel tried to fuse traditional telephony, such as voice, with the internet and applications that would operate over the internet. The idea was to provide a unifying solution architecture for disparate networks – including voice, data, internet/intranet, wireless, fax, video, and integrated multimedia. The end result was solution that did not do any one function exceptionally well and did not provide customers with a compelling reason to adopt the solution. Nortel quickly retooled their solution set, and as we will see, realized tremendous success during the ITO Revolution providing specific, compelling solutions for optical networks.

By 1995 the structure of the market ecosystem had begun to change the size and scope of investments in technology, computers, and networking. Voice services had been a predominant driver of service provider investment for the previous one hundred and ten years using the date of AT&T's incorporation of March 3, 1885 as a starting point for the telecom industry in the United States. By 1995, the proliferation of the personal computer, the debut of the Windows 1995, the existence of 8 million indexed web pages, and the founding of Yahoo and the IPO of Netscape begin to alter the flow of capital in the Market Ecosystem circa 1995. Computer connectivity was becoming more important than voice connectivity in the enterprise market and the penetration of computers within the consumer market supported the thesis of the growing importance of data services to the consumer market. Even with the emerging demand for data services within the consumer market, the flow of capital between markets was healthy in 1995. See **Chart 5: 1995 Market Ecosystem** in the Chart and Model section.

In 1995 the questions concerning the internet and the personal computer focused on the adoption rate of the technology by the consumer and enterprise markets. Televisions could be found in 63% of American households by 1955. That penetration rate level of U.S. households required eight years to achieve. The current percentage of U.S. homes with a television is about 98% and this level was achieved in 1985 – an additional growth period of thirty years. In 1995 the ITO markets were looking for metrics to help understand how big and fast the ITO markets would grow. To size the new economy, analysts looked that the adoption rates of the television and the telephony. It was assumed that the personal computer and the internet would experience faster rates of adoption [see *Price, Value and Risk*]. Television was the natural technology with which to compare the internet and PC. In 1992, George Gilder published a book called *Life After Television*. In this book he wrote of the coming of the ITO revolution and that technology will emerge in a way that *"…will change the way we do business, educate our children and spend our leisure time. It will imperil large, centralized organizations: television networks, phone companies, government bureaucracies and multi-national corporations … The United States has only to unleash its industrial resources to command the 'telefuture,' in which new technology will overthrow the stultifying influence of mass media, renew the power of individuals and promote democracy throughout the world."* The concept of measuring the size and scope of the ITO Revolution in terms that non-technical people could easily understand goes back to the discussion of framing [see *Price, Value and Risk*] and behavioral economics. Certainly an investment looks really attractive if it is framed as bigger than television and will replace all the major media and entertainment corporations.

As the early 1990s progressed into the mid 1990s, the macro conditions required to support the ITO Revolution where formed. Economically, the United States was coming out of the recession that marked the end of the first Bush Administration. President Clinton's policies of deficit reduction and fiscal responsibility spurred lower interest rates and began to transform the economy of the United States. Unemployment began to decline, small businesses expanded, and the economy began to grow.

Within America, there was a belief that with the end of the Cold War the era of big government was over. This belief was translated into political power at the voting box and set the legislative agenda for the next several years. The governmental structures that had been created under Franklin Roosevelt and expanded by Lyndon Johnson and Richard Nixon were part of the problem – not the solution. America was confident. America was the undisputed leader of the world and her armies had returned from Kuwait victorious – yet people wanted change. They wanted change because they felt confident. Revolutions occur when people are full of self-confidence and are empowered to dream of great expectations. Inflation and stagnation that had plagued America in the 1970s was a distant memory, if a memory at all. The baby boomer generation was maturing and the people had excess capital to invest in the stock market. From America's inherent confidence in her ability to be a global leader, developed the class antagonism that produced the ITO Revolution. There is no question that the ITO Revolution was clearly shaped by the political process that had started in the early 1980s and evolved into the mid-1990s.

There is a reason why a President of the United States loses a midterm election and control of both houses of Congress. That reason was that people wanted and expected more from their government. Political leaders rarely act on their own accord – but rather to facilitate their own careers by seeking to satisfy the demands and aspirations of their constituents. When Newt Gingrich and Republican Party won control of Congress during Clinton's mid-term election, it was a seminal moment in the post-Cold War history of the United States. It signaled a massive change in the power structure of government of the United States. Overnight, the Republicans had control of all the legislative committees and the ability to appoint leaders of the functional elements of the government. The 1994 mid-term election was a signal by those people in America who participate in the political process that they wanted change. This single event set the overriding macro condition that would govern its political thinking for the next several years. Americans wanted change and their desire for change produced the structural weakness within the government that enabled change to take root. Americans wanted less government and more freedom to pursue the rewards of their own accomplishments. President Clinton understood the message and it came at a time when an important bill was working its way through Congress.

As 1995 ended, a legislation candidate was moving through Congress. This legislation was called the Telecom Reform Act. On January 27, 1996 President Bill Clinton addressed the nation and said that the "...*era of big government is over, but we can't go back to a time when our citizens were just left to fend for themselves.*" In February of 1996, the Telecom Reform Act of 1996 was passed by Congress. The telecom revolution of the 1990s does indeed have its Bastille

Day; a day that is equivalent to April 19, 1775 in Concord or February 1917 in St. Petersburg. The Telecom Reform Act was signed into law on February 8, 1996. In the coming weeks, the revolutionaries would seize their day and start the ITO Revolution. It would be a revolution that few people, if any, could comprehend in the early weeks of 1996.

CHAPTER THREE:
Changing the World

Man is the child of custom, not the child of ancestors. - Ibn Khaldun

During ITO Revolution of the 1990s, the Eternal Figaro that fueled the flames of revolution was the revolt against the established methods and infrastructure of business and communication. The revolution studied in this discourse is the transformation in the network equipment and telecom service markets that was driven by technology advancement, deregulation, and the abandonment of established business practices. This revolution would have never been possible without the personal computer, networking technology, the assemblage of the internet and optical networking technology, and the deregulation of the U.S. telecom industry. Combined, these four technology markets forced a regulatory shift that provided the foundation for the ITO Revolution of 1990s and made possible the *Six Years that Shook the World*. The next stage of the G3 Market Model is called the Change stage.

Change: This is the phase in which a market undergoes a change event. Change can come in many forms, but it must be forceful enough to enable a shift in the market structure and enable market share to become dynamic and flow between companies. A change event is often called a revolution and occurs when a market, technology, and regulatory forces converge to dynamically alter the competitive structure of a market. It is this convergence that releases the inherent value of the market – whether that value is derived from regulation or the creation of a new value (i.e. market share). In the case of the ITO Revolution, deregulation enabled existing market share to become dynamic and deregulation enabled the organic creation of new market share by enabling new companies to be created who now had an ability to capture the pre-existing market share. See **Chart 9: G3MM Change Stage for ITO Revolution** in the Chart and Model section.

In the business world, the Eternal Figaro does not stand to admonish the second estate – but rather to admonish the old regimes, which are the ruling corporations of the established markets. Our Figaro's plight is to banish the products of the old regime and their methods of business. This is an ongoing cycle in nearly every segment of every market. An important differentiator for technology companies is the cost of technology development and the value placed on the intellectual property rights of the technology created. Technology companies that provide innovation, traditionally have a high entry cost. This is why significant attention is paid to intellectual property rights or IPR. Traditional market models for technology adoption have short and extreme market adoption curves.

A well known model for technology adoption developed by Geoffrey A. Moore was termed the Technology Adoption Life Cycle [see Geoffrey A. Moore, *Inside the Tornado*, 1995, page 25]. This model was developed for use by companies who are introducing a new technology or managing the adoption and migration of a new technology. The model does not address market share, economic conditions, and the affect that technology and competitors have on technology acquisition, service cost and profitability levels. During the 1990s, the Technology Adoption Life Cycle became a mainstay of companies in Silicon Valley and Boston. Venture capitalists and entrepreneurs used this model to project the next hot technology, with the hope of funding the next Cisco Systems. Moore describes the model has having six distinct phases. The first is the Early Market period, in which there is real excitement concerning the technology, but no real commercial deployments of the new technology. A good example of this is a technology called ATM or Asynchronous Transfer Mode. ATM was a hot technology in the early 1990s. So much was expected of this technology that an ATM Year 1 conference was held. It was followed by ATM Year 2, ATM Year 3, ATM Year 4, and eventually everyone moved on to a new technology. ATM was a big technology in the 1990s and many companies profited from its deployment – but it never achieved the life altering expectations that attendees at the ATM conferences had expected.

The second phase is The Chasm in which initial interest in the new technology has waned and companies need to prove in the new technology to return to the excitement levels of the Early Market stage. The Bowling Alley stage is when the technology is deployed for niche applications, by mainstream companies before a broad market adoption of the technology occurs called the Tornado Stage. Main Street is the period after the technology has been developed, proven, and deployed on a broad scale. The End of Life period is the mature market stage of the technology, revenues are in decline for the technology, but sales are still occurring and companies are managing the latter life-cycle stage of the technology.

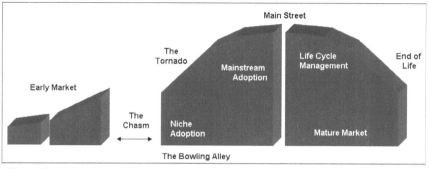

Figure 9: Technology Adoption Life Cycle by Geoffrey A. Moore
Source: *Inside the Tornado*, Geoffrey A. Moore, HarperBusiness, 1995, page 25

Moore's Technology Adoption Life Cycle has been adopted and adapted by many companies, consultants, and industry researchers to exploit of the notion of Moore's Law, as in Gordon Moore (Intel Founder) not Geoffrey Moore. There is a theory that technology markets have a fast, cyclical life-cycle that is unique to technology markets. The supposition is that innovation in the cookie industry is less competitive than innovation in the computer, networking and technology industries. Emerging, innovative computer and networking technology is consistently being invented that begins the process of obsolescing the existing technology before that technology has reached the Main Street stage. Sometimes, the new technology does not proven in, while other times the technology is not adopted as quickly as anticipated. The following chart is a product of Gartner, Inc. and is called the Gartner Hype Cycle for Identity and Access Management Technologies, 2005. The illustration below draws on the stages of a technology adoption life cycle to illustrate how various technologies flow through a model of market adoption. Technologies begin with the triggering event and progress through the early adoption period, before having to cross what Moore defined as the "The Chasm" and Gartner terms the "Trough of Disillusionment." Once a technology has been proven in and adopted for some applications, the market begins to accept the broader applicability of the technology and mainstream adoption of the technology will occur. The Gartner Hype Cycle is another example of creating a market adoption model for technology using a lifecycle approach to technology.

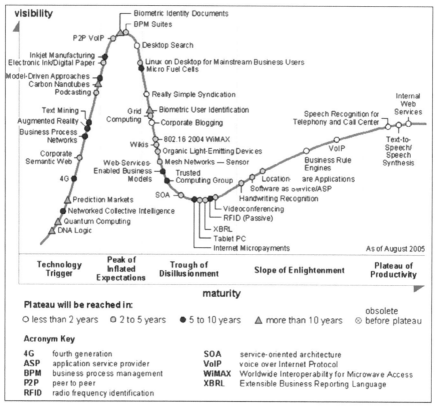

Figure 10: Gartner Group Technology Hype Life Cycle

Source: Reproduced with permission from Gartner Group [see *Gartner's Hype Cycle Special Report for 2005*, August 2005, Jackie Fenn and Alexander Linden]

The revolutionaries of technology (i.e. startup companies or old regimes with intrepreneurial programs) place large value on their technology and ability to bring innovative IPR to market. The value of being a market first mover with innovative technology that is timed to market adoption curve is that objective of all technology companies. Bad market timing with innovative products results in FiberWorld, where innovative products matched to perfect market timing is what occurred in the late 1990s when Nortel stole the 10G long-haul optical market [see *Essay One, Chapter Five*] from Lucent and others. IPR direct translates into customer wins, market share, revenues, earnings per share, and value. If we go back to our basic definition that business is the act of making money, then IPR is a key component for technology revolutions. Cisco Systems has traditionally had product margins in the high sixties to the low seventies. Nortel and Lucent traditionally received margins in excess of seventy percent for their telephony switches. High margins can be commanded because intellectual cost required to develop these products is high. Not everyone is capable of developing networking products. For those companies that can develop technology that is revolutionary to the existing market, they can command a sizable premium for their efforts.

As we detailed in previous chapters, the revolution we are studying is the telecom revolution of the mid to late 1990s and how the personal computer, internet, and optical revolutions fueled the revolution in telecom. The telecom revolution occurred because there was an Eternal Figaro for telecom. Our Figaro sought the right to offer long distance as well as local telephony services and high-speed networking services – but this struggle would only result in a revolution when it became bigger than life. Revolutions do not occur because someone wants to start a competitive phone company or offer an identical product or service at a lower cost. Revolutions start because people believe that they are missing something in their lives that is dramatic enough to cause them to accept personal risk. Our Figaro's struggle was elevated by the PC, networking technology, and the internet. Our Figaro was not only seeking just to offer competitive telephony services – but rather to usher in a new digital age and a new social order. Revolutions are all about changing the world – they are not about small changes. The struggle for our Figaro was nearly forty years long. *"'What's going on is a revolution in telecom,' says Joseph Nacchio, Qwest's CEO and a former AT&T exec. 'It's going to be as dramatic as the shift from the telegraph to the telephone,' echoes Nayal Shafei, Qwest VP and a graduate of the MIT Media Lab. 'We aren't a telco, we're a multimedia carrier.'"* {see *Wired*, Steve G. Steinberg, March 31, 1998].

In the telecom world of the United States, the old regime was AT&T and the many companies spawned from AT&T. The revolution against AT&T started with Microwave Communication Incorporated, or MCI. MCI was an early revolutionary who used microwave technology to build private networks that bypassed the legacy copper local loops used by AT&T's local telephony divisions. Over time, what MCI gained that was significant was the right to offer long distance telephone services. Initially, MCI had limited market coverage and the service was not to the same quality level as AT&T's, but in the fullness of time MCI built a business by offering discount long distance services. MCI raised debt and continued to build an improved network. By the early 1980s, MCI was becoming a global company and a worthy competitor to AT&T. The litigation between AT&T and MCI is what led to the eventual ruling by Judge Harold H. Greene that AT&T was a monopoly. To the settle the case, AT&T leaders decided to break up the company. A breakup would satisfy the government complaint that AT&T was a monopoly and it would provide a solution to the problem of the legacy local copper loops. The legacy of the local loops had been considered a plague on AT&T since the end of the Second World War, by the executive leadership team. AT&T had lobbied against microwave technology because it could be used to rapidly build an inexpensive alternative to AT&T's networks – thus destroying their investment in the copper local loops. By breaking up the company, AT&T's executives found a solution to the legacy local loop, their perceived Sword of Damocles, as well as a solution to their legal dispute with the U.S. Government.

The Telecom Act of 1996 was the moment of spontaneity that launched the ITO Revolution. Before we can analyze the first stages of the ITO Revolution, we must understand the Eternal Figaro of our revolution. As the early 1990s closed, there was a belief that we were on the doorstep of a new digital age and that this new age would be better served with open market competition for telecom services. The Telecom Act of 1996 was intended to open this market. Representative Ed Markey of Massachusetts said of the Telecom Act of 1996, *"This bill unleashes a digital free-for-all..." "America's economy is even better suited for today's rapidly changing knowledge-based economy that it was for the mass production, industrial economy of earlier times. The new bottom up economic environment is tantamount to a giant information processing system that enhances the its capacity to absorb, adapt to, and manage ongoing revolutions in technology, information, and logistics that to dynamic and complex to be handled by a top-down system, no matter how talented its bureaucracy, government, or corporate oligopoly. The marriage of a new economy and an older American culture promises a comparative advantage that will endure,"* see *A Second American Century*, Foreign Affairs, May/June 1998, Mortimer B. Zuckerman, page 23].

For those of you who do not remember the signing of the Telecom Act of 1996, it was quite a significant affair, for rarely had an act of legislation be signed into law with such high expectations. The expectations were so high, that some people called this bill revolutionary. Vice President Al Gore said of this act, *"What we've seen in the last decade is amazing. But it's nothing compared to what will happen in the decade ahead. The word revolution by no means overstates the case. But this revolution is based on traditions that go far back in our history."* During the signing of the Telecom Act into law, President Clinton said *"Today our world is being remade yet again by an information revolution, changing the way we work, the way we live, the way we relate to each other. Already the revolution is so profound that it is changing the dominant economic model of the age. And already, thanks to the scientific and entrepreneurial genius of American workers in this country, it has created vast, vast opportunities for us to grow and learn and enrich ourselves in body and in spirit. An industry that is already one-sixth of our entire economy will thrive. It will create opportunity, many more high-wage jobs and better lives for all Americans. Soon, working parents will be able to check up on their children in class via computer. Families heading off on vacation trips will be able to program the fastest route in their car computers, thanks to the work the Department of Transportation is now doing. On a rainy Saturday night, you'll be able to order up every movie ever produced or every symphony ever created in a minute's time."* Both of these statements are quite dramatic in their description of the revolution that was upon us in February 1996. President Clinton and Vice President Gore were two of the intellectuals who transferred their allegiance from the old economy and the old regimes and embraced the ITO Revolution. The old regimes had lost the battle for influence with the regulatory bodies of the Government of the United States. When the leader of the most powerful nation-state sets such high objectives, people will be attentive and business will act upon the opportunity being created by their government.

In his speech announcing the signing into law of the Telecom Act of 1996, President Clinton noted the historical parallels of the Act. He said, *"It is fitting that we mark this moment here in the Library of Congress. It is Thomas Jefferson's building. Most of you know President Jefferson deeded his books to our young nation after our first library was burned to the ground in the War of 1812. The volumes that line these walls grew out of Jefferson's legacy. He understood that democracy depends upon the free flow of information. He said, 'He who receives an idea from me receives instruction himself without lessening mine. And he who lights his paper at mine receives light without darkening me.'"* We can also see the close relationship that revolutionary acts have with opportunity. Figaro's complaint was that he was denied opportunity by class divisions and privileges of French society, President Clinton realized that by opening the telephony markets to competition this would answer the call of Figaro for the ITO Revolution. He said, *"This historic legislation in my way of thinking really embodies what we ought to be about as a country and what we ought to be about in this city. It clearly enables the age of possibility in America to expand to include more Americans. It will create many, many high-wage jobs. It will provide for more information and more entertainment to virtually every American home."* Revolutions are about change, opportunity and expectations. Al Gore communicated this same message in his remarks, *"As we enter this new millennium, we are learning a new language. It will be the lingua franca of the new age. It is made up of ones and zeros and bits and bytes. But as we master it ... as we bring the digital revolution into our homes and schools ... we will be able to communicate ideas, and information – in fact, entire Toni Morrison novels – with an ease never before thought possible."* With the ITO Revolution started, our Figaro's plight had been solved. Open competition had come to the U.S. telephony services market. Soon, we would have thousands of television channels and movies to choose from and every book in every library would be on line for all to enjoy. A new digital age was upon us and we would all soon be rejoicing in its many splendors. To build on a phrase from Wordsworth, there stands America on top of golden hours and with the birth of the digital age, her future seeming born again.

In fueling our perfect storm of a revolution, two networks collided in early 1990s. The first network was the vast collection of private networks that had been built by the Fortune 5000. Born in the furnaces of IBM, these networks had fuelled the rise of Cisco Systems, Synoptics, Wellfleet, 3Com, Cabletron, and numerous other networking companies. The wealth produced by these companies for their goods and services, was committed to a continuous deployment of computer and networking technology. Before the client/server revolution of the 1980s, companies made technology investments that lasted for years. The pace of computing change was measured in years – not days and months. The PC revolution and the client/server network evolution accelerated the pace of change. Technology adoption and deployment cycles went from years to months. The percentage of private capital committed to technology programs within the private sector increased exponentially from the 1980s to the new millennium.

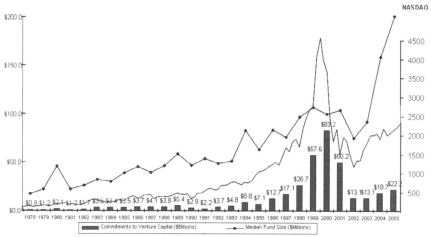

Figure 11: Venture Capital Commitments, Average Fund Size Superimposed on NASDAQ Composite Index
Source: Dow Jones VentureOne (www.ventureone.com)

The second network that collided with the private network of the Fortune 5000 was the internet. Before 1994, the internet was an obscure network used by university researchers and government agencies. The opening of this network for commercial use fueled the Figaro of change. Before the internet, companies built wide area networks from dedicated private lines. Computer networking for the Fortune 5000 was about private networking and the in sourcing of networking technology. Private lines are the key element to identify, as they are the source of a vast amount of predictable revenue for telecom service providers. The threat to AT&T's private line business posed by microwave technology in the 1960s, motivated them to develop the Telpak Tariff [see *Essay One, Chapter One*]. Thirty years later, a new network based on a collection of technologies (i.e. IP, Frame Relay ATM, WDM, Optics) emerged as a threat to the biggest beneficiaries of private line revenues: RBOCs and IXCs. This network was called the internet. Seemingly overnight, companies could bypass costly private line services and network remote facilities through the internet. The opening of a public network that could support a new method of business called "Business to Business," or "B2B," had important ramifications for the telecom industry. The internet was believed, by industry visionaries, to become an impacting force of growth on the telecom services, computing, and technology markets by the mid to late 1990s. Jeff Bezos commented, on his discovery of the internet's growth rates that *"It was pretty clear that anything growing at that rate might have been invisible then, but would certainly be ubiquitous in the future,"* [see Jeff Bezos, March 1999 Red Herring]. The internet did provide companies, post the Telecom Act of 1996, the ability to outsource networks and leverage the internet as a public, global asset. An important transition point for the commercial industries was the ability to use the internet and by-pass private networks. The internet enabled telecommuting and the networking of small, remote offices with high-speed data connections, which were not affordable prior to deregulation. There was a fundamental belief that commercial businesses would outsource their networks to the dearth of service providers that were created post the Telecom Act of 1996. These many new service providers created post the Telecom Act of 1996 were investing in new networks rich in leading edge technology that provide a wide range of services which were not available in the prior market structure. These new services would be cost-effective enough to obligate business to abandon owning networks and outsourcing their networking needs. *"I think the spread is opening up between the players. I think from my perspective that Nortel was the first from our cadre – Nortel, Cisco, and Lucent – to start doing acquisitions. And this group is now spreading out. Nortel has rapidly moved to the top of that, and that has corresponded to the rate at which we embraced the Web. Cisco is trying to follow the traffic. As corporations are saying, 'I don't want to build networks anymore,' Cisco is realizing that the business they have enjoyed from enterprises is really going to flip toward service providers"* [see John Roth, InfoWorld, January 24, 2000, by Martin LaMonica, Jennifer Jones]. In hindsight, this observation that enterprises had a high desire to outsource their networks, was really an example of inductive reasoning. If the global economy is accelerating towards structure that relies on and requires technology infrastructure, why would corporations want to surrender control of a critical asset? This was just a limited observation of occurrence that was based upon the heightening excitement and unrealistic expectations of the technology bubble as it neared its peak in 2000.

In 1993, there were approximately 600 web sites accessible via the internet. By 1995, the number of internet web sites had grown to more than 100,000 and would top one million sites by 1997. In the minds of the revolutionaries and the old regimes, this was credible evidence that a significant paradigm shift was underway. If the internet could grow from 600 sites to more than one million in three to four years, this had the potential to enable corporations to reduce their private network infrastructure and costs by using the public internet. Businesses could expand their networks to include their customers as well as their suppliers. Electronic data interchange (EDI) was viewed to have a huge potential for reducing the fundamental costs of business transactions and improving corporate efficiencies. Less than twenty years earlier, companies were trying to find networking technologies that would enable their employees to utilize computers spread across multiple offices. Now companies were contemplating networking their computers with the computers of their suppliers, partners, and customers. This was only possible by reducing the cost of the telecom infrastructure. In the mid-1990s, the private and public internet collided in a confluence that would create a global market valued in the trillions of dollars.

The Telecom Act of 1996 opened up local telephony markets to anyone who could raise money to start a competitive business to the Incumbent Local Exchanges Carriers (ILECs). The ILECs are the local telephone companies that were in existence pre-1984 in addition to the Regional Bell Operating Companies (RBOCs) because they were part of the AT&T breakup in 1984. When AT&T was broken up, seven regional companies were created: PacBell, Ameritech, Nynex, Bell Atlantic, Southwestern Bell (SBC), US West, and BellSouth. The seven RBOCs are essentially regulated businesses within their operating regions, wherein they own the vast majority of local telephone lines both copper and fiber optic. There are two primary types of phone lines or circuits. Local circuits serve to provide service in the metropolitan markets and these are generally referred to as "local services." Long haul circuits are used to interconnect regions and global markets and this is generally referred to as "LD" or "Long Distance." When AT&T decided to breakup in 1982, the long distance portion of the company looked upon the breakup as an opportunity to divest AT&T of the legacy copper infrastructure in the local loop. There was a fundamental belief that the copper infrastructure was a liability – not an asset. Over the next twelve years, this belief would be proved wrong by three market trends. The first trend was the price of long distance voice services. AT&T was becoming a provider of only long distance services, or out of region consumer and business services, which already had competition from MCI and Sprint. Throughout the late 1980s and into the 1990s, AT&T and MCI engaged in an aggressive price war for long distance services. AT&T was using their diversified and healthy balance sheet as a weapon against MCI. The result of this price war between long distance suppliers was that the price of long distance services would steadily decline into late 1990s. The following chart from the FCC shows erosion in revenue generated on a per call basis. Over a ten year period, from 1992 to 2002, interstate call revenue per call declined by 50%.

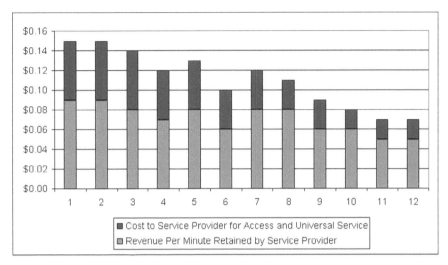

Figure 12: Revenue Per Minute for Interstate Calls
Source: Federal Communications Commission, Study on Telephone Trends, June 21, 2005, Chart 13.1

The seven RBOCs that were saddled with the liability of legacy copper local loop infrastructure, realized that had to deal with government regulation – but no real competitors of any significance. This market reality was one of the driving elements to deregulate the local telephony market and encourage competition to reduce consumer cost and improve services, as seen in the long distance market. The second reality that moved against the long distance providers and new entrants who entered the market after the Telecom Act of 1996 was that the RBOCs controlled access to the customer. In the world of business, the best position to be in is the original producer of product and the direct seller of that product or service to your customer. This is the most desirable position because it enables the acquisition of the highest percentage of margin dollars. Margin dollars (i.e. profit) is why businesses exist. The RBOCs controlled access to the consumer in the form of the local loop. The exception to RBOC was the ~1300 incumbent local exchange carriers (ILECs), primary found in second and third tier markets and rural areas.

All the other service providers were forced to pay the RBOC for telephony access to the consumer. This is the reason why cable service providers are a legitimate threat to the RBOCs – they have their own local loop access to the end consumer. In the service provider business, a direct sale of services or capacities to the end-user is the crown jewel of the business. Wholesale services are a nice complement to a profitable direct business – but not a substitute for having many end-user customers directly buying services. The third force that moved against the long haul providers was the creation of the internet. The internet reduced the need for private line services. Businesses could use the public internet to network their offices.

The Telecom Act of 1996 forced the RBOCs to open their local access lines to competition. RBOCs are treated in the U.S. as a regulated monopoly, which means they must publish their service rates in the form of a "tariff" and seek government approval for their tariffs. The framers of the Telecom Act of 1996 believed that by forcing the RBOCs to open their circuits to competitive use, a vibrant, competitive market would be created. The result was that it did foster the creation of many companies and it did open local telephony markets to competition – but it did not create a vibrant and self-sustaining market. Two charts from the FCC illustrate the affect of the Telecom Act of 1996 on local loop ownership. These charts show (a) a decline in the total number of local loops or access lines reported by ILECs and (b) potentially a plateau of number of access lines provided to other carriers at around 16%. If this is true, then end user access lines for telephony voice services is in decline and the Telecom Act of 1996 has resulted in the ILECs retaining 84% market share, or ownership of the local loops they owned in January 1996. In nine years they have lost 16% of their market share, which is not a total loss because the other carriers are leasing the local loop from the ILEC. The ILEC may not be receiving the service revenue – but they are receiving a fee for the local loop connection from the competitive service provider who is leasing the loop to sell their own telephony service.

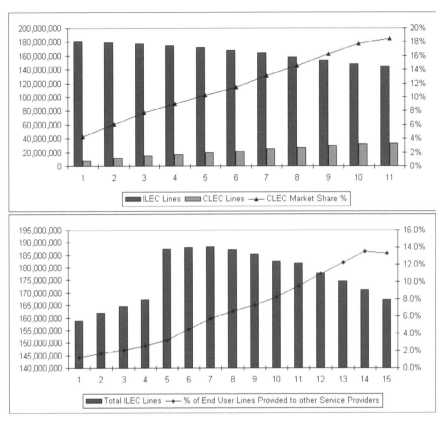

Figure 13: ILEC/CLEC End User Lines and ILEC End User Lines Provided to other Service Providers
Source: Federal Communications Commission, *Local Telephone Competition Report*, July 8, 2005, Charts 1 and 4

The Telecom Act of 1996 enabled new service providers to lease local access lines from the RBOCs, put services on these lines, and sell these services to customers in their territories below the published tariffs of the RBOCs. The deficiency with this model was that these new companies, called Competitive Local Exchange Carriers (CLECs), had to build new networks and facilities. They could get access to the physical lines owned by the RBOC by paying for these lines at a discounted rate, but they had to install their own switching equipment. Building new networks is a capital-intensive process. The new CLECs would be forced to incur heavy debt loads and to support their debts on smaller margins (i.e. profit) compared to the RBOCs. To win customers, CLECs had to undersell the RBOC for local phone services. Additionally, the new CLECs were building a business on the same legacy infrastructure that AT&T had viewed as a liability. To make the business problem more difficult to solve, the new CLECs had to offer the same service as the RBOC, on the same legacy infrastructure, at a lower cost, and find a way to survive on smaller margins (i.e. profits). In hindsight, this conclusion is easily identifiable – but in 1996 the lure of gaining access to the lucrative telecommunications industry was too hard to pass for entrepreneurs and investors. The event that occurred post the Telecom Act of 1996 was a large investment of capital for building competitive networks to the ILECs. Hundreds of CLECs spent capital buying telephony equipment and building networks. In the mid-1990s, if you wanted to be in the business of offering telephony services, you had to build a network or purchase some elements of telephony network. This is why Lucent and Nortel realized a renaissance in their telephony switching business at a time thought leaders were predicting the demise of telephony due to VoIP.

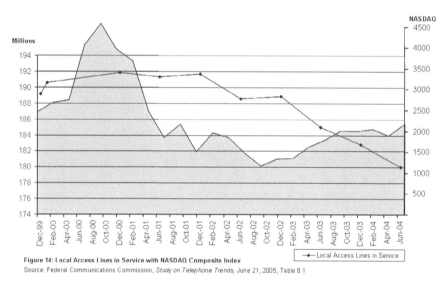

Figure 14: Local Access Lines in Service with NASDAQ Composite Index
Source: Federal Communications Commission, *Study on Telephone Trends*, June 21, 2005, Table 8.1

It took a few years for the networks to be built and another year or more for the new service providers to market their service and acquire customers – but in time the new CLECs began to acquire market share. By June of 2004, CLECs accounted for 16% of the end-user switched access lines in the U.S. market. More alarming is that from 1999 the overall number of end-user switch access lines declined from 189 million to 180 million. The CLECs have slowly made progress acquiring market share – but long term trend reflected in the chart above is a decline on overall market share.

The Telecom Act of 1996 failed because it did not deregulate the local telephony market in the United States. The framework of the law was sufficient to trigger competition and investment, but the result was catastrophic because the local telephony market was still regulated at fixed costs. An underlying premise of the Act was the assumption that the millions of installed copper phone lines that connect the homes and businesses of America could never be replicated and therefore, to foster competition the government must force the RBOCs to give access to their copper lines to competitive companies below the retail market value. This belief had three fundamental fallacies.

The first fallacy is that the millions of copper access lines would never be replaced. It is true that the copper local loop will be functional for many decades to come, but the RBOCs and ILECs can make headway by replacing the copper infrastructure if they choose to. In mid-2005, after committing to a fiber upgrade to support video services, Verizon reported *"...by the end of the second quarter, the company was deploying or selling Fios fiber-to-the-premises (FTTP) broadband services in 15 states. Verizon plans to introduce Fios TV services in the second half of the year and is currently pursuing cable TV franchises in about 200 communities."* SBC made the same commitment to offer video services and reported in mid-2005 *"We are investing $4 billion in Project Lightspeed to upgrade our wireline network, increasing the available bandwidth to provide consumers with the next generation of high-speed data, voice and video services. We will deploy an additional 40,000 miles of fiber in our networks — in some cases taking the fiber directly to the premises — enabling a full range of IP services and features. This will deliver bandwidth of 20 to 25 megabits ... more than four times as fast as our fastest broadband speeds today. That's more than enough to provide high-definition IPTV, superfast broadband and video on demand — and just about any other application you can think of. Within three years, about 18 million SBC households will have access to this network. That makes CES the ideal venue for unveiling a new service that captures the universe of choices and options available, putting you at the center. That's why we call it SBC U-verse. U-verse ensures that the entire universe of communications and entertainment works for — and around — you. U-verse marks a new beginning for SBC and millions of American consumers. We are using the power of the Internet to finally achieve the convergence of voice, data and video that consumers deserve, and we are taking the confusion out of communications with easy-to-understand choices. U-verse delivers the simplicity of bundling communications and entertainment services that fit each customer's needs."* The many cable service providers that have existed in the U.S. have wired millions of homes at least two times since the dawn of cable TV. If the cable service providers can deploy fiber networks to the home, there is no reason why the RBOCs and several well-funded new entrants could not solve this problem.

The second fallacy is that it is generally a bad business practice to allow competitors to use your assets against you in business. This is the result of the Telecom Act of 1996. If you are an RBOC, you must provide competitors access to your network in order for them to deploy services to sell against you. The construct of this business arrangement is anti-innovation and anti-revolution. If the RBOCs were forced to give access to their network assets to their competitors, why would this provide them with an incentive to invest in upgrading their assets that they are being forced to share with competitors? In reality, it forces them to slow innovation. If Sprint and MCI could build competitive networks to AT&T in the 1970s and 1980s, there is no reason to believe that a few well funded CLECs and cable service providers could not do the same in competition against the RBOCs.

The third fallacy of the Telecom Act of 1996 is that it fails to foster the competitive nature of America and does not believe in the American desire to compete. Americans find competition irresistible. We have always been a nation that seeks challenges. We do not shun from that which is difficult – but rather we seek to overcome the greatest of odds as long as we have the ability to compete freely and openly. This does not mean we are without fault – but rather we are about worthiness of the challenge and the knowledge of the rewards. If America can successfully complete the Manhattan Project and land a man on the moon and return that man safely, we should be able to effective deploy broadband to the millions of homes in America. The ability of Americans to respond to a challenge is truly a national asset. In the end, the Telecom Act of 1996 will be remembered as a failure because it did not open markets to free and unregulated competition. It failed because it did not live up to the spirit of America, which is echoed so strongly in the words of John F. Kennedy, *"We dare not forget today that we are the heirs of that first revolution. Let the word go forth from this time and place, to friend and foe alike, that the torch has been passed to a new generation of Americans – born in this century, tempered by war, disciplined by a hard and bitter peace, proud of our ancient heritage – and unwilling to witness or permit the slow undoing of those human rights to which this nation has always been committed, and to which we are committed today at home and around the world. Let every nation know, whether it wishes us well or ill, that we shall pay any price, bear any burden, meet any hardship, support any friend, oppose any foe to assure the survival and the success of liberty...So let us begin anew – remembering on both sides that civility is not a sign of weakness, and sincerity is always subject to proof. Let us never negotiate out of fear. But let us never fear to negotiate. Let both sides explore what problems unite us instead of belaboring those problems which divide us...In your hands, my fellow citizens, more than mine, will rest the final success or failure of our course. Since this country was founded, each generation of Americans has been summoned to give testimony to its national loyalty. The graves of young Americans who answered the call to service surround the globe. Now the trumpet summons us again--not as a call to bear arms, though arms we need – not as a call to battle, though embattled we are – but a call to bear the burden of a long twilight struggle, year in and year out, 'rejoicing in hope, patient in tribulation' – a struggle against the common enemies of man: tyranny, poverty, disease and war itself....And so, my fellow Americans: ask not what your country can do for you--ask what you can do for your country. My fellow citizens of the world: ask not what America will do for you, but what together we can do for the freedom of man."*

These words were spoken in the context of our nation's foreign policy, but they are equally applicable to our nation's domestic and economic policies. The spirit of the framework of President Kennedy's words should govern the economic policies of our nation-state.

The response of the RBOCs to the Telecom Act of 1996 was to consolidate and seek permission to provide long distance services. By 2001, only four RBOCs remained and only two had their original name. Bell Atlantic and Nynex had merged, then acquired GTE and changed their name to Verizon. SBC had acquired Ameritech and Pacbell. Qwest had acquired US West and Bellsouth remained as the only original baby bell without any major changes from the day it began operating on its own in 1984. By mid 2003, all of the RBOCs had beaten the threat of the CLECs and had achieved, or begun to seek, regulatory approval to offer long distance in addition to their local telephony services.

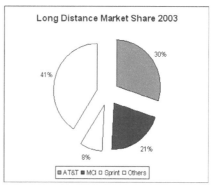

Figure 15: Long Distance Market Share 1984 to 2003
Source: Federal Communications Commission, *Study on Telephone Trends*, June 21, 2005 Chart 9.2

The part of AT&T that remained, post the 1984, breakup was the long-distance component of the company. Devoid of its local telephony services, AT&T had become an Interchange Carrier (IXC). An IXC is a Service Provider who specializes in long distance, or out of region transport. The RBOCs, ILECs, and CLECs provide in-region transport or local services, but customers, whether consumer or business class, make long-distance calls and require out of region connectivity to many parts of the world. Typically, RBOCs, ILECs, and CLECs would hand off voice and data traffic to IXCs who would then transport them to their destined region in the world and hand them back off to the local RBOC, ILEC, or CLEC. Post 1996, competitors started to develop in the IXC market to challenge AT&T, MCI/Worldcom, and Sprint. Companies such as Global Crossing, Level 3, Qwest, 360 Networks, Tycom, and Williams, to name a few, built huge continental or global fiber networks and purchased billions of dollars of switching equipment to service their customers, who would soon be filling their networks to capacity. This is how the telecom bubble of the late 1990s was created. Before the telecom bubble of the 1990s could begin to grow, the industry needed a bell weather event that signaled to all that the revolution was underway. Every revolution needs a Bastille Day or shot heard around the world. For the ITO Revolution, the event that captured the immediate attention of the everyday citizen was the IPO of small software company in California.

The initial public offering of Netscape was the revolutionary act for the internet component of the ITO Revolution. The California based Netscape issued five million shares of stock that were targeted to trade at $28 dollars per share. By the close of trading day on the first day, August 8 1995, the price of Netscape's shares had raised to $72 a share, giving the company a market capitalization of $1.96 billion. A market cap of nearly $2 billion dollars is quite an achievement for a company that was less the five hundred days old and had but a single software based product that within a year would be offered for free. In terms of value creation, Netscape was able to create $125 million in value per month during its first sixteen months. Netscape's IPO initiated a stampede towards the internet. All levels of the thought leadership within the market embraced the internet after Netscape's IPO. Investors, entrepreneurs, bankers, consultants and venture capitalists, wanted to be part of the revolution. There was no need for the intellectuals to transfer their allegiance to the new economy and the internet, Netscape pulled everyone into the internet.

Three months before the IPO of Netscape another important internet company went public. UUNet was founded in 1987 as a non-profit company that provided Arpanet (i.e. early variation of what would become the internet) connections for individuals and organizations seeking a means to provide email interchange. Email was considered by many people to be the first "killer application" for the internet. In their famed *Internet Report*, Mary Meeker and Chris DePuy of Morgan-Stanley declared that *"at a minimum, e-mail should become pervasive. So should Internet/Web access: **Email is the "killer application of the Internet today**, and browsing through information services the "killer app" of tomorrow,"* [see, *the Internet Report*, Mary Meeker and Chris DuPuy, February 1996, page 1-2]. In 1990 UUNet became a for profit company and in 1992 received its first venture capital investment. As interest in the internet and connections to the internet began to accelerate in the early 1990s, private capital and revolutionary leaders found their way to UUNet. John Sidgmore joined UUNet as CEO in 1994. John was a veteran from GE Information Systems and had sold his former company to Computer Sciences Corporation. One of the major wins for UUNet was they became the backbone internet provider for Microsoft's MSN network, which came with an investment from Microsoft. UUNet was the first company to offer commercial connections to the internet when the internet was privatized. UUNet went public on May 25, 1995. Goldman Sachs was the lead underwriter and the company raised $68 million dollars. UUNet was not the only provider of commercial internet connections. Companies such as Netcom on-line and PSINet were in business as the internet connectivity market was gathering momentum. Less than a year after their IPO, UUNet was acquired by MFS Communications for $2 billion. A few months later Worldcom would acquire MFS Communications and with it UUNet, which would become a very public component of the Worldcom value proposition and positioning of the company through the NASDAQ run-up in the late 1990s.

As 1995 ended and 1996 began, the forces of change for the ITO market had been marshaled to the point of revolution. The internet was privatized and open for commercialization. The government had deregulated the telephony market and opened it to free market competition. Financial capital was positioned for investment in the emerging markets of the ITO Revolution as well as in the technology that would enable the digital revolution. There was a substantial belief that the new technologies that the ITO Revolution was bringing to the market, were close to commercialization and thus the market adoption of new technology would occur quickly. This is the mob mentality of revolutions. Expectations do get ahead of reality and perception is often stronger than reality. Great expectations and boastful predications become the new reality of the day – rather than the facts.

Thus, the ITO Revolution of our generation passed from the intellectuals and leaders who had championed the forces of change, to the revolutionaries who were responsible for managing and enacting change. The companies (i.e. revolutionaries) who were formed in the hot fires of revolution still had to establish their businesses, secure their markets, and prove themselves to be worthy successors to the old regimes. In the ITO Revolution, this would prove to be remarkably difficult for some and easy for others. Thousands of dotcom companies were formed in 1996 and 1997 as all the words in the English language were registered as internet domain names. Nearly every segment of the economy was affected by the internet revolution. From books to pets to janitorial supplies, if you wanted to buy it, someone was offering it on the web. Many of these early attempts to capitalize on the internet would find commercial success difficult to achieve, but the spectacular success of a few early dotcom companies fueled the fire of revolution. People believed it could be done and the spectacular success of some only served to validate the revolution and drive others to the banner of change.

On the telecom side of the ITO Revolution, more than three hundred competitive local exchange carriers (CLECs) were formed in the United States. Some CLECs targeted major markets while others focused on second and third tier U.S. markets. The capital required to create and build three hundred CLECs is enormous. It has been estimated that the CLECs in the U.S. market have raised and spent in excess of $56 billion since the passage of the Telecom Act of 1996 through mid-2001. Ravi Suria, was an analyst at Lehman Brothers and in August 2000 released a report entitled *The Other Side of Leverage*. In this report he estimated that new economy telecom and media companies had raised an estimated $240 billion in debt. *"The endgame for these companies was always to sell out. Nobody was looking to run a telecom services company 15 years down the line. The money allowed companies to go out and build networks and go after customers in competition with the old-line telecom companies, which had networks that were 30 to 40 years old. The argument of the new economy companies was that the Old Economy companies had the customers and the revenue base, but they didn't have the networks. The new guys said, 'We can borrow money from the markets, build out the networks and then sell to the guys who have the customers,'"* [see Ravi Suria, interview with Thestreet. com, March 28, 2001]. The following chart is brief summary of ten CLECs and the total amount of funds raised and their debt levels by mid-2001.

Company	July 2001 Debt Levels ($Millions)	July 2001 Funds Raised to Date ($Millions)
Net2000 Communications	$225	$603
Birch Telecom	$310	$105
Adelphia Business	$1,500	$461
ITC-DeltaCom	$515	$150
Time Warner Telecom	$1,400	$1,584
McLeod USA	$3,000	$750
XO Communications	$5,200	$4,800
WinStar	$3,600	$1,020
Teligent	$1,440	$1,700
e.Spire	$980	
Totals	$18,170	$11,173

Figure 16: Selected 2001 CLEC Funding and Debt Levels

The formation of three hundred new telecom service providers, many in tier one cities, created a dramatically different market for telecom equipment suppliers compared to the market that existed prior to 1996. Three hundred new telecom service providers added market share to the overall market size for telecom equipment. The legacy market of incumbent telecom service providers (i.e RBOCs, IXCs, CAPs) was now challenged by a number of new service providers who possessed vast sums of capital, who were willing to spend their capital quickly, and who made a mandate to invest in new technologies. From an entrepreneurial and venture capital perspective, this was a dream come true. Private capital could be put to work to develop products for the telecom equipment market created by the need of the new service providers to deploy new technology that provided a technical advantage over the legacy technology used by the old regimes – AT&T, SBC, Nynex, Bell Atlantic, US West, BellSouth, and MCI. In turn, the rapid pace of the ITO Revolution forced the incumbent equipment suppliers (i.e. Nortel, Lucent and Cisco) to react by acquiring technologies, products, and customers that they could not obtain through their internal, legacy processes. Revolutions change the way people act. Revolutions in business change the method in which companies act. This change is reflected in the rapid rise in merger and acquisition (i.e. M&A) activity post 1994. As the internet, then telecom and optical revolutions commenced, companies were compelled to increase strategic activity levels to maintain pace with the markets.

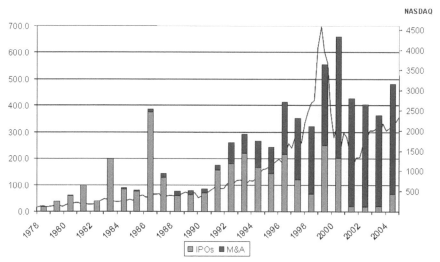

Figure 17: Venture Capital IPO and M&A Exits with NASDAQ Composite Index
Source: Dow Jones VentureOne (www.ventureone.com)

The Cisco Systems acquisition model, as well as the merger and acquisition (M&A) activity conducted by Nortel Networks and Lucent Technologies became an important component of the investment model, relied on by the venture capital industry during the ITO Revolution. The expectation that privately funded corporations could rely upon M&A as a viable exit option created a pseudo-ecosystem that in time would prove to be fleeting. One of the proofs of this ecosystem was a company called Ardent Communications.

Ardent Communications and the Rise of Made To Order M&A

Ardent Communications was founded in 1996 as a planned "spin-in" startup focused on building a specific product designed for Cisco Systems. The spin-in model was a method to create a startup that could attract top talent that, in turn, would build a product defined by Cisco in short period of time. To capitalize the new company, Cisco invited Sequoia Capital to participate in the funding of the new venture. To foster the entrepreneurial atmosphere, the employee and management pool was sized at 55% [see *Cisco Systems: A Novel Approach to Structuring Entrepreneurial Ventures*, Stanford University Graduate School of Business, Case Number EC-15, February 2000]. The trigger mechanism on the deal was a put/call feature that gave Cisco the option to purchase the company at a specific time or upon a product deliverable at a specified price of $232.5 million in cash or stock. The first round of funding for Ardent closed on August 11, 1996. Less than a year later, on June 11 1997 Cisco announced the acquisition of Ardent Communications for $156 million, which does not includes the 32% of the company already owned by Cisco bringing the total transaction value to $232.5 million. The significance of the Ardent acquisition was multi-fold for the venture capital industry. Ardent was a made to order M&A transaction. It combined venture capital and a publicly traded stock to build a product outside of the corporate structure and process of Cisco Systems. The real beauty of transaction was the minimal risk incurred by Cisco and Sequoia Capital. Unless the development team failed to develop the product, it was a guaranteed exit strategy using M&A. Over the next few years M&A transactions would dramatically rise as venture capitalists and private equity teams would utilize strategies that closely coupled the stock of a public company and venture capital to realize gains and exit strategies. As the stock markets continued to increase in value, these artificial strategies became accepted and legitimate business strategies for private capital.

As the ITO Revolution gathered momentum from 1996 through 2000, M&A activities had never been higher. This activity level provided investment exit strategies for venture capitalists. The return on investments from acquisitions and IPOs were invested back into new ventures. New companies, in turn, developed new technologies and continued to pressure the market and push the revolution forward. To create new companies, the venture capital industry raised more money. Bankers worked long hours on the many companies poised to go public. Companies with technologies that few people truly understood went public with spectacular success. Revolution was in the air and the Figaro of our time stood ready to exact revenge on the old regimes. Class privilege, which for decades was the purview of the old regimes was no more. Revolution was the means to an end that had been sought for a long time. Our world was changing and those who could not adapt would soon fall to the revolutionaries who were deploying new technologies and new methods of business that would soon chase the old regimes from the market.

The Story of Excite@Home

In the ITO Revolution, a prime example of two early revolutionary companies, started during the Change Stage, which did not survive the full cycle of ITO Revolution, was Excite and @Home. Excite was started in early 1993 by a group from Stanford with the goal of developing a marketable software tool for searching large databases. When the internet burst on the mainstream global market, Excite had found the largest, most complex and disordered database in the world. It was a natural extension to evolve their product from a database tool to a public search engine for the web. This also changed the business model for Excite. Instead of selling their search engine to companies, they turned their search engine into a public web site wherein revenue would be generated by selling advertising on their web page. As long as they attracted web users, they could command revenue to promote products or other web sites from their web site. As Excite evolved their business plan, they teamed with Vinod Khosla of the venture firm Kleiner Perkins Caufield & Byers in 1995. Two years later, Excite had emerged from a group of companies to become the number two search engine on the web. They were still behind the Yahoo brand, but Excite and Yahoo were rapidly transforming their search engine business into portal sites wherein users could access all kinds of information including stock portfolios, address books, and user groups. By 1998, market consolidation had begun within the internet search engine market vertical. AOL bought Netscape in 1998 and Excite needed to diversify its revenue source by adding a complementary revenue source to its advertisement revenue generated by its web portal. It was at this point that the Excite team connected with another Kleiner Perkins Caufield & Byers company called @Home.

@Home was started in 1995 by Kleiner Perkins Caufield & Byers venture capitalists John Doerr and William Randolph Hearst III. Many considered Doerr to be the star venture capitalist in California. His resume of success as a venture capitalist includes: Compaq, Cypress, Intuit, Macromedia, Netscape, Lotus, Millennium Pharmaceuticals, S3, Sun Microsystems, Amazon.com, and Symantec. The @Home business plan was to become a provider of high-speed data services (i.e. cable modem service provider) for consumers using cable television networks. From the beginning, the @Home team set lofty goals *"Most of all, I wanted to build a new network, from scratch, that will change society, and how many places can you go to do that?"* [see Milo Medin, Senior VP Engineering & CTO, Excite@Home, January 1996, *Wired 4.01*].

During the time that @Home was created, there were two fundamental network challenges to overcome to enable the @Home business plan. The first was that cable service providers needed to upgrade the physical plant that locally connected their consumers to the cable network to support two-way digital traffic. The early generation cable network used analog technology and thus had limited capacity (i.e. channels). The desire to use the cable footprint to provide high speed data services added another challenge, in that cable networks that were typically unidirectional networks. This meant that the cable networks to the home must be upgraded to support two-way traffic which is fundamental to high-speed internet access. Essentially, the cable service providers faced the same problem that RBOCs faced with the legacy copper local loop. The second challenge that @Home had to overcome was that the internet was not equipped to handle the vast amount of data requests and content streaming requirements that a higher speed cable network with millions of users would generate. In the early days of the internet, the public infrastructure supporting the internet would become clogged with data requests. The network would simply slow and users would find sites unavailable for some period of time. The solution to these problems was two-fold. @Home would build a 15,000 kilometer nationwide IP backbone, thus providing the cable service providers with a fast, high-capacity network that they could use to bypass the internet for their customer specific content and the cable service providers would upgrade their local fiber plants to support high-speed services to the home. *"This announcement {IP backbone deployment} is not only a milestone for Excite@Home, but also a significant benefit to companies who are looking for cost-effective, reliable access to run their businesses. The deployment of our backbone is the first phase in an on-going initiative to continue to scale our capacity in order to provide and support world-class broadband services for five million broadband users throughout North America."* [see Milo Medin, Senior VP Engineering & CTO, Excite@Home, November 3, 1999 http://newsroom.cisco.com/dlls/fspnisapief48.html]

The @Home team started aggressively signing a five year exclusive deal with the cable company TCI to provide high-speed internet access via cable modem. In 1996, Will Hearst commented in the January 1996, 4.01 issue of *Wired* magazine that @Home would have one million subscribers within a year and that this would allow @Home to *"...exist as an advertising-size entity when you hit a million customers, I think this business has to expend its energy while growing as fast as possible and not conserving cash"* [see http://www.wired.com/wired/archive/4.01/medin.html?pg=4&topic=]. By early 1998, @Home had signed agreements with eight major cable service providers: Tele-Communications Inc (TCI), Cablevision Systems Corp., Comcast Corporation, Cox Communications, InterMedia Partners, Marcus Cable, Rogers Cablesystems Limited, and Shaw Communications. As with Excite, business looked good as the ITO Revolution marched forward and everything became about the web and executing as fast as possible – but the business was not scaling as fast as predicted. *"Back in January 1996, as @Home was about to launch, Will Hearst predicted in Wired that it would have 1 million customers within a year. This proved embarrassing when a back-of-the-envelope calculation showed that even with every cable truck in America working 24 hours a day for the next 365 days, doing 1 million installations was simply not possible. In fact, it would be almost four years before @Home got its millionth customer - and yet, by the beginning of 2001, it would have nearly 3 million subscribers, a figure that has since grown to more than 3.7 million,"* [see Wired, *The $7 Billion Delusion*, Frank Rose, January 2002, 10.01].

Unfortunately for @Home, the revenue structure of their business presented significant operating challenges. When @Home signed partnerships with cable service providers, the cable service providers were given equity positions in @Home that were equal to the number of homes they passed, rather than the quality of the local network to these homes. In addition, @Home and the cable company split the revenue from the subscriber. TCI had the most homes passed of any @Home partner, yet they had many of the oldest networks that required upgrading. Other cable service providers that were further along with their cable plant upgrades viewed the equity arrangement as unfair as they had more subscribers contributing to the success of @Home. The @Home business structure began to present problems. Due to the partnership arrangement with the cable service providers, advertising revenue for the service was difficult to generate because @Home retained the national advertising revenues and the cable service providers retained the local advertising revenues. The split in advertising dollars meant that coordinated, nationwide advertising revenues where difficult to generate. Even if @Home had one million subscribers, it was a challenge to market the value of a nationwide advertising campaign when the local cable providers may not be supportive. @Home viewed itself as a hot Silicon Valley technology venture. The cable service providers viewed @Home as a cable specific service subsidiary. When there was a problem with the @Home service, customers were sent back and forth between @Home and the cable company call centers as neither @Home nor the cable service providers had a proven system to resolve service issues. While @Home and Excite were working to improve their business models, AOL was fast becoming a major internet powerhouse, passing twelve million subscribers in 1998. Developing an alternative to AOL was a prime directive because AOL was securing market share and in Silicon Valley, it was believed that a fundamental lesson was *"... that market share now equals revenue later, and if you don't have market share now, you are not going to have revenue later"* [see Marc Anderseen, as quoted by Robert Reid, *Architects of the Web: 1,000 Days that Built the Future of Business*, page 31].

The idea was formed to unite Excite's users, portal revenues, and content with @Home's subscribers with the intention of building a broadband based alternative to AOL. The vast majority of AOL's subscribers accessed AOL via dialup modems at 56k speeds. Excite@Home would combine content with a high-speed network that would deliver an unmatched browsing experience that was rich in active content. On January 19, 1999, @Home announced the acquisition of Excite for $6.7 billion in stock. Within the story of @Home and Excite, there is an interesting business corollary that is, in many ways, similar to the macro causes of the ITO Revolution.

Cable service providers are government sanctioned franchises or monopolies in their designated service areas. @Home was an internet service provider business in which they provided an exclusive service to customers of cable service providers. The addition of Excite changed the business model of @Home from providing just access, to providing access and content. The question that the Excite acquisition put into the play was the question of equal access. Local telephone companies were required to give access to any ISP who wished to offer service in their local serving area; would the same not be true of cable service providers? There were no rules which governed how cable service providers provided competitive access, but now with Excite@Home providing service and content, the question concerning competitive access was in play. AT&T was the first company to challenge Excite@Home and it began negotiating deals with MSN, Yahoo, and AOL to provide them the same rights that Excite@Home enjoyed with AT&T customers. Ultimately, the FCC did not impose any restrictions or rules for internet based content – but a competitor to Excite@Home clearly put the issue of equal access into play. When AT&T agreed to purchase TCI, they were forced to petition for cable service license transfers within each state and each community. AOL aggressively pushed a grassroots marketing campaign at the community level to promote equal access. The executives of Excite@Home were suddenly confronted with a serious threat to their business that did not exist when they were a portal only business.

Five months after the merger between @Home and Excite was completed, Excite@Home agreed to acquire Bluemountain.com for $780 million. The bluemountain.com web site generated minimal revenue, but it did average nine million visitors a month and most of them were female, which was a desired market demographic. It was after this transaction that Excite@Home began its free fall into ITO Revolution oblivion. The revenue goals for Bluemountain. com were never realized. Advertising revenues for the Excite portal site began to rapidly decline in early 2000 as internet based companies began to eliminate advertising expenditures to conserve cash. While revenue was declining on the Excite side of the house, service trends were no better on the @Home side of the house. Customer dissatisfaction with the @Home service continued to be a problem. By January 2001, Excite@Home announced a $4.6 billion dollar write-off of its media ventures. Then the company announced a loss of $850 million on revenue of $150 million. Excite@Home was trapped in a difficult business model of their own making. They did not own the connection to the customer

– that was owned by the cable company. The content they owned through the Excite portal business was overvalued and in the end, their customers were the cable service providers – not the consumers they targeted. Excite@Home was a wholesale business – not a retail business. This leads back to the tenet that a wholesale business is a nice business to have as a complement to a retail business, but it is not a core business. In September 2001, Excite@Home filed for bankruptcy protection. Its media assets, which included Bluemountain.com, were sold for $35 million. The @Home network was sold for $307 million to AT&T. The number two web search engine/portal that was acquired by @Home for $6.7 billion in 1999 was sold thirty three months later to Infospace for a mere $10 million. This might seem like a great financial tragedy, but it most likely worked out for the limited partners at Kleiner Perkins Caufield & Byers, as the three equity events (i.e. two IPOs and the merger) experienced by Excite and @Home enabled the distribution of proceeds to the limited partners. Excite@Home never turned into the success that its founders had envisioned.

Where the Leaders of the ITO Revolution Came From

Within revolutions and the human social change process there is an element called the transfer of the allegiance of the intellectuals. The term intellectuals is used to describe a collection of people who provide industry thought leadership. They hold positions as consultants, analysts, and corporate leaders and are often key note speakers at conventions, or publish there ideas in letters or trade publications. The intellectuals are the people who influence and shift public opinion from the status quo to the future. When markets, technologies consumer fades and consumer marketing changes occur, there are people who champion the change before the general market or population adopts the new trend. The change of loyalty by the intellectuals is called the transfer of allegiance. The intellectuals are the visible, publicly known people who have the ability to influence others by lending credibility to change. When we look for the transfer of the allegiance of the intellectuals within the ITO Revolution from the regulated market structure that predated the Telecom Act of 1996, to the creation of an unregulated market, we are identifying people in many different roles who had an affect on the industry state of mind. A revolution is a process in which a new thought pattern is accepted. The process in which a new idea is accepted migrates through three levels of thought leadership. Thought leadership is provided by many people in many roles at various times during the revolutionary process. In the ITO Revolution, as well as any industry undergoing revolutionary change, thought leadership comes from people in positions such as industry pundits, analysts, and consultants as well as corporate leaders, public officials, and elected government leaders.

Within technology revolutions, the first thought leaders are the revolutionaries, who are typically technical people who are pioneering research and development of a new technology. Entrepreneurs and visionaries are also part of the first group of thought leaders.

The next level of thought leadership comes from the intellectuals who are the forefront of market development and market evolution. These intellectuals are the consultants, long-term planners and venture capitalists – otherwise known as the risk takers. By the time that the idea for a revolution moves beyond the second level, the revolution is close to occurring. At the third level, we find the operating leaders within market. These are the corporate leaders in the old regimes who depart the old regimes to assume active roles in the revolution. The operational leaders are the group that assumes the least amount of risk. They prefer to wait and see if the revolution is really going to happen before committing themselves and forfeiting their positions of power within the old regimes and the old market structure.

@Home was started by two prominent venture capitalists, which at the time of the ITO Revolution played prominent roles in creating, growing, and promoting @Home. There is a second group of people that come after the intellectuals and they are called the leaders. The difference between the intellectuals and the leaders is implementation. The intellectuals espouse ideas – while the leaders implement ideas. The intellectuals who empowered the revolution came from many backgrounds, but they all sought change because they believed in the higher ideals and principals that ITO Revolution would achieve. Vice President Gore promoted ideas of a new economy and new governing force that would drive global integration and break down political and social barriers.

Thought leadership for any revolution or change event can be broken down into three groups of people who represent the leading edge of market change and the trailing edge of market change. These groups appreciate different levels of risk and possess different scopes of view for the future. Revolutions and change are driven by loyalties of the people classified in the Though Leadership Model (TLM). Technologies are adopted by the market, until they are promoted and championed by all levels of the TLM. The structure of a market does not change unless leaders influence and convince others in the model to accept the change. When the intellectuals within the TLM switch their loyalty from one technology, business, or method to another that is when revolutions become possible. Change must have credible champions, who are trusted, to provide leadership. Leadership rarely comes from the revolutionaries; revolutionaries are often not the long term builders who perfect and refine the changes enacted by revolution. This is the task of the operating leaders and intellectuals.

Figure 18: Thought Leadership Model (TLM)

The intellectuals who had helped bring about the ITO Revolution would soon realize the great trap of any revolution. The leaders may have changed and new companies may have been created – but the legacy problems that existed before the revolution still exist after the revolution. In terms of the ITO Revolution, America was still wired with a majority of copper local access loops in 1996 and by 2003 America homes were still wired with copper local access loops. Almost twenty years after AT&T's leaders decided to breakup the company, to rid themselves of the legacy local loops that were holding back the company, the dilemma of the local loop still exists. It is true that the cable service providers have been making progress in deploying higher speed conduits to the home – but for the vast majority of the telecom infrastructure of America, the legacy of the copper still rules as the method by which the average consumer and small to medium sized business accesses the new digital age.

In comparison, Korea has achieved the broadband revolution that initially the ITO Revolutionaries and intellectuals were seeking in the United States. By mid-2005, Korea had more than eleven million homes on-line or 73% with broadband access rate of at least one megabit to each home. A broadband penetration rate of 73% is not expected in the United States until 2010 or later. Korea has become a nation-state with nearly ubiquitous broadband access, broad third generation wireless handsets in use, and on line activism significant enough to affect the election of their President. In 2004, U.S. subscribers using broadband to connect to the internet exceeded those using a dial-up connection (narrowband) for the first time and the gap continues to increase – but the rate of broadband adoption and deployment in the U.S. is rapidly falling behind other developed nation-states. In 2000, the U.S. ranked third amongst the largest economies in the world for broadband connections to the internet. By mid-2005, the U.S. ranked tenth according to the Organization for Economic Cooperation & Development (OECD). The U.S. now ranks behind Korea,

Canada, Iceland, Denmark, Belgium, Netherlands, Switzerland, Sweden, and Japan.

The leaders that emerged during the ITO Revolution came from the old regimes; our government, our universities, and our industries. Often the initial leaders came from the social elite and from within the established industries associated with the revolution. In the ITO Revolution, this point can be illustrated by the departure of senior executives from the old regimes with the intent of creating companies with the mission of overthrowing the old regimes. Perhaps the best single example is the departure of executives from AT&T. AT&T is the quintessential old regime of the ITO Revolution. From within her ranks of executives, revolutionary leaders would come forth and revolutionary companies would be formed. Some of the more prominent leaders who left AT&T to assume leadership positions within ITO Revolution companies were:

- James Barksdale
- Joe Nacchio
- Daniel Hesse
- Bob Annunziata
- Alex Mandl
- David Nagel

When AT&T divested its local telephony businesses in 1984, it certainly did not know that it was creating a breeding ground for future revolutionaries within its former subsidiaries. Within the baby bells, AT&T had divested some of its best and brightest leaders who would guide their companies into positions that directly threatened their former parent. The fertile ground for revolution provided by AT&T should was not the only breeding ground for revolutionaries; ITO Revolutionaries came from universities, the government, and the industries of America. Looking back on our Excite@Home example, the founders of Excite were from Stanford University and one of the key founders of @Home was Milo Medin who came from NASA and was a key architect of the NASA internet that linked researchers in sixteen countries through a high-speed global network.

We can find a near perfect corollary in the story of Excite@Home. After the close of the Excite@Home merger, AT&T began negotiating access contracts with MSN, AOL, and Yahoo. AOL began to view @Home as no longer a provider of access, but a competing content provider via the Excite portal site. Excite and @Home had evolved from positions of differentiation or leadership within their market segments, to weak moderates of the ITO Revolution vulnerable to attack. In the case of Excite@Home, within thirty-three months they would be eliminated from the ITO Revolution in a grab for power. Today, Yahoo and AOL are still around while @Home is a footnote and the old Excite search engine is a weak competitor to Yahoo and Google.

The Three DSL Providers during the Perigee Stage

When the Telecom Act of 1996 was signed into law, it was the act that created many telecom service providers across various segments of the U.S. telecommunications industry. Some companies focused on long distance services for voice and data, some focused on local voice services, while others focused on high-speed data services for businesses and consumers. One of the many sub groups within the overall group of telecom service providers was the data only DSL providers. The DSL providers were a group of companies that focused on high speed data transmission over the traditional copper local loop – rather than voice services. Although there were several companies in this sub group, three companies stand out as early ITO Revolutionaries. These three companies were formed with private venture capital, built what seemed to be flourishing businesses – if not businesses with vast potential – and all three successfully completed initial public offerings. These three companies were Covad Communications, Rhythms NetConnections, and Northpoint Communications. As we go through the history of the ITO Revolution, we can identify the various stages of the revolution through the history of these three companies.

Covad Communications was formed in October 1996 with venture capital from Intel, CrossPoint Ventures, and Warburg-Pincus. The founding executives where from one of the strongest Silicon Valley companies that was founded by revolutionaries and with venture capital: Intel Corporation. Covad was the first of a new generation of post-Telecom Act of 1996 service providers to offer DSL services in a major metropolitan area. With $26 million in venture capital and headquarters in San Jose, Covad's first target market was the San Francisco metro area. By the end of 1997, Covad was able to offer services to more the 1.2 million households, 140,000 small businesses, and 10,000 medium to large size businesses in the San Francisco area.

Building a competitive telecom service provider requires massive amounts of financial capital. By the end of 1997, Covad needed far more capital than typical venture capital firms were comfortable providing in 1997 – although this would change by 2000. The solution was found in the high-yield market wherein Covad was able to raise $135 million in bonds with warrants. The three original venture capital investors also contributed another $17 million, bringing the total amount of capital raised by Covad before going public to $178 million. This capital enabled Covad to expand into additional markets and begin the process of building company momentum for an IPO.

As the company moved towards an IPO in 1998, the regulatory environment for telecom services was still in its formative and influential post revolutionary stage. Charles J. McMinn, then CEO of Covad, testified before the U.S. Senate Commerce, Science, and Transportation Subcommittee on Communications that, *"Failing to ensure a competitive environment would condemn the deployment of crucial next-generation digital communication services to the unfettered whims of the ILECs; precisely the opposite of what Congress intended sections of the Telecommunications Act of 1996 to accomplish."*

Covad went public on January 26, 1999 raising more than $140 million dollars. The company then returned to the high-yield market, raising an additional $390 million in February of 1999, bringing the total capital raised in 1999 to more than $500 million. This is quite an accomplishment for a company that had revenues of $27,000 dollars in 1997 and $5.326 million dollars in 1998. Any time more than $500 million in capital can be raised on a business plan that to date had generated less than six million dollars, it must be considered to have substantial future value. Covad's first annual report, dated March 31, 1999 stated on page 4, *"The passage of the Telecommunications Act of 1996 ('1996 Act') created a legal framework for competitive local exchange carriers ('CLECs') to provide local analog and digital communications services in competition with the ILECs. The 1996 Act eliminated a substantial barrier to entry for CLECs by enabling them to leverage the existing infrastructure built by the ILECs, which required a $200 billion investment by ILECs and ILEC ratepayers, rather than constructing a competing infrastructure at significant cost. The 1996 Act requires ILECs, among other things: to allow CLECs to lease copper lines on a line by line basis, to collocate DSL and other equipment in the ILECs' central offices to connect to the leased copper lines, to lease access on the ILECs' inter-central office fiber backbone to link the CLECs' equipment, and to use the ILECs' own operational support systems to place orders and access the ILECs' databases. The 1996 Act in particular emphasized the need for competition-driven innovations in the deployment of advanced telecommunications services, such as our DSL services."*

The second of the DSL providers was founded by a US West executive named Catherine Hapka. She left the old regime of US West to take advantage of an unprecedented market opportunity – the revolution initiated by the Telecom Act of 1996. Rhythms NetConnections was founded in February of 1997 with capital from four powerful venture capital firms. These firms where: Kleiner Perkins Caufield & Byers, Enterprise Partners, The Sprout Group, and Brentwood Ventures. Rhythms moved quickly to expand into targeted markets and by the time of the first annual report in March of 1999, stated *"... we have made substantial progress in implementing a scalable nationwide network. We began offering commercial services in San Diego in April 1998, and have subsequently begun service in nine additional markets: San Francisco, San Jose, Oakland/East*

Bay, Chicago, Los Angeles, Orange County, Boston, Sacramento and New York. We intend to continue our network rollout into an additional 23 markets in 1999 and a further 17 markets by the end of 2000. Upon completion of this network expansion, we anticipate providing services in 50 of the nation's largest metropolitan areas, which we believe contain 60% of the nation's local area networks." As a company philosophy, Rhythms embraced the mantra to move quickly and seize the first mover advantage. In the 1999 Annual Report, the company stated *"We intend to exploit our early market entrance to deploy our network and establish strong relationships with business and service provider customers. As of January 31, 1999, we provide service or had installed our network equipment in nearly 200 central offices. Installation on this scale requires significant time and resources; therefore, we believe our progress to date provides us a significant time-to-market advantage over would-be competitors. We have gained significant build-out experience, which we believe will streamline our further expansion. We plan to construct our network rapidly so that we are an early mover in our other target markets. We intend to exploit our early mover advantage to gain significant market share in our target markets."*

Rhythms was financed from inception through a combination of venture capital ($31 million) and senior notes ($144 Million). In early 1999, Microsoft and Worldcom invested a combined total of $60 million and on April 7, 1999 Rhythms went public, raising gross proceeds of $196 million. By the end of 1999, Rhythms would have a market cap of $23 billion. With $430 million in working capital raised in the span of twenty-six months on revenues from the previous year of $528,000, Rhythms was poised to move aggressively into their target markets. The market driver for Rhythm's business plan was the belief that *"The value of goods and services sold through the Internet will grow from $2.6 billion in 1996 to $400 billion in 2002."* [see page 3, http://www.sec.gov/Archives/ edgar/data/1065869/0001047469-99-012897.txt] Rhythms was betting their business plan on the belief that this market would develop and as a provider of high speed data services, Rhythms would be in a position to be a leading data service provider for internet access. Interestingly, there was a note of caution in their 1999 Annual Report, *"We have not validated our business model and strategy in the market. We believe that the combination of our unproven business model and the highly competitive and fast changing market in which we compete makes it impossible to predict the extent to which our network service will achieve market acceptance and our overall success. To be successful, we must develop and market network services that are widely accepted by businesses at profitable prices. We may never be able to deploy our network as planned, achieve significant market acceptance, favorable operating results or profitability or generate sufficient cash flow to repay our debt. Of the 9,800 lines that we have committed to deliver to date, we committed approximately 8,700 to only two customers. None of our large business customers has rolled out our services broadly to its employees, and we cannot be certain when or if these rollouts will occur. We will* *not receive significant revenue from our large customers unless these rollouts occur. Any continued or ongoing failure for any reason of large business customers to roll out our services, failure to validate our business model in the market, including failure to build out our network, achieve widespread market acceptance or sustain desired pricing would materially and adversely affect our business, prospects, operating results and financial condition."*

Northpoint Communications was the third of the three data DSL service providers. It was founded in May of 1997 with venture capital raised from three prominent venture capital firms. These firms were Benchmark Capital, Greylock Capital, and Accel Partners. The founders of Northpoint were six former executives of MFS. MFS was a voice and data service provider that focused on the commercial and governmental sectors. It was acquired by Worldcom in August of 1996 for $14 billion in Worldcom stock. At the time of acquisition, it was viewed as a shrewd deal on behalf of Worldcom because one of the companies in the MFS family was a company called UUNET. UUNET was generally recognized as the first commercial internet service provider and at the time of the Worldcom acquisition a coveted asset.

Northpoint's business plan was to target commercial businesses using DSL technology to provide internet access as well as private line connectivity. As part of Northpoint's business plan, they targeted companies which could be customers as well as investors. Initial success was achieved with *"...Microsoft, Tandy (the parent company of the RadioShack stores), Yahoo!, Excite@Home, SBC/Pacific Bell Internet Services, Intel, Verio, Cable & Wireless, Frontier Corporation (a subsidiary of Global Crossing Holdings Limited), Concentric Network, ICG Communications, Enron Communications, Network Plus, Netopia, GTE, iBeam, Equinix, and High Speed Access Corporation, among others. Most of these companies and The Carlyle Group, Vulcan Ventures, Accel Partners, Benchmark Capital, Greylock and others have invested in our company"* according to their 1999 Annual Report.

Northpoint went public on May 5th, 1999, raising net proceeds of $386 million dollars. The company then obtained a credit facility of $250 million and issued senior notes for an additional $400 million in working capital. Early 1999 was a good time for Northpoint as they had access to more than one billion dollars of capital after they had finished 1998 with revenue of $931,000. A vast majority of the capital raised in early 1999 was targeted for capital expenditures to expand and build out the Northpoint network presence in the United States, Canada, The Netherlands, Germany, and Belgium. In the go-go days of the ITO Revolution during the Perigee Stage, working capital was easy to obtain and leadership teams were pressured by investors to move quickly to secure markets and customers. Interestingly, a review of Northpoint's first annual report in 1999 reveals an interesting disclosure by the company, concerning competition, *"We face competition from many competitors with significantly greater financial resources, well-established brand names and larger customer bases. We also expect competition to intensify in the future. We expect significant competition from traditional and new telephone and telecommunications companies, including national long distance carriers, cable modem service providers, Internet service providers, on-line service providers, and wireless and satellite data service providers. Other Competitive Telecommunications Companies, Some With Greater Financial Resources, Compete in the Same Markets for the Same Customers. Other competitive telecommunications companies have entered and may continue to enter the market and offer high speed data services using a business strategy similar to ours. Some competitors, including those focusing on data transport such as Rhythms NetConnections Inc., HarvardNet Inc., @Link Networks L.L.C., New Edge Networks, Covad Communications Group, Inc., BlueStar Communications, JATO, Telocity, Vitts Network, DSL.net and Network Access Solutions Corporation, have begun to offer DSL-based access services, and others are likely to do so in the future. Finally, traditional voice-based telephone companies such as BTI Telecom, Hyperion, MCG, McLeod Communications, Allegiance and Network Plus, are entering the DSL market. Certain of our customers have made investments in our competitors, which may enhance their relationships with these competitors at our expense...Traditional Telephone Companies With Greater Resources Than Ours May Directly Compete in Our Markets. The traditional telephone companies have an established brand name and reputation for high quality in their service areas, possess significant capital to deploy DSL equipment rapidly, have their own copper lines and can bundle digital data services with their existing analog voice services to achieve economies of scale in serving customers. In addition, most traditional telephone companies have established or are establishing their own Internet service provider businesses, and all of the largest traditional telephone companies that are present in our target markets are conducting market trials of or have commenced offering DSL-based access services. For example, Bell Atlantic, BellSouth, Cincinnati Bell, Pacific Bell and Southwestern Bell are offering commercial services in some territories in which we offer services, U S WEST is offering commercial DSL services and Ameritech has announced commercial DSL services in some areas of Michigan and Illinois. We recognize that the traditional telephone companies have the potential to quickly deploy DSL services and are in a position to offer service from central offices where we may be unable to secure space in traditional telephone companies' central offices. In addition, the FCC is considering establishing requirements for separate subsidiaries through which the traditional telephone companies could provide DSL service on a largely deregulated basis. As a result, we expect traditional telephone companies to be strong competitors in each of our target markets...National Long Distance Carriers May Begin to Compete for Our Small- and Medium-Sized Business Customers. Many of the leading traditional national long distance carriers, including MCI WorldCom, Inc., AT&T Corp. and Sprint Corporation, are expanding their capabilities to support high speed, end-to-end data networking services...The newer national long distance carriers, such as Level 3 Communications, Inc., The Williams Companies, Inc. and Qwest Communications*

International, Inc. are building and managing high speed fiber-based national data networks and partnering with Internet service providers to offer services directly to the public...Cable Modem Service Providers May Offer High Speed Internet Access at More Competitive Rates Than Ours, Forcing Us to Lower Our Prices. Cable modem service providers, such as At Home Corporation and Road Runner, Inc. (with their cable partners), are deploying high speed internet access services over hybrid fiber coaxial cable networks. Where deployed, these networks provide similar and in some cases higher speed Internet access than we provide. They also offer these services at lower price points than our services. Actual or prospective cable modem service provider competition may have a significant negative effect on our ability to secure customers and may create downward pressure on the prices we can charge for our services... Internet Service Providers, Our Targeted Customers, May Begin to Provide DSL Services Directly. Internet service providers, such as Verio Inc., GTE Internetworking, UUNET (a subsidiary of MCI WorldCom, Inc.), Sprint, Concentric Network Corporation, MindSpring Enterprises, Inc. and PSINet, Inc., provide Internet access to residential and business customers, generally using the existing telephone system. On-line Service Providers, Our Targeted Customers, May Begin to Provide DSL Services Directly. On-line service providers, such as America Online, Inc., Compuserve (a subsidiary of America Online), Microsoft Network, Prodigy, Inc., and WebTV Networks, Inc. (a subsidiary of Microsoft), provide, over the Internet and on proprietary on-line services, content and applications ranging from news and sports to consumer video conferencing. These services are designed for broad consumer access over telecommunications-based transmission media, which enable digital services to be provided to the significant number of consumers who have personal computers with modems. In addition, on-line service providers provide Internet connectivity, ease-of-use and consistency of environment. Many of these on-line service providers have developed their own access networks for modem connections. AOL has announced that it will purchase DSL services from Bell Atlantic and SBC Communications. If these on-line service providers were to extend their owned access networks to DSL, they would be our competitors." In summary, the 1999 Northpoint Annual report declared that the company had competitors contending for its customer from all segments of the telecom service provider business. Many of these companies had stronger brands, better financing, and a base of customers from which to operate.

Conclusion

In the Change Stage of the ITO Revolution it was the new economy versus the old economy. Companies such as Toys R' US were at risk because eToys. com had been created. Barnes and Noble bookstores were now threatened by Amazon.com. Webvan was a threat to grocery stores. Nearly a billion dollars of private capital went into a series of online pet supply initiatives and none of them were commercially successful. General Electric and other Fortune 1000 companies were suddenly challenged with the need to develop a successful online presence.

New thought leaders emerged from the ranks of consultants, analysts, venture capitalists, and bankers. Almost overnight the world was teaming with ecommerce and internet experts. The fact that this was an evolving market with no prior history should have called into question the legitimacy of the revolution furor – but as with all revolutions, people are easily consumed by the excitement of the moment as the revolution strips away all prior barriers that had left them unfulfilled. In some cases, the extremists of the revolution emerged from within the ranks of the large public technology companies. The CEOs of Lucent, Nortel Networks, and Cisco Systems were consumed by the revolution as their companies began to exploit highly unusual market conditions that supported a nearly continuous and significant revenue growth.

In the technology business, there is a belief that the first company to introduce a new technology or method of conducting business has what is termed a first mover advantage in the market. During the first four years of the ITO Revolution, many internet and optical startups were founded with the mandate to get to market quickly. Even the new leading revolutionary telecom service providers such as Global Crossing had the mandate of speed. Speed in the construction of their networks would enable new revolutionaries to capture customers and market share, thus enabling them to be the leading companies in the new economy. In March of 1997, Gary Winnick, co-chairman of Global Crossing stated in a company press release, *"Due to the overwhelming demand for the internet and other new multimedia applications, coupled with market changes driven by deregulation and accounting rate decreases, we expect an explosive growth in telecommunications traffic worldwide, we expect the North Atlantic Region to be particularly dynamic due to the advanced economies that it services."* There is clearly some advantage to being a market first mover, but in reality, the advantage is minimal when compared to being the first to market with a sustainable solution that generates profitable revenue. George Gilder remarked about Global Crossing in 2000, *"Just as MCI pioneered single-mode fiber in the U.S., TCI transformed cable, and McCaw launched a national wireless system, Global Crossing will pioneer the first integrated global fiber-optic network, fulfilling my decade-old predication of a 'worldwide web of glass and light.'"* [Gilder, *Telecosm*, page 192]. Global Crossing declared Chapter 11 bankruptcy on November 18, 2002, five years after its founding. To their credit, Global Crossing emerged from chapter 11 bankruptcy on December 9, 2003 and has since enjoyed annual revenues in the mid-two billion dollar range. For the balance of 2004 and into 2005, Global Crossing has maintained a market capitalization of between three hundred and four hundred million, which is reflective of an annual turn over of approximately $1.7 billion, limited cash reserves of approximately $200 million, and $700 million in debt.

In terms of the ITO Revolution and the DSL providers, the 1999 Annual Report for Northpoint foreshadowed this development. In that report, Northpoint stated, *"Traditional Telephone Companies With Greater Resources Than Ours May Directly Compete in Our Markets. The traditional telephone companies have an established brand name and reputation for high quality in their service areas, possess significant capital to deploy DSL equipment rapidly, have their own copper lines and can bundle digital data services with their existing analog voice services to achieve economies of scale in serving customers. In addition, most traditional telephone companies have established or are establishing their own Internet service provider businesses, and all of the largest traditional telephone companies that are present in our target markets are conducting market trials of or have commenced offering DSL-based access services. For example, Bell Atlantic, BellSouth, Cincinnati Bell, Pacific Bell and Southwestern Bell are offering commercial services in some territories in which we offer services, U S WEST is offering commercial DSL services and Ameritech has announced commercial DSL services in some areas of Michigan and Illinois. We recognize that the traditional telephone companies have the potential to quickly deploy DSL services and are in a position to offer service from central offices where we may be unable to secure space in traditional telephone companies' central offices."*

During the Change Stage of the ITO Revolution, optimism was abundant. The warning in the Northpoint annual report was written in 1999 – not 1996. During the Change Stage of market revolutions – the impossible seems possible. Revolutionary fervor has the ability to strike down barriers and motivate the uninspired to become the inspired. Often rational forethought as to the real challenges that lay ahead is not part of the thought process of early revolutionaries. It is much easier to simply join the revolution.

CHAPTER FOUR:
The Glory Days

Government, even in its best state, is but a necessary evil; in its worst state, an intolerable one. - Thomas Paine

The period of time from 1997 through 1999 was an amazing time to be involved with the ITO Revolution. Companies were going public, companies were being acquired, fortunes were made, and new companies commanded hundred million dollar valuations overnight with a web site and biography page. *"My view is big companies are not positioned well to deal with this changing environment. In this industry, the next ten years belong to the entrepreneurs... even though they have smaller revenues, the companies deploying the newest technologies will exert a disproportionate amount of influence on how the industry shapes itself,"* [see, Joseph P. Nacchio, CEO of Qwest, *The New Entrepreneurial Elite*, Jerry Useem, Inc Magazine, December 1997]. The three years between 1997 and mid 1999 are represented in the G3MM by the phase called Perigee. The term Perigee is used to represent the point at which the revolutionary frenzy is peaking and market share reaches its most diffused point.

Perigee: A dynamic market condition. Market barriers to entry and success are low. Investment in new companies, new technologies and high-risk high reward business ventures are occurring at a rapid pace. Market size is growing as new companies and consumers are added to the overall market. The new companies and consumers are uncommitted market share. Uncommitted market share is unlike pre Change stage market share in that it has not built any loyalties to preferred suppliers. Market share is fluid and dynamically changes amongst the competing companies. This is the phase at which the intellectuals who had extolled the revolution declare victory and validation. The Perigee phase of the revolution is all about the success of the day as the inherent value of the prior structure of the market is released and realized via the public markets. In markets that were previously regulated, the new companies created during this phase of the revolution capitalize on lower market barriers and the financial market's eagerness to capture the inherent value released by the removal of regulatory controls. See **Chart 10: G3MM Perigee Stage for ITO Revolution** in the Chart and Model section.

In relation to the ITO Revolution, the Perigee phase of the G3MM represents the most optimistic phase of the revolution. The removal of regulatory controls resulted in the creation of many new companies focused on exploiting the changing structure of the telecom services and networking equipment markets. The intellectuals who had extolled and promoted the need for a change declare that removal of regulatory controls has now been vindicated by the emergence of many new and exciting companies. On the surface of the ITO Revolution it did appear as if a new era for telecom services had emerged within the Unites States. Many new service providers emerged thus providing market based competition and new services such as broadband services were now being offered. The Perigee phase of the ITO Revolution can also be identified by the lowering of market barriers. The barriers to entry within a regulated market that had kept companies out of the ITO markets are lower during the Perigee phase. The effect of lowered market barriers is two-fold. The first is it enables the creation of new companies within the industry to be formed and compete for business. The second is it enables companies in other businesses who serve adjacent or different markets to cross-over into the newly deregulated market and compete for business. Within the ITO Revolution, this later aspect is aptly represented by the various energy companies that entered into the ITO Revolution post the Telecom Act of 1996.

From Power to Light and the Story of Touch America

The story of Touch America is in many ways a microcosm of how the Perigee Phase of the G3MM enables companies to enter new markets and what can happen to new entrants who do not fully comprehend the G3MM cycle. Montana Power Company was the power industry in Montana and a traditional old economy company. For ninety years, it provided inexpensive electricity, was conservatively led, paid a good dividend, and provided quality benefits for its employees and the communities they served. As the ITO Revolution gathered momentum throughout 1996, the leadership team of Montana Power decided that it was time to evolve the company. Montana Power Company existed as a state authorized monopoly. As long as it provided the citizens of Montana with cheap and reliable services, the state of Montana allowed it to exist without competition. In short, Montana Power was a perfect Keynesian structure – but there was the siren call of a revolution. A great opportunity existed to become a telecom services provider, instead of an average, reliable producer of power. After all, power generation was clearly a part of the old economy and everyone wanted to be in the new economy.

In April 1997, the governor of Montana signed into law Senate Bill 390. This legislative act deregulated the power industry of Montana. The belief was that deregulation and privatization of the energy sector was a natural extension of a twenty year long process to privatize uncompetitive sectors of the economy. Other sectors of the economy had been deregulated such as transportation and telecommunications. In case of Montana, deregulation of the power industry was viewed as a way to avoid the potential issues surrounding energy issues in California as well as provide consumers with a choice. Once regulation went into affect, it enabled Montana Power Company to divest its power assets and invest in telecommunications.

Montana Power moved quickly to divest its legacy power generating assets. The first Montana Power assets sold were thirteen power plants which included 11 hydroelectric plants for $1.586 billion to Pennsylvania Power and Light. When the selling was done, Montana Power had sold $2.7 billion in assets. The next step in the evolution, or revolution, at Montana Power was to exit the power generation business and become a telecom service provider called Touch America. Touch America was started with capital acquired from the selling of the power generating assets. In their first annual report, filed on April 1st, 2002 Touch America stated; *"Touch America Holdings, Inc., was incorporated on September 27, 2000 under the laws of the state of Delaware. We are the publicly traded successor to The Montana Power Company (MPC), which prior to the reorganization discussed below, provided telecommunications and energy products and services. With our transition to Touch America Holdings, Inc., we are now a national broadband telecommunications company, providing services including customized voice, data and video transport through our principal operating subsidiary, Touch America, Inc. On March 28, 2000, MPC's Board of Directors announced its decision to divest its multiple energy businesses, separating them from Touch America, Inc. The Board of Directors decided to divest the energy businesses based on a belief that the divestiture would allow the company to focus on Touch America, Inc.'s telecommunications business, while enabling the energy businesses to continue under new ownership. The Board of Directors concluded that the existing structure, which had been created to be responsive to the demands of a regulated utility business, could not continue to meet the demands and ensure the success of the different energy and telecommunications businesses. Consequently, MPC implemented a restructuring plan to transform from an energy and telecommunications business to Touch America Holdings, Inc., a telecommunications business,"* [see Touch America filings http://www.sec.gov/Archives/edgar]. The primary objective was to evolve into a nationwide telecommunications provider *"As Touch America Holdings, Inc. (Touch America), we develop, own, and operate a 22,000-mile high-speed fiber optic network through our subsidiary, Touch America, Inc., a national broadband telecommunications operating company. We expect our network will span 26,000 route miles and 40 states by early 2003,"* [see Touch America filings http://www.sec.gov/Archives/edgar].

Touch America's entry into the telecom service provider business could not have been timed worse. They entered the market and committed the company to the revolution at time in which the market was changing. The Perigee Stage was coming to end and soon the extremists of the ITO Revolution would assume power and Touch America was not part of the extremists of the ITO Revolution. The goal to transform a company from the Keynesian high ground of the economy and emerge from Montana as a telecom service provider can only be achieved in revolutionary times. Companies simply do not exit their traditional line of business and shift to a completely different line of business without a fundamental change to their operating structure. To perform such a feat requires a revolution. In the case of Touch America, the government had to deregulate the power industry in Montana and financial capital had to be accessible to fund the transformation from power to telecom. Each of these events occurred in the heart of the ITO Revolution, in a stage called Perigee, when the market barriers were low and optimism for the future had never been higher.

After Touch America emerged from the burdens of the heavy industry, it began to build its nationwide fiber network. Unfortunately, the market drivers which Touch America had based their business plan began to fail in the market place. By early 2001, a number of competitive nationwide long haul fiber optic networks were operating in the U.S. market by companies such as Qwest, AT&T, Worldcom, Sprint, Level 3, Global Crossing, 360 Networks, and Williams Communications. Each of these companies had based their business plans on the assumption that CLECs, ILECs, and the Fortune 5000 would drive business from the local markets into the long haul networks. As 2001 dawned, this market simply failed to materialize and the financial support for Touch America's business plan began to erode. By mid 2003, Touch America was unable to realize positive progress with their business plan and declared bankruptcy on June 19, 2003.

The breakup and sale of Touch America highlights an interesting element of the ITO Revolution. When Qwest offered to acquire US West for $41.3 billion in June of 1999, the government gave approval to the transaction only after Qwest agreed to sell US West's in region long distance network and certain assets to Touch America for $200 million. The assumption was that Qwest had built a new nationwide long distance network and by combining with US West, a legacy RBOC, the new company would have a monopoly on local as well as long distance services within the US West region. The solution was to allow Qwest to retain their nationwide network, acquire the local telephony business of US West, but sell US West's in region long distance services to another company in order to promote in region competition. At the time the transaction was announced, Robert P. Gannon, Chairman and CEO, Montana Power/Touch America stated; *"This milestone acquisition fits well with our strategy to add customers, sales force and increase revenues on Touch America's rapidly expanding national fiber-optic network. The service area is a part of the country we know well, as we have had infrastructure in place for some years that matches much of the service region Qwest is divesting. We look forward to providing our new customers the same superior service that we have been offering others for the past 16 years."* The assets that Qwest was divesting were the legacy, in region network that served US West customers for long distance services. This included the 1+ and related wholesale and private line services for approximately 250,000 customers. After the deal closed, Qwest executed on a strategy of gaining regulatory approval to sell long distance services within its fourteen state service region.

The move to offer long distance services to its customers initiated a dispute between Qwest and Touch America. Both companies sued each other alleging billing disputes and anti-competitive practices. Qwest was eventually fined $6.5 million by the FCC in May of 2003. The result of the Touch America's bankruptcy was two fold. Qwest acquired the private line data assets and services it had sold to Touch American in November 2003. The remaining assets of Touch America, including 10,300 fiber route miles were sold to 360 Networks in January of 2004 for $28 million.

The creation of Touch America and the transformation of Montana Power Company affected the ITO Revolution in two important aspects and left a lasting legacy in Montana. The easiest observation is that Montana no longer has a regulated power industry that provides inexpensive power to its citizens. This has had a significant impact on the state and its economy – but that is a story for another study. As for the ITO Revolution, the creation of Touch America enabled Qwest to gain government approval to acquire US West. It can be argued that if it was not Touch America who acquired the in region long distance and private lines services of US West then it would have been another company, but the fact remains that Touch America had the financial resources and desire to acquire these assets and enable Qwest to take control of US West. In the end, Touch America spent their $2 billion – raised from exiting the power industry and Qwest made $200 million of the sale of assets and services to Touch America, only to gain the right to sell the same services and acquire back the assets in 2003 for pennies on the dollar. Touch America and its financial backers were left with the financial obligations.

Enron: From Natural Gas, to Power, to Broadband

The story of the ITO Revolution would not be complete without a discussion regarding Enron Broadband Services or EBS as it was known. To understand the complete Enron story, see *The Smartest Guys in the Room*, by Bethany McLean and Peter Elkind. For the purpose of this discourse, we will contain our Enron discussion to the portion of their business that attempted to capitalize on the ITO Revolution. Enron found their way into the ITO Revolution via the acquisition of public utility called Portland General. Enron was acquiring Portland General to as a key component to their ability to provide consumer electricity. Inside Portland General (i.e. PG) was a telecom group called FirstPoint Communications that had laid fiber in the existing power delivery right of way, owned by PG. This was a common activity as many energy companies leveraged their right of ways for the dual purpose by laying fiber and building a telecom services business within their energy company. By 1999, ITO stocks had taken off and the leadership team at Enron made the decision to position Enron as a major player in the telecom service business by creating Enron Broadband Services. To head the new service, Jeff Skilling, who was COO of Enron, named Ken Rice as CEO. Ken was a long time Enron employee and prior head of their Enron North America division, which was the core natural gas pipeline business, to lead the new division.

In late 1999, Enron decided to build a large fiber optic network and create a product called the Enron Intelligent Network. The objective of this network was to transform the internet by providing a mechanism to deliver broadcast quality TV via the internet. This network would also provide the backbone for creating a network that would enable bandwidth trading in the same way Enron traded natural gas and energy.

At Enron's investor conference in January 2000, the company pushed the broadband message. The company told analysts that Enron had already deployed the Enron Intelligent Network using a middleware mechanism that could identify applications on the internet that required large amounts of bandwidth and configured the network dynamically to support these applications. This was not true. Enron told the investor community that they expected bandwidth mediation to be a $68 billion business in 2004 [see *The Smartest Guys in the Room*, by Bethany McLean and Peter Elkind, page 243]. The guest speaker at the event was Scott McNealy, CEO of Sun Microsystems, who announced that Enron had committed to purchase 18,000 Sun systems. Enron was also planning to be in the content delivery business and Jeff Skilling projected annual revenues of $18 billion by 2008. In the wake of the conference, industry analysts gushed over the Enron Broadband story. The following quotes from intellectuals of the ITO Revolution are reprinted from McLean and Elkind, page 244:

- *"Impressive story"* Carol Coale, Prudential Securities

- *"We see validation in the sheer technical excellence that was obvious from our walk-trough of the Enron facilities,"* Ray Niles, Schroder and Company

- *"For Enron to say we can do bandwidth trading is like Babe Ruth's saying, I can hit that pitcher...the risk is staggeringly low and the potential reward is staggeringly high,"* Steven Parla, Credit Suisse First Boston

- *"Absolutely it will succeed."* Brownlee Thomas, Giga Information

- *"All we can say is WOW!"* Deutsche Bank

- *"Although this is still an energy company, in our view, Enron fits the description of a new economy stock..."* Donato Eassey, Merrill-Lynch

Enron was not bashful about promoting the prospects for the EBS business. CEO Jeffery Skilling even went as far as to say *"If we can maintain or build a 25 percent market share worldwide, this business by itself could have revenues of over a quarter trillion dollars a year!"* The reality was that Enron's desire to become involved in the ITO Revolution was based on a full adoption of the new economy and the digital revolution. The business plan that @Home was executing against assumed that the cable service providers would not have the capital to build a nationwide backbone for the new generation of digital video and internet access. Enron's business plan was the extreme opposite of the @Home plan. They were betting on a full adoption of the ITO Revolution and the hypothesis that user demand for capacity would outpace any single service provider's ability to fulfill. If Enron could embed their business as a broker between networks, they could become an arbiter of bandwidth and build a business trading bandwidth. The idea is great – but it is completely impractical as Enron did not own networks, they did not own content and had no alternative to the local loop controlled by the RBOCs and cable service providers to end-user.

Enron promoted an intellectual advantage around their software architecture called the Enron Intelligent Network (EIN) that would embed itself in the operating system of service providers, thus providing the data points around bandwidth needs and bandwidth capabilities. The concept of the EIN was good – but the reality is that service providers run a business based on fixed costs and they prefer to lock customers into contracts. This is why service contracts have traditionally had early termination fees. The end result of Enron's foray into the ITO Revolution was a tremendous amount of hype generated by the Enron public relations machine – but not a lot of business. Eventually the entire EBS business collapsed with the now famous story of Enron's implosion. EBS was as much a dream as Enron was a Ponzi scheme to promote the value of their stock. The unfortunate aspect for the ITO Revolution was that EBS helped promote the frenzy around the ITO Revolution and the belief that a new digital based economy was taking hold.

The Evolution of the ITO Revolution during the Perigee Stage

Markets evolve through the same process as revolutions because markets and revolutions are products of human intentions and are subject to the same tendencies of the human condition. Markets and revolutions share a common bond in regard to the role of the extremists. The extremists of historical revolutions desire absolute power, which means control of the resources of the nation-state which are then applied to controlling the territory of the nation-state. The extremist in a business revolution want absolute power and power in the business world is achieved by controlling markets through dominant ownership of market share and the resources used to derive revenue from markets. By controlling market share, the extremist in business can project power and prevent competitors from gaining power. The internet

In our analysis of the ITO Revolution, we are at the stage of the G3MM wherein the extremists begin to systematically assert market pressure, which is the beginning of their assumption of power. The timeline is early 2000 through mid 2001. The revolution has occurred, the initial euphoria has spawned numerous companies to capitalize on the explosive growth in the internet, telecom, and optical markets and there is a near universal belief that a great cultural change has occurred. *"The Internet has launched a technological revolution that is changing the way individuals, as well as organizations, live and interact. Imagine combining the power of printing press (and most newspapers and magazines on earth) with the power and speed of the telegraph, telephone, radio, television and computer. Then you make this package easy to use and cheap enough for the mass market. You would then have the potential of the Internet in its most usable form, the World Wide Web (known as the "web") for short,"* [see Michael A. Cusumano and David B. Yoffie, *Competing on Internet Time*, 1998, page 1].

The intellectuals of the ITO Revolution are still promoting a new economy versus and old economy – but evidence is beginning to accumulate to question the long-term viability of the assumptions made by many of the leading intellectuals of the ITO Revolution. At this stage of the ITO Revolution, the non-extremist companies in the ITO markets begin to find barriers that prevent them from being successful. A good example we reviewed to illustrate this point was Touch America. The barriers encountered by the revolutionaries have been erected by a diverse set of market players. The old regimes are still in contention for the market as well as the revolutionaries who rule during the Perigee phase of the G3MM – but a new group begins to exert pressure on the market and this group is called the extremists.

The ITO Revolution played an important role in changing how critical financial information was publicly disclosed and it enabled accessibility of financial information in a timely manner. Before the SEC adopted the fair disclosure law or Regulation FD on September 23, 2000, companies were allowed to brief selective members of the financial community with information that enabled these people and institutions to take advantage of market conditions before the information became generally available to the public. The ITO Revolution was a driving force that provided access to information and acted as a socializing force within society. It enabled financial information that was difficult to obtain in a timely manner before 1996 to be easily accessible on demand and forced the SEC to adopt rules that provided for the equitable distribution of sensitive financial information. The ironic aspect is that the financial community played an important role in the creation and decline of the ITO Revolution. During this cycle the ITO Revolution wrought dramatic and dynamic change on the first estate. The world of the financiers that emerged from the end of the ITO Revolution looks very different from that which preceded the revolution.

Over the past seventy-years, corporate governance in the United States has undergone a steady tightening process. The process has been accelerating since the 1980s. The result of the new regulations covering disclosure, internal controls, and checks and balances has been a rise in shareholder litigation, improved access to corporate information, and an increase of information disclosed from corporations – yet questionable relevancy of the information released. In April 2000, at the near peak of the ITO Revolution, George Gilder wrote a short essay, published in the Wall Street Journal attacking the fair disclosure regulation as an unfair regulation. *"Ultimately ruling markets are data about the remorselessly real facts of supply and demand, the empirical realities of finance and the intricate, unforgiving details of technology paradigms and performance. Yet the conventional wisdom is that stock markets ride on tides of greed and fear. From the Tulip mania of the 17th century to the crash of 1987 and now the plunge of 2000, chaos and volatility have all too often ruled. The promise of the Internet, however, is the instant spread of information. More information is available about more companies and securities than ever before. Why then, in the midst of an information age, do markets for technology stocks still behave like tulip auctions in 1630?...Less information about companies means more volatility and more vulnerability to outside events. Inside information -- the flow of intimate detail about the progress of technologies and product tests and research and development and daily sales data -- is in fact the only force that makes any long-term difference in stock performance. Yet it is precisely this information that is denied to public investors...Entrepreneurial information from deep inside companies, not from the investment counsel or PR firm, is the most important real knowledge in the economy. Acquiring and comprehending it is the chief work of inside entrepreneurs...By excluding inside news from influencing the day to day movements of prices, the U.S. effectively blinds its stock markets...In an environment where inside information is banished from markets, much of the value is harvested not by the public but by organizations like General Electric, Cisco and Berkshire Hathaway that increasingly are not companies at all but portfolios of assets, whose strength is full access to inside knowledge about their holdings. Similarly, venture capitalists command full intimate knowledge of their target firms. Meanwhile the average investor is left in the dark...Even on the World Wide Web, blind markets are covered by blind pundits. With inquiring analysts barred from any "material" information not divulged at once to the world, reporters focus on the personalities of executives and on financial data, necessarily retrospective and thus of little value in predicting future prices. This is the reason that the huge expansion of financial coverage on the Internet has not resulted in more rational and informed pricing of stocks. This is why the market feeds chiefly on rumors and momentum and 'technical' analysis. In an information economy, inside information is the basis of share value. Yet inside information is barred as much as possible from the markets...To realize the benefits of the World Wide Web on those information markets that focus on stocks, the current rules on the disclosure of material information should be rescinded. They are in clear violation of the First Amendment. Fraudulent manipulation of shares will remain a criminal act, and it can be prosecuted without stultifying the flow of information from companies. Information wants to be free, and the more of it that is incorporated in the prices of shares, the more robust, and the less subject to manipulation, euphoria and panic, the market will be. Through the Internet, stock exchanges can escape the popular Keynesian characterization as a 'casino,' and can fulfill still better their real role in the intelligent investment of capital. Greed and fear can give way to knowledge only if knowledge is not illegal,"* [see, *The Outsider Trading Scandal*, George Gilder, The Wall Street Journal, April 19, 2000].

An interesting hindsight view of Gilder's protest against regulation FD is the affect of Sarbanes-Oxley on disclosure of corporate information. The intention of Regulation FD and SOX was to provide information equality and ensure proper internal corporate controls to avoid fraud and theft. The net affect seems to be that less information is released by public companies. Executive leadership teams are acutely aware of disclosure level events and manage their business to be risk adverse and are increasingly focused on avoiding engagements that can be considered a future commitment of the corporation. Over the past hundred years, there has been an increasing level of accountability and equanimity through corporate governance.

- 1914: Clayton Act passed, prohibits a person of serving as a director and director of a competitor
- 1919: Dodge v. Ford Motor: Court decides a public company is organized for the profit of shareholders

- 1924: Barnes vs. Andrews: Court ruling on duties of a corporate director
- 1926: NYSE bans non-voting stock from the exchange
- 1933: Securities Act of 1933 which imposes civil penalties on company directors for material defects in filings
- 1934: Securities Act of 1934creates the SEC
- 1940: SEC Recommends the creation of audit committees
- 1942: SEC adopts the Shareholder Proposal Rule requiring shareholder resolutions to be voted upon
- 1947: SEC v. Transamerica: Court rules businesses are bared from omitting governance orientated measures from proxy statements
- 1973: Founding of the Financial Accounting Standards Board (FASB)
- 1974: SEC requires disclosure of whether or not a company has an independent audit committee
- 1977: Congress passes the Foreign Policy Corruption Act
- 1978: NYSE requires companies to have audit company composed of independent directors
- 1978: SEC requires that proxy statements disclose financial or personal relationships between directors and the company boards on which they serve.
- 1979: First Fortune 500 firm acquired by a Private Equity/LBO Firm
- 1985: Delaware forces boards to craft due diligence procedures
- 1992: SEC enables easier communication between shareholders before proxy votes
- 2000: SEC enacts auditor independence rules that force companies to publicly disclose consulting ties that have the potential to be a conflict of interest
- 2000: Regulation Fair Disclosure (FD) enacted
- 2002: Sarbanes-Oxley Act
- 2003: SEC changes stock exchange rules that force boards to be composed of independent directors
- 2005: Enron and Worldcom directors pay personal penalties to settle litigation

Prior to the ITO Revolution, the world of venture capital was a small and quiet element of the financial industry that stayed within its click. Information about private investments was difficult to obtain if you were not in the venture capital industry or the business of privately funded startups. Once the internet came to be, nearly every venture capital firm created a web page to tout their firm, describe their investment strategy, and promote their investments. The successful closing of a private venture fund was news. New startups that had never before promoted their funding status, suddenly realized a sense of accomplishment in the act of closing a funding round. As soon as a new company was funded, they would create a web page to tell who they were, what they were focusing on, and what they had accomplished in prior business lives. The ITO Revolution provided a cruel irony for the venture capitalists and ITO startups. During the first three phases of the G3MM, there was a sense of elitism and honor to be part of the revolution. Very little risk was associated with being part of the revolution. As the ITO Revolution progressed into the later stages, the culture of promotion by the revolutionaries became a catch-22. Venture backed startups suddenly were viewed as risks – not agents of change blazing a path in the new economy. Venture firms that realized honor by publicly touting private investments, suddenly found that these investments had no exit strategies and thus were viewed as liabilities.

During the Perigee stage of the ITO Revolution, there was an open market for new companies to create businesses outside the traditional metrics used to determine value and outside of the market conditions that were familiar during the period prior to the Telecom Act of 1996. The investment bankers of the first estate used the lowering of market barriers to take companies public. The revolutionaries (i.e. new companies) raised cash to continue building their businesses and the financial community reaped substantial rewards in form of investment banking fees. With the lowering of market barriers came the raising of expectations; after all the first three phases of the G3MM are a time of revolutionary fervor. The companies of the new economy, as well as the old regimes that were evolving into the digital age, had to demonstrate growth within their peer group of the revolutionaries. During the Perigee stage, market share becomes diffused amongst the competitors. The diffusion of market share is the result of new, uncommitted market share being added and the fluid exchange of market share. To be successful during this stage, it is critical for new companies entering the market to demonstrate market share acquisition. This is what Enron was doing during 2000 and early 2001 before the market collapsed [see *Essay One, Chapter Four*].

The pressure to maintain high growth rates in order to maintain stock price levels is the driving force that led to financial scandals at Enron, Worldcom, Qwest, Nortel, Lucent, Anderson, and many, many other companies that were major players in the ITO Revolution. The net result of this pressure was that the governmental system in the United States reacted, and has begun to regulate the accountability standards for U.S. based corporations. The mechanism with which this regulation is being enforced is called the Sarbanes-Oxley (SOX) Act and the specific section of the Act numbered 404. Section 404 sets forth regulations on internal controls and auditing. Specifically, it outlines rules that public companies must follow for:

- Establishing and maintaining internal control structures
- Assessing the effectiveness of the controls and structures
- Preparation of a management report on the structure and its effectiveness
- Securing an attestation from an external auditor on the effectiveness of your controls

The extremists of the internet element of the ITO Revolution revealed themselves to be the old regimes that pre-dated the Netscape IPO. Microsoft and AOL played the role of the extremists in the ITO Revolution as well as the traditional bricks and mortar companies such as Wal-Mart, Barns and Noble, General Electric, traditional banks, and other major financial institutions. The internet did provide a new method for consumers to perform commerce, but it did not fundamentally change the economy. The economy did change during the Perigee stage of the ITO Revolution, because vast amounts of capital were invested in the internet and telecom market segments. Anytime hundreds of billions of dollars are invested in a market segment, it will have an affect on economics of that market – but in retrospect, the internet did not change the habit of consumers on the scale and speed predicated. Consumers still went to stores to purchase products. The internet did provide a new method of interaction for services such as online banking and stock trading and it had a tremendous impact on the travel industry, but the internet is really a channel to a market – not necessarily a market unto itself. No new internet-only banks grew to dominant the banking industry. A quick check of the five largest U.S. banks in early 2004 reveals that all have an extensive online presence via the internet, but none of them started as an internet only bank. The old regimes of banking simply developed internet based banking access for their customers.

Within the consumer brokerage market, a number of on-line based trading companies emerged. Companies such as Charles Schwab, Etrade, Ameritrade, Datek, DLJDirect, TD Waterhouse, Web Street, and others all started in the Perigee stage of the ITO Revolution as early revolutionaries in the online trading revolution. As online trading became popularized, the old regimes of brokerage business emerged with online trading components to their business. The old regimes were companies such as Fidelity, Morgan Stanley, and Merrill-Lynch. At the end of the ITO Revolution, consolidation occurred within the online trading market segment and the ability of the old regimes to add equal or better capabilities negated the early advantages that online brokerage revolutionaries possessed.

Bank	Assets	Employees
Citigroup	$1.36 Trillion	260,000
JPMorgan Chase	$771 Billion	94,335
Bank of America	$736 Billion	133,549
Wachovia	$401 Billion	87,000
Wells Fargo	$391 Billion	139,000
BankOne	$326 Billon	71,200
Washington Mutual	$286 Billion	55,000
FleetBoston	$200 Billion	50,000
US Bancorp	$182 Billion	51,673
Suntrust	$125.4 Billion	27,650

Figure 19: Sampling of Largest US Banks, Jan-2004

Five interesting companies that evolved out of the early stages of the internet revolution are eBay, Amazon.com, Dell Computer, and Microsoft. These five companies are important because they each developed an important consumer aspect of the internet revolution. eBay was the first to develop a highly successful, profitable, and repeatable business model based solely on consumer access via the internet. Amazon.com was the first company to build a recognizable consumer orientated brand via an internet only sales channel. Dell was the first company to perfect a "build-to-order" or "just in time" supply chain based on sales via the internet and linkage to their supply chain. Microsoft is an interesting case study because it was an old regime that emerged from the internet revolution as a major internet power by embracing the opportunity of change that the internet provided and marshalling its resources to respond to competitive threats. AOL is the historical bridge from an ITO revolutionary extremist, to the social model overlay found in the succeeding essay. AOL was the only early internet extremist to emerge from the ITO Revolution with control of an old regime and a charter member of the old economy. Beyond all that revolutions are supposed to do and represent, in the end the one product they provide in abundance is opportunity. Confusion is the breeding ground for opportunity and revolutions cause confusion. From within this confusion, the winners find opportunity. By adapting to the changing environment (i.e. market conditions) and perfecting the ability to deal with incomplete information, successful companies engaged in a revolutionary cycle drive their business plan to success.

The business model developed by eBay is without question the best application of the internet revolution to a quality, revenue generating business. eBay makes money by providing a service that facilitates consumer to consumer transactions. Revenue is earned from the transaction between the consumers or businesses without taking possession of the products. eBay is an internet based marketplace that facilitates transactions between consumers and businesses. Customers pay a commission to eBay for using their market place to perform a transaction. A mall could do the same by charging stores a percentage of their transactions in lieu of rent. The real value of eBay is not that their service is unique, although they have secured trademarks and patents to certain aspects of their service and technology to prevent competitors from providing the same consumer experience – but rather that eBay has developed a strong brand. People know the eBay brand and consumers are willing to pay for the service because they believe in the strength of the eBay marketplace. The eBay brand draws consumers to their site and eBay is able to generate revenue from the brand value. Beyond the company, eBay has created a sub-culture of businesses based on the eBay web site. Today there are books on how use eBay, how to make money on eBay, and on any given day one can find seminars in hotels given by consultants on how to make money using eBay. Beyond the business model, eBay can be credited with the contribution of a sub-tier culture

Amazon.com provides the clearest example of why the internet revolution was not the dawn of a new economy – at least not yet. Amazon.com started as a provider of books purchased through its web site. Jeff Bezos, founder and long time CEO, chose to focus on books because books are a product that consumers would purchase without the need to physically review the product before it is purchased. Customers will purchase books without reading or evaluating the product before the purchase decision is made. This is an important foundation to the initial business plan of Amazon.com. People rarely purchase high priced goods such as furniture, automobiles, or real estate without firsthand experience with the product or property – but there are products they will purchase without first hand experience. Books and CDs fall into this category and it was from books that Amazon.com built a strong consumer brand. Today, Amazon is a full fledged consumer retail business. They possess a broad cross-section of products with multiple warehouses from which they supply their customers. At the end of 2004, Amazon.com enjoyed a market cap of nearly $17 billion, with annual sales approaching $9 billion per year. In comparison to the old regimes of retail, Amazon.com is less than one third the annual revenue of the top ten retail companies in their peer group. Wal-Mart leads the top ten companies in the retail sector with sales approaching $250 billion per year. Clearly, the new economy did not disrupt the retail order that had been set during the period of the old regimes, during the old economy days.

If there is another company that can be placed next to eBay as a shining example of how the internet could be harnessed to change their business model it was Dell Computer. Dell was formed by a true ITO revolutionary – Michael Dell. Michael started selling computers when he was in college. Serendipity occurred when Dell Computer and the internet collided. The rapid growth of the internet and the growing demand for personal computers, created a model wherein Dell could have a cost effective method of interacting with the end-user of their product. Traditionally, computers had been sold through specialized resellers who were the conduit to the consumer. Dell was the leading company who perfected a method of access to the consumer market via the internet as well as pioneering a just-in-time manufacturing process that utilized a minimal stock supply chain. Dell's objective was to build exactly the number of computers they needed for their customers using as much of the company's inventory as possible each quarter, leaving the company with minimal inventories. As the model expanded with the internet, customers could place orders via the web and actually watch the progress of their computer through the manufacturing process into the shipping systems and track the delivery to their doorstep. Dell built a phenomenal company that managed a tight expense line, found innovative ways to interact with their customers and a predicable, highly scalable, and cost effective sales model that leveraged the internet. Much of the Dell success has to do with the growth of personal computing, the proliferation of servers, and the high demand that both these markets experienced due to the internet and overall networking.

The real extremists of the internet component of the ITO Revolution turned out to be Microsoft and AOL. Without question, Microsoft is the best managed technology company in the world, if not the best company in the world. With a cash balance of more than $53 billion in early 2004, they have immense market power. It is believed that Microsoft was late to invest in the internet revolution, but in retrospect, we find that Microsoft was an early advocate of the ITO Revolution; they simply believed the revolution would start in a different medium and did not anticipate the impact of deregulation in the U.S. telecom market. Microsoft envisioned that the revolution that would have the biggest impact on the world was going to be an evolution of the television medium. Television was going to evolve from a fixed time slot broadcast medium to an interactive, on demand model. This was the market that Microsoft was focusing on in the early 1990s.

In June of 1990, the United States Federal Trade Commission (FTC) began an anti-trust investigation into Microsoft's business practices. The government was pursuing a case that alleged Microsoft exploited its dominance of the PC operating system (i.e. DOS and Windows) market to contain and eliminate competitors within other software markets. The government alleged that by controlling the underlying personal computer operating system, Microsoft had a competitive advantage for the development of productivity applications such as word processors, and spreadsheet and personal finance management applications. Competitive products may not work as well as competitive programs from Microsoft and that Microsoft was further able to exploit their vast market share in the operating system business to ensure that their productivity applications were promoted ahead of competitive products by the distributors of computers such as Dell, IBM, Packard Bell, HP, Compaq, and Gateway. At the time, one of the potential outcomes speculated in the press by industry pundits was a division of Microsoft into two companies. One company would own the operating system business which included DOS, NT, and Windows. The other company would own the productivity applications such as Word and Excel. This outcome would have been analogous to the division of AT&T's local and long distance business in 1984 and thus seemed very plausible in the early 1990s.

In August of 1993, the Justice Department took control of the investigation from the FTC and settled with Microsoft in July of 1994 with the signing of a consent decree. The basis of the consent decree was an agreement by Microsoft that it would not use its computer operating system to unfairly block competitors from using computers operated by a Microsoft operating system. It was not until a year later that U.S. District Court Judge Thomas Penfield Jackson officially approved the 1994 consent decree in August 1995. Consider the fact that investigations by the FTC are a time and resource consuming process. IBM was investigated by the FTC for thirteen years and it had a measurable impact on the culture and structure of their business. The prolonged nature of the FTC's investigation into IBM actually contributed to the development of an internal culture that, in the long term, hurt the company [see *Building IBM: Shaping an Industry and Its Technology*, by Emerson Pugh]. The anti-trust investigation of IBM created a compartmentalized business culture that was managed and approved by staffs of corporate attorneys. IBM was vigorously fighting the government's investigation and as such became lost in a malaise of bureaucracy designed to defeat the government. During the investigation and eventual trial, 974 witnesses were called to testify and over 100,000 pages of transcript were produced. The result of the investigation was an enormous amount of wasted money and it left in its wake a dysfunctional corporate culture that drove IBM into a precarious condition in 1993.

In contrast to investigations by the FTC, investigations by the Justice Department bring the potential for imprisonment as well as fines and have an emotionally draining affect on the leaders of any target corporation. During the time that Microsoft was under investigation, the leaders of the company were heavily engaged in developing the concept of interactive television as well as the development of a new operating system. The settlement of the Microsoft anti-trust case in 1994 marks an interesting confluence of events that had a significant impact on the ITO Revolution. In April of 1994, the company that would eventually become known as Netscape Communications was founded. During the early 1990s, Microsoft was increasingly interested in the online bulletin board or BBS market that was dominated by AOL, Compuserve, and Prodigy. As part of its next desktop operating system, Microsoft began development of its own online service in 1993. The objective was to time the launch of their online service with the introduction of its new operating system in mid 1994.

In the time period from 1993 to 1994, Microsoft was consumed with readying one of the most significant product launches in the company's history as well as developing an online service to rival AOL, Compuserve, and Prodigy. The impending new product launch would be a significant driver of Microsoft revenue and would secure Microsoft's position as the dominant supplier of operating systems for the PC market. This product was called Windows 95 and in August of 1994 when the product was launched, it was difficult to avoid the global marketing campaign developed by Microsoft around the Rolling Stones' song, *Start Me Up*. It was just a few short months before the launch of Windows 95, that Microsoft made a commitment to the web. In April of 1994, Bill Gates wrote an important memo to the key leaders of the company entitled, *"Sea Change."* In this memo, he outlined the importance of the web and set Microsoft on a rapid development plan to integrate a browser into the Windows 95 product, which was scheduled to launch in a few short months [see *Speeding the Net*, Joshua Quittner and Michelle Slatalla, 1998]. Before the April memo from Bill Gates, the web was not a top priority for Microsoft and its best resources were not aligned to capitalize on the emergence of the web. Although Microsoft did start work on its browser in late 1993, it was not a top development priority within the company. Following the launch of Windows 95, the MSN Network, and Internet Explorer 1.0, Microsoft began some initial investments in the internet revolution, but the company was still focused on the anticipated revolution in the consumer market of television. As part of their investment in the internet, Microsoft became an investor in UUNET in 1995, but the main investment focus of the company was in area of interactive television. Microsoft envisioned a world in which the personal computer and television would become fused. This belief guided Microsoft to be an early investor in next generation cable television as well as to be a creator of broadcast content. Three significant cable and broadcast media investments set the foundation for what would later become more than $10 billion in follow-on investments in the network infrastructure of cable television to carry high-speed internet data and enhanced video services.

The first major investment that Microsoft made in the cable industry was investing in TCI. The same TCI was the first customer of @Home. Microsoft's next investment was in a company called WebTV that was developing a form of interactive television. The idea behind WebTV was to provide internet capabilities to a cable television set top box for the consumer who wanted internet access, but did not own a computer. Microsoft eventually acquired WebTV, on April 6, 1997, for $425 million. In the press release announcing the acquisition, Bill Gates said, *"This partnership with WebTV underscores our strategy of delivering to consumers the benefits of the Internet together with emerging forms of digital broadcasting."* Before the acquisition of WebTV, Microsoft made a major move into the broadcast media, well before anyone ever envisioned AOL buying Time-Warner. In 1995, Microsoft launched Windows 95 and started a broadcast network with NBC that would become known as MSNBC.

1995 was just the beginning for Microsoft and the cable industry. The next four years would see Microsoft invest nearly $10 billion in the cable industry worldwide. The first big deal announced after 1995, was a $1 billion investment in Comcast in June of 1997. Bill Gates said of the deal, *"Our vision for connecting the world of PCs and TVs has long included advanced broadband capabilities to deliver video, data and interactivity to the home. Comcast's integrated approach to cable distribution, programming and telecommunications complements that vision of linking PCs and TVs. Today's announcement will enhance the integration of broadband pipes and content to expand the services offered to consumers."* Brian Roberts, then president of Comcast said of the investment, *"I am pleased to have Microsoft's participation as we shape and advance the integration of the PC and the TV. Microsoft's investment is a strong endorsement of Comcast's vision to use its cable networks as a broadband vehicle to homes, schools and businesses. Comcast's customers will be the beneficiaries of the innovations that America's most advanced computer and cable companies can offer. In addition to a significant cash infusion, this investment gives us access to Microsoft's expertise, which will help us facilitate the deployment of high-bandwidth applications and lead to more sophisticated services."* Microsoft was making a major play for the interactive television and internet market accessed via cable networks. At the May 1998 NCTA show, Bill Gates said of the internet and cable industry, *"By early '99 we should be rolling out hundreds of thousands, even millions of set-top boxes that combine PC technology with these Internet connections. Now, the information that people will deal with will be in many different places. You'll have a pocket-sized device that you can take with you. You'll have your pager or telephone. You'll have your intelligent set-top box. And you'll continue to have PCs that you keep in your den, or that you have as portable devices, or that you use at work. Now, through all these devices you'll want to get at the same information. And the value of having that information online will continue to increase. It's really stunning, if you go out on the Internet, to see all of the things you can find out there. You can see what's going on in Congress. In fact, whenever you go and browse a news site, if you've provided your zip code, it automatically appends onto any news stories about the Congress, specific information about how your representative voted. There's even a link that's included now, where if you disagree with what they did, or if you want to provide feedback, you simply click, and you can provide electronic mail to your representative. And so we're going to get interactive democracy, letting people participate in new ways. Electronic commerce across the Internet is also exploding. Companies like Amazon.com are achieving very high valuations, as people see the incredible growth there. Whether it's finding books, finding records, booking travel, all of these things, the interfaces continue to improve. And I think that a substantial part of all of those activities will be done over the Internet. And therefore, give the cable industry a chance to participate, participate in the transaction fees, and participate in owning the companies that are going to make this happen"* [see, Bill Gates, http:// www.microsoft.com/billgates/speeches/ncta'98.asp].

The one billion dollars invested in Comcast was just the beginning. Microsoft next invested $212.5M in Time-Warner's Road Runner cable modem service. Time-Warner was one of the few cable service providers that did not use the @Home service, but rather built its own cable modem service. A look at the June 15, 1998 press release finds two typical ITO Revolution quotes from the two Cable Company CEOs involved in the deal. Gerald M. Levin, CEO of Time-Warner said *"Today's investments by Microsoft and Compaq validate the cable architecture as a premier Internet distribution medium, which will benefit consumers nationwide. This combination of world-class companies will enable us to develop a powerful, branded package of content that will become the high-speed online service of choice for our customers. Microsoft's and Compaq's expertise complements perfectly the strengths of Time Warner and MediaOne."* Chuck Lillis, who was chairman and CEO of MediaOne said, *"With this combination of industry leaders, the venture will be well-positioned to rapidly deploy a wide range of high-value content and services to our customers. As network-based services become ever more integral to our lives, providing a network that will allow us to ensure the performance, connectivity and interoperability to any network in the world will be critical. This venture provides the ideal platform to build both the online service of choice and the network."*

As Microsoft pushed into 1999, their investment in the cable infrastructure as a broadband delivery mechanism increased. Interactive active television, the internet, and the legacy service of telephony became targets for Microsoft money. In January of 1999, Microsoft made a $500 million dollar investment in NTL, the largest cable provider in the United Kingdom. Barclay Knapp, then CEO of NTL said, *"Microsoft believes in our vision of bringing advanced digital Internet, telephone and television services to consumers and businesses throughout the UK via all platforms. NTL's pioneering marketing, network and back-office resources, coupled with Microsoft's world leadership in personal computing and digital television, will make for a great combination."*

Following the NTL investment, Microsoft made two international cable investments and one of the largest single investments in the company's history. The two international cable investments were in the cable arm of Portugal Telecom (PT) and Rogers Communications in Canada. The investments were $38.6 million in PT and $400 million in Rogers, which is the largest cable operator in Canada. On July 12, 1999, Microsoft and AT&T announced a $5 billion dollar investment by Microsoft in the cable business of AT&T, known as AT&T Broadband. In the press release, Bill Gates was quoted as saying, *"Our agreement today represents an important step in Microsoft's vision of making the Web lifestyle a reality. Working with AT&T, a leader in the delivery of cable and telephony technologies, we will expand access to an even richer Internet and television experience for millions of people."* In turn, AT&T used the proceeds from this transaction on capital expenditures to improve their cable network. This infusion of capital to build their own network occurred four months after the merger of @Home and Excite.

@Home had billed itself as a service provider for cable service providers that was building an internet overlay network. @Home never viewed Microsoft as a competitor, but this is why the extremists win. While @Home was building a nationwide network to sell to the cable service providers and struggling with their business model, Microsoft was providing capital from its vast financial reserves in form of investments to enable the cable service providers to afford the capital expenditures required to upgrade their own networks. Additionally, telecom deregulation lowered the barriers for capital and the old regimes and new revolutionaries who provided services for the internet backbone and were able to rapidly acquire the capital to expand and improve their internet backbones. Microsoft was offering a far better business proposition to cable service providers than @Home. In the end, Microsoft was using its capital to build strategic business relationships with the cable providers. This is why the extremists win. @Home was a service provider to a cable company that slightly increased revenues. Microsoft invested in the business of cable with proposition of (a) here is the capital you need to improve your network, (b) improvements will in turn improve revenues, and (c) a better network and improving revenues will increase your stock price thus making the company wealthier. In the old regimes of Europe, the royal families intermarried to create bonds of loyalty and alignment. In the business world of the ITO Revolution, bonds of loyalty and alignment were created at the executive and board levels through the exchange of money and ownership in the pursuit of wealth and power.

The Rise of AOL

AOL is the poster child for the *Six Years that Shook the World*. Here is a company whose founding employees covet many of the characteristics we find in the extremists of the great western revolutions. AOL predated the ITO Revolution by nearly fourteen years. Its founders had worked to develop online communities for the Commodore and Apple computers. They had toiled in the background of the industry for many years with, at best, modest success. The founders and employees of AOL were true believers in online communities. Long before the public discovered chat rooms and web sites, the employees of AOL were trying to build online bulletin boards for the various computers that seemed to do well in the home market. This is why they first focused on the Commodore and then Apple computer markets. The convergence of the internet and the evolution of the clone PC makers into strong brands such as Dell, Gateway, Micron and Compaq, changed the market that AOL was addressing. The name America On-Line (AOL) was not used by the company until 1987 and yet this small group of fanatical extremists built their business and waited until the revolution provided an opportunity. Luck can be defined as where planning meets opportunity and for the extremists of AOL, this is exactly what happened when the internet marketing hype exploded on America in the mid-1990s.

Fundamentally, AOL could not have accomplished what it did without a massive structural shift in the markets they served. This massive shift is called a revolution. The ITO Revolution enabled, legitimized, and empowered AOL. AOL toiled in the background of the market for many years before realizing substantial success. When the opportunity came for AOL to seize territory (i.e. market share), they were successful from within the revolution. AOL did not create the internet. AOL did not create telecom privatization. AOL did not create the computers and networks used to launch their assault on the old regimes – yet AOL exploited these events to their advantage.

As the 1990s progressed towards the year 2000, AOL became the marketing machine for the acquisition of subscribers to their online world. Through subscriber growth and marketing, AOL developed into the premier online brand. When AOL passed twenty million subscribers, it was producing an astounding $400 million per month in subscriber revenue. Not including their advertising revenue, AOL had a predictable yearly turn over of $4.8 billion in subscriber revenue alone. This type of cash flow generated from their commanding market share, powered AOL's stock price higher and provided AOL with the resources (i.e. assets, people, and technology) and right (i.e. money) to acquire other companies. The asset that AOL acquired was a venerable component of the old economy, a company called Time-Warner. *"The idea behind merging the world's leading online services provider with the world's biggest media and entertainment company is that together they can set the pace for what AOL chair Steve Case likes to call 'the Internet century.' As Merrill Lynch analysts Henry Blodget and Jessica Reif Cohen put it in their fervent endorsement of the deal, AOL Time Warner will provide the 'operating system for everyday life' in our fully interactive future - involving the way we communicate, get news and entertainment, go shopping, manage our money, do almost everything except eat and sleep."* [Wired 8.09, September 2000]

Time-Warner is a classic example of an old economy company that had been seeking a strategy to access the new economy created by the ITO Revolution. The marriage between AOL and Time-Warner was founded in the belief that a strong internet brand should be married to content. The internet was going to evolve into an interactive content delivery medium. To be the dominant company in this revolution, the leaders would be required to own content and have the ability to deliver that content. AOL provided Time-Warner with a strong internet brand, increased cash flow and the one of the most popular internet portal destinations. Time-Warner provided content for AOL subscribers as well as a large cable company with a network to millions of homes in the Untied States. In this merger, the power of revolution can be identified. Time-Warner was a company with a vast stable of media companies that include Time, CNN, Warner Brothers, Sports Illustrated, People, HBO, TBS, TNT, Cartoon Network, Warner Music Group, Fortune, Entertainment Weekly, The WB, Time Warner Cable, Road Runner, and Looney Tunes. These brands required decades to build as they are pillars of the entertainment, cable, music, and media industries of the Untied States. In the span of six years, from 1994 to 2000, AOL grew from a small online provider in the suburbs of Washington to a giant company that had the ability to purchase the world's largest media company. *"This strategic combination with AOL accelerates the digital transformation of Time Warner by giving our creative and content businesses the widest possible canvas. The digital revolution has already begun to create unprecedented and instantaneous access to every form of media and to unleash immense possibilities for economic growth, human understanding and creative expression. AOL Time Warner will lead this transformation, improving the lives of consumers worldwide,"* [see Gerald Levin, CEO, Time-Warner, January 10, 2000].

In January 2000, Time-Warner and AOL agreed to a merger worth $109 billion. AOL shareholders ended up owning 55% of the combined company at close. AOL, the company that toiled for years in pursuit of their revolution, became the extremists of the internet revolution. As an extremist, AOL acquired their nearest rival, CompuServe, and the first of the great internet revolutionaries, Netscape. They would parlay their success and leverage the power of the ITO Revolution to win control of a pillar of the old economy in a company called Time-Warner. This is the power of revolution; AOL realized that the revolution was not won or lost on the day of revolution. AOL exploited a continuation of revolution by focusing on their market segment, eliminating the competition, and building a position of power that enabled AOL to exploit the market conditions to gain control of assets that were part of the old economy. In this behavior, AOL deserves credit as a preeminent, successful extremist of the ITO Revolution that resulted in an online service provider becoming the largest media company in the world.

The RBOCs Rule

Within the telecom component of the ITO Revolution, the extremists reveal themselves to be the regional bell operating companies (i.e. RBOCs) – the same seven companies that were divested from the old regime AT&T, in 1984 to settle the government's allegation that AT&T was a monopoly. The extremists in our market model are reflective of the role that the RBOCs played in the ITO Revolution – not a commentary or assessment of their intentions. We are not equating the moralities or actions of any participant in the ITO Revolution with the actual actions of any historical group or person. As the ITO Revolution approaches, the extremists have been bidding their time, seeking strategies to change their businesses. The ITO Revolution creates an environment that enables the RBOCs to take advantage of their strengths as extremists to consolidate market share and assume power. Although many supporters of the Telecom Act of 1996 view it as an agent of change destined to open closed markets to competition and bring new services to the disenfranchised consumer – the reality is that the Telecom Act of 1996 is a mechanism for the RBOCs to access new markets, provide new services and consolidate power.

The extremists in G3 Market Model are successful for many reasons, but the foundation of their success is set by the pre-existing market conditions. Power (i.e. market share) is less concentrated following a revolution. During the days of old regimes (i.e. pre-1996 Telecom Act), the market for telecom services in the U.S. was primarily a stable oligarchy. We define an oligarchy as: *A form of government in which the supreme power is placed in the hands of a few persons; also, those who form the ruling few* [see HyperDictionary.com]. There were a small number of suppliers who controlled the majority of services within the total market. Post the Telecom Act of 1996, there was an exponential increase in the number of suppliers of telecom services within the total market. Market share became less concentrated and diffused amongst the many service providers during the first three stages of the G3MM. During the Perigee stage of the ITO Revolution, it seemed as if the new revolutionaries were making substantial progress in developing their business. Specific to the telecom market, this was an indication that the revolutionaries were either taking market share from the old regimes (i.e. RBOCs) or they were winning a vast number of new, uncommitted customers who were entering the market and choosing service providers. New competitive local exchange companies (CLECs) were successful in acquiring capital, building networks, and entering markets that had been closed to local telephony competition. In turn, the CLECs were new, uncommitted market share for the network equipment providers such as Nortel, Lucent, Cisco, Ascend, and many other companies.

It appeared as if the business model of the revolutionaries was being validated – but in reality, the market was changing while they were creating their businesses. The extremists of the ITO Revolution simply did not stand idly by and let the revolutionaries enact their vision of the future. The extremists acted and used the new market conditions to fundamentally change their businesses, thus alternating the market conditions and competitive pressures. Successful revolutionaries think not of the market today, but of the market of the future and what they need to do today to acquire power in the future. The Telecom Act of 1996 altered the market conditions for the RBOCs of the ITO Revolution. Before the act, the RBOCs lived in a well-defined market silo – post the act, they were able to use the revolution around them to change their businesses in ways they had only dreamed of before 1996. When the CLEC, CAP, and IXC revolutionaries began to enact their plan as part of the revolution, they found that market conditions had changed and they had the wrong plan for a new market they did not anticipate. The result of the unanticipated market conditions was a collapse in the ability of the new entrants to sustain their businesses. When the revolutionary companies lost the ability to sustain their businesses projections, they become vulnerable to pressures of the financial extremists of the ITO Revolution. When new companies that require extensive capital are unable to meet their growth projections, it has a severe affect on the viability of their business.

In the telecom component of the ITO Revolution, it is the RBOCs that have a fanatical devotion their business. From a historical perspective, the RBOCs own a near monopoly in their markets. This might lead one to believe that they are the old regime of the ITO Revolution, but when we look at their business, we realize they are not the old regime. The RBOCs are few in number and pre-date the revolution. They were once part of the old regime (i.e. AT&T), but they had been divested from the old regime and resigned to operate in their isolated markets, regulated by the government, and confined to minimal expansion. In reality, they were cast off to live with the liability of the copper local loop and slow market growth. For the twelve years before the Telecom Act of 1996, the RBOCs struggled to gain approval to sell new services and expand their markets. The ITO Revolution changed the structure of the market conditions and created an opportunity for the RBOCs to become an end-to-end provider of services within, and outside, of their markets.

When the RBOCs were divested from AT&T, they became independent regulated monopolies. As such, they where limited in the services they could offer and limited as to where they could offer those services. The Telecom Act of 1996 changed the operating environment of the markets that the RBOCs served. They were still regulated monopolies, but they had the ability to add new services and enter or acquire new markets. In return for this ability, they were forced to open their infrastructure for use by competitors within their markets. This was the market change that the CLECs were expected to exploit. From the RBOC perspective, they wanted to provide more services to their customers, including long distance services that had been the domain of AT&T, MCI, GTE, Sprint, and a handful of smaller companies. With their infrastructure being forced open and new market challengers, the RBOCs were faced with a new set of challenges. They always wanted to be a player in the long distance market, but they also had to protect their local telephony market. To accomplish both goals, it required the RBOCs to protect the value of their copper local loop and maintain market status quo. They would do this through a fanatical devotion to their cause that would force out competition and use the threat of competition to change government regulation to allow them to offer new services.

The RBOCs are probably the most disciplined revolutionary in the ITO Revolution. This is a by-product of culture, regulation, and process. The RBOCs do not deploy new technologies quickly and they prefer to adopt solutions that are stable and can be sourced from the large telecom suppliers such as Lucent, Nortel, Alcatel, and Fujitsu. The loyalty that the RBOCs give to these vendors is for several reasons. RBOCs typically deploy new technologies on a large scale and the deployment process is completed over several years. Supplier stability and support capabilities are critical decision points for an RBOC. If an RBOC is going to deploy hundreds of millions of dollars of technology, train thousands of support people, and operate the equipment for eight to fifteen or more years, then it is important that the suppliers be part of the process on day one as well as the fiftieth year. The RBOCs are unified because they all share the same market conditions, have the same need to expand their markets and must go through the same internal processes. For the most part, the RBOCs do not compete with each other in their regions. This is changing as markets evolve – but the level of competition between RBOCs in each other's home region is minimal when analyzed on a total revenue perspective.

The RBOCs successfully realized two important objectives out of the ITO revolution. The first objective was the ability to offer previously prohibited services such as long distance. The second objective was the ability to enter new markets and change their business model. The Telecom Act of 1996 enabled the RBOCs to achieve these objectives. What the RBOCs had not counted on was the rise of the cable service providers, growth in wireless phones, and emergence of AT&T and MCI in their local telephony markets. As the year 2000 dawned, the ITO Revolution stood on the brink of a great change. Few people realized in January of 2000 how dramatic, severe, and swift the change would occur.

A Viewpoint from 2000

The early weeks of 2000 were an interesting time for the ITO Revolution. Optimism still abounded, yet the ITO Revolution was about to go through a dramatic and sudden change. The transition from the Perigee stage to the Decline stage of the ITO Revolution occurred quite quickly. Companies that were not cash flow positive and were running low on cash began to rapidly cut staff and services in order to remain solvent. Growth targets were missed and business expectations were unfulfilled because companies were unable to capture market share or the projected market share never materialized. When the metrics for growth and business development did not occur along the expected timelines, then investors began to reconsider the valuation of the new internet, telecom, and optical companies. In the ITO Revolution, the transition from Perigee to Decline is neatly marked by the stock prices and the market caps of the revolutionaries in the stock market. The companies who were making money survived and those who were not making money began a rapid descent. The Decline stage of the ITO Revolution begins with the failure of companies to grow their revenues and is highlighted by the consolidation of market share by the extremists of the revolution.

The transition from Perigee to Decline within the ITO Revolution was preceded by a phenomenon known as Y2K readiness. Y2K readiness is important because it serves as a defining moment in the ITO Revolution. Revolutions need expectation setting events. Revolutions are a sequence of momentum events. When expectations are exceeded, revolutions increase in speed and power. When revolutions begin to slow or fail, it is usually because expectations of the revolutionaries were not achieved. Few events in modern time have had as much publicity as Y2K. During the Y2K readiness process, International Data Corp. (IDC) provided numerous reports on the spending required to prepare the global IT infrastructure for the Y2K event. Their estimate was that from 1995 to 2001, nearly $300 billion was spent worldwide, with $122 billion of that spending occurring in the United States, to prepare for the Y2K event. It has been argued that this spending only represented a small fraction (~5%) of overall IT spending during the period. This is probably true, because during this period the ITO Revolution was peaking and companies were building millions of networks and the associated support infrastructure – but Y2K was important. The IT spending in the mid 1990s was so significant that the U.S. Department of Commerce commented, *"In 1996 and 1997, declining prices in IT industries lowered overall inflation by one full percentage point. Without the contribution of the IT sector, overall inflation, at 2.0 percent, would have been 3.1 percent in 1997* [see *The Emerging Digital Economy*, U.S. Department of Commerce April 15, 1998].

Y2K was a bell weather event within the ITO Revolution as it marked the boundary between an Orwellian fantasy world and business reality. When the New Year passed around the world and nothing out of the ordinary happened of great magnitude within the IT infrastructure of the world, the ITO Revolution began to lose some of its apocalyptic specter. Companies began to move beyond Y2K and slow their spending. Y2K spending began to end just as the first phase of the internet and telecom revolutions where beginning to move to a new phase. 1999 was all about getting the new infrastructure built and the old infrastructure ready for Y2K. When the year 2000 dawned, the financial community of the ITO Revolution began to examine the financial performance of the new economy companies. Companies needed to perform and metrics such as cash flow, cash balances, market share, and cash burn became important in assessing value.

The transition from Perigee to Decline occurred during mid to late 2000. Within the internet component, AOL had already made the leap from a new economy revolutionary to an old economy hybrid with the acquisition of Time-Warner. Other internet companies began to collapse as their business models began to fail. Consolidation amongst the internet market segments began to occur. It was in mid-2000 that the first cracks in the telecom component of the ITO Revolution became visible. Many of the new revolutionaries struggled with making their business models successful. As business was slow to grow, the new telecom companies began to slow the rate at which they were purchasing telecom equipment. This slowing of capital equipment expenditures began to be reflected in the results of the telecom equipment suppliers. The result was a massive chain reaction. As the internet companies failed, the new telecom companies began to lose sources of revenue and thus slowed their spending on network equipment. When the new revenue sources did not materialize for the service providers, they started to conserve cash and began to stop the purchase of new telecom equipment. The slowing of capital expenditures on networking equipment began to impact the financial valuations of the network equipment suppliers. This was the beginning of the collapse of the telecom bubble. Even the intellectuals who once touted the ITO Revolution became skeptics. *"Seventy-five percent of all Internet companies will cease to exist in the next three to five years. Amazon could buy eToys because it has expertise that Amazon doesn't have,"* [see Henry Blodget, February 2000].

As we look back on 2000, what we find is that the extremists of the revolution were growing stronger. The extremists wanted more change, as they wanted the revolution to continue. As such, they were making it as difficult as they could on their competitive revolutionaries. While this was happening, the eventual survivors of the ITO Revolution were beginning to emerge and draw new lines of battle. The RBOCs had always used their control of the local loop and the revenue provided by local telephony as the foundation of their business. In late 2000, the first real threat to that business began to emerge. The threat came from the providers of wireless telephones and cable broadband. Internet access via dialup modems had driven the sales of local telephony lines during the early stages of the ITO Revolution. As 2000 progressed, internet access via cable modems began to affect the number of the local lines in service. Customers also discovered that wireless or mobile phones were not novelties. The wireless providers began to offer aggressive price plans that made it possible to cost-effectively use mobile phones anywhere in the Untied States. Consumers were not tied to their local telephone number. In this example we find the power of revolution.

The growth of local telephony lines in the 1990s drove the need to create many overlay area codes. Overlay area codes had a social impact on America. People had lived their entire lives in the same area code – now they were divided overnight. Revolutions divide people and families. When a new area code was introduced to market, it would be preceded by months of marketing and public awareness campaigns, which is how a revolution is marketed. The unintended result of the new area codes was that it changed social habits in America. The world outside of the Untied States is very familiar with country codes and ten digit dialing – but in America, local seven digit dialing is taken for granted. When the old social habit of seven digit dialing was broken and people accepted new area codes, they naturally came to the conclusion that they did not need a telephone at home. The social impact was significant enough that it was even portrayed in a *Seinfeld* episode. In reality, area code changes did have a significant local impact on people and businesses even if they were not caught up in the ITO Revolutions. Companies were forced to print new letter head, update business cards and general billing and contact information. This is an expense that was generated by the ITO Revolution and it changed social habits. The result is that a telephone number is no longer significant to social standing or status. Hence, the ITO Revolution enabled people who live in Arizona, but had once lived in Massachusetts, to keep their Massachusetts area code and number. This is the beginning of global mobility as part of a global community. It starts small, but the ITO Revolution clearly began to break down social structures and habits that had been ingrained in the people for decades.

As we look at the success and failures from the ITO Revolution, we will find that successful companies that emerged from the fires of revolution were the companies that possessed great leaders. The leaders many not have been recognized at the time of the revolution, but in the end, their greatness was evident to all. The leaders who emerge at the end of the revolution are not always viewed as the great leaders at the time of revolution. Revolutions mold great leaders. When times are complacent and predicable – great leaders are not molded. The history of revolutions shows us that great leaders are shaped and elevated by revolution. In the ITO Revolution, Michael Dell, Bill Gates, John Chambers, Jeff Bezos, and Steve Case were shaped and elevated by the ITO Revolution. Clearly the world knew of Bill Gates before the ITO Revolution of the 1990s, but it is a testament to his leadership skills that Microsoft emerged more powerful after the ITO Revolution – than before the revolution.

The Three DSL Providers during the Transition from Perigee to Decline

The transition from Perigee to Decline is marked by the transfer of market share to a smaller, dominant group of companies. In the business world of the ITO Revolution, the transition is identified when revolutionary companies begin to fail. The failure of the average companies empowers the extremists, but also provides the trigger for the progression from Decline to the next stage of the revolution known as the Apogee. This sequence is neatly illustrated in the ITO Revolution by the fate of three DSL providers. An unfortunate aspect of the Decline stage of the G3MM is that it can be considered an isolated event if it is not viewed in the context of the entire market model. *"This is the last big hiccup out of this shakeout that we've seen over the past few months. I don't think we'll see anything this dramatic or traumatic after this, unless Covad or Rhythms fail to pull through. The unfortunate thing about the whole NorthPoint situation has been that it gives the whole industry a black eye"* [see Adam Guglielmo, DSL Analyst at TeleChoice, http://news.com.com/2100-1033-255086.html?legacy=cnet, March 30, 2001].

By the end of 1999, the three DSL providers had each completed successful initial public offerings, raising a combined total of $722 million from the public markets. With listings on the NASDAQ, the three DSL providers were viewed as a new breed of revolutionary companies that were leading the transformation of the telecom infrastructure of the old economy to the infrastructure of the new economy. These new telecom service providers were not burdened with the legacy networks and bureaucracies of the old regimes – therefore they would have better operating (i.e. OPEX) cost structures. The three DSL providers would move faster than the old regimes and capitalize on the transfer of market share from the old economy to the new economy. The three DSL providers were leaders in the internet revolution. They understood the internet and deployed new technologies that provided advantages that would take the old regimes years to realize. Unfortunately, this revolutionary fever sounded great to the masses, but it had little to do with reality.

The first of the DSL providers to collapse was Northpoint. Northpoint's business model was focused on providing high-speed internet access to web centric companies that were part of the new economy. Northpoint's business plan focused on internet businesses such as internet service providers, web hosting companies, and web centric software and service companies. By design, Northpoint stayed out of the consumer internet access business. Unfortunately for Northpoint, they were dependent on access by the RBOCs to the local loop in order to gain access to their target customers. Northpoint was renting access on the RBOC network to acquire customers. The problem with this business model is that RBOCs have to (a) be inclined to provide access for Northpoint to access customers, (b) when access is provided Northpoint must pay a monthly fee to the RBOC for use of the local loop, and (c) Northpoint's business was dependent on the internet component of the ITO Revolution. It was the internet component of the ITO Revolution that was first to collapse. Northpoint's business model, which was created by the Telecom Act of 1996, simply did not work. The RBOCs had no incentive to move quickly in granting access to the local loops and as Northpoint began to fall behind their financial projections, the financial community of the ITO Revolution began their assault on the company. In early 2001, Northpoint collapsed, due to the inability to grow revenues, make profits, raise capital, and service their debt. Northpoint closed operations in March of 2001. At its peak in 2000, Northpoint employed over a thousand people.

The startling aspect of the Northpoint's collapse was it was hastened by an extremist of the ITO Revolution. In August of 2000, Northpoint agreed to merge its DSL business with Verizon and the Verizon OnLine business unit. Under terms of the agreement, Verizon agreed to invest a total of $800 million. $450 million would be used to fund Northpoint's operations and continued network expansion while the remaining $350 million would be used to acquire the outstanding shares of Northpoint. At the time of the announcement, Northpoint posted a $112 million dollar loss on revenues of $24.4 million. Verizon was paying $350 million for a business generating approximately $25 million in top line revenues that still required hundreds of millions of dollars to expand their business. The $112 million dollar loss indicated that profitability was still far off in the future.

On November 29, 2000, just a little over three months later, Verizon terminated the merger agreement with Northpoint. In the press release Verizon stated that; *"Under the terms of the agreement, Verizon's obligation to complete the merger was conditioned upon Northpoint's business, operations and financial condition each remaining materially the same as they were at the time the agreement was signed.*

Northpoint recently reported a continuing decline in revenues, an erosion of its customer base, an increase in expenses due to write-offs for increased bad debt, and, as a result, a material increase in net losses. Verizon said that given the material adverse changes, it has terminated the agreement as permitted under the terms of the contract." The termination of the Verizon merger was a terminal event for Northpoint. From the time that the merger agreement was struck, Northpoint's business was undergoing a turbulent change as the extremists of the ITO Revolution were assuming power. Unforeseen bankruptcies within Northpoint's base of internet customers had caused the company to revise downward revenue estimates for the current quarter after the merger was announced, from $30 million to $24 million. By this time in the merger process, Verizon had used their due diligence time to fully study Northpoint's network, cost models, and market conditions. When Northpoint's market began to erode, Verizon decided to pull out of the merger. Paying $800 million for a declining business that required hundreds of millions of dollars of capital investments was not a sensible business strategy. The result of Verizon's withdrawal from the Northpoint merger was material and swift. A little over three months later, Northpoint stopped operations, declared bankruptcy, and its assets were sold.

Rhythms began a similar collapse in the same timeframe as Northpoint. As Northpoint watched its internet business customers go bankrupt and disappear in mid to late 2000, Rhythms found that the consumer market simply did not materialize fast enough to enable the successful execution of their business plan. Rhythms suffered under the burden of two challenges in the market. The first was the slow adoption of DSL service in the consumer and small business markets and the second was the slow pace of installation. In order to use the copper local loop to service their customers, Rhythms had to apply for a loop from the RBOC. The slow bureaucratic processes of the RBOC served the end-goals of the extremists well. The business model employed by Rhythms continued to deteriorate throughout 2000 and into 2001. In April 2001, Rhythms received a delisting warning notification from the NASDAQ. CNET reported on April 2, 2001; "*We may not be able to compete effectively in our target markets. The independent local exchange carriers are larger, better capitalized, have stronger brand recognition, offer a wider range of products and services, own the copper lines, and have many more existing relationships with potential end users than we do,*" the filing said. *Rhythms may already be in trouble with its lenders. According to the SEC filing, one of the company's leasing companies has notified Rhythms that a default has occurred for failure to maintain certain covenants. As of Dec. 31, Rhythms had approximately $832.3 million of long-term debt and approximately $451.3 million of mandatory redeemable preferred stock*" [see CNET, http://news.com.com/2100-1033-255109.html?legacy=cnet]. After watching Northpoint collapse, Rhythms was unable to meet the financial standards required by the

NASDAQ and was de-listed in May 2001. In June of 2001, Rhythms began to decommission equipment in 150 central offices throughout its markets. The company filed bankruptcy protection on August 2, 2001 and most customers were disconnected by the end of August. By the beginning of September 2001, only one of the original three DSL providers remained.

Covad led the most charmed life of the three DSL providers. It was the first of a new breed of data LEC (DLEC) revolutionaries and the only one not to cease operations – but it did experience the same set of difficulties as Northpoint and Rhythms when the extremists took control of the ITO Revolution. On May 24, 2001, Covad announced that its quarterly revenue for the quarter ending December 31, 2000 was $55.2 million dollars. It lost from operations $854.1 million. Revenue for the year ending on December 31, 2000 was $158.7 million, which resulted in a net loss of $1.44 billion. The financial community reacted by punishing Covad's stock. By the end of 2000, Covad had been in operation as a company for a little more than four years. As the result of their efforts they had acquired 274,000 DSL customer lines. Although Covad passed nearly 40 million homes, they had a DSL penetration rate of .000695%. The good news is they had massive potential for growth – the bad news is they were not meeting the expectations set by the ITO Revolution and new economy status. The financial community punished Covad's stock and on June 1, 2001, Covad was notified that the company had fallen below the minimal standards required for listing on the NASDAQ. On August 15, 2001, Covad filed for Chapter 11 bankruptcy protection with the intent to retire $1.4 billion in debt. By December 20, 2001 Covad had reached agreements with their primary bond holders to eliminate $1.4 billion in debt and had enough of a business to successfully exit chapter 11. Charles E. Hoffman, Covad President and CEO at the time, stated in the company press release, *"A year ago, Covad refocused the company to accommodate the change in capital markets and began reducing expenses. We have now finished restructuring our balance sheet, are fully-funded and essentially debt free. We are focused on refining our business plans to continue to innovate with new services, strengthening our distribution channels, maintaining quality service and financial discipline and keeping the customer at the center of what we do."*

By mid 2005, Covad was still a public company listed on the OTC BB of the NASDAQ. Quarterly revenues are around $110 million. Customer subscriber lines have increased to 417,000. By all accounts, Covad is beginning to show signs of a company that, over the long term, can be successful – but rational people simply do not spend a couple of billion dollars to build a $500 million a year business. Covad could only have built their network and business in a time of revolution. The Perigee stage of the ITO Revolution was a magical time when market barriers were lowered, people dreamed impossible dreams, and all that was happening seemed as if it was part of a new era. Entrepreneurs and companies attempted impossible business plans that would never have seemed plausible in the years preceding the ITO Revolution. The structure of the ITO markets was changed by the power of revolution and the Perigee stage was the time in which the boundless energies and visions of the ITO Revolution were exhausted. It is during the Perigee stage of the G3MM that risk factors are discounted as the constraints of the market conditions are unknown and the prevailing belief is that great value can be created through by being quick to market.

Conclusion

The period known as Decline in the G3MM, is often referred to by industry analysts as a period of market shakeout or market consolidation. As markets progress through their natural cycle, they force a period of market share consolidation. The strong companies come to the fore and the weak companies retreat from positions of power. Market share is voluntarily or involuntarily transferred to the extremists. During the period of the Decline, the intellectuals and moderate leaders of the revolution are removed from positions of power. Companies that had entered the market as an adjunct unit to their core business, typically divest from the market when business becomes difficult and barriers to entry rise. If the company is large enough it may sell or divest their interest in the revolutionary market to focus on their businesses from its days as an old regime – but often the course taken for the weaker revolutionaries is bankruptcy.

There are several examples within the ITO Revolution of companies that fled the telecom markets as a result of the changing market conditions found in the Decline stage. Tyco divested their telecom division called Tycom. Many of the power companies that built telecom networks determined that the cost to build and maintain these networks was too high and the revenue contribution too small. Williams divested their interest in their telecom division. The former telecom arm of Williams is now called WilTel and stands as a separate company from its former parent. Williams was a company that retreated from the ITO Revolution and is now focused on their core business of energy delivery including its oil and natural gas pipelines. Williams and the WilTel story highlight the impact that the ITO Revolution had to create new markets and motivate substantial capital investment. Williams never went as far as Montana Power in completely divesting their old regime – old economy business of energy delivery – but they did make substantial investments in the ITO Revolution and at one time they were considered a leader in the telecom revolution in the United States. Other energy related companies that made or envisioned substantial investments in the ITO Revolution where Enron,

Progress Energy, and El Paso. Enron went bankrupt from the business model they employed during the revolution and today, Progress Telecom is a jointly owned subsidiary of Progress Energy still in the telecom business.

A natural gas pipeline company called Dynegy also made a late foray into the ITO Revolution. Dynegy acquired a small facilities based backbone provider called Extant in 2000 for $151.3 million. Based on this purchase and further investment in their network, Dynegy was attempting to build a network to provide wholesale bandwidth options to CLECs and other service providers who did not have an optical backbone. The service was called *Dynegyconnect Internet Service* and offered customers a variety of connectivity options. As with many companies who entered the ITO Revolution as an extension to their core business, when the Decline stage took full control of the market, these companies exited the telecom services market. Dynegy sold their network which consisted of *"...more than 16,000 route miles and access points in 44 U.S. cities,"* to 360 Networks in March, 2003.

The Decline stage is the gateway to the most violent and tumultuous period of the revolution cycle. The smart money companies that will not end up as the dominant companies realize the pending course of the revolution and begin to exit their business strategies. This is the start of market consolidation. The market and business barriers are on the rise. Sustaining growth is not as easy as it was during the Perigee stage. As such, companies begin to merge. The strongest companies, the extremists of the revolution, are looking to acquire companies that increase their market share and provide them additional strength. The weakest of the revolutionary companies become desperate as market conditions begin to move against them. For the weak companies caught in the movement of stronger market forces, the situation slowly and steady moves against them. The weak companies are caught in a situation that has the peculiar feeling of slipping down a declivity; a deep hole in which the company is clinging to the sides for survival, but cannot muster enough strength to pull itself up. Slowly the company is falling to the bottom. A dark, deep bottom and there is nothing the company can do to alter its fate. The leaders of the company struggle to avoid their fate, but all they can do is look up at the fading light and struggle against the forces pulling the company down. Customers and employees begin to abandon the company. At times, the leaders of the company can still see some light, which fosters hope, but this in time this light fades and the company falls into the dark hole of bankruptcy. This is how revolutions end for those who are not the final arbiters of power. This is how the ITO Revolution ended for Northpoint. The potential acquisition of Northpoint by Verizon was merely a glimmer of light as Northpoint slipped to the bottom of the pit. Customers abandoned the company and Verizon decided to release their hold on Northpoint's hand.

CHAPTER FIVE:
All Glory in Fleeting

Victorious warriors win first and then go to war, while defeated warriors go to war first and then seek to win. - Sun Tzu

The Terror within the ITO Revolution began with the first days of spring in the summer of 2000. The term "Terror" is taken from the historical context used to describe a period during the French revolution that will be discussed in the following essay. For the ITO Revolution, the term Terror can be aptly substituted for the Decline stage of the G3 Market Model. It was during this stage that companies went bankrupt, hundreds of thousands of people were unemployed, 9/11 occurred, and the world seemed to change from a magical time of revolution to a time of Terror. As with the beginning of the ITO Revolution, the time at which the extremists seized control of the ITO Revolution occurred on a serial time line that lagged each other by several months. For the internet element of the ITO Revolution, the spring of 2000 was clearly the beginning of the Decline stage of the G3MM. The telecom and optical elements did not yield power to the extremists until late 2000 and into early 2001. During the years before 2000, the extremist forces had been working stealthily against the ITO revolutionaries. These forces began to exert a change in the ITO Revolution that was unanticipated by the other companies (i.e. revolutionaries) in the market.

As the year 2000 progressed and slipped into 2001, the market conditions changed, which enabled the extremist companies to assume power. Once the extremists had assumed power, the terror began for those who were not in power. The first element of the terror for the ITO Revolution that we will examine is the economic crisis that descended. Unlike the financial crisis facing the U.S. Government [see *Essay One, Chapter Two*] that had laid the seeds of ITO Revolution in the mid-nineties, the economic crisis facing the ITO companies was real and had a dramatic affect on all the companies in the ITO Revolution. The economic crisis that descended in the year 2000 was real and came in several forms. It started with the inability of the new economy companies to meet their financial objectives, thus failing the expectations set by the equity markets and their investors, and it ended when many of these companies ran out of cash, declared bankruptcy, and closed their doors. *"We've come out of a big-bang period, where investors have been willing to fund anybody with a business plan. The recent pullback in the market is probably going to temper that enthusiasm. {There will be} a pretty brutal shakeout in which valuation is going to become a lot more important. I think you'll see probably 75% of these companies disappear"* [see Henry Blodget, 2000].

Many of the internet based auction houses (e.g. eBay and Dovebid) would spend the next few years liquidating hundreds of millions of dollars of networking and telecom equipment. The gray market hangover from the ITO Revolution for telecom and networking equipment lasted into early 2005. The three years between 2000 and mid 2003 are represented in the G3MM by the phase called Decline. The term Decline is used to represent the period of time post the peak of the revolution, which can be identified by the intensifying occurrence of market consolidation and a retreat from the extreme optimistic peak of the revolution, which occurred during the Perigee stage.

Decline: Market conditions continue to be dynamic, allowing for market share exchange – but unlike the Perigee stage, market share ownership has begun to contract to a fewer companies – rather than continue to expand amongst many companies. New, uncommitted market share being added to the market size has slowed to minimal levels or stopped. In most cases, the Decline stage can be identified because the market size has begun to contract. Investment in new companies slows, and then stops and eventually a withdrawal from the market by investors and companies begins. It is at this point that the intellectuals, who had previously extolled victory and validation, now become despondent and dismayed at the course of the revolution. The Terror begins with layoffs, bankruptcies, financial loses, high profile departures of senior executives, and the eventual appearance of investigation and lawsuits. See **Chart 11: G3MM Decline Stage for ITO Revolution** in the Chart and Model section.

The value of the new economy companies that led the internet revolution was determined in large part by their ability to grow rapidly in expanding markets that had the potential to become larger than the legacy markets of the old economy. The markets that internet companies focused on were labeled "hyper growth" and "hyper competitive." The demand for products or services from internet related companies that were labeled "hot" was abnormal in a historical context, but enough leading intellectuals of the revolution were able to justify the valuations that people believed in the revolution. Many leading intellectuals, who were influential in the creation of the revolutionary buzz of the internet, believed that traditional forms of economic valuation mattered little in the creation of new markets. Revolutions create a new environment, therefore legacy methods and procedures from the old regimes and old markets do not apply. Henry Blodget commented in 2000, *"I think valuations matter, but less in the big-bang stage of an industry, where you have few metrics to get comfortable with. But as an industry starts to mature, it starts to matter more, and you need to get a better handle on, say, Yahoo! and what it could earn in three years."* The internet market was considered revolutionary and therefore the growth potential and expectations of the leading companies did not conform to previous market dynamics. When companies began to miss their revenue and growth targets, retribution from the extremists and the public was swift and severe. Companies that were public had their valuations slashed to mere fractions overnight. Companies in similar market segments suffered when competitors failed to meet expectations as market segmentation and grouping began to take hold. In October 2000, Blodget commented on the progress of Amazon.com, *"We continue to be discouraged by…a steady increase in our loss estimates without a correspondingly large increase in revenue or profitability estimates. Bottom line, it continues to cost Amazon more than we ever imagined to generate revenue. Although management has now committed to demonstrating that the basic business model works, we are simply exhausted by the endless postponement of financial gratification."*

As detailed in the history of the three DSL providers, the failure to achieve the expectations of the business plans throughout 2000 and into 2001 accelerated the pace of the Terror within the Decline stage. Companies began to approach positions of low cash reserves and began to take dramatic actions to reduce their cash burn rates. As these actions became public, the financial industry began to punish the failing companies. Stock prices declined and some companies with enormous debt loads with debt covenants tied to their stock price were forced into liquidity issues and many slipped below the minimal financial metrics required for maintaining their stock listing. When the public companies begin to fail, it limits the exit strategies for the privately funded companies. *"Venture capitalists backed 8,101 new companies between the start of 1998 and the first half of this year, according to VentureOne, a Dow Jones & Co. publication that tracks the industry. (Dow Jones also publishes The Wall Street Journal.) Excluding companies that were acquired or went public, 1,924 were shut down by venture capitalists or went out of business, costing investors at least $36.4 billion, according to VentureOne. Of the 4,672 that still are alive, about half initially were funded at the top of the market in 1999 and 2000. Many now are being recapitalized or relaunched with a new business model as 'restarts' as venture capitalists pick through those with the most promising technology – and least risk – to see if they can turn a profit. They often can get a larger stake in a company on the cheap,"* [see *The Wall Street Journal*, August 16, 2004, Ann Grimes].

In the private company market, the pain was equally severe. Investors began to question exit strategies as public and private valuations began to decline. Vast fortunes were committed to companies and markets that in a short period of time appeared to be worthless. When access to financial capital closes, this is when the Terror becomes real for the business world. Hundreds of technology startups were closed [see *Foundations*] during the Decline stage of the G3MM. Venture capitalists, as well as leading technology leaders were shocked at the swiftness of the market correction. In December 2000, Crosspoint Venture Partners turned down $1 billion in commitments for a new fund it had from top shelf institutions such as Harvard University and the Rockefeller Institution. The reason for the cancellation of their ninth fund was two-fold. Crosspoint still had $500 million to invest from its last fund and the leadership team did not see a viable market that would enable the firm to invest the new money with reasonable expectations for success. Most of the leading venture capital firms had just closed new and record size funds in 2000 and 2001. The money had been raised and it was their job to put this money to work for their clients – but the Decline stage had begun. Venture capitalists were suddenly faced with the challenge of finding suitable investments that had a plausible exit strategy. The Terror had closed the public equity markets and devastated the stock price of the companies that were public. Companies such as Cisco, Lucent and Nortel, who had been leaders in the acquisition frenzy of the late 1990s, where suddenly out of the acquisition business. If startups could not go public and large corporations where not acquiring venture back startups, then the startup venture capital pseudo-model refined during the ITO Revolution, had become obsolete. The model was broken. The ecosystem that had pushed for faster innovation cycles, in turn consuming capital to sustain itself, came to rapid halt. The ITO Revolution was no longer a challenge of faster, bigger, spend more money. It was now a question of how to build a real business. How does a startup develop a sustainable competitive edge? Real business drivers had returned to the venture capital industry and the private companies were being measured by increasingly difficult business metrics that were a direct result of the contraction of power within the ITO Revolution. The market barriers that had declined during the early stages of the revolution were now on the ascent. If business was difficult for a company the size of Cisco, Lucent, or Nortel, it was near impossible for small venture backed startup with 100 employees and $80 million in debt.

Death in business is unemployment and foreclosure. The extremists of the ITO Revolution go about creating shock to achieve death in business. The extremists in business want to influence customers to change the criteria of their buying decision. By creating fear, uncertainty, and doubt (i.e. FUD) in the mind of customers, the extremists drive customers from the weak competitors in the market to the strong suppliers, the extremists. During the Perigee stage of the ITO Revolution, the new economy companies portrayed the old regimes as slow, trailing edge companies that were resigned to the pasture. Once the extremists begin to accelerate their acquisition of market share, the pressure on the weak companies of the revolution dramatically increases. The revolutionary companies are not only missing their market growth targets, their competitors see a visible increase in market share and this calls into question the viability of the business model of the weak companies. The tables are turned and it is the large companies who portray the new economy companies of the ITO Revolution as weak and devoid of a long term future. This is the strategy that the extremists use to eliminate competitors from the market.

When the extremists take market share from their competitors it calls into question the entire business model and exit strategy. When the revolutionary companies fail to achieve their objectives, their financial backing is eliminated. The business model and the assumptions upon which it was based are called into question. If the revolutionary companies that suddenly find themselves in a changing market do not correct their business quickly, a death spiral begins. Companies begin reducing expenses in order to conserve cash. This is a prudent strategy that is fraught with challenges because the reduction of expenses means the assumption of a dramatically different business model than originally intended. Everything changes when capital reserves are no longer accessible. When a private company with limited cash reserves and an unprofitable business model slows product development and the drive to create intellectual property value [see *Essay Three, Chapter Eleven*], it is essentially putting the company to sleep.

The extremists want to shock the weak companies trying to survive in the Decline stage. They do this by creating untenable market conditions for the weaker companies. The result of their direct actions is that the market conditions are affected and altered and it is these new and unanticipated market conditions that the revolutionary companies cannot overcome. The three DSL providers encountered this problem when the RBOCs were slow to find and provision local loops for the DSL providers to use to access their customers. The slow growth of the business, coupled with their extended financial condition put the DSL providers is a precarious position. The three DSL providers differentiated their business model from the old regimes by promoting speed, agility, rapid growth and better cost structures than the old regimes. This is how they justified the value of their business in a time of revolution. When the market conditions changed, the value of the new economy business model was eliminated. Revolutionary companies that have not perfected their business model and are relying on capital reserves acquired from venture capitalists, convertible debt or IPOs become particularly vulnerable. Companies have a limited number of actions that directly engage their competitors. Companies inflict pain on their competitors through their customers, products, services, and channels to market. By altering the conditions of these four elements, they can affect their competitors. It was the changing market conditions created by various competitors within the ITO Revolution that created the Decline period and started a reign of Terror within the ITO markets.

The decline of the internet and telecom bubble of the ITO Revolution was the civil war that tore apart the technology and telecom business sectors throughout 2001 and into 2002. As the stock market correction began to accelerate in 2001, its impact was magnified by the events of 9/11. The market conditions created by a deteriorating economy and the collapse of the technology bubble were coupled with a real war post 9/11. Wars are events that change and strain the economy of a nation-state. The events of 9/11 were clearly an attack on the first estate of the United States and mechanisms that support the first estate. The terrorists who attacked the Untied States were trying to disrupt the economy of the United States and make a stand against what they believed was a globalization effort that was being led by the United States on many levels. Globalization is often used as an all encompassing term for global economics, but it also can be linked to political, religious, and sociological forces. When we look at the events of 9/11, we can identify all of these elements as being part of global revolution and as such they play an important role in the progression of the ITO Revolution.

As the ITO markets emerged into the new millennium, the market ecosystem was changing. Internet access via dialup modems was beginning to fade as broadband connections were coming to market. As cable service providers continued to make progress in upgrading their asynchronous cable plant to support two-way high speed data, the foundation for broadband internet connections via cable and voice over IP was being laid. Mobile operators began to offer limited data services – but technically the innovative cycle was being started that, in time, would bring market broadband internet access via wireless. Within the enterprise market, growth in frame relay and ATM WAN connectivity began to slow. IP VPN was a growing business and the optical capacity that was being deployed throughout the Perigee stage and into 2000 began to affect the market. This would eventually be known as the fiber glut, but in 2000 and into 2001 there was growth in high-speed connections that were supported on SONET and optical WDM networks. Two primary segments of fiber capacity were deployed in the U.S. market. The first was numerous nationwide fiber backbones that were built by companies such as AT&T, Worldcom, Sprint, Level(3), Qwest, Williams, IXC, and others. In addition to the backbone networks, a number of regional or metro fiber networks were built by smaller competitive access providers. See **Chart 6: 2000 Market Ecosystem** in the Chart and Model section.

In the March 2000, the Federal Communications Commission released their annual *Trends in Telephone Service Report*. In this report, the FCC highlighted the emerging growth of fiber deployments by CAPs, or competitive access providers, who are alternative service providers. The FCC used this data to highlight the emerging trends towards data. *"Chart 9.1, Chart 9.2, and Table 9.1 compare nationwide fiber deployment and revenue data for ILECs with data for local competitors. While consumers in a particular market can take service only from carriers that actually provide service in that market, the nationwide data serve as an indicator of broad trends. Chart 9.1 presents data on fiber miles, which are calculated by multiplying the number of miles of fiber cable by the number of fiber strands per cable. ILECs added about 2.1 million fiber miles in 1998, an amount larger than the local competitor inventory at the end of 1997. Chart 9.2, however, shows that competitors have had a much faster rate of growth. At the end of 1998, competitors had at least 16% of the total fiber optic system capacity (measured by fiber miles of fiber) that is potentially available to carry calls within local telecommunications markets and to deliver calls to long distance carriers."* What these charts do not reflect is the massive amount of fiber deployed by CAPs in 1999 and 2000. In the subsequent years the FCC did not release any further updates to the trends in the March 2000 report. The interesting trend that these charts reflect is that the ILEC rate of fiber deployment was decreasing from 1993 to 1998. The deployment of fiber by CAPs increased from 200k miles in 1993 to 3.1 million miles in 1998, a deployment of 2.9 million new miles. In the same time period ILECs deployed 8.6 million new miles of fiber – but retained majority ownership of the fiber deployed in the U.S. market with 83% percent market share in 1998.

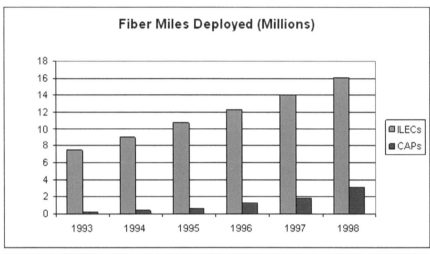

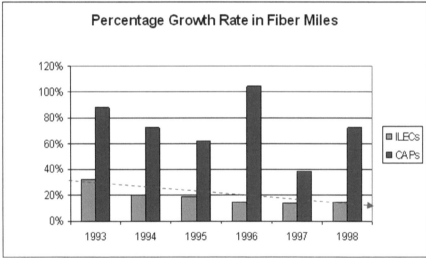

Figure 20: US Fiber Deployments 1993-1998
Source: Federal Communications Commission, *Study on Telephone Trends*, March, 2000 Charts 9.1 and 9.2
FCC Source: Industry Analysis Division, *Fiber Deployment Update*

Lucent and the Right of Self Determination

The birth, rise, decline and acquisition of Lucent Technologies by Alcatel in 2006 is one of the most dramatic stories in American business history. At the time of the writing of this discourse, Lucent was still in business – but it is effectively a shell of its former self and trapped in a position that offers little prospect for significant growth and hence agreed to be acquired by France's

Alcatel for $13 billion. The ITO Revolution was the reason to value Lucent as a growth stock. It was also the reason to spin Lucent out of AT&T as a stand alone company. When the ITO markets stopped being the growth markets of the new economy and Lucent returned to revenues within historical norms, there was little reason to value Lucent as growth stock. For Lucent, their leadership team was unable to diligently work through significant internal challenges within a rigid market structure to avoid the fate of Wang and Digital Equipment Corporation (DEC). Both Wang and DEC were innovative technology companies that grew into giant technology companies that, for a time were rivals to IBM. Wang started as a small technology company that found its way as a pioneer in desktop calculators, then word processing, and eventually into the development of mini-computers that rivaled the systems from DEC, Prime Computer, and Data General. When the mini-computer market began a decline in favor of PCs, Wang was without a product for the emerging PC market. The personal computer devastated Wang's business. By 1990, Wang was a fraction of what is was during the mid-1980s. Wang's stock debuted on the stock market at $12 per share, rose to $800 and fell to zero as the Wang was eventually acquired [see *Riding the Runaway Horse*, by Charles C. Kenney, 1992].

There are those who believed that Lucent's prospects would turn around, as it would undergo a similar change of fate as IBM under the leadership of Lou Gerstner – but the reality was that Lucent faced far greater challenges than those that faced Gerstner when he joined IBM. As of 2005-2006, Lucent averaged quarterly revenues of a little more than $2 billion, giving it a yearly turnover of $9-11 billion. When Gerstner assumed the position of CEO, IBM had revenues of $75 billion. IBM needed to have their internal processes reformed, costs contained and new revenue streams developed. It was a daunting challenge – but the framework of a solid business was present to build upon. As it is constituted today, Lucent does not have the same framework that IBM had when Gerstner took command. Lucent has become a stable company with annual revenues of approximately ten billion dollars – but is no longer the innovative, leading research company that retains the dominant global market share for telecom equipment.

In terms of the ITO Revolution, Lucent was a revolutionary, born from the old regime. They were a prodigy of AT&T when Lucent was spun out of AT&T on April 2, 1996. At the time that this essay was written Lucent still ranked as the tenth largest U.S. based IPO with a debut value of three billion dollars. As a product of an old regime and a leader within the ITO Revolution, we can identify many of the same liabilities that brought about the downfall of other companies that were created during the ITO Revolution – but few of these companies had the size and scale of Lucent. In the end, Lucent's downfall was not due to the adoption of a new technology that Lucent failed to adopt, as in the case of DEC and Wang, but rather to a changing market that was influenced by extremist companies intent on complete and total victory and the inability of Lucent to execute their business model.

Within the overall ITO Revolution, Lucent was the intellectual leader best positioned to reap the rewards of the markets created by telecom deregulation. From the start, Lucent was a global company with customers in nearly every nation-state in the world. It had everything a company needed to be successful in a global market wherein telecom privatization was a driving force. Lucent was a market leader in many market segments and technology vertical markets on a global basis with a customer list that contained nearly all the names of the premier telecom service providers in the world. Lucent had more than a hundred thousand employees, excellent research facilities, and intellectual property rights covering thousands of patents and vast reserves of financial capital. How could it all go wrong? The answer to that question lies in the cycle of ITO Revolution and leadership team that guided Lucent.

Lucent's leadership team that guided the company during the spinout from AT&T had strong similarities to the leadership of AT&T. In many ways, Lucent's leadership team leading the company into the new era of telecom deregulation, had more in common with the old regime of AT&T than any new company such as Cisco Systems. On October 12, 1995, AT&T issued a press release announcing the leadership team for the soon to be created Lucent Technologies. The team AT&T announced was; Henry Schacht as CEO and Rich McGinn as President and COO. Henry Schacht was joining Lucent from a senior advisor position at Warburg-Pincus. He had been a long-time board member at AT&T. having previously held the position as CEO of Cummins Engine Company, Inc. Schacht was an outsider to the world of telecommunications and telecom equipment – but that was not a liability. Schacht was there to shape the leadership team, post the spinout, and help form a new identity apart from AT&T. He was to help Lucent transition to a large publicly traded company separate from AT&T. McGinn, eleven years younger to Schacht, was a popular senior executive who had worked his way up the ranks of AT&T's Systems and Technology business unit. McGinn and his team were the true revolutionaries who had spent most, if not all, of their careers inside Lucent and the world of telecom equipment. They had dreamed of convincing AT&T to spin out the systems business unit as a separate company for many years. A little over a month after the Schacht and McGinn announcement, AT&T announced the top leadership selections for what would become Lucent Technologies. In the AT&T press release, the following leaders were announced [http://www.lucent.com/press/1195/951120.cha.html]:

- Bill Marx, 56, was named senior executive vice president of the new company.

- Dan C. Stanzione, 50, was named president of Bell Labs.

- Carleton S. Fiorina, 41, was promoted to executive vice president for corporate operations, with responsibility for strategy, business development, mergers and acquisitions, all external affairs, and new ventures.

- Patricia F. Russo, 42, would continue in her role as president of Global Business Communications Systems.

- James K. Brewington, 52, was promoted to president of product realization. He would have responsibility for the design, development, and manufacturing for all of Network Systems' product units, including Global Public Networks, Wireless, Network Cable Systems and Applications Software.

- William T. O'Shea, 48, joined Network Systems in July as president of all international operations, would continue to lead the Network Systems business outside the United States.

Ten years later, only four of the original fourteen team members announced in 1995, would still be with the company. With the exception of Henry Schacht, the entire team was long time employees of AT&T and the Bell System. They were revolutionaries who were taking advantage of market conditions produced by the ITO Revolution – but they were not the hard-core extremists of the revolution who had been toiling in secret to someday bring about their vision of a better world. The hard core revolutionaries could be found in other places like San Jose, Boston, and Maryland. Lucent's first management team were moderates who had once been part of the old regime and now found an opportunity to exploit the changing structure of political power and the dynamic nature of market share within the telecom market as well as AT&T. See **Chart 12: North American Service Provider CAPEX Model** in the Chart and Model section.

The ITO Revolution was the reason why AT&T spun out Lucent Technologies. If the market had remained a stable oligarchy of state owned and regulated telecom service providers throughout the world – there would have been no reason to create Lucent. Lucent was created to take advantage of a dynamic, global deregulated telecom market wherein the pace of technology adoption and market creation was accelerating. To be successful in this market, the old regime of AT&T entrusted the leadership of Lucent to executives who only had experience in the market structure of the old regimes. The chart above illustrates the evolution of the ITO Revolution in terms of CAPEX. Static markets (i.e. Old Regimes of G3 Market Model) becoming fluid release value. Lucent was spun out of AT&T to capture the new value being released by the changing structure of the market ecosystems. If Lucent had remained part of AT&T, it is unlikely that competitive service providers would have purchased equipment from Lucent, as AT&T was a competitor. In order to ensure Lucent's ability to compete in a deregulated, privatized global market, Lucent had to be a stand alone company with a brand wholly separate from AT&T. The explosive growth in CAPEX by telecom service providers in the North American market was driven by the internet, optics, and telecom deregulation in the form of the Telecom Act of 1996. The years between 1996 and mid-2000 was the market that Lucent and thousands of other companies were contending to gain control of during the ITO Revolution. Few, if any, companies expected this market to decline as fast as it did post 2000. From the years 1997 through 2000, new market share was added and existing market share was as fluid and dynamic as it had ever been in the history of the telecom equipment business. New technologies and new competitors created a fast pace of business throughout the late 1990s.

There is no question that the collapse of the ITO Revolution markets had a detrimental affect on Lucent Technologies – but the fact remains that Lucent was not the only company affected during the Decline Stage of the ITO Revolution. Every company in the ITO Revolution was affected by the Terror of the Decline stage – but some companies were able to execute and avoid disaster. Lucent was not one of these companies. In their quarterly report filed on August 8, 2000, Lucent reported that *"On June 30, 2000, Lucent employed approximately 155,000 persons, including 76.3% located in the United States."* By the end of 2004, Lucent would have less than 32,000 employees. The Terror of the Decline stage of the ITO Revolution had claimed 120,000 employees or 77% of the workforce of Lucent Technologies – Lucent experienced the Roman fate at Cannae during ITO Revolution.

As the Decline stage of the G3MM set upon the ITO Revolution, whole markets and companies that were customers of Lucent began to collapse or disappear. From a market perspective, Lucent's leadership team failed to perceive these market changes and lead the company through the impact of three major market forces. The first of these forces is known within the technology community as the collapse of the bubble era spending – or the progression from the Perigee to the Decline Stage of the G3MM. The bubble era spans the period from the day of revolution, which is the passage of Telecom

Act of 1996 through the Change and Perigee stages of the G3MM. The bubble era ends when the extremist companies take command of market share during the Decline stage. During the bubble era, Lucent achieved unrivaled success in comparison to its peers – but this success was fleeting because it was driven by market dynamics that were unsustainable. The bubble or revolutionary era was witness to dramatic changes driven by never before seen drivers of the internet, personal computer, and telecom deregulation. The market changes wrought by these three forces were historically unsustainable. Lucent's leadership team viewed these dramatic departures from the norms of their historical business as permanent market changes – when in reality they knew that the market conditions required to sustain changes of this magnitude would require years rather than months to develop. If anyone should have known that the market for new telecom equipment providers was fleeting, it should have been the leadership team at Lucent. They had the most experienced team, in terms of industry tenure, in the business and they had access to real time data to assess the success or failure of new service providers because of the Lucent's role in financing a number of new telecom service providers.

Few people in the summer of 2000 realized the changes that the ITO Revolution was undergoing. The first visible signs of the transition to the Decline Stage occurred in mid-2000. Revolutionaries had yet to be sent to the guillotine, but the time for public executions was fast approaching. On July 20, 2000, Lucent Technologies announced their third quarter results. In the press release, Lucent publicly acknowledged for the first time that they had missed a major product cycle. This was the first outward sign from an ITO revolutionary that all was not well. Rich McGinn stated *"The fourth quarter expectations reflect product transition issues associated with a faster- than-expected decline in circuit switching sales, which is not expected to be offset as quickly by the ramp-up of newer products; a longer-than-expected, full-volume ramp-up in optical networking; and the substantial reduction of a major long-term foreign project…The company expects to see these factors offset in the following quarters as Lucent hits full volume production and executes on its product cost reduction plan."* Less than three months later, Lucent again warned that their Q4 2000 results would not meet previous guidance. *"As a result of the review, the company expects a pro forma loss of 25 to 30 cents per share on continuing operations1 in the first fiscal quarter of 2001, ending Dec. 31, 2000, and will initiate a business restructuring program to drive out in excess of $1 billion in costs as the company re-designs its internal systems and processes for long-term, sustainable growth. The company has also completed the revenue review it announced on Nov. 21. As a result, its fourth fiscal quarter 2000 revenue will be $8.7 billion and its pro forma earnings will be 10 cents per share on continuing operations. This is lower than the previously announced $9.4 billion in revenues and pro forma earnings of 18 cents per share on continuing operations for the quarter ended Sept. 30, 2000. For fiscal* *year 2000, the adjusted results will be $33.6 billion in revenue and pro forma earnings per share of 93 cents on continuing operations. 'Fiscal year 2001 will be a rebuilding year, a turnaround year for Lucent,' said Lucent Technologies Chairman and CEO Henry Schacht. "We have identified the issues we must tackle, and we are undertaking a major re-tooling of the business. We are looking for a fresh start in the new year as we implement our restructuring and get our company back on track,"* [see Lucent Press Release, 12.21.2000]. The product transition and retooling that Lucent was referring to was a competitive situation wherein Lucent made a quality technology decision – that was trounced by a better business decision.

In the game of telecom equipment sales, companies employ a strategy in which the objective is to intersect the market with the leading technology at attractive price points when the telecom service providers are entering into a spending cycle. Typically, once a product selection is made, the equipment suppliers who are chosen can generate sales through the spending cycle over several years. The equipment suppliers who are not chosen reset their technology and sales plans to prepare for the next spending cycle. The ITO Revolution increased the speed in which service providers progressed through their spending cycles. The Telecom Act of 1996 greatly increased the number of telecom service providers across all market segments and the result was old regimes of the telecom business had to commercialize and deploy technology faster. One of the important technology developments was commercialization of dense wave division multiplexing or DWDM products in the mid 1990s. DWDM is a method for multiplexing multiple wavelengths (i.e. individual colors) onto a single strand of fiber, thus dramatically increasing the capacity of the fiber to carry traffic. The ability of DWDM to provide capacity for optical networks was a key technology foundation of the information superhighway.

From the service provider perspective, many were building or planning to build nationwide optical backbones as the foundation of their networks. Interchange carriers (i.e. IXCs), who were building or had announced intended builds of a nationwide optical backbone in the late 1990s, were WiilTel, Qwest, Level(3), Touch America, Sprint, Worldcom, WinStar, Enron, Dynegy, 360 Networks, Cable and Wireless, Global Crossing, and others. There was a significant optical backbone build occurring, not only in the U.S. market, but also Europe and Asia. This was the market wherein billions of dollars were spent on long-haul optical networks. Spending by these service providers on core optical equipment dramatically affected the fortunes of Nortel, Lucent, Ciena, Sycamore, and Corvis.

By 1998 Lucent was the leading supplier of DWDM optical equipment in the world and the optical division of Lucent was the fastest growing business unit of the company. This should not have been a surprise to anyone who followed Lucent. Many of the technological foundations of optical technology had been developed at Bell Labs and with the dawn of the ITO Revolution, Lucent enjoyed a superior position from which to supply the leading telecom service providers in the world with optical technology.

In 1997, at their strategic planning and investment meeting, Rich McGinn and the leadership team at Lucent made the decision to focus the company's investment capital on the OC-48 optical standard. The Lucent leadership team was convinced that the next evolution of optical transmission technology called OC-192 or 10G, would not be needed for another four to five years [see *Optical Illusions*, Lisa Endlich, 2004 pages 164-171]. McGinn and the leadership believed that the market was simply not ready to go from 2.5G to 10G in the span of a few short years. All of their market studies, customer data points and third party industry consultants agreed that for the next few years, OC-48 (i.e. 2.5G) would be more than sufficient to address the bandwidth requirements of the service providers building optical backbones. This was a sound technical decision that had one flaw which was the assumption that the next evolution of technology called 10G was too expensive to deploy and thus service providers would deploy 2.5G for a few years until the cost of 10G systems were reduced.

At the time that McGinn and his team of revolutionaries made this decision, they did not realize the full scope of the revolutionary cycle that was sweeping through the global telecommunications industry. There were other companies and other revolutionaries who were playing by a different set of rules. All over the world, the revolution launched by the personal-computer, the internet, and optics was viewed as a once in lifetime opportunity. Fortunes could be won and destinies changed. When you are the leader of a company that has lived in the shadow of AT&T/Lucent Technologies, the ITO Revolution was the event that you had been waiting for your entire career. This was the time to go all in and make a massive bet that held the prospect of altering the global telecom equipment supplier balance of power. The man who made this bet was John Roth. It can be said of John that he is not afraid to bet and in the mid 1990s, John Roth and the Nortel team bet big on 10G – while Rich McGinn and the Lucent team bet safe on 2.5G. These two business decisions might have been resigned to a footnote in the history of optical technology if it were not for the ITO Revolution. These two diverging decisions resulted in an explosion that propelled the spending of billions of dollars and changed the course of business history.

Lucent's choice was to supply the optical long-haul market with 2.5G products that would more than satisfy their customer demands. What Lucent did not consider was that Nortel Networks had made a decision to bypass 2.5G and go for a 10G system. When Nortel began to promote their 10G optical long haul system, potential customers could not justify the price of Nortel's 10G systems over competitive 2.5G systems from Lucent and Ciena. Then the power of revolution took over. The urban legend of the internet's phenomenal growth became the mantra of the ITO Revolution. The statistic that the *"internet was doubling every hundred days"* became the equivalent of *"give me liberty or give me death."* During the early phases of the ITO Revolution, including the Change and Perigee stages, many revolutionaries cited the statistic that internet traffic doubles every 100 days [see *Internet Traffic Growth: Sources and Implications*, Andrew M. Odlyzko, University of Minnesota, Minneapolis, MN http://www. dtc.umn.edu/»odlyzko]. This statistic was widely promoted and touted as the litmus test for the impact that the new economy was going to have on the lives of every citizen in the world. A November 17, 1997 Business week article stated *"All is not well on the Internet. Delays, disruptions, and missing messages can make life miserable for millions who work and play there. Traffic is growing about 100% a year. And coming soon is a tsunami called electronic commerce, in which companies replace paper transactions with electronic messages. By 2002, Forrester Research Inc. in Cambridge, Mass., expects E-commerce to balloon into a $327 billion phenomenon."* Market sizing by Jupiter Media in 2002 estimated the market for ecommerce to be only $47.8 billion [see *Market Forecast Report*, Jupiter Media Matrix, January 2002, page 6], which is well short of $327 billion – but during the Perigee stage of the ITO Revolution, bold market predictions, such as the internet doubling every hundred days, was the driving force for business and investment decisions within the ITO Revolution.

Even as late as November 27, 2000, Fortune magazine had two references to the statistic that internet traffic was doubling every hundred days. The hundred day urban myth became a common belief amongst the revolutionary masses of the ITO Revolution. Not only was internet traffic doubling every hundred days, but companies needed to be on internet time. Development cycles must be accelerated to match competitors who were on internet time. Important leaders of the ITO Revolution were promoting the fact that the internet's growth was going to drive massive capital spending (CAPEX). On March 6, 2000 Bernie Ebbers, then Worldcom CEO, stated at the New Economy Summit at Boston College that Worldcom was adding capacity of 800 percent annually to keep up with growth of the internet and that Worldcom's CAPEX spending would exceed $100 billion a year by 2003. On the panel with him was Desh Deshpande, who was co-founder and Chairman of Sycamore Networks and former CEO of Cascade Communications. When Ebbers reiterated Worldcom's need to spend $100 billion annually on routers, switches, and optical regeneration, Desh responded *"we'll take it all"* [see *Boston Globe* archives, March 7, 2000, Peter J. Howe]. Other proponents of the digital economy were citing the phenomenal growth of the internet such as the April 15, 1998, U.S. Department of Commerce report entitled, *"The Emerging Digital Economy."* The FCC Chairman during the passage of the Telecom Act of 1996 and the subsequent stages of Change and Perigee was Reed Hunt. After he retired, he published a book recounting his years as FCC Chairman. *"The communications revolution has had technological, economic, and political dimensions that are each and all beyond precedent or expectations. This multifaceted revolution would not have had such a grand scale and scope but for the new laws that, in an era of extreme political disharmony, were enacted in the first term of the Clinton-Gore Administration. These laws – the 1993 Omnibus Budget Reconciliation Act and the 1996 Telecommunications Act – reversed one hundred years of pro-monopoly policy in the telephone and cable industries,"* [see Reed Hundt, You Say You Want a Revolution, 2000, page ix].

The market for 10G optical long-haul systems collided with myth of internet growth and a shrewd business strategy by John Roth. When Nortel commercialized their 10G optical systems, they were betting that the growth of the internet would rapidly drive telecom service providers to deploy 10G systems faster than projected – but when they went to sell the 10G system, they did not find any buyers for their more expensive 10G system. This is the point when Roth decided to go all in and bet on 10G. He made deal with Joe Nacchio, CEO of Qwest and former AT&T executive. Nortel would sell 10G systems to Qwest at 2.5G prices and when the traffic on the 10G systems exceeded the capacity of the 2.5G systems Qwest was considering, Qwest would pay Nortel a premium for use of the capacity above 2.5G. It was a win, win deal. If Qwest's network never needed the capacity that Nortel's 10G system provided, then they had not over paid – but if the network usage grew, Qwest had the bandwidth installed in the network to support the unanticipated demand. From Nortel's perspective the deal was not a good deal if Qwest never needed the capacity, but if their bet was correct, all the major carriers would need more capacity. Nortel believed it was only a matter of time.

What happened next was the point at which the ITO Revolution changed the world order of telecom equipment suppliers. After installing Nortel's 10G systems at 2.5G prices, Qwest soon realized that demand was increasing beyond their expectations and Nortel started receiving their 10G premium checks. Qwest had a network that was built around 10G and their competitors had networks built around 2.5G. Every other major service provider in the U.S. and around the world had to respond to the competitive advantage that Qwest had with their 10G network. The result was a sudden boom in the optical market for 10G long-haul systems. Nortel was first to the market and reaped the benefits. Revenues in Nortel's optical division went from one billion to four billion to ten billion in three years. Lucent missed out on $15 billion of optical spending because John Roth had bet on 10G, priced the system at 2.5G prices, and timed the market perfectly. The added benefit for Nortel was that $15 billion in optical long-haul orders provided enough business to reduce the cost of their 10G system and make the optical business quite profitable. Nortel had gone from the poor step child of Lucent who was cast off, many years before, to the preeminent supplier of optical systems in the world that bested their long time rival. For the first time Nortel's market value as a company surpassed Lucent. To do so it took a revolution and a bold bet by a revolutionary leader who was playing to win.

The result of Nortel capturing such a large amount of market share in the optical market had a huge impact on Lucent. The revenue warnings that Lucent was issuing in mid 2000 were a direct result of missing the optical spending on 10G systems. Not only was Nortel reaping a benefit from having a majority of the 10G optical market – Lucent was being wounded by a sudden decline in the 2.5G optical revenues. Rich McGinn had pushed the company hard throughout the Perigee years of the ITO Revolution. The revenue warnings issued by Lucent in 2000 had a dramatic affect on Lucent's stock. From mid 2000 through late 2001, Lucent's stock began a decline from more than $60 per share to less than $4 per share over a period of approximately twenty-seven months. When it was clear to Lucent's Board of Directors that the company had missed a major optical market and the company required a significant restructuring to reduce costs and improve product planning, the decision was that Rich McGinn was not the man to lead the company through the turmoil ahead. Lucent announced on October 23, 2000 that Rich McGinn had stepped down as CEO and his replacement was Henry Schacht. Rich was not the last causality of the Terror, but he was the first major revolutionary to fall. He spent thirty years in the telecommunications business and his entire career at AT&T and Lucent. He was a revolutionary and for a time the undisputed leader of the ITO Revolution – but he was outmaneuvered by revolutionaries playing a bolder game to win.

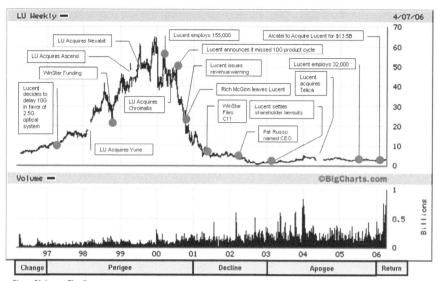

Figure 21: Lucent Timeline
Source: BigCharts.com + Author's Research

WinStar and Lucent's Role in Vendor Financing

The story of WinStar Communications, its role in the ITO Revolution and the history of Lucent are embolic of the ITO Revolution. Revolutions create environments in which unsound principles become sound. Business plans that have a high degree of risk when market conditions are stable during the Start and Change stages of the G3 MM become plausible in times of revolution. WinStar Communications represents a business plan with a high degree of risk and it also represents how to create the image of a pseudo-healthy company and market. This is represented by the activity of vendor financing, which Lucent heartily endorsed.

Vendor financing played an important role in the ITO Revolution. Lucent, Nortel, and Cisco used their vast cash reserves and balance sheets to lend or acquire investment capital for new telecom service providers. A service provider receiving vendor financing, in turn, was required to purchase products from the equipment supplier providing the financing. These purchases were usually at price points higher than the market price points. After all, if you are loaning a customer hundreds of millions of dollars of your own money to purchase products from your company, you might as well have high margins on those purchases. The equipment suppliers were not the only companies to engage in this process. Microsoft put their capital reserves to work to improve market conditions for their products. Microsoft was not engaging in vendor in its purest form, but its activities were intended to use their capital reserves to improve market conditions that fostered growth for the overall market in which their products were used. The Microsoft investment premise was this: if there were more companies providing broadband connections to the internet, then more computers would be sold to the users of these network connections and thus more copies of Windows and Microsoft Office would be sold. Lucent, Nortel, and Cisco to a lesser degree, elevated vendor financing from the minor activity of venture capital type investments, to an art form of large contractual cash loans that were directly tied to specific volume purchase agreements. In short, equipment vendors would loan a new telecom services providers several hundred million dollars and then require that the money be returned via scheduled equipment purchases.

Much of the negative aspects of vendor financing can be found in the agreement that Lucent and WinStar Communications entered into in 1998, which was during the Perigee stage of the ITO Revolution. The five year agreement called for Lucent to provide network design and build-out services in addition to being the primary supplier of equipment for WinStar's fixed wireless business. The terms *"fixed wireless"* may seem to be an oxymoron, but the terms refer to the WinStar plan which was to equip roof tops with towers that used wireless technology to deliver voice and data services. These services were then sent to collection points that had fiber access to the nationwide WinStar network. Customer traffic would depart a building via a wireless connection, then be converted to WinStar's fiber network for transportation to the next city and then back into the metro wireless network for delivery to the destination building. Hence, WinStar was building a nationwide fiber optic network in the U.S. and using wireless technology to bypass the local loop, which was controlled by the RBOC or ILEC. The structure of the deal was a five year term and two billion dollar loan that could be accessed by WinStar in increments not exceeding five hundred million dollars. Lucent would, *"...provide network design, integration and buildout services for WinStar's end-to-end global network, encompassing a flexible, scaleable architecture to accommodate WinStar's present and future voice and data service offerings. WinStar will continue to operate and maintain final design authority for its network. Lucent will provide its superior technology and equipment for this state-of-the-art network. Lucent will also access, test and integrate all elements in WinStar's network, including equipment from other manufacturers."* Winstar's executive team was equally excited with the deal, *"We are proud and excited that WinStar selected Lucent to design and build the kind of feature-rich network that will enable it to serve its customers better. WinStar is revolutionizing the way that businesses receive and use broadband telecommunications services and we are excited about furthering that revolution through this strategic relationship. This complete network solution will showcase the breadth of Lucent's product lines, the value of Bell Labs innovations and our unmatched expertise in helping customers design, build and turn up their networks quickly and profitably,"* [see Lucent Press Release, 10.22.1998]. The problem with this arrangement is that it has the potential for abuse. In theory, if Lucent's sales were short of their target during any given quarter, they could receive a five hundred million dollar order from WinStar using the money loaned by Lucent. This is not how the loan was intended to be used, but the structure of the deal did provide for the possibility that this type of arrangement of interests could occur.

As the Decline stage of the ITO Revolution took hold in 2000, WinStar's business model began to fail. They were excellent at spending money, but they were not as skilled at making money. WinStar continued to raise money in 2000 by selling convertible debt to a host of companies such as Microsoft, Compaq, and Credit Swiss First Boston. As the market continued to move against WinStar and Lucent, Lucent decided to end loan payments to WinStar. With the bank of Lucent closed, Winstar could not make payments on the debt that they had raised. On April 18, 2001, WinStar filed chapter 11 after missing a $75 million payment on their debt. The company collapsed and was sold to IDT for $42.5 million. At the time of the collapse WinStar had debt of approximately $6.3 billion, of which they owed Lucent $700 million.

The result of WinStar's failure was a lawsuit by WinStar against Lucent for $10 billion. In the lawsuit, WinStar claimed that Lucent's default on loan payments to Winstar was the event that resulted in WinStar's inability to make a loan payment and thus the cause of their bankruptcy. There was second issue raised when Lucent stopped loaning money to WinStar. That issue was whether WinStar had done a favor for Lucent. To Henry Schacht's credit, he had the finance team at Lucent investigate the revenue recognized from WinStar. Lucent announced on November 21, 2000 that the company had improperly recognized orders from WinStar totaling $125 million. One month later, Lucent revealed the following in a press release *"Lucent found that in one case there had been misleading documentation and incomplete communications between a sales team and the financial organization with respect to offering a customer credits in connection with a software license. It was done with disregard for the clear revenue recognition procedures that Lucent has in place. Appropriate disciplinary action, including the dismissal of an employee, is being taken. As a result, Lucent will reduce its fourth fiscal quarter 2000 revenues by $125 million…In the course of the review, Lucent identified two other cases in which the sales teams had verbally offered credits to be used at a later date, but that may have been related to transactions in the fourth quarter. Lucent has decided to reflect those credits in the fourth quarter, reducing fourth fiscal quarter revenues by an additional $74 million…In one case, Lucent found that revenue had been recognized from the sale of a system that had been incompletely shipped. Accordingly, Lucent reduced its fourth fiscal quarter revenues by an additional $28 million…During the course of the review, Lucent decided to take back $452 million in equipment that had previously* *been sold to certain systems integrators and distributors, but not utilized or passed on to customers due to changes in business strategies and the weakening of the emerging service provider market. In the interest of preserving customer and distributor relationships, and because there was some evidence that there may have been verbal agreements that led them to expect Lucent to do so, Lucent has decided to take the equipment back and resell it in the future. As a result, revenues for the fourth quarter will be reduced by an additional $452 million. Revenue from the resale of this equipment will be recorded as it occurs"* [see *http://www.lucent.com/press/1200/001221.coa.html*].

At the time, the approximately $700 hundred million restatement of earnings was viewed as shocking by the technology, telecom, and financial communities. As time would show, seven hundred million would seem respectable in comparison to the disasters at Enron, Worldcom, and Nortel. In retrospect, the concept of vendor financing seems poor in the context of a Chicago School view of the market. Vendor financing (a) locks customers into fixed pricing structures (b) limits the ability of customers to continuously evaluate technology options and, (c) eliminates open competition between suppliers to ensure market based pricing and technology options.

Traditionally, Lucent's largest source of revenue came from the sale of telephony voice switches. Nortel and Lucent sold the most advanced line of voice switches in the world. The internet and the Telecom Act of 1996 produced three phenomenal drivers of switching business. The first was the creation of 300 new CLECs in the U.S. service provider market. To be in the phone business requires the use of a telephone switch. Lucent's addressable market increased dramatically following the Change stage, as about 300 competitive local exchange carriers (CLECs) were created in the United States. The second driver of Lucent's growth was the internet. Using AOL's subscriber growth post 1995 as a benchmark, it indicates that thousands of people where dialing into the internet with their computers. Consumers and businesses needed far more local phone circuits than they had in the past. Many new overlay area codes were introduced as consumers had multiple phone lines in the home for the kids, the home office, the fax line, and the computers. If you are a telephone service provider that averages 1.5 lines per subscriber and suddenly that average goes to three or four lines per user then you will need to expand your switching capacity by three or four times. The internet drove the sales of legacy products, especially the sales of switching products, because the increasing amount of personal computers in the home, were connecting to the internet via the traditional circuit based telephone network. Unfortunately for Lucent and Nortel Networks, this was not a long-term trend, as broadband services would supplant modem technology over time.

The second major market shift that Lucent missed and Cisco Systems realized was the evolution from circuit technology to packet technology. In the first few years of the ITO Revolution there was an increase in the traditional circuit switching business that had been the core business of Lucent and Nortel. This increase was due to (a) a large number of new CLECs who wanted to purchase their own voice switch and (b) the increase in demand for local access lines as consumers added additional phone lines for modems and fax machines. All told, the traditional circuit switching business experienced a renaissance in the mid to late 1990s. Even with strength in their traditional lines of business; Lucent was unable to position the company to compete in the market of the future, which was packet switching. It was not as if Lucent did not try to be a player in this market, they simply were unable to organically develop a competitive product to Cisco and Juniper, nor was Lucent able to acquire a competitive product and development team. Lucent's development arm of Bell Labs was simply too ingrained in the technology they knew, which was telephony centric technology, and they could not cross the chasm to become an innovative and competitive supplier of packet technology that was driven by functionality and price – not carrier class product requirements. Even in 2005, Lucent's answer to address this market is a partnership with Juniper Networks, which is Cisco's nearest rival.

Lucent's leadership team is directly responsible for the collapse of the company. Only one metric is needed to support this conclusion and that is Lucent's cash to debt ratio as the telecom bubble began to collapse. It is unfair to criticize Lucent's leadership team for missing a major market decline that nearly every industry leader, analyst, and participant missed – but it is not unfair to criticize the leaders who led the company to $194 billion in sales, debts of $6.2 billion, a cash position of $4.1 billion, a stock price of $3.46 per share, and a market cap of $14.83 billion. Lucent was being run by a leadership team that did not have experience leading technology companies through boom and bust cycles. Lucent's leadership team was shielded from market cycles as part of AT&T and the regulated market structure that pre-dated 1996. It stark comparison, Cisco Systems and Microsoft have amassed vast cash reserves in the boom and bust market cycle. The difference between the leadership teams of Cisco Systems and Lucent Technologies is the industry experience and imbued fiscal responsibility of the Cisco leadership team. The Cisco and Microsoft leadership teams were composed of leaders who had experienced the creation and destruction cycles of technology [see *Essay One, Chapter One*]. Lucent's leadership team inherited a company and culture that was born and raised in the culture of AT&T. Closed markets that are regulated by the government are not the best environments to train leaders to understand the concepts of market creation and destruction. Fiscal responsibility is not created in markets that are slow, stable monopolies, as that of AT&T prior to 1984. Cisco's leadership team and company culture was honed in the hot competitive fires of the personal computer, networking, and internet revolutions.

In hindsight, the mistakes made by Lucent's leadership team are dramatic and damning. We examined the leadership of Lucent because leaders are responsible for the manner in which companies act. The culture and structure of a company are direct reflections of the leadership team. In Lucent's case, the actions of the leadership team are a direct reflection of culture from which Lucent was born – AT&T. Lucent's leadership team did not understand the market in which they were inserted by AT&T. Without the old regime, Lucent was defeated by a group of extremists who were far more fanatical than Lucent's leaders. The extremists Lucent was facing had been waiting decades for this opportunity and they were not going to fall. Lucent was a company to be beaten and looted until it was a mere shell of its former self. In the world of business and war, that objective cannot be faulted. What can be faulted is the fact that Lucent's leadership team let it happen.

Lucent was not a fanatical extremist who championed technical change. Cisco was an extremist. Lucent's leadership was reared in the protective womb of an old regime. The Cisco leadership team, especially John Chambers, was veterans who had experienced failure before in their careers. When Chambers was at Wang, he had experienced the losing end of a revolution. At Cisco, John Morgridge and John Chambers led a company that was fiscally lean, commercially aggressive, and played the game of business with a brutal intensity. Cisco acted as an extremist and used the Decline stage of the ITO Revolution to eliminate competitors. Lucent acted as the mirror opposite of Cisco. Lucent practiced the art of massive spending in their operational model to support the bureaucracy they inherited and maintained post their spin out from AT&T.

Cisco was a much smaller company than Lucent and Nortel Networks in 1995, yet six years later Cisco is the dominate company. The reason they are the dominate company is they became the extremist. Cisco developed an obsessive culture, based on a paranoid fear of failure and crafted in the hot fires of the evolution from a startup to a successful public company. Lucent had no such defining cultural events. The leadership of Lucent came from a competitive market environment, but they were always the company to beat – never the company looking up to, and learning how to beat the competition. As such, Lucent's leadership team was ill equipment intellectually and inexperienced in the skills required to enact the cultural changes and retool Lucent to be an extremist of the ITO Revolution. The inefficiencies and bureaucracy of Lucent was not corrected during the Perigee stage of the ITO Revolution. Lucent's leadership team only began to correct the culture of Lucent when the ITO market collapsed and their problems were exposed by the extremists.

Unfortunately for Lucent, their inability to shape the company to the market conditions of the ITO Revolution put Lucent in a vulnerable position vis-à-vis the extremists.

Lucent's leadership failed to act decisively against market forces. When Lucent emerged from AT&T and began to use their stock and cash to acquire companies, the strategy was unconnected to the company and ineffective in the market. Lucent acted indecisively and their leadership team never decided what the company would become after the spin out from AT&T. This fact is revealed in the acquisition strategy that Lucent' leadership employed.

In May 2004, Lucent acquired the thirty-ninth company in their eight year history as a stand alone company. This acquisition came three years and eight months after their last acquisition. The name of Lucent's thirty ninth company acquisition is Telica. This is an interesting acquisition because Lucent was acquiring a company that produced, "...*high-capacity, second-generation softswitch-based, fault-tolerant packet switch for both TDM and VoIP switching, supporting traditional and next-generation services.*" Within the Lucent umbrella of business units is an organization named Bell Labs. Bell Labs was founded in 1925 and is one of the greatest research organizations of the twentieth century. A quick look at the inventions of Bell Labs shows how this one organization has shaped our lives. Bell Labs is credited with the following inventions:

- 1923 - The first cathode ray tube, a predecessor of the television tube is invented
- 1925 - Harald Friis developed the first superheterodyne radio receiver
- 1926 - H.M. Stoller and A.S. Pfannstiehl invented the first machine to synchronize motion picture sound, thus beginning the end to the silent movie era
- 1927 - Herbert Ives and Frank Gray developed the first long distance television transmitting and receiving equipment
- 1928 - Bell Labs demonstrated color television
- 1930 - Harvey Fletcher produced a stereophonic reproduction system.
- 1930 - Lloyd Espenshied and H.A. Affel developed a coaxial cable carrier system that provided a very wide bandwidth capable of carrying thousands of telephone channels or several video signals.
- 1934 - W.M. Bacon originated the automatic store and forward switching concept, providing fast and efficient handling of teletypewriter message traffic. An architectural mainstay in today's packet switching systems.
- 1946 - Harald Friis and A.C. Beck led the development of microwave

radio transmission using JA. Morton's invention, the close-spaced triode, a vacuum tube microwave amplifier. Until the availability of optical fibers some thirty-five years later, microwave radio was the dominant long distance communications facility.

- 1948 - William Shockley, John Bardeen, and Walter Brattain won the Nobel Prize for their invention of the transistor in 1948, probably the most significant development in the field of electronics in this century.
- 1954 - D.M. Chapin, C.S. Fuller, and G.L. Pearson invented the solar battery, the first efficient means of directly converting a significant amount of the sun's energy into electricity.
- 1958 - Charles Townes and Arthur Shawlow invented the LASER, which revolutionized telecommunications in the 1990s
- 1958 - P.W. Anderson received a Nobel Prize for his theoretical work in physics dealing with the nature of electrical conduction and magnetism.
- 1954 - John R. Pierce conceived the idea of communications satellites, several years before artificial satellites of any sort had been launched. $60 million later, Telstar was launched in 1962.
- 1956 - Bell Labs and the Bell System of companies had designed, manufactured, and installed the first transatlantic telephone cable. More than 100 optical amplifiers were required to complete the link. The project cost $50 million dollars.
- 1965 - The first viable electronic central office switching system went into service. It took ten years of research and development at a cost of more than $500 million dollars.
- 1966 - Andrew Bobeck invented magnetic bubble technology.
- 1970 - Class 4 Switch to route long distance calls is commercialized. Development cost an estimated $400 million.
- Unix and C Computer languages
- Optical communications

Nearly all the elements of the ITO Revolution find some linkage to the innovations of Bell Labs. The ironic aspect of the Telica acquisition is that Lucent created many of the original technical innovations for telephony patents and found itself in a position that it must acquire another company whose technology was being used to replace legacy Lucent products. Just seven years earlier, on the eve of Lucent's first day of trading as an independent company, Henry Schacht, chairman and chief executive officer said, *"Tomorrow we begin our new life as a wholly independent company, one that starts out as the 35th largest in the U.S., we have 125 years of experience and leadership in communications and the opportunity to compete in a huge and growing global market."* Rich McGinn, COO added, *"This is the opportunity of a lifetime for us, creating this new company has released a tremendous amount of energy in our people, who look forward to bringing innovations in communications to our customers around the world."*

A component of Rich McGinn's strategy of bringing innovation to customers around the world involved acquiring companies. During McGinn's tenor, he would lead Lucent through thirty-eight acquisitions for a reported public value of $46.1 billion. Of this sum, $42 billion of stock value and $3.5 billion in cash were used to acquire the following companies.

Date	Company	Business Unit	Value / Currency
May-04	Telica	Lucent	$295 Million / Stock
Sep-00	Spring Tide Networks	Lucent	$1.3 Billion / Stock
Jun-00	Herrmann Technology, Inc	Agere	$428 Million / Stock
Jun-00	Chromatis Networks	Lucent	$4.5 Billion / Stock
Mar-00	Ignitus	Lucent	Undisclosed / Undisclosed
Apr-00	DeltaKabel	Lucent	Undisclosed / Undisclosed
Apr-00	Ortel Corporation	Agere	$2.95 Billion / Stock
Apr-00	Agere	Agere	$415 Million / Stock
Mar-00	VTC, Inc.	Agere	$100 Million / Cash
Feb-00	SpecTran	Lucent	$64 Million / Stock
Dec-99	Soundlogic CTI	Avaya	Undisclosed / Undisclosed
Nov-99	Xedia Corporation	Lucent	$246 Million / Stock
Nov-99	Excel Switching	Lucent	$1.7 Billion / Stock
Oct-99	International Network Ser.	Lucent	$3.7 Billion / Stock
Jul-99	CCOM	Avaya	Undisclosed / Undisclosed
Jul-99	Nexabit Networks	Lucent	$900 Million / Stock
Jul-99	Mosaix	Avaya	$145 Million / Stock
Jun-99	Ascend Communications	Lucent	$24 Billion / Stock
Jun-99	Batik Equipamentos	Lucent	Undisclosed / Undisclosed
Jun-99	Zetax Tecnologia	Lucent	Undisclosed / Undisclosed
Mar-99	Div of Enable Semi	Agere	$50 Million / Cash
Mar-99	Kenan Systems	Lucent	$1.48 Billion / Stock
Feb-99	Sybarus	Agere	Undisclosed / Undisclosed
Jan-99	WaveAccess	Lucent	$50 Million / Cash
Nov-98	Pario Software	Lucent	Undisclosed / Undisclosed
Oct-98	Quadritek	Avaya	$50 Million / Cash
Sep-98	JNA	Lucent	$70 Million / Cash
Aug-98	LANNET	Lucent	$117 Million / Cash
Jul-98	Mass Media	Lucent	Undisclosed / Undisclosed
Jul-98	SDX Business Systems	Avaya	$200 Million / Cash
May-98	Yurie Systems	Lucent	$1 Billion / Cash
Apr-98	Optimay GmbH	Agere	$65 Million / Cash
Mar-98	TKM Communications	Avaya	Undisclosed / Undisclosed
Mar-98	HP LMDS Wireless Bus.	Lucent	Undisclosed / Undisclosed
Jan-98	Prominet Corp	Avaya	$200 Million / Stock
Dec-97	Livingston Enterprises	Lucent	$650 Million / Stock
Sep-97	Octel Communications	Avaya	$1.8 Billion / Cash
May-97	Triple C Call Center Comm	Avaya	Undisclosed / Stock
Oct-96	Agile Networks	Avaya	Undisclosed / Undisclosed

Figure 22: Lucent Acquisitions
Source: Lucent Web Page

Analysis of this list reveals that Lucent acquired twenty-one of these companies, while the business unit of Avaya acquired ten companies and the business unit of Agere acquired seven. Several of these acquisitions sharply illustrate Lucent's confusing market strategy, technology strategy, indecisiveness, and apparent unwillingness of the leadership team to reduce the scale of the Lucent's bureaucracy. In hindsight, Lucent's acquisition strategy appears to lack a greater vision of what the leadership team wanted Lucent to evolve into in the form of markets and technology offerings. The acquisitions appear to be justified on the basis of what Lucent thought customers would buy next rather then a plan to intercept the future direction of the market and technology with a solution. This was, in part, because of the size of the company and many competing interests inside Lucent, but it is also reflective of the culture from which Lucent was created. The processes and cultural imprint that the old regime AT&T had left on Lucent clearly put Lucent in the camp of the revolutionary moderates – not the revolutionary extremists.

- In 1997 Lucent acquired Livingston Enterprises for $650 million in stock. Livingston provided Lucent with a portfolio of remote access products at the time when remote access was a hot market. When Lucent acquired Ascend eighteen months later, they acquired a strong ATM business as well a better remote access portfolio than Livingston possessed. Ascend's ATM and Frame Relay product portfolio came through its acquisition of Cascade communications. Lucent had acquired an ATM company in May of 1998 called Yurie Systems for $1 billion in cash.

- The dual acquisitions of Ignitus and Chromatis networks in mid-2000 are specifically interesting. Lucent was spending $4.5 billion for Chromatis at the very point of the market that the ITO Revolution was transitioning into the Decline stage. Ignitus and Chromatis had clear portfolio overlaps with each other and with existing products within the Lucent portfolio. At the same time, Lucent was spinning out another optical company called Internet Photonics that would be acquired by Ciena in 2004. In the metro optical market segment Lucent was buying, selling, and owning at the same time. The ironic aspect of these acquisitions is that in 2004, Lucent would complete an OEM deal to resell the WDM products from Movaz because Lucent did not have a competitive portfolio of products in the WDM market space, despite spending a few billion dollars.

- In June of 1999, Lucent spent $900 million to acquire a small, privately held company called Nexabit Networks to provide Lucent with a core router. In the press release, Curt Sanford, president, InterNetworking Systems, Lucent Technologies said, *"The communications revolution is fueling tremendous demand for more bandwidth in core networks, this merger gives Lucent not only a leading product for ultra high-speed IP core networks, but a terrific lead in delivering terabit-speed switch/routers that connect directly to optical networking systems. Now Lucent's data networking portfolio will include the leading IP core switch/router technology for next-generation networking, the leading multiservice ATM technology delivering absolute quality of service, the leading core optical networking technology, the leading software capabilities to integrate these networks together, plus the unmatched capability to service and support it all, this sets a new standard for internetworking capabilities for the industry."* It did not quite work out that way and in May 2003, Lucent announced a strategic partnership with Juniper to source Juniper's routing technology to Lucent's core customers.

- On October 2, 2000 Avaya began trading as an independent company from Lucent. As Lucent had done four years earlier from AT&T, Avaya spun out of Lucent. Avaya took from Lucent much of the traditional enterprise focused telephony and networking products. In short, Lucent was exiting the market for traditional office telephony and internet access products targeted at businesses. In February 2003, Lucent announced an alliance with Enterasys to provide solutions to the enterprise security market.

- When Lucent spun out of AT&T, it counted Northern Telecom (Nortel), Siemens, Fujitsu, and Alcatel as its primary and historical competitors. The first few years of the ITO Revolution revealed that a new competitor had emerged and this competitor was an extremist whose goal was complete domination of its markets. The competitor was named Cisco Systems and for much of Lucent's first few years, the companies waged a bitter war against other. Cisco fought the battle from its strength in the enterprise market. Lucent fought the battle from its strength within the service provider market. The two companies clashed within the new telecom service providers, created after the Telecom Act of 1996. The winner of this battle was Cisco Systems. In January of 2003, Lucent and Cisco announced a joint agreement wherein Lucent agreed to integrate and resell Cisco packet data and media gateway products. After a long battle, the company that invented cellular technology had surrendered to the extremist that had won the ITO Revolution. Cisco was now a key supplier of technology to Lucent for the evolution of next generation mobile voice technology.

It was not extraordinary that Cisco beat Lucent. Cisco was a smaller, better organized, and a far more focused company. Wherein Cisco was fanatical about protecting and growing their market share – Lucent was trying to expand and grow into Cisco's markets through acquisitions. Lucent, Cisco, Nortel and Alcatel clashed during the Perigee stage driven by acquisitions and investments. Above all the networking companies, these four companies played a deadly game of acquisition brinkmanship to seize control of their markets and eliminate the competition. When the Perigee staged transitioned to the Decline stage, Cisco Systems was left as the extremists who had won the war. A large portion of the new market share that was created during Perigee stage was eliminated during the Decline stage. Cisco was the company that was left with control of the remaining market share. For a company that had a history of more than seventy years of innovative brilliance when they went public in 1996, Lucent turned out to be especially poor at evaluating technical innovation and bringing products to market. When Lucent did acquire successful product lines from Ascend and Cascade, Lucent's leaders were more successful in stifling future evolution of these product lines than continuing the enhancement of these products and growing their market share.

Of the many acquisitions that Lucent completed, few of them found a happy home inside Lucent. Lucent's old regime cultural roots did not match with the new revolutionaries that Lucent was acquiring. Bell Labs did not appreciate the rival research and development cultures. The biggest question of Lucent's actions post their spin out from AT&T is: why did Lucent not act as a mentor and Sheppard for the technology industry in and around New Jersey? Lucent never acted as part of the venture community, supporting former employees and acting as an anchor to the overall ecosystem of technology companies in and around their corporate headquarters. In fact, Lucent often had an adversarial relationship with former employees and technology startups in their local market. Perhaps this cultural quirk came from the AT&T culture of a monopoly and resistance to any competitor and all potential threats, regardless of size to the company. The acquisition of thirty-eight companies produces an indecisive and massive leadership team. Unlike Cisco Systems, who can point to key leaders inside the company that were part of their very first acquisition, few, if any, of Lucent's leadership team today came from the acquisitions they made during the period from1996 to 2000.

Nortel and the Conquest of Optical

In 2000, Nortel Networks had $30,275 billion in annual revenues. It was a record year. They closed the final quarter of 2000 with revenues of $8,818 billion and a reported a profit of $4,014 billion. In their January 18, 2001 earnings press release, John Roth, CEO stated, *"We see continuing strong market demand in our target industry segments. Even with the current economic uncertainty, Nortel Networks, with our global reach and industry leading portfolio, is ideally positioned to continue to outpace the market and gain profitable market share. Our focus on high-growth markets will be balanced with optimizing profitability and driving efficiencies in our business."* Additional, Nortel's CFO Frank Dunn stated *"Considering the current economic environment and tightening of capital within the telecom sector, we are projecting growth in revenues and earnings per share from operations (b) in 2001 over 2000 of 30 percent. For the first quarter of 2001, we expect revenues of US$8.1 billion and earnings per share from operations(b) of US$0.16 on a diluted basis. Our views for the quarter and the year are within the ranges we previously communicated. We will continue to focus on optimizing profitability and driving efficiencies in our business in 2001 by eliminating redundancies, managing technology transitions, and streamlining operations and activities that are not aligned with our core markets and strategies."* Nortel's top two executives were still bullish on their ability to expand in a market wherein other companies such as Lucent were struggling and Cisco was cautious.

On February 15, 2001, Nortel issued a press release offering new market guidance. Twenty-eight days after confirming guidance for the quarter, Nortel warned that their new analysis was indicating that their business was not as strong as previously indicated. In this press release, John Roth, CEO stated, *"While we previously noted that economic uncertainties and capital constraints were impacting our outlook, we are now seeing a faster and more severe economic downturn in the United States which we now expect will result in a slower overall market growth of approximately 10 percent in 2001. We are seeing longer than expected delays in spending by our U.S. customers as they continue to assess the impact of the economic and market conditions on their businesses. We now expect the U.S. market slowdown to continue well into the fourth quarter of 2001. Partially offsetting the impact of the U.S. market slowdown is the continued solid growth we are seeing in Europe and in the Asia Pacific and Latin America regions. Even with the current economic and market uncertainty, we continue to believe that Nortel Networks, with our global reach and industry-leading portfolio, is ideally positioned to gain market share and continue to grow revenues faster than the overall market growth rate. We now expect growth in revenues and earnings per share from operations(b) in 2001 over 2000 of 15 percent and 10 percent, respectively. For the first quarter of 2001, we expect revenues of US$6.3 billion and a loss per share from operations(b) of US$0.04 on a diluted basis. No other company is as well positioned in the market today with our leading portfolio and management bench strength as Nortel Networks,"* concluded Roth. *"We are strengthening our hold on being the world's leading* *provider of profitable, high-performance Internet and communications solutions for our customers around the world. We are seen as a company that our customers can confidently move forward with. There should be no confusing the current economic downturn in the United States, and the adjustment we are announcing today, with Nortel Networks overall health and our market leadership position."*

Three weeks later, John Roth issued an open letter to Nortel shareholders stating, *"Much has been said and written about Nortel Networks in recent weeks. I recognize that this has been of concern to our shareholders. It has also been a concern to me and all those associated with the company. That is why I want to review and update you on what has transpired since we issued a press release on February 15 revising our guidance for the first quarter and year 2001. When issuing that release, we stated that Nortel Networks was not immune to the current economic downturn in the United States. Based on previous experience, we had anticipated a longer lead-time for the effects of a downturn to be felt by our sector and by our company. The current downturn occurred with unprecedented suddenness and severity. Our decision to revise guidance on February 15 occurred as soon as the effects of this downturn were clear to us. We were among the first to recognize the severity of the downturn occurring in the U.S., our largest market. Since February 15, a growing number of technology companies with heavy dependence on the U.S. market have also revised their forecasts. This is clearly a broad market/economic slowdown that has affected companies in our sector with unprecedented speed. At the same time, I want you to know that our position as an industry leader and innovator remains strong, despite the unfavorable economic and market conditions we are facing. Our fundamentals remain sound and we offer an industry-leading portfolio of end-to-end communications solutions. We have a diverse and strong base of customers throughout the world. And we have some of the most talented and committed people in the world working to provide those customers with breakthrough technologies that create value and competitive advantage for our customers around the world."*

Nineteen days after the open letter, Nortel pre-announced lower than expected Q1 2001 sales. In the March 27 press release, John Roth stated, *"We continue to feel the impact of the economic downturn in the United States and are now seeing customers globally assess its effect on their businesses. Reduced and/or deferred capital spending and increased pricing pressure (sic) are resulting in lower overall revenues, particularly in the United States. Given the poor visibility into the duration and breadth of the economic downturn and its impact on the overall market growth in 2001, it is not possible to provide meaningful guidance for the Company's financial performance for the full year 2001. We continue to align our cost structure and industry leading product portfolio with our customers (sic) priorities and plans. It is our belief that Nortel Networks continues to be the best positioned high-performance Internet and communications equipment vendor for the customers we serve, and that our global leadership position combined with our agility will enable us to weather the current economic storm and come out of it a stronger company."* For Q1, 2001 Nortel's revenue declined to $6,177 billion with profits of $1,860. Forty-five days later, Nortel announced that their COO and successor to John Roth, Clarence Chandran was leaving the company immediately for medical reasons. John Roth was back for another year with plenty of time to find a new successor. For the balance of the year, Nortel Networks achieved $17 billion in revenues. Their revenues continued to decline and finally leveled in 2003 and will probably not exceed $12-13 billion annually for many years to come. How could this happen? In a few short months, Nortel's revenue declined by more than 50%. The "Perfect Storm" of the Decline stage had arrived.

During 2001, John Roth once again assumed day to day control of the company as well as leadership of the search for a new CEO. A five month search ended when Nortel named their current CFO Frank Dunn, who was a twenty-six year veteran of the company, as their new CEO. John Roth then assumed the role of Vice-Chairman. John and Frank were the revolutionary leaders of the most significant period of growth and change in the history of Nortel Networks. John Roth was named CEO of Nortel in 1997 and Frank Dunn was named CFO in January 1999. Under their leadership as CEO and CFO, Nortel embarked on the most aggressive period of change in the history of the company. John Roth referred to this as the *"right angle turn,"* a turn away from the traditional telephony business to the business of the internet. *"If Nortel had not been successful in moving ourselves to the data side, this could have been devastating. But we are so well-planted now in optical, in wireless Internet, in ATM, {and} in high-capacity routing. So if the growth in my voice products is flat, but these things are growing so rapidly at 30 to 40 percent a year, {then} we are not going to have a long eulogy about a 3 percent business. That was the right-angle turn that Nortel took."* [see John Roth, InfoWorld, January 24, 2000, by Martin LaMonica, Jennifer Jones].

Roth's fabled right angle turn came to him one night when he was surfing the web and realized he could order rare automobile parts from an obscure supplier thousands of miles from his home. *"I started poking around and within five minutes I'm in a little garage north of London, England – a four man operation – and he's got my parts. How would I have found this person if he wasn't on the Web? The idea that some guy north of London can carry out a business transaction with someone he's never met in Canada – it struck me what a powerful force this was, and how could something like this ever be stopped,"* [see John Roth, *Nortel's Driving Force*, McLean's, August 2, 1999 by Ross Laver]. This epiphany was his realization of the perceived power of the internet to change lives, ergo the power of the ITO Revolution, and from that day forward, he set Northern Telecom on a path to secure revolutionary glory. *"Obviously we're faced with great challenges as we move from the dial tone to webtone. But we're presented with even greater opportunities. And as we approach the turn of the century, what could be better than facing that world of opportunities and realizing the potential of the digital economy, which has reshaped business and is already touching every aspect of our personal lives."* [John Roth, Don Tapscott, *Blueprint to the Digital Economy*, 1998, page 297].

John Roth was not the only intellectual to realize the power of the ITO Revolution, many leaders of technology companies and analysts saw a tremendous opportunity in the years following telecom deregulation and the globalization of the internet. *"Yes, they saw an enormous opportunity over time, and there's a few fundamental underpinnings of the growth and demand. So they believed that there was a whole new economy, a whole new way of doing business. There were going to be tremendous productivity enhancements. People were going to continue to spend on technology more than they would spend on anything else. Technology was going to become a bigger and bigger piece of the GDP, the gross domestic product, of the economy, and that even if the economy grew 6 percent, telecom and technology could grow significantly faster. That was the underpinning of the entire movement of capital toward the telecom industry. It was assumed that all the buyers -- that is, corporations and consumers -- that are buying cable television, that are buying Internet services, that are buying e-business applications, would continue to buy at tremendous rates."* [see Susan Kalla, interviewed by FRONTLINE correspondent Hedrick Smith on Jan. 13, 2003].

To support the right angle turn, John Roth and Frank Dunn began to radically remake Northern Telecom. As witnessed in many revolutions, Nortel embarked on a name changing crusade. The company name changed to Nortel Networks and the number of employees went from 57,064 in 1994 to over a 100,000 in 2000. Revolution was in the air at Nortel as evidenced in the 1998 Annual Report, *"The global communications industry has experienced more than two decades of revolutionary ferment. As we approach the end of the twentieth century, the pace of change has never been more rapid nor the changes more profound. The marketplace is being dramatically reshaped by deregulation, technology, and mobility, compounded by the explosive growth of the Internet, as both a communications medium and a business phenomenon. Powerful drivers of change are transforming network economics, creating new customer relationships, and generating massive investment in network infrastructure, services, and applications. These are the characteristics of a new era of networking that will define the global economy and society of the next century. The new era of networking excites the imagination in many ways. Sometimes it's the little things that capture our attention, such as getting a better deal on a new car after comparison shopping on the Web, or effortlessly reaching the office through a wireless laptop connection. But the new era of networking is about big things, too. It offers a panoramic vision of a networked society that allows our ideas and aspirations to soar around the globe and into cyberspace. Telecommunications is the "killer app" driving the Internet revolution. This is good news for a company like Nortel Networks that understands both telecommunications and the Internet. It puts your company at the heart of the revolution = the coming together of public and private networks with the Internet. High-performance optical technology is powering the Internet revolution that's changing the way the world communicates...After just a few short years, the Internet is becoming part of everyday life. It eliminates the constraints of time and distance and gives us global access to information, not only in online libraries, but in businesses and in people's minds."*

In November 2000, Susan Kalla, who was industry analyst at BlueStone Capital, released a report on the telecom equipment sector, including the optical equipment segment, predicting a significant market correction and recession for this market segment. Her report was roundly criticized by those who were willing to consider her report, but mostly her report was ignored and her warning went unheeded. November 2000 was the time in the ITO Revolution when Lucent restated their first earnings. CLECs began to run low on cash and the first signs of a massive spending decline were becoming visible to the network equipment suppliers.

When the ITO Revolution entered the Decline stage of the G3MM, Nortel's leaders were forced to radically scale down the size of the company. The numbers are staggering when examined over a ten year period. From 1994 to 2004, Nortel hired or fired 117,000 employees. That is an average change of 17,000 employees per year. If we examine Nortel's employee number in a narrower period of time from the late Perigee stage through the Decline Stage (i.e. 1999 – 2002) Nortel experienced an employee turn over of 82,000 employees during a 36 month period. Assuming each employee worked at least 1.5 years at an average salary of $40,000 per year that equates to $4.96 billion in salary cost. Not included in this number is the cost of computers, work tools, benefits, physical building space, and the basic administration costs required to handle the hiring and firing of 82,000 people. When the ITO Revolution began to exit the Decline stage, Nortel had returned to employment levels in the mid to low 30,000 range; an employment level the company had not maintained since the 1980s. The table below is a compilation of Nortel employment statistics from their public financial statements. The number of employees mirrors the same market share curve for the ITO Revolution revealed in the G3MM. Nortel was steadily adding employees through the early stages of the ITO Revolution and then rapidly accelerated this pace in 1999. Nortel employment figures peaked in 2000 when the Perigee stage ended and then employment levels began a rapid descent in 2001 as the ITO Revolution transitioned from the Decline stage to the shock and pain of the Apogee stage. During 1999, Nortel added 29,288 employees. Of this number, it appears that about 2,000 came from acquisitions in 1999.

Year	# Employees	Change	Note
1994	57,064	-	Source: Company SEC Filings
1995	63,715	6,651	Source: Company SEC Filings
1996	67,584	3,869	Source: Company SEC Filings
1997	68,341	757	Source: Company SEC Filings
1998	71,296	2,955	Source: Company SEC Filings
1999	76,712	5,416	Estimated 2k New Employees from Acqusitions
2000	106,000	29,288	Estimated employment peak
2001	94,500	(11,500)	First Year of RIFs
2002	52,600	(41,900)	Major Force Reduction
2003	37,000	(15,600)	Last Major Force Reduction
2004	36,960	(40)	Announced 3,500 Force Reduction in August
2005	35,370	-	-
2006	34,270	(1,100)	7-06 1,100 Layoff, Last Reported Employee Count

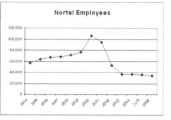

Figure 23: Nortel Employee Timeline

1. Between 1994 and 2004, Nortel hired/fired ~117,000 employees
2. Average of 17,000 adds/subs per year
3. Betweeen 1999-2002 (36 Months) 82,000 employees came or left
4. Assuming they worked 1.5 years at NT for $40,000 per year = $4.96B

As part of the right angle turn, Nortel became a major player in the acquisition frenzy of the mid to late 1990s. Before 1997, Nortel's last major acquisition was Standard Telecommunications and Cable (STC) in 1991. The STC acquisition brought optical expertise to Nortel as well as additional inroads into an important customer called British Telecom [see *Nortel Networks*, Larry MacDonald, page 100]. For decades, STC was considered the British equivalent of AT&T's Bell Labs and Northern Telecom's Bell Northern Research (BNR). To acquire STC, Nortel paid $4.1 billion, issuing shares and raising $1.7 billion in debt. This acquisition was done under the leadership of CEO Paul Stern. Nortel would not attempt another major acquisition for six years. When Nortel did resume acquiring companies, it advanced on a historically unprecedented run of acquisitions designed to (a) change the culture of Nortel, (b) bring new products and technology into the company, as well as (c) position Nortel to reap rewards from the new market opportunities presented by the ITO Revolution. Revolutions are once in a life time event. They are remembered as defining moments. Milestones that people look back on in future years to remember where they were and what they were doing. Revolutions also force leaders to make decisions outside of their traditional processes. Because global market revolutions are not frequent events, business leaders are not familiar with the revolutionary cycle. Inexperienced revolutionary leaders who are accustomed to the decision making process of the Start stage market structure, find the revolutionary cycle challenging as they are not familiar with the reasoning aspect of the decision making process in the midst of a revolution cycle. Revolutions drive a sense of urgency and clearly John Roth and Frank Dunn viewed the ITO Revolution as an opportunity to remake Nortel and position the company as a global supplier and global brand beyond the telephony world. For years Nortel had struggled to match the size of Lucent and the ITO Revolution presented an opportunity to seize the initiative as market barriers declined globally [see *Essay One, Chapter Two*] and market share became fluid for the first time in decades. The ITO Revolution was a vehicle that Nortel's leaders could use to significantly increase the size of the company as well as the global presence and brand of Nortel Networks.

Date	Company	Value	Currency
6-Feb-01	JDSU Zurich Plant	$2.5B + $500M	65.7M Shares
15-Aug-00	Sonoma Systems	$540M	4.8M Shares
28-Jul-00	Alteon WebSystems	$7.8B	82M Shares
14-Jun-00	EPiCON, Inc	$275M	4.26M Shares
23-May-00	Photonic Technologies	$35.5M	Cash
19-Apr-00	Architel Sys. Corp.	$395M	6M Shares
19-Apr-00	CoreTek, Inc	$1.43B	14.5M Shares
14-Mar-00	Xros, Inc	$3.25B	53M Shares
9-Feb-00	Dimension Enterprises	$64.7M	Cash
6-Jan-00	Promatory Comm.	$778M	6.15M Shares
15-Dec-99	Qtera Corporation	$3.25B	5M Shares
10/18/1999	Clarify, Inc.,	$2.1B	31.7M Shares
24-Aug-99	Periphonics Corporation	$436M	8.4M Shares
20-May-99	X-CEL Communications	Not Disclosed	Not Disclosed
16-Apr-99	Shasta Networks	$340M	Stock+$22M Cash
15-Dec-98	Cambrian Networks	$360M	Cash
31-Aug-98	Bay Networks	$9.1B	135M Shares
18-Mar-98	Aptis	$305M	2.5M Shares+$5M Cash
2-Nov-97	Broadband Networks Inc.	$593M Cdn	5.6M Shares+$213M Cdn Cash

Figure 24: Nortel Acquisitions
Source: Nortel Web Page and SEC Filings

Over a thirty-eight month period, Nortel Networks closed 19 acquisitions worth more than $33 billion dollars. Nortel was acquiring companies at the rate of $850 million per month – but this number is somewhat deceiving because the acquisition rate over the last eighteen months was higher. During the last half of Nortel's acquisition run, the company spent $22 billion, or $1.2 billion per month. This is important because it is evidence that Nortel's leaders were not perceptive to the rapid changes occurring in their markets on a global scale. This is a tell tale sign of the Decline stage of the G3MM. When the Extremists assume power, it is swift and often comes as a shock to the moderates of the revolution. This is what happened to Nortel in late 2000 and into 2001.

When Frank Dunn assumed the position of CEO of Nortel Networks, he had a sizable mess to manage. To his credit, he spent much of 2002 and into 2003 managing to keep Nortel from collapsing under a large debt level, too high of an expense line and dwindling cash reserves. In January 2003, Nortel surprised the world by announcing a profit. In the press release, Dunn stated, *"As we enter 2003, the focus on profitability will continue. Our differentiation continues to be technology leadership and customer engagement. We are focused on the delivery of multimedia services and network infrastructure that will allow our customers to grow their business and reduce overall costs. We saw continued momentum in all of our focus areas in the quarter."* It appeared that Nortel had begun to stabilize their business from the impact of the Decline stage of the ITO Revolution.

Unfortunately, the appearance of Nortel as a healthy company was false. On April 29, 2004 Nortel Networks announced that Frank Dunn (CEO), Douglas Beatty (CFO), and Michael Gollogy (Controller) had been terminated for cause. On August 19, 2004 Nortel announced that an additional seven individuals responsible for financial reporting within the lines of business had been terminated for cause. Specifically Nortel's press release stated, *"As previously announced on April 28, 2004, the Company terminated for cause each of its former president and chief executive officer, chief financial officer and controller. Today, the Company announced that seven individuals with significant responsibilities for financial reporting at the line of business and regional levels have also been terminated for cause. Four of these individuals had previously been placed on paid leaves of absence, as announced on April 28, 2004. In making these and the previous determinations, the Board of Directors found that each of these ten individuals had primary, or substantial, responsibility for the Company's financial reporting; that if not aware, each ought to have been aware that the establishment and/or release to income of such accruals and provisions were not in accordance with applicable generally accepted accounting principles; and that the improper application of generally accepted accounting principles with respect to these accruals and provisions misstated the Company's financial statements. The Company will demand repayment by these individuals of payments made under Company bonus plans in respect of 2003, and will take further additional action with respect to these individuals, if appropriate."*

With the dismissal of Frank Dunn, Nortel began an extensive audit of the company's financials. As 2004 progressed, the extent of the investigation became larger and in more depth. By December of 2004, Nortel could still not release accurate financial results. The ongoing investigation into accurate financial results was going as far back as 1999. Nortel announced in December 2004 that, *"As previously announced, the Company has identified adjustments to revenues, primarily in the Company's Optical Networks and Enterprise Networks businesses. Based upon the work done to date, these adjustments have resulted in a net reduction in revenue of approximately US $430 million and US$2.8 billion in 1999 and 2000, respectively (adjusted from US$600 million and US $2.5 billion previously announced). The Company currently does not expect a material change to the previously announced approximate amount of permanent revenue reversal in 2000, which is largely due to collectibility issues. The remaining revenue adjustments in 1999 and 2000 will be deferred and recognized in subsequent years. The impact of these revenue adjustments is currently estimated to result in a net increase in revenues of approximately US $1.5 billion, US $265 million and US $460 million in 2001, 2002 and 2003, respectively (adjusted from US $1.35 billion, US $450 million and US $450 million previously announced). The adjustments to date would also result in additional deferred revenue* *on the Company's balance sheet as of December 31, 2003."* This is clear evidence that the leadership team of Nortel used aggressive accounting techniques to meet the pressure and expectations of the ITO Revolution at the very time the extremists were taking command of the revolution.

In January 2005, Nortel announced that, *"As a matter of corporate leadership and integrity, twelve senior executives of Nortel's core executive leadership team have voluntarily undertaken to pay to the Company over a three year period the amount of their Return to Profitability bonuses awarded in 2003 (net of tax withheld at source) aggregating the equivalent of approximately US$8.6 million, and to disclaim any potential award of the remaining two installments of the 2003 Restricted Stock Unit Plan, in each case regardless of whether the profitability metrics for these bonuses or awards were met on a restated basis."* Nortel had sought and received repayment of the bonuses that were paid through the manipulation of financial reporting to alter the fiscal appearance of the company. In addition, Nortel announced that it had appointed a Chief Ethics and Compliance Officer. All seemed pointed in a positive direction. In March of 2005, Nortel announced that Gary Daichendt would be appointed COO and heir apparent to Bill Owens as CEO. Gary was coming out of retirement after a long and distinguished career at Cisco Systems. In the press release, Owens stated, *"We are playing to win and Gary will play a critical role in our doing so. He is a world class leader with unquestioned integrity and one of the top technology executives in the world. Gary's deep involvement in the spectacular growth of some of the world's leading technology powerhouses and his unique track record have given him a special perspective and experience that will optimally position our great Company for our customers, shareholders and employees. All of us at Nortel are very pleased with his decision to join us."* Twenty-seven days later Nortel announced that Gary Kunis had been appointed CTO. His career background included holding the position of Chief Science Officer at Cisco Systems. Gary Daichendt commented that, *"We're thrilled to have Gary join our team. He's an acknowledged Internet pioneer with a solid record of accomplishment and I know he will provide an outstanding contribution to Nortel's technology leadership. His track record in leading the building, servicing and selling of network technologies globally will be a strong addition. He's an excellent senior leader who throughout his career has consistently demonstrated his ability to link technology innovation with business success both internally and externally."*

Eighty-seven days after announcing the appointment of Gary Daichendt, Nortel announced that both Gary Daichendt and Gary Kunis had left the company in apparent disagreement with CEO. In the June 10 press release, Bill Owens stated, *"It has become apparent to Gary and me, however, that we have divergent management styles and our business views differ. I respect him for his decision and I wish him every success in his future endeavors."* Four months later Nortel named Mike Zafirovski President and CEO. At the time of the appointment, Zafirovski was

51 years old with a twenty-five year career at General Electric and a five year career at Motorola with the last three years as COO of Motorola.

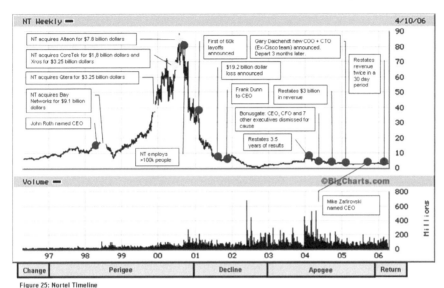

Figure 25: Nortel Timeline
Source: BigCharts.com + Author's Research

In the first five months at Nortel, Mike Zafirovski began to radically remake the leadership team, gain closure on outstanding litigation from the Perigee Stage of the ITO Revolution, and place Nortel on a path to become competitive in the new global order. Zafirovski recruited an almost entirely new leadership team from General Electric and Motorola. Long time Nortel leaders, who had prominent roles publicly and internally during the boom years of the 1990s, were quietly retired. By March of 2006 Nortel had reached a tentative agreement to settle the shareholder class action suit stemming from the decline of Nortel stock. Throughout the first few months of 2006, Nortel made three public announcements regarding revenue restatements. By May of 2006, Nortel had restated $1.5 billion of new revenues going back three years in addition to the $3.1 billion announced in 2003. Another act that marked Nortel passage from past to the future, was the announcement of a joint venture (JV) with Huawei Technologies of China to leverage the cost points of China Inc in the North American market. During the Decline Stage of the ITO Revolution, Nortel sold its access and broadband product lines to Zhone Technologies in August of 2001. A little over five years later Nortel was back in the access and broadband business with products designed and manufactured in China.

Post Nublia Phoebius

Examining the Decline stage within the ITO Revolution the terror came in many forms and many guises, but it was always the terror. Within the community of people who had chosen the field of telecom services and telecom equipment for their career, the Decline stage was especially difficult. Thousands of employees left long standing careers at established companies such as Bell Labs, Northern Telecom, RBOCs, and AT&T to start new companies at the height of the telecom bubble – only to find their dreams of building a new company destroyed in the winds of the terror. Many employees who did not have long careers at Lucent or Nortel, but did enjoy reliable jobs that paid them well, found that the terror of ITO Revolution was inescapable. The result was that these people exacted their revenge on the message boards of websites that covered the ITO industry. Web sites such as www.fuckedcompany.com/ were created for disgruntled employees to traffic in company gossip, innuendo, and outright character assassination.

If you were a CEO of a startup that was on the verge of closing, it was quite likely that your employees or former employees had been contributing to an early form of a web blog that detailed the trials and travails of the company. Character assassination via message boards is the guillotine of the ITO Revolution. Decency and decorum were not the hallmarks of these message boards. Disgruntled employees found these boards to be their outlet to vent frustrations over lost careers, lost fortunes, and the impact that the terror had on their families. Within the networking community a web site called www.lightreading.com was created in the late 1990s. This web site became one of the most famous sites for telecom equipment industry people to monitor and contribute. A company called Tachion collapsed under the weight of the Decline in 2002, but the company became famous as the subject of one of the longest, most vicious message boards on www.lightreading.com. The *"Tachion Trolls for Cash"* message board began on June 26, 2001. More than four hundred and fifty-two posts later, messages were still being posted in early 2006. This single thread about a company that went bankrupt in 2002 generated over four years of messages attacking the leadership team and mocking all aspects of the company.

Much of the terror seen in the ITO Revolution can be linked to the old regimes. Many of the leaders who emerged from the old regimes to assume positions of leadership within revolutionary companies were simply not prepared for the challenge. During the Perigee stage, it seemed that thousands of executives who held vice president level positions or could claim to have held a position close to that level within an old regime (i.e. AT&T, Northern Telecom, Bellcore and the 7 RBOCs), were shopping a business plan to venture capitalists. Venture capitalists started so many new companies, that there was a shortage of executive level talent. The result was that salaries rose to attract talent of all levels, and executives who had modest career experience used the ITO Revolution to accelerate their career paths. When the Decline stage of the ITO Revolution began, many of these executives where ill equipped to lead companies through the challenges of the market conditions.

It was not unexpected that many of the executives leading ITO companies did not posses the skill sets required to lead their companies. The newness of the companies and the ITO market that emerged after the day of revolution was unfamiliar to nearly all the leaders of companies and their customers. Expectations for a new global economy that were set in the early days of the ITO Revolution never materialized on the scale and scope predicted. The internet clearly made it easier to access information and had dramatic affects on some industries, but in the end it never really lived up to expectations. The real legacy of the ITO Revolution is that trillions of dollars of wealth were eliminated during the Decline stage. Hundreds of thousands of people were laid off and the intellectuals who had been the leaders of the revolution in the early days had little to say and in some cases were hard to located post the crash. To their credit, several of prominent revolutionaries such as George Gilder had the gumption to admit mistakes and stay involved with the industry that he had a role in changing.

With the sunset of the Decline stage, the Apogee stage of the G3 Market Model begins for the ITO Revolution. One of the most visible reactions to the rise of the Perigee stage and its counterpart the Decline stage is the passage of the Sarbanes-Oxley (i.e. SOX) Act of 2002. SOX is an attempt by the government of the United States to provide legislative structure designed to prevent abuse of corporate power and finances such as those seen at Enron, Nortel, and Worldcom. According to the Wall-Street Journal, public companies in the U.S. spent $5.4 billion in 2004 preparing to meet SOX and it is estimated that an additional $5.8 billion will be spent in 2005 [see *The Wall Street Journal*, July 14, 2005, page C1] The effects of the ITO Revolution will be long lasting and have a global affect. The high expectation levels of the ITO Revolution seen during the Change and Perigee stages, were tempered by the extreme lows seen during the Decline stage. Only a revolution can waste trillions of dollars, destroy companies and force thousands of people into unemployment. A few lowlights from the Decline stage of the ITO Revolution include:

- Estimates in excess of $7 trillion of investor wealth eliminated by internet company failures

- Top ten Wall Street investment banks settle lawsuit initiated by

Elliott Spitzer, alleging conflict of interest between their investment and research groups within their companies for $1.4 billion. Going forward, investment banks and accounting firms agree to separate research, investment, and accounting practices.

- Arthur Anderson eliminated in the wake of Enron scandal; a firm that had been in existence since 1913 years and had originally built their reputation on the highest standards of professionalism, morals, and incorruptibility. Arthur Anderson was, for a long time the Robespierre of the accounting business [see *Essay Two, Chapter Eight*].

The legal efforts by Elliot Spitzer, the destruction of Enron, the public trials of executives from Worldcom, Enron, Adelphia, and others are classic examples of extreme reaction to when revolutions fail. When revolutions fail to meet the expectations set by the revolutionaries and intellectuals, the public seeks to find people to blame, to hold responsible for the failures, and seek retribution against. As the ITO Revolution moved into the Apogee stage, it was marked by the return of rational business practices. Eventually, the public outcry began to fade. Old leaders from more stable times return to lead the cleanup of companies from the effects of revolution.

CHAPTER SIX:
The Age Long Strife

Strategy…is the art of bringing the greatest part of the forces of an army upon the important theater of war or of the zone of operations. - Jomini

As the year 2003 dawned, an unprecedented collapse had occurred within the telecom services, telecom equipment, and technology markets of the United States as well as their global counterparts. As we conclude this chapter, we will provide some additional detail regarding market conditions within the North American telecom services market and its technology suppliers. This will help frame the sequence of events from 1994 through 2003 using the G3 Market Model, and enable the extension of the G3MM to include the evolution of regulated markets when disruptive events, such as deregulation and new technology, change the structure of the market. The final stage of the G3MM will be detailed in following chapter. To appreciate the scope of the devastation within the U.S. technology markets, let us begin with a quote. *"In 1994, three million people, most of them in the United States, used the Internet. In 1998, 100 million people around the world use the Internet. Some experts believe that one billion people may be connected to the Internet by 2005. This expansion is driving dramatic increases in computer, software, services and communications investments,"* [see U.S. Department of Commerce, *The Emerging Digital Economy,* April 15, 1998].

The second to last stage of the G3 Market Model is called Apogee. Apogee is time of market settlement and extreme market consolidation. During the Decline stage, companies, leaders, employees, and customers are struggling to remain secure. The market conditions are changing with such rapidity, that it becomes a cruel game of musical chairs. The music keeps stopping and fewer and fewer chairs are left in the room. Companies go out of business when the money runs out. Layoffs are occurring at such a rapid and large pace that there is no time for social justice. For the large companies trying to size their business to market changes during the Decline stage of the ITO Revolution, the task was enormous due to the size of the company of the swiftness of the decline of the market. Employees were notified that they had been terminated by email thousands at the time. There was no time for employee ranking or agonizing decisions. Employees were terminated by groupings. If you were in the wrong group, you were terminated. Few options existed to save a job.

Apogee: Market conditions have become less dynamic. Market share is beginning to reach a point of maximum concentration as the extremist companies capture as much market share as they can effective manage. Investments in new companies comes to a near halt as venture capitalists, equity firms, and the extremists look at options to consolidate market share or roll up competitors at a significant discount to the Perigee stage. It is at this point that the intellectuals retreat from the market in utter disbelief, as it appears that the market has come nearly full circle. For the companies left in the market, competition for customers reaches its most intense peak, as customers are life. In order to capture market share, companies unable to differentiate their value proposition begin to compete on price. Price becomes the governing decision making point for customers. During the Perigee stage of the G3MM, power is in the hands of the sellers as they have new technologies and services that the buyers want to purchase in order to remain competitive in the new market structure. During the Apogee stage, the buyers have assumed the advantageous position in the market structure. The remaining suppliers are desperate for market share and as such, they drive the cost of goods and services to its lowest point. See **Chart 13: G3MM Apogee Stage for ITO Revolution** in the Chart and Model section.

In September 2002, Larry Ellison commented in the Financial Times, *"Silicon Valley will never be the same. Those who believe this is merely a cyclical downturn are mad. They cannot see what is happening in front of their eyes. Our industry is going to mature and as something matures, the rate of innovation does slow."* His statement focused on one element of a profound change that was occurring within the technology industry. The market ecosystem for telecom and technology companies is bound by one common characteristic: innovative technology. The creation of new technology drives the cycle of market revolution; in the words of Schumpeter, a cycle of creative destruction. The telecom industry would not exist if the technology to enable telephony was not invented and patented. The emphasis is on the patent because intellectual property rights (i.e. IPR) are a fundamental element to the creation of value. Intellectual property creates a market advantage, which in turn enables the acquisition of capital, which can be translated into value. The process of creating innovative technology requires an investment of capital that is made at considerable risk. If the technology can be proven and the intellectual property rights secured, then great value will be created and returned to those who provided the initial investment capital. The accelerated revolution frenzy that occurred in the 1990s is the direct result of a massive infusion of capital into an industry that traditionally evolved at a managed pace. The pace at which the internet, telecom, and optical networking markets evolved during the mid to late 1990s was unprecedented and unnatural. Competitive pressures created market conditions that many had never been experienced before, but assuredly would be witnessed again in the future – albeit at a more managed pace.

As for the pace of innovation, it may have paused, but it did not decline to a rate below the historical pace of innovation. Using telecommunication patents as a measurement of the pace of innovation, the statistics published by the U.S. Patent and Trademark Office, there was a decline in the number of patents issued in 2001, but the historical pace resumes in 2002 and 2003. The pace of patent issuing is probably a reflection of two forces. The first driver is that many of the technology startups funded in 1999 and 2000 were far enough along in the process of product and technology development to apply for and receive patent grants in the years 2002 and 2003. The second plausible driver is concentration of market share. As the ITO markets collapsed and the extremist companies took command of market share, these companies have the resources to fund patent initiatives. The large companies undertook the patent process because a library of patents is a powerful force with which to defend market share in a static market structure. Companies use patent libraries to keep small competitors out of markets, control market share, broker détente with large rivals, and to wage war against rivals. Patents and intellectual property rights are a tangible measurement of corporate value.

In August 2005, Qualcomm paid $600 million with a potential for another $205 million for a venture backed private company called Flarion Technologies. With the acquisition of Flarion, Qualcomm acquired an extensive patent library covering a technology called orthogonal frequency division multiplexing, or OFDM. Flarion was another company spun out of Lucent Technologies – but the acquisition by Qualcomm was not based on the prospect of a mass deployment of Flarion technology y mobile service providers. Qualcomm was acquiring Flarion for their patents that could be used as an alternative to WiMAX. WiMAX is an emerging technology that potentially threatens the patent and chip CDMA revenue stream of Qualcomm. Qualcomm's acquisition of Flarion is continued proof that the cycle of innovation in technology markets is alive and well. The following chart is adopted from the Federal Communications Commission, *Trends in Telephone Service Report*, June 21, 2005 Chart 17-1:

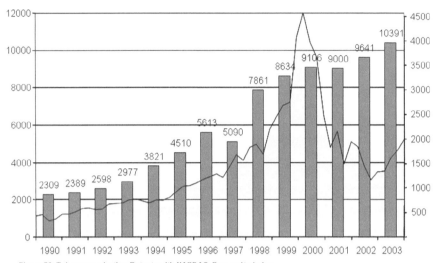

Figure 26: Telecommunication Patents with NASDAQ Composite Index
Note: 1996 total reflects one-time change in law affecting patents.
Source: U.S. Patent and Trademark Office, Patent Counts by Class by Year, January 1977-December 2003,
Telecommunications Classes 370, 375, 379 and 455 (March 2004).

The capital made available to the internet, telecom, and optical revolutions was based on the belief that a fundamental set of changes had occurred to these markets and an opportunity existed to accelerate the process of building value. The traditional telephony markets pursued by Lucent and Nortel that had evolved at a slow and predicable pace were changed in a material manner. Research and development into new technologies was accelerated. In order to be successful in an accelerating market (i.e. Perigee stage) companies were required to shorten the cycles of product development and for securing intellectual property rights for innovative technology. New markets and new technologies were being introduced at a pace unparalleled in the prior history of telecom services and networking technology. There was a near dizzying pace in the creation of companies to access the new markets. The due diligence cycles by venture capitalists and investment banks were reduced to a matter of weeks and days. Executives with successful career backgrounds, built over many years within the established industry companies, were provided with an opportunity to accelerate their career track. The vast number of new companies needed CEOs, CFOs, CTOs, CMOs, and Vice Presidents to fill their ranks. As part of this process, talented executives who were not prepared for expanded rolls were put into positions of leadership for which they were not ready and pushed immature companies into the public equity markets at a dizzying pace. *"They've got the muscle to make sure the deal happens,' said David Menlow, president of IPO Financial Network. 'They've been lining up interviews for the CEO on the big TV finance shows. That's very unusual for a company that's not even public yet. This seems to* *be a very seriously choreographed process.' The number of shares, pricing information, or an offering date weren't disclosed. The company lost $10.2 million against $652,000 in revenue in its sole quarter of operation. Since there's just the one quarter on the books, it's impossible to gauge growth. No matter, said Menlow. 'I'm surprised to see them come out, because of the short time they've been around, but it makes sense given all the attention they've been getting.' "* [see David Bicknell commenting on the Drugstore.com IPO, *Wired*, May 20, 1999]

The technology industries centered near San Jose (i.e. Silicon Valley) California and the suburbs of Boston Massachusetts and to a lesser extent, Holmdel New Jersey and Dallas Texas have been the places where new networking companies are born. Companies were created by one of three methods: spinout, venture funded startup, and bootstrap startup. In the case of Lucent, Agere and Avaya, they were created by divesting divisions or business units from larger companies. All three of these companies were at one time, part of AT&T. The second strategy is to create a business plan and acquire venture capital backing. Successful companies who have used this strategy are Juniper Networks, Cascade Communications, Ciena, Tellabs, Ascend, and Intel. The third strategy is to privately fund the company by the founders or employees. This strategy is typically called boot strapping. Many technology startups begin as boot strapped startups and then acquire venture capital as they begin to grow. Examples of boot strapped companies are Hewlett-Packard, Microsoft, and Cisco Systems. During the Perigee Stage of the ITO Revolution, the attractiveness of the telecom services, networking, and optical markets had never been better. It was a significant event that many companies and leaders did not want to miss. *"Obviously, we are in one of the most opportunistic public markets ever. The bar has never been lower. I think a company needs two things to get out these days. First, it has to have discernible momentum. Momentum is subjective, but Wall Street wants to see a path to profitability and some solid revenue growth. Second, the market is rewarding CEOs who can tell a good story -- not a falsehood, but a story that will convince everyone that this new company is going to be the next big thing, even if it isn't. If the window for IPOs gets tight, that skill loses its importance. But composure and the ability to tell a story convincingly are definitely assets in a CEO. In this environment they make a company extremely valuable,"* [see Tony Perkins, R*ed Herring*, January 1, 1997].

Regardless of the strategy used to create a company, one common resource is needed to grow the company, and that resource is capital. If small companies can sell their products and become self-funded early in their life cycle, it is a clear advantage to the company, its employees and leaders. What occurred in the 1990s was an unimagined confluence of events. Markets with a massive potential for value creation were formed in a very short period of time. Private capital flowed into California and Massachusetts as new companies were created with this private capital. It became common place for local newspapers to publish quarterly venture capital funding commitments along side the quarterly mutual fund performance reports. Venture capitalists committed massive amounts of capital to these emerging companies with the intent to accelerate the life cycle of the company. By accelerating the life cycle, the time required to experience an equity event was shortened, whether that equity event was an acquisition or initial public offering. At some point in the late 1990s, a viewpoint developed in the technology and venture capital communities that building a profitable business should be a second priority to the development of products and market introduction. The intent was to accelerate the life cycle of the company to prevent missing a market window. A market window is defined as a period of time in which the barriers to entry are lowered, or there is going to be an adoption of a new technology and the dominant suppliers of that technology have not been determined.

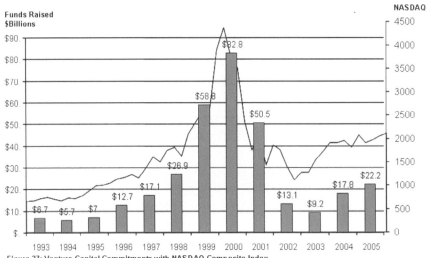

Figure 27: Venture Capital Commitments with NASDAQ Composite Index
Source: Dow Jones VentureOne (www.ventureone.com)

The previous chart illustrates the amount of capital committed to venture capital funds with an overlay of the NASDAQ composite index. The dramatic rise in venture capital commitments, illustrates a desire to capitalize on the internet, telecom, and optical revolutions. *"While the month of October offered a relative lull in technology IPOs, the Internet promises to make the close of 1995 extraordinarily active. Thirty IPOs may be priced by the middle of December, when the capital markets shut down. That would bring the total for the year to 120 technology IPOs priced at greater than $20 million. Last year was considered very busy with only 90 such IPOs. The public offerings of '95 have been sturdy, too -- all but one priced within* *or above the filing range; 80% have since appreciated. And the average appreciation of '95 IPOs is 65%. As Goldman Sachs' Brad Koenig put it, 'When you have that kind of performance, there is an almost insatiable demand for more IPOs.' His firm was the lead underwriter for 10 technology deals this year, more than twice the number it underwrote in its best year. Equally impressive, Robertson Stephens will do more deals in this year's final quarter than in good previous years. Robertson is so swamped, it's pulling bankers out of other industries to work the technology beat....Matt Thompson of Wheat First Butcher Singer estimates, 'There is an ability for companies to go public today whereas a year ago there wasn't.' His firm has been working with a good number of East Coast Internet companies which he says are trying to ride Netscape's coattails,"* [see Red Herring, January 1, 1996]. Even as the ITO Revolution was entering the Decline stage in late 2000 and into 2001, capital was flowing into the venture funds. The extent of the changes to the ITO market structure wrought by the Decline stage was not fully realized by industry insiders, analysts, and consultants until 2002.

In the United States, for much of its history, the telecom industry had been a regulated industry. Any industry that is regulated by the government is not subject to dynamic rates of change forced upon it by market conditions such as competition and new technology. If we start with the Telpak Tariff, we find that the government of the United States in the form of the FCC, required ten years of deliberation to determine that this tariff was anti-competitive. The traditional suppliers of telecom related equipment in the United States, Lucent (formally AT&T), Nortel Networks (formally Northern Telecom), Fujitsu, and Siemens, are very large multi-national corporations. When large incumbent telecom service providers such as AT&T, Verizon, SBC, BellSouth, MCI, GTE, and Sprint deploy new technology, it is a slow and laborious process. A typical cycle of technology adoption can be summarized by the following:

- Business Case Planning (6 to 12 Months)
- Request for Information (RFI) or Proposal (RFP) (3-6 Months)
- Request for Quote (RFQ) (3 Months)
- Shortlist of Suppliers and Lab Test/Certification (6-18 Months)
- Deployment (12-36 Months)

The high-level process to introduce new technology to an incumbent telecom service provider is a twelve to thirty-six month process before substantial revenue is realized by the equipment suppliers. This type of business is difficult for a small company to win as the sales cycle is long enough to be a substantial barrier to entry. Small companies simply do not have the capital and life-cycle support structures in place to be able to compete and win business from large companies – unless there is a substantial shift in the market structure. This is a fundamental reason why large incumbent telecom service providers have typically favored solutions from large telecom equipment suppliers who will be in business for the next ten to twenty years to support the installed base of technology. If it takes two years to win the business and another three years to finish the bulk of the deployment, an incumbent telecom service provider is not going to throw away equipment that it just invested five years of time deploying. That equipment is going to be around for another ten to twenty years. This fact gives a new technology project a life cycle of ten to twenty five years – which is certainly not a challenge that a company that is only two to three years old can address. The inverse of this challenge is, should a new equipment supplier win a contract with an incumbent telecom service provider, that the rewards are significant, as long term value will be created because of the length of the spending cycle. In terms of the Decline and transition into the Apogee stage of the ITO Revolution, it came as a shock to many equipment suppliers how quickly the CAPEX spending stopped. It was not a gradual process. Service providers and the Fortune 5000 simply stopped buying IT equipment at the start of 2001. Nortel and Lucent employed more than 100,000 employees each in 2000 – twelve months later they had laid off tens of thousands of employees. Throughout the entire industry, every company in the ecosystem began a rapid reduction of workforce in 2001.

In the mid to late 1990s, two interesting market drivers collided that changed the structure of the telecom market in the United States. The first was the passage of the Telecom Act of 1996. Overnight, there was a market of new telecom service providers that did not possess the same barriers to entry as the incumbents. These new telecom service providers were actively seeking an edge over the incumbents, the old regimes of telecom service provider market such as AT&T, Verizon, SBC, and MCI. They wanted new systems, new methods of operation, new strategies, and new technologies to avoid the bureaucratic overhead of the incumbents. The adoption of new technologies by the new service provider entrants (i.e. CLECs, IXCs) forced the incumbents to accelerate their process for technology adoption. In total, these two forces opened a market that was traditionally closed to new suppliers. The venture capitalists realized that this could be a once in a lifetime opportunity to create new telecom equipment suppliers. To capitalize on this market opportunity, new equipment suppliers had to move faster, get bigger quicker, and access the public equity markets in order to acquire the capital needed to build the critical company size and scale required to compete for business from the new service providers as well as the old regimes. During the Perigee stage of the ITO Revolution, a new strategy for company building took hold that was an offshoot of the internet time concept. *"Most startups now hope to go from formation to IPO in 18 months, We'll do it in 15 months."* [see Mouli Ramani, Vice President of Business Development, Jasmine Networks, November 9, 2000] Hence, it was in the mid 1990s that the creation of a new market created by telecom deregulation collided with the venture capital market. Historically, the U.S. telecom equipment market had high barriers to entry for new suppliers and required massive amounts of capital resources that were only available to large public companies such as Lucent, Nortel, Fujitsu, and Siemens.

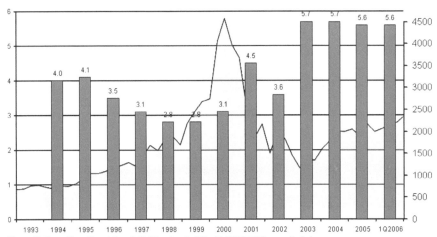

Figure 28: Mean Time (Years) from Initial Funding to IPO with NASDAQ Composite Index
Source: Dow Jones VentureOne (www.ventureone.com)

Typically, technology companies require years to build. Microsoft was founded in 1978; it went public eight years later in 1986. Cisco Systems was founded in 1984 and went public eight years later in 1992. Intel was founded in 1968; it went public more than three years later in 1971. By the late nineteen nineties, companies were going public in a matter of months – not years. Venture capitalists, as well as company leaders, used expressions such as "*fastest company to IPO*" and "*IPO within eighteen months*" to motivate their employees as well as to secure large infusions of capital needed to scale the business beyond accustomed metrics. The process of building and growing a company was being accelerated. The acceleration of the growth process required company leaders to develop their companies with the ability to support the full product life cycle earlier in the growth curve of the company. To support the full product life cycle at an earlier point, the corporate growth curve required a greater amount of working capital and the infusion of this capital earlier in the process. The ability to accelerate growth required new companies to operate faster within their market cycle. Markets as well as companies developing within markets have well defined cycles. During the ITO Revolution, the overall ITO markets and their sub-markets were developing at an extraordinarily fast pace. Venture capitalists, as well as industry leaders, had never experienced market conditions like this before. The combination of (a) fast developing markets, (b) intense market competitiveness, and (c) the ability to create value and exit investments quickly created a market that consumed capital. More capital was needed to accomplish more within a shorter lifespan than ever before. To support the capital needs of the market; more venture capital firms were created with ever-larger funds. *"I don't think Internet valuations are crazy, I think they reflect a fundamental embrace of huge opportunities. Virtually all forecasts estimate something like a thousandfold rise in Internet traffic over the next five years. That means that if you are an Internet company today, you are dealing with only a tenth of 1 percent of your potential traffic in just a couple of years. In 10 years, at this rate, there would be a millionfold increase,"* [see George Gilder, *Wired 7.09*, September 1999].

	1980	1990	2001
Number of VC Firms in Existence	87	375	761
Number of VC Funds in Existence	124	734	1627
Number of VC Professionals	1220	3794	8891
Number of First Time VC Funds Raised	23	14	66
Number of VC Funds Raised This Year	56	82	299
VC Capital Raised this Year ($MM)	$2,100	$3,130	$40,300
VC Capital Under Management ($MM)	$3,100	$32,000	$250,000
Average VC Capital Under Management Per Firm ($MM)	$42.5	$85.3	$333.2
Average VC Fund Size to Date ($MM)	$29.8	$43.6	$155.9
Average VC Fund Size Raised This Year ($MM)	$37.4	$38.2	$134.7
Largest VC Fund Raised to Date ($MM)	$1,000	$1,775	$5,000

Figure 29: Rise of Venture Capital Firms and Committed Capital
Source: Dow Jones VentureOne (www.ventureone.com)

In 1990, there were 375 venture capital firms in the United States. By 2000, the number of those firms had grown to 693 firms and would peak at 761 firms in 2001 – which was the beginning of the Decline period of the G3MM for the ITO Revolution. The capital raised by these firms in a single year had grown from $3.2 billion in 1990 to $105 billion in 2000. If we assume the average size first round financing of a new company in 2000 was ten million dollars, then 10,500 new companies could be created with the venture capital raised in 2000. A more realistic analysis would be to examine how this capital was employed by venture capitalists. At the beginning of the 1990s, the generic model for funding a company was radically different from what it would be some eight years later.

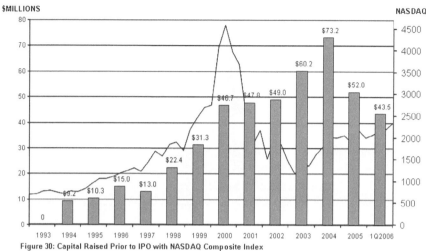

Figure 30: Capital Raised Prior to IPO with NASDAQ Composite Index
Source: Dow Jones VentureOne (www.ventureone.com)

In the early 1990s, startup technology companies were typically funded in two to three funding rounds with an expectation that $10-20 million in capital would be required to grow the company, assume good execution, and be in a position that would enable the company to have created enough value to be acquired or to go public. Venture capitalists call this an equity event. By the late 1990s, the typical VC funding model had radically changed. Startups were no longer thinking that they had to create value on $20 million, but rather had $80 million or more to work with. Looking back on the $105 billion raised in 2000, this was enough to support more than twelve hundred separate companies throughout their planned funding lifespan, assuming $80 million of total funding. In reality, $85 million would not be enough for many companies capitalized at the height of the technology bubble. In 2003, Calient Networks, founded in 1999, closed its fourth round of financing, bringing the total value of private capital committed to this company, to more than $300 million. This is an astonishing amount of capital committed to a single company as it represents an enormous amount of capital committed to the idea that Calient Networks will be able to sell new technology to large incumbent service providers.

Round	Average 1990 Round	Average 1999 Round	Calient Networks
Seed	$100k	$500k	-
1st Round	$3M	$10M	$6M (1999)
2nd Round	$8M	$25M	$50M (2000)
3rd Round	$12M	$50M	$225M (2001)
4th Round	-	-	$35M (2004)
Total	$23.1M	$85.5M	$316M

Figure 31: Calient Networks Funding Rounds

Calient Networks is classic example of startup funded by venture capital during the Perigee stage of the ITO Revolution. The company was created to build a new generation of optical switches designed for the large service provider market. The growth of the services using the internet would require service providers to increase the switching capacity of their networks. All optical switches were perceived as the future of networking. *"'Service providers today suffer from the Overbuild Syndrome,' said Tim Dixon, Calient Vice President of Marketing. 'They build out their infrastructure with one generation of technology, services and speed, and then in two years, they have to churn that infrastructure to meet new needs. It is devastating to their balance sheets. With an all-photonic infrastructure, we break the overbuild cycle. Not only will providers experience lower first costs, but by building a photonic layer that does not churn with every change in interfaces, speeds or formats, providers will lower their lifecycle costs by orders of magnitude. This is the big payoff from what we call Photon-Economics, as compared to legacy Electron-Economics.' Calient Networks aims to build industry leadership in all-photonic switching systems, photonic network migration, and next-generation network intelligence. Because the company's targets include mainstream carriers as well as next generation packet providers, the Calient architecture will support applications as diverse as SONET crossconnect relief and fiber frame upgrades, as well as wavelength management and multi-protocol lambda switching. The company's deep carrier network experience, progressive architecture and applications-oriented software approach enable this wide-ranging service set,"* [see Calient Networks Press Release, May 22, 2000]. By 2006, Calient Networks still exists as a company – but they have few options to grow the company to control a meaningful amount of market share. The challenge that Calient faces is that demand for the products is not substantial enough to provide a viable exit strategy. They are not a large company, therefore, the large service providers are unwilling to purchase and depend on core technology from a small company that is perceived as risky and this eliminates the ability to access the public equity markets. The speculative period of the ITO Revolution is over and Calient must perform by acquiring market share and building a profitable business in order to access the public equity markets. The other option for Calient is to be acquired by a large equipment supplier such as Lucent, Nortel, or Cisco. Unfortunately, the market for Calient's type of technology has been dormant throughout the Apogee stage, thus providing few, if any, acquisition options for the company.

A different perspective of the opportunity that venture capitalist were focusing in the mid-1990s is to look at the number of companies funded by venture capital firms. From 1995 to 2000, there were 14,463 private companies funded by venture capitalists. Of this number 978 went public, 1,529 were acquired, and 1,180 were closed. That left 10,776 companies to resolve their outcome in the post-technology bubble world. In order to obtain a fifteen (15%) percent success rate for the remaining 10,776 companies, 1,616 equity events would be required. Cisco Systems set the bar for technology-related equity events by a networking company in 2000 with 21 acquisitions. Hypothetically, it would require thirty companies similar to Cisco acquiring twenty-one or more companies (646) a year and the opportunity for another 969 companies from this group, to go public. No market could possibly sustain or support this rate of equity events.

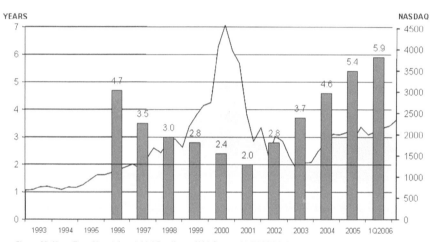

Figure 32: Mean Time (Years) from Initial Funding to M&A Event with NASDAQ Composite Index
Source: Dow Jones VentureOne (www.ventureone.com)

When we look back on the mid to late 1990s, we can identify five basic investment drivers that drove venture capital into the internet, telecom, and optical markets. These five themes can be linked to the five behavioral attributes defined in the lead chapter on Price, Value, and Risk.

Behavioral Attributes	Investment Drivers	Examples
Need for Thought Anchors	**Once in a Lifetime Opportunity**	*Market Barriers Lowered*
Image Transfer	Telecom and Internet Deregulation	*Telecom Act of 1996*
Labeling	Rise of Technology and Science	*Available Investment Capital*
Power of Story and Legends	**Belief in New Market Paradigm**	*Digital Revolution*
Emotional Decisions	Old Economy versus New Economy	*George Gilder*
Decisions Based on Story and Myth	Globalization	*Internet Doubling Every 100 Days*
Overconfidence and Ignorance	**Irrational Exuberance**	*Bull Market of the 1990s*
Induction	Overall Market Conditions	*Economic Conditions*
Lack of Research and Knowledge	Cadence and Endless Opportunities	*Blodget and Grubman*
Herding Behavior	**Greed, Missing Market of Lifetime**	*Easy Investment Exits*
Following the Crowd	Never Before Experienced Market	*Billion Dollar IPOs*
Stationarity	Easy Money	*Many M&A Transactions*
Denial, Not Accepting Mistakes	**Unachievable Expectations**	*NetScape IPO*
Stationarity	Inflated Valuations	*AOL buying Time-Warner*
Refusal to Learn from Errors	Financial Engineering	*Worldcom and Enron*

Figure 33: Behavioral Attributes and Technology Bubble Drivers

Each of these investment drivers played a role in the creation of the ITO bubble and the market downturn that followed. To appreciate the rise and fall of the ITO bubble, we can examine some financial statistics to help define the size and scale of the bubble. There were approximately 1,300 incumbent local exchange companies in the United States before the Telecom Act of 1996. These companies varied in size from small rural phone companies with a few thousand customers to the largest RBOCs. Three hundred CLECs were created and well over one hundred of these CLECs would be bankrupt within five years. In 1996, there were 244 technology related IPOs that generated $13 billion. This number declined in 1997 to 147 technology IPOs generating $6.54 billion. From mid-1998 through the end of 2000, technology related IPOs raised $165 billion and generated $8.7 billion in underwriting fees [see http://www.corante.com/reports/ipo]. $165 billion is an enormous amount of working capital. The war in Iraq and subsequent occupation is estimated to cost the U.S. $251 billion [see http://costofwar.com/numbers.html]. In October 2003, The World Bank estimated that it would cost $55 billion to rebuild Iraq. Subsequently in October 2005, the Congressional Research Service concluded that $251 billion had been spent or obligated for the war in Iraq. Allowing for errors, the total amount of capital raised from technology IPOs from mid-1998 through 2000 would be enough to pay for 65% of Gulf War II and the rebuilding of the nation-state of Iraq. Consider for a moment how these monies were an important driver of the U.S. economy in the late 1990s. *"When you analyze the 370-plus Internet companies that have gone public since Netscape's debut in August 1995, the collective bunch reached a combined market valuation on March 9 of an incredible $1.5 trillion. This number is truly amazing when you figure that it* *was supported by a meager $40-something billion in total sales — most of which were concentrated into the hands of a few companies like Qwest Communications, America Online and Amazon.com. It is also clear that a major day of reckoning came just before taxes were due: on April 14, many of these Internet companies saw their stock prices take a 50 to 70 percent whack. And since April 14, a Darwinian shakeout of Internet businesses has ensued, with almost daily reports of once-promising public and private companies slamming their doors for good. As we sort through the ashes, the debate over the status of the Internet stock bubble rages on. The most immediate question is, of course, Has the bubble completely popped?"* [see Tony Perkins, R*ed Herring*, November 13, 2000]

Outside of the telecommunications industry and investment community, many people probably do not fully comprehend the speed and scale at which the ITO bubble burst. The reason for the public unawareness is that the ITO industries are relatively obscure from a public perspective. Until the personal computer and the internet, most people not working in the technology field had little comprehension of the networking and telephony industries. Before the internet, the telephony services, technology, and networking industries were relatively small in size and did not market consumer based products. They did market consumer services – but as long as the phones and the internet connections are working, most networking companies rarely touch the lives of the average person who is not employed in the ITO industry. In comparison, when the automobile industry began to decline in 1970s, it took nearly twenty years for the membership in the United Auto Workers (UAW) union to decline from 1.5 million members to 732,000. When the ITO markets began to decline, estimates are that 500,000 people lost their jobs in eighteen months. The following is a brief and incomplete summary of work force reductions announced in early 2002:

- SBC Communications; 9,000 jobs by the end of 2002 and another 2,000 in early 2003

- Verizon Communications; eliminated 14,000 jobs in 2002 and another 8,000 in 2003

- BellSouth eliminated 5,000 jobs in 2002 on top of 4,200 jobs reductions in 2001

- AT&T announced the elimination of 3,500 positions in addition to the 10,000 in 2001. Overall employees will be around 68,500 by mid-2003, down from a peak of 128,000

- Sprint announced that it will eliminate 2,100 positions

- MCI-WorldCom announced job cuts of 17,000 in 2002

- Deutsche Telekom (Germany) plans to slash 55,000 jobs over the next three years.

- Cable and Wireless announced it will cut 3,500 jobs in its global division, ending most service on the continent and in North America

- Lucent announced plans to cut another 10,000 jobs, the new layoffs will reduce the company to just 35,000 employees, down from 123,000 in 2000

- Nortel Networks announced it will eliminate another 7,000 jobs. When complete, Nortel's workforce will stand at 35,000, down from 106,000 in 2000

- Alcatel announced it would eliminate an additional 10,000 workers next year on top of the 17,000 employees the company plans to eliminate in 2002. At the end of 2000, Alcatel had 113,000 employees, but only 60,000 will remain by the end of 2003.

- Corning will eliminate another 2,200 jobs on top of the 4,600 jobs cut so far this year.

- Siemens announced plans to cut another 4,000 workers in its fixed-line telephone business, ICN. Siemens' ICN unit is already in the process of eliminating 17,000 jobs this year.

The summary of the job cuts on this list is 205,300. In October 2001, ComputerWorld Magazine reported that telecommunication job cuts for 2001 stood at 225,231 and computer companies had eliminated another 131,658 jobs. Since the ITO market peak in mid-2000, a span of eighteen months, we can identify more than 500,000 positions eliminated by companies in the ITO markets. These jobs are traditionally well paying jobs. Assuming an average salary of $50,000 per year, it amounts to a $25 billion reduction in annual salaries. This is $25 billion less money put into the economies and governments of the nation-states that drove the ITO markets. During the Perigee stage of the ITO Revolution, it was generally believed that a new, digital technology based economy was developing. The support for this belief could be found in the stock market, from intellectuals, analysts, and the government of the United States. *"The impact of IT is also reflected in the capital IT firms currently represent. The collective market capitalizations of five major companies, Microsoft, Intel, Compaq, Dell and Cisco, has grown to over $588 billion in 1997 from under $12 billion in 1987, close to a fifty-fold increase in the space of a decade,"* [see U.S. Department of Commerce, *The Emerging Digital Economy,* April 15, 1998]

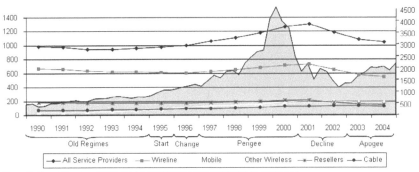

Figure 34: Annual Number of Employees in the Service Provider Industry (in thousands)

Source: Author's adaptation of Federal Communications Commission, *Trends in Telephone Service Report*, June 21, 2005 Chart 5-3

The chart above reflects the employment trends in the telecommunications industry as published by the Federal Communications Commission. Clearly reflected in this chart is the rise of the industry post the Change stage of the ITO Revolution. What is also reflected in this chart is the shrinking size of the industry in terms of employees during the Decline state as well as the first signs of a leveling of employees during the Apogee Stage. It appears that the leveling of the employee pool identified in the later stages of the ITO Revolution is settling near historical employment levels at the beginning of the Change Stage.

The Transition to Apogee Stage of the ITO Revolution

The ITO Revolution entered the Apogee stage during the year 2003. There was no single event to mark the transition, but rather a series of events that signaled the beginning of the convalescence of the revolutionary spirit. Within each component of the ITO Revolution, a single company could be identified as the strongest company. There was a clear competitive imbalance in the market place as one or perhaps two companies were far more dominant than their nearest competitors. In the networking equipment segment, Cisco Systems stands far above Nortel, Juniper, and Lucent. AOL remains the dominant on-line content provider. Yahoo and Google are the two dominant search engine companies. Microsoft has vanquished all rivals and stands as the undisputed provider of computer operating systems and productivity applications. Verizon and SBC are the two strongest telecom service provides in the U.S. market. Comcast provides cable service to more than twenty million subscribers, which is more than double the next largest cable service provider. Even within the mobile phone market, Verizon Wireless has forty-two million subscribers and Cingular has forty-six million subscribers. The nearest rival is the $35 billion dollar merger between Nextel and Sprint called SprintNextel, which will yield a combined subscriber base of thirty-five million – which is approximately one thousand dollars in shareholder value per mobile subscriber. Each market shows that a single company or a duopoly of companies that dominate their market segments. In the business world of the ITO Revolution, these companies are the dictators of their revolution. They are Napoleon, Stalin, Cromwell, and Washington. All the other companies are looking at these companies as the tyrants of their market segment.

In the year 2003 the first signs emerged of a lessoning of tensions produced by the tribunals of the ITO Revolution. Elliot Spitzer's investigations into the many banks and brokerages that played prominent roles during the first five years of the ITO Revolution were on the wane. ITO companies that had been the target of shareholder lawsuits began to settle these lawsuits. Lucent settled all their class action lawsuits stemming from the ITO Revolution in March, 2003 for "…*$315 million in common stock, cash or a combination of both.*" Revolutionary companies and old regimes emerged from the revolutionary carnage with new organizational structures and accountability standards. Nortel's CEO, William Owens, announced in April 2004 that Nortel would "…*meet the highest standards of integrity and transparency in its financial reporting.*" In November of 2005, Qwest announced that it had reached an agreement to settle all shareholder lawsuits for $400 million in cash in three payments. The lawsuits had alleged that Qwest, its board, and former officers had hid information before the company restated $2.2 billion in 2000 earnings and $2.5 billion in 2001 earnings. These earnings had been financially engineered by swapping network capacities at inflated values to make the appearance of capacity and revenue growth. The 2005 settlement was in addition to a 2004 settlement in which Qwest agreed to pay the SEC $250 million, in regard to the same allegations.

Fear of indictment and public scandal began ebb. It is true that the leaders of Enron, Worldcom, and Adelphia were still concluding their day in court, but the public outrage had been tempered by Iraq and the politics of the 2004 presidential election. The country was moving away from the furor of ITO Revolution. A few of the more prominent ITO leaders who felt the backlash of the Decline stage during the period of Apogee were:

- **Bernie Ebbers**: Found guilty in March 2005 of securities fraud, conspiracy, and filing false documents with regulators. On July 13, 2005, Bernie Ebbers was sentenced to twenty-five (25) years in prison for presiding over the largest accounting fraud in U.S. history. There is no parole, but he can reduce his sentence by 15% for positive behavior. Mr. Ebbers was found guilty that, at his direction, WorldCom overstated its results by more than $5 billion over seven quarters and in total masterminded $11 billion in fraud. During his tenure as Worldcom CEO, he borrowed $366 million to cover stock losses, received $772 million in loans to purchase property, and netted $140 million in Worldcom stock sales.

- **Scott Sullivan**: Former WorldCom CFO Scott Sullivan pleaded guilty in March 2004 to three criminal charges. He was sentenced to five year in prison. He made in access of $25 million in Worldcom stock sales.

- **Worldcom Directors and Auditors**: Ten former members of the Board of Directors have agreed to pay $54 million dollars to settle a shareholder law-suit. Trial is waiting to begin for the directors and auditors who have not settled.

- **Jeffrey Skilling**: Former Enron CEO Jeffrey Skilling was indicted on 19 counts of fraud, conspiracy, and insider trading. If convicted on all counts, Skilling faces a maximum sentence of 325 years in prison and millions of dollars in fines, as well as the forfeiture of $66 million in earnings, allegedly received through insider trading. He pleaded not guilty to all charges.

- **Andrew Fastow**: Former Enron CFO, Andrew Fastow, chief architect of the off-the-books deals that brought down Enron, pleaded guilty in January 2004 to two counts of wire and securities fraud. He agreed to a ten-year prison sentence.

- **Rigas Family**: Founder John Rigas and son Timothy Rigas were convicted of corporate-looting and accounting-fraud in 2004. Federal prosecutors in mid-2005 asked a U.S. judge to impose 215-year prison sentences on both family members for their role in the corporate scandal. On June 21, 2005 John Rigas, age 80, was sentenced to 15 years in prison. His son, Timothy Rigas, age 49, was sentenced to 20 years in prison.

- **Jack Grubman**: Agreed to a lifetime ban from the securities industry and to pay a $15 million fine without admitting wrongdoing.

- **Henry Blodget**: The securities fraud investigation brought by New York State Attorney General Elliot Spitzer, resulted in a $1.4 billion settlement with Merrill Lynch. Henry Blodget, the former internet analyst for Merrill Lynch, was fined $4 million and received a lifetime ban from working in the securities industry.

- **Joseph Nacchio**: In March 2005, the SEC filed a civil lawsuit against Joseph P. Nacchio, the former CEO of Qwest Communications International Inc., alleging that he and other executives engaged in a *"massive financial fraud"* to mask the failing financial condition of the company from investors, during a four year period from 1999 through 2002. The SEC alleges that through capacity swaps, Qwest falsely generated revenue on intangible assets to produce $3 billion in revenues over three years to cover short falls in revenue projections. In 2004, Qwest agreed to a $250 million settlement with the SEC to settle corporate charges – but this settlement did not include former executives. In addition to Nacchio, the following were named as part of the complaint: Corporate Officers Robert Woodruff and Robin Szeliga; former Chief Operating Officer Afshin Mohebbi; former Executive Vice President of Qwest's wholesale business Gregory Casey; and two former finance executives James Kozlowski and Frank Noyes.

- **Frank Quattrone**: The National Association of Securities Dealers charged him with IPO spinning. Federal prosecutors charged him with obstructing investigations by a federal grand jury and by the SEC, and witness tampering. In May 2004, he was found guilty on three counts of obstructing justice and witnessing tampering. He was sentenced to 18 months in prison, two years of probation and fined $90,000. In March, 2006 Mr. Quattrone had his sentence remanded and a new trial ordered, due to improper jury instructions. This will be his third trial.

When we examine many of the companies that were major players during the ITO Revolution, we find that old leaders have returned to the industry as well as new leaders having been installed with the mission of resurrecting the company and fixing the shame of scandal or failure. Leadership is a key element in any company's success or failure. In mid-2005, nearly all the companies that struggled during the Decline and Apogee stages of the ITO Revolution have new leaders, while many of the extremist companies that excelled post the Decline stage have not made significant leadership changes. The following is a brief summary of leaders at prominent ITO companies in mid-2005. A common characteristic shared by all is significant experience in the extremists or old regimes of the ITO Revolution.

- **Lucent**: Is led today by Patricia Russo who was with Lucent when it was spun out of AT&T. She was named in the leadership team press release that AT&T released in October of 1995. She left Lucent for a stint at Eastman-Kodak, only to return to replace Henry Schacht during the darkest days of the Apogee Stage of the ITO Revolution. In late Match 2006, Lucent and Alcatel announced that they would merge the two companies. The acquisition of Lucent by Alcatel will leave the United States without a major telecom equipment provider. For nation-state that invented the telecommunication industry, we will no longer have a major innovator in the field. The major telecom centric companies will all be foreign companies: Alcatel, Ericsson, Nokia, Siemens, Nortel and Huawei.

- **Nortel**: Is led by Mike Zafirovski as President and CEO. Prior to Nortel, Zafirovski spent 25 years at General Electric (GE), including 13 years as president and CEO of five businesses in the industrial (GE Lighting) and GE Capital businesses. After GE and before Nortel, Zafirovski spent five years at Motorola including the last three years as COO.

- **Qwest**: In led by Richard Notebaert. Before joining Qwest, Notebaert was president and chief executive officer of Tellabs. Prior to Tellabs, he was Chairman and Chief Executive Officer of Ameritech, which was acquired by SBC. Prior to his role as CEO of Ameritech, Notebart had a long and distinguished career in the Bell System including president of Indiana Bell.

- **CMGI**: Is led by Joe Lawler as Chief Executive Officer. He joined CMGI in August 2004. Prior to CMGI, he was Executive Vice President at RR Donnelley (RRD) – an $8 billion global printer with 30,000 employees. Prior career stops included The Gillette Company, President and CEO of Gander Mountain and Fingerhut Companies.

- **Cisco**: John Chambers leads Cisco Systems.

- **Microsoft**: Bill Gates and Steve Ballmer still lead Microsoft.

- **at&t (Formerly SBC)** Edward E. Whitacre Jr. has been chairman of the board and chief executive officer of SBC Communications Inc since 1990. He began his career at Southwestern Bell Telephone Company in 1963.

- **Verizon**: Is led by Ivan Seidenberg, who has served as CEO since 2002. His career spans 38 years with stops as CEO of Bell Atlantic, NYNEX, and AT&T.

- **Global Crossing**: Global Crossing is led by John Legere. His background is reprinted from the Global Crossing web page, "*As chief executive officer of Global Crossing Limited since October 2001, John steered the company from its entrepreneurial roots to its current operational focus with the completion of the world's first integrated global IP-based network. He kept Global Crossing's network, customer base and employees intact through 681 days of restructuring, emerging on December 9, 2003 with a streamlined cost structure, improved customer satisfaction scores and near-perfect network operations. The company is now a leading provider of IP services worldwide. At AT&T, where John began his telecommunications career, he rose rapidly through the ranks to become one of the telecom giant's youngest officers. He served as head of global strategy and business development and led the company's expansion in Asia as president and chief executive officer of AT&T Asia/Pacific from April 1994 to November 1997. From 1997 to 1998 he was president of worldwide outsourcing at AT&T Solutions, the unit that provided customized support to the company's largest customers. From AT&T John moved to Dell Computer Corporation, spearheading its expansion in Asia so successfully as president of Asia-Pacific from 1998 until February 2000 that he was also named president for Dell's operations in Europe, the Middle East and Africa as well. He then took on the challenge of president and chief executive officer of Asia Global Crossing from February 2000 until January 2002, building a new company from scratch, conducting its successful initial public offering and overseeing construction of its leading-edge fiber-optic network before taking the top spot at Global Crossing.*"

- **Sprint/Nextel**: Sprint is led by Gary Forsee. His background is reprinted from the Sprint web page, "*Gary D. Forsee is chairman and* *chief executive officer of Sprint Corporation. He became chairman of the Board of Directors in May 2003 following his appointment as chief executive officer in March 2003. He has been designated chief executive officer and president of Sprint Nextel when that merger closes, which is expected later in 2005. Forsee has spent more than 30 years in the telecommunications industry. Under his leadership as chairman and CEO, Sprint has emerged as one of the telecommunications industry's strongest competitors. Forsee transformed Sprint's operational structure by moving from product-focused divisions to a customer-centric model, allowing Sprint to more effectively market its broad portfolio of services and to focus on innovative retail and wholesale strategies that emphasize strategic partnerships. He combined Sprint's two tracking stocks into a single stock representing all of the company's assets. In 2004, Sprint's equity value increased by 74 percent, far outpacing the performance of every major industry competitor and outdistancing the major indices by significant margins. BusinessWeek magazine recognized him as one of the 19 best managers of 2004. Prior to taking Sprint's top position, Forsee served as vice chairman of BellSouth Corporation where he had responsibility for all of BellSouth's domestic operations and chaired the Cingular Wireless joint venture. Upon joining BellSouth in September 1999, Forsee managed staff functions throughout the corporation and subsequently was president of BellSouth International. Forsee initially joined Sprint in December of 1989 in the Government Systems Division, where he was president. Over the next nine years, he served as president-Business Services Group, interim chief executive officer of Sprint PCS, and president and chief operating officer of Sprint's Long Distance Division. In 1998, Forsee assumed the position of president and chief executive officer of Global One located in Brussels, Belgium, a joint venture of Sprint, France Telecom and Deutsche Telekom. Prior to joining Sprint, Forsee was with AT&T and Southwestern Bell for almost 18 years. The position he held prior to moving to Sprint was vice president of government sales and programs in AT&T's Federal Systems division.*" It the declining world of unprofitable wireline voice revenues, Sprint and Nextel agreed to a $35 billion merger that was approved by shareholders on July 13, the same day that Bernie Ebbers was sentenced to prison. As the onetime pursuer of Sprint who valued the company at $115 billion goes to prison, the current leaders of Sprint have decided to evolve the company into a mobile provider powerhouse and move away from wireline and broadband services.

- **AOL**: AOL/Time-Warner is today led by a person who does not have an ITO career background. Richard Parsons was named CEO is

2002. His background is reprinted from the AOL/Time-Warner web page, *"Richard D. Parsons is Chairman of the Board and Chief Executive Officer of Time Warner Inc., whose businesses include filmed entertainment, interactive services, television networks, cable systems and publishing. He became CEO in May 2002 and Chairman of the Board in May 2003. Since becoming CEO, Mr. Parsons has led Time Warner's turnaround and set the company on a solid path toward achieving sustainable growth. In the process, he has put in place the industry's most experienced and successful management team, strengthened the company's balance sheet and simplified its corporate structure, and carried out a disciplined approach to realigning the company's portfolio of assets to improve returns. In its January 2005 report on America's Best CEOs, Institutional Investor magazine named Mr. Parsons the top CEO in the entertainment industry. Before becoming CEO, Mr. Parsons served as the company's Co-Chief Operating Officer, overseeing its content businesses-Warner Bros., New Line Cinema, Warner Music Group and Time Warner Book Group-as well as two key corporate functions: Legal and People Development. Mr. Parsons joined Time Warner as its President in February 1995, and has been a member of the company's Board of Directors since January 1991. As President, he oversaw the company's filmed entertainment and music businesses, and all corporate staff functions, including financial activities, legal affairs, public affairs and administration. Before joining Time Warner, Mr. Parsons was Chairman and Chief Executive Officer of Dime Bancorp, Inc., one of the largest thrift institutions in the United States. Previously, he was the managing partner of the New York law firm Patterson, Belknap, Webb & Tyler. Prior to that, he held various positions in state and federal government, as counsel for Nelson Rockefeller and as a senior White House aide under President Gerald Ford. Mr. Parsons received his undergraduate education at the University of Hawaii and his legal training at Union University's Albany Law School."*

In the early days of the ITO Revolution there was significant attention lauded on the old economy versus the new economy. Companies had to transition to web time or internet time and required a presence on the web to capture the millions of customers who were in the process of abandoning the old ways of business. This is one of the two fundamental reasons why so many competitive telecom services companies were created. A large market was created through government deregulation that was enabling subscriber mobility. Before the ITO Revolution, how many choices for local telephone service did a consumer have? The answer is very few if they had a choice at all. Web based retailers now had a conduit to potential customers on global basis. Amazon.com did not have to build thousands of stores to compete with Wal-Mart. All that Amazon.

com needed was a good web site, a warehouse full of products to sell and consumers from across the U.S. and around the world would forgo the hassle of the shopping mall on the day after Thanksgiving to surf Amazon's virtual store in the comfort of their home.

The transition from Decline to Apogee includes the realization that the new ways do not fully supplant the old ways and that many of the revolutionary theses do not prove to be accurate. Barnes and Noble did not go out of business because of Amazon.com. If Amazon.com had remained a retailer of only books and CDs, it most likely would be valued equal to or less to Barnes and Noble. Amazon.com is projected to have revenues of roughly $8 billion in 2005 and Barnes and Noble is projected to have revenues of $6 billion – yet Amazon.com has a market capitalization of $18 billion to Barnes and Noble's market capitalization of $2.2 billion. One of the fundamental differences between the two companies is that Amazon.com has $1.1 billion in cash with a debt of $1.7 billion, compared to Barnes and Noble who has $190 million in cash and $245 million in debt.

When the CLECs ran out of money and their business models did not fulfill expectations, it became clear to the many investors in the telecom services market that little had changed during the period from 1996 to 2004. Trillions of dollars were spent, fortunes were won and lost, but in reality the competition for the local loop simply does not exist on a broad and vast scale. The majority, roughly 85% of the 185 million local loops in the U.S, are controlled by the four, going to three, baby bells. At the time when AT&T announced the divesture of the baby bells, they had a combined market cap of $47.5 billion. In late 2004 the combined market cap of the four remaining bells is $258 billion dollars. It is very likely that if you were a customer of Bellsouth in 1988, you are still a Bellsouth customer in 2005. Bell Atlantic and Nynex are now called Verizon, but customers in Texas are still getting phone bills from SBC as they did in 1985. Microsoft is still the most important software company in the U.S. Netscape did not put Microsoft out of business. People still shop at Wal-Mart, Barnes and Noble, and Target and the new economy never really materialized as an entity to supplant the old economy. What the new economy did become is an adjunct method of commerce to supplant the old economy. People still prefer to socialize. We are a world of browsers and that is why people enjoy going to Barnes and Noble and Starbucks. The internet did bring many new and creative services that provide access to information, but the internet did not supplant the old ways of doing business. The cutting of the Gordian knot occurred when the realization that a wholesale replacement of the old economy was not going to occur nor was the internet going to be the genesis of vast new economic markets. The same companies that controlled the local loop in 1984, that AT&T was committed to divesting, still own those local loops in 2005 and there are now three of them instead of seven. Wal-Mart, Target, Barnes and Noble, and many other bricks and mortar retailers are doing just fine.

The election of 2004 in the United States might have served as transition event for the ITO Revolution from Decline to the Apogee stage. The reelection of George W. Bush was an event that was different from the election in 2000. The long disputed end to the 2000 presidential election in the United States was the event that defined the transition from the Perigee to the Decline stage. President Clinton's polices ended when George Bush assumed the Presidency. The economy of the U.S. began to enter into a recession. The markets served by the ITO Revolution all began a rapid decline. Then 9/11 happened, followed by the wars in Afghanistan and Iraq. When Bush won reelection in 2004, there was sense of finality in the society. The war in Iraq was over – yet the peace still needed to be won and nation-state rebuilt. The election of 2004 also ensured that Bush's policies would extend for another four years. When President Bush made his first State of the Union address on February 2, 2005, *"In these four years, Americans have seen the unfolding of large events. We have known times of sorrow, and hours of uncertainty, and days of victory. In all this history, even when we have disagreed, we have seen threads of purpose that unite us. The attack on freedom in our world has reaffirmed our confidence in freedom's power to change the world. We are all part of a great venture: To extend the promise of freedom in our country, to renew the values that sustain our liberty, and to spread the peace that freedom brings. As Franklin Roosevelt once reminded Americans, "each age is a dream that is dying, or one that is coming to birth." And we live in the country where the biggest dreams are born. The abolition of slavery was only a dream -- until it was fulfilled. The liberation of Europe from fascism was only a dream -- until it was achieved. The fall of imperial communism was only a dream -- until, one day, it was accomplished. Our generation has dreams of its own, and we also go forward with confidence. The road of Providence is uneven and unpredictable -- yet we know where it leads: It leads to freedom."* These are not the words of a revolution – but rather the words of reconciliation and settling. It was time to transition from uncertainty to certainty. It was time to begin a settling process which is the end-result of the Apogee stage of the G3 Market Model.

The New Economy Companies Funded in Perigee

Starting new companies and venture capital investments were an important aspect of the ITO Revolution. Understanding the business outcome of these companies and the success and failure of their business plan is a critical element to understanding the revolutionary cycle for technology and business markets. Startup companies that were started late in the G3MM of the ITO

Revolution had few exit options once power started to concentrate in the hands of the extremists during the Decline stage. Three startups that became public companies late in the ITO Revolution highlight the challenges of the market when power is concentrated in the hands of the extremists. The four companies to be examined are interesting because each was led by a successful ITO Revolutionary and all had their business plans and technology lauded by leading intellectuals of the ITO Revolution. The intellectuals who were early voices of change that lauded the ITO Revolution viewed these four companies as important examples of the ITO Revolution. The four companies are TeraBeam, Tellium, Sycamore, and Zhone Technologies.

TeraBeam started life as an early player in the free space optics market. The free space optics technology market vertical, of the ITO Revolution, is a perfect example of an investment idea that never lived up to the expectations. During the Perigee stage there were several prominent startups building products for the free space optics market that was about to explode upon the world. These companies were AirFiber, MRV, Maxima, TeraBeam, AOptix Technologies, Laserbit, CableFree, PAV Data, and LightPointe. Two notable companies from this list that failed were AirFiber, which closed down in February 2003 after burning through $92 million in venture capital, and TeraBeam, which raised $526 million.

TeraBeam was another company developing disruptive technology that was going to revolutionize the telecom services industry. An investor in TeraBeam and their technology was Lucent Technologies. In an April 11, 2000 press release, Lucent announced that it was *"...investing cash, certain research and development assets, intellectual property, and free-space optical products valued at $450 million. TeraBeam is contributing research and development assets, manufacturing assets, intellectual property, and free space optical products."* TeraBeam was also the subject of high praise from George Gilder, a leading intellectual of the ITO Revolution. The company was prominently featured in chapter 17 of his book Telecosm, which was named the *"Terabeam Era"* [see, Gilder pages 232-241]. In the chapter, Gilder describes the technology that Terabeam was developing and how the company was planning to provides systems for a nation-wide rollout of wireless, optical technologies that would revolutionize the last mile.

George Gilder was not the only leading intellectual of the ITO Revolution to champion the TeraBeam story. Jack Grubman, Salomon Smith Barney telecom analyst and former AT&T executive, said TeraBeam might have the *"...best senior management team of any telecommunications start-up in history... My hunch is that {TeraBeam is} the next meteoric rise in the emerging telecom space. . . This is the first example of revolutionary technology I've seen in twenty-three years."* This quote from Jack Grubman was cited in many articles written about TeraBeam in 2000, but the quote varies from article to article and no author really cites the actual text from the research report that Grubman allegedly produced on the company. In another article written about TeraBeam, Jim Friedland of Robertson Stephens was quoted to have said; *"Terabeam could be as disruptive to telecom services as Microsoft and Intel were to technology."* A few analysts were uncertain as to the potential of TeraBeam. *"This is something that makes too much sense to stand alone in the marketplace, so they'll see competition, but they'll have the first-mover advantage, and they'll have the opportunity to dominate. Five years from now, if Terabeam has not been acquired, they'll either be a hero or a zero. I don't think you'll ever see them limp along,"* [see Jeff Kagan, an independent telecom industry analyst, February 26, 2001].

Adding to the aura around TeraBeam was the well published arrival of Dan Hesse who left the position of President and CEO of AT&T Wireless Services and Executive Vice President of AT&T. Prior to this position, Mr. Hesse had a long and distinguished career at AT&T. He had previously held positions as Vice President and General Manager for the AT&T Online Services Group and as President and CEO of AT&T Networks Systems International, which became the international business unit of Lucent Technologies. The interesting aspect of Mr. Hesse's arrival at TeraBeam was that it occurred prior to the spin off from AT&T of AT&T Wireless. It was also widely reported that he left $20 to $50 million in stock options that would have occurred with the AT&T Wireless spinout to join TeraBeam. Thus, we have a company that has acquired a significant investment and relationship with Lucent, hired a high-profile CEO from AT&T, and was lauded by the most powerful banker and the leading futurist of the ITO Revolution. If there was ever a company poised for success, it was TeraBeam. This is the reason we are studying TeraBeam. TeraBeam seemed to have all the ingredients needed for success. Why was it a failure?

In 2000, the market for free space optics (FSO) was still an unknown. In May of 2001, Merrill Lynch published a report that estimated the market for FSO equipment would grow from $100 million in 2000 to more than $2 billion by 2005. In September of the same year other industry analyst groups made similar predictions of a $2-3 billion dollar market by 2005. The challenge that TeraBeam would face was two faceted. The first was that their technology did not live up to the hype that surrounded the company. The second was that their target market disappeared during the Decline stage of the ITO Revolution. TeraBeam was developing a competitive access technology that used free space optics to bypass the local loop. *"'Periodically technology is developed that has the power to significantly change the landscape,' said Rich McGinn, chairman and CEO, Lucent Technologies. 'TeraBeam's Fiberless Optical Network system is such a disruptive technology. We are pleased to be working with TeraBeam to help them bring their gigabit speed Internet access to customer.'"* {see Lucent Press Release, April 12, 2000}.

The customers who were interested in bypassing the local loop were the new revolutionaries who did not own any local loops. TeraBeam's technology missed the spending window that occurred during the Perigee stage. When TeraBeam was ready with their technology to solve the problem of the local loop, the extremists were taking control of the market and they did not need to procure technology to bypass the local loop.

Unfortunately for TeraBeam the promise of their technology did not meet the expectations of the company and their customers. As market conditions continued to worsen throughout 2002, TeraBeam's investors quickly soured on the prospects for the company. TeraBeam still had a sizable cash position, but the relationship with Lucent was terminated in September. Seventeen months after Rich McGinn and Dan Hesse hailed Lucent's investment as a pillar for a bright future for TeraBeam; the relationship came to end as Lucent was struggling to survive the Decline stage of the ITO Revolution. Buried in a September 2002 Lucent quarterly filing, was this reference to the TeraBeam investment, *"On April 9, 2000, Lucent and TeraBeam Corporation entered into an agreement to develop TeraBeam's fiberless optical networking system that provides high-speed data networking between local and wide area networks. Under the agreement, Lucent paid cash and contributed research and development assets, intellectual property and free-space optical products, valued in the aggregate at $450. On September 26, 2001, Lucent and TeraBeam agreed to terminate most of the existing arrangements between the parties. Pursuant to the agreement, the 30% interest held by Lucent in the venture that develops the fiberless optical networking system was exchanged for a 15% interest in TeraBeam Corporation in the second quarter of fiscal 2002. As a result of exiting the original arrangement and an evaluation of the restructured investment as of September 30, 2001, the remaining investment and goodwill and other acquired intangibles of $328 were written-off and included in the fiscal 2001 business restructuring charge. In the fourth quarter of fiscal 2002, the remaining 15% interest was sold for $5 and included as part of the fiscal 2002 business restructuring charge,"* [see *Lucent 10-K*, December 12, 2002, page 108].

The final outcome of the TeraBeam story involved an acquisition by an unlikely company. On April 14, 2004 YDI Wireless announced that it was merging with TeraBeam. The acquisition of TeraBeam by YDI Wireless was completed on June 22, 2004 for approximately $48.1 million. For a company that at one time commanded investments of more than five-hundred million dollars and valuation well more than a billion dollars, this outcome was a disappointment. Ironically, the acquisition of TeraBeam was completed by a microwave radio system provider – which is the technology that TeraBeam was intending to replace with their high-speed, WDM free space optical equipment. In his March 2000 newsletter, futurist George Gilder commented that microwaves were *"...mostly a default paradigm. But now that episode is over, and the TeraBeam era begins."*

Tellium was founded in early 1997 by a group of Bellcore veterans. Bellcore was the research business unit of the Regional Bell Operating Companies (RBOCs) that were divested from AT&T in 1994. Bellcore was acquired by SAIC in 1997. As part of the acquisition agreement, the RBOCs required that Bellcore drop the "bell" portion from the name of the company. The founding of Tellium by revolutionaries from the old regime of Bellcore provide us with further evidence that the fundamental shift in the U.S. telecom market that opened never before opportunities. Revolution was the game in 1997 and the diffusion of power, coupled with the market, opportunity was a combination that many intellectuals from the old regimes could not pass up.

Tellium provides another fascinating case study for the ITO Revolution. The company was founded by revolutionaries from an old regime. They successfully designed, built, and sold an optical switch to large telecom service providers. Even more impressive was Tellium's ability to secure major commitments from customers to purchase an enormous amount of Tellium product in their short history. Tellium even completed an IPO, thus raising a vast amount of working capital and positioning the company for the future. Yet today, Tellium does not exist. It products are discontinued; its employees work at other companies, and their once bright future was swept away in the furor of the Decline stage of the ITO Revolution.

Although founded by revolutionaries from Bellcore, Tellium's CEO came from a different background. Harry Carr was named Chairman and CEO of Tellium in January 2000. He arrived at Tellium with a career background that included time at a familiar old regime and two revolutionary companies of the ITO Revolution. As with many of the corporate leaders of the ITO Revolution, Harry Carr had a significant and prominent career at AT&T. In 1997, Harry Carr joined Yurie Systems as Chief Operating Officer, which was the ninth company acquired by Lucent Technologies on May 29, 1998, for approximately one billion dollars in cash. At Lucent, Mr. Carr served as Chief Operating Officer and then President of Lucent Technologies Inc.'s Broadband Carrier Networks business unit, which focused on selling data switching products to the service provider market. This is significant, because by all accounts Harry Carr was an extremely successful ITO Revolutionary when he assumed the responsibilities of CEO at Tellium. He was winner. He had evolved from a role at an old regime to a leadership role at prominent revolutionary which was acquired for a vast sum of money by another revolutionary leader by the name of Lucent Technologies. Still the siren call of revolution pulled Mr. Carr back to another ITO Revolutionary in January 2000.

In September 2000, Tellium filed to go public. On the dawn of the Decline stage, Tellium filed to rise $250 million from the public equity markets. In the S-1 filed by Tellium, there were three important commercial deals reveled as well as an equity reward structure that had become common during the frenzied early stages of the ITO Revolution. Tellium's lead customer was a company called Extant. In April of 2000, Tellium reported that Extant had deployed nine of its optical switches with a planned deployment of another 41 switches through 2001. This is a significant achievement for a company the size of Tellium – but there was a forbidding warning in the Tellium S-1. The warning stated, *"Moreover, while Extant has agreed to purchase its full requirements for optical switches from us for the first three years of the contract, Extant is not contractually obligated to purchase future products or services from us, and may discontinue doing so at any time. Extant is permitted to terminate the agreement for, among other things, a breach of our material obligations under the contract. Extant has announced that it is being acquired by Dynegy, Inc., a publicly traded company. Dynegy may determine not to proceed with Extant's planned network build-out on a timely basis, or at all. Accordingly, Dynegy's acquisition of Extant creates additional uncertainties regarding our existing arrangements with Extant and may adversely affect our ability to derive future revenues from Extant."*

The Tellium S-1 also revealed two additional wins for the Tellium product. These wins were with Cable & Wireless for $350 million and Qwest for $300 million. Tellium had scored two big contracts, worth $650 million over the next five years. This is how a startup goes public. The only caveat to these contracts was they both contained mechanisms to reduce their contract value or outright terminate the purchase agreement. At the time of the deals, termination was the last option that anyone was willing to predict. Tellium looked like a winner and clearly they were going to go public at the very end of the Perigee stage of the ITO Revolution. *"We closed this deal completely on our own, no vendor financing, no equity. We won this account on our own merits,"* [see Harry Carr, Chairman and CEO of Tellium, September 12, 2000].

When Lucent, Nortel, and Cisco used their balance sheets to provide vendor financing, it changed the competitive nature of the telecom equipment market. Smaller companies could not compete. Using the example of Winstar, why would Winstar turn down the loan of $2 billion from Lucent to spend their own money on products from a company such as Tellium? The answer is; they would not, as along as the terms of the loan were agreeable. Revolutions and markets, whether technical or financial, are about action and reaction. When the big public companies provided loans to secure deals, the private companies responded by providing stock options. Stock options were the anti-vendor financing move by the startups. Interesting to note is that both strategies are really only viable in extremely positive market conditions. Stock options are worthless if their value is not appreciating and companies are not going to loan money to customers if their balance sheet is weak. Both actions occurred because power during the Perigee stage was diffused. If market share (i.e. power) was concentrated in the hands of the few suppliers, as it was during the old regimes, there would be no need to provide vendor financing. The corollary is that private companies could not use stock options to entice buyers if the buyers did not have a reasonable expectation that the stock options would be of value. These stock options become valuable when they are liquid; when they become publicly traded. Private companies, fraught with risk, only go public in times of revolution, when power is less concentrated and market barriers are lower.

When Tellium published their S-1, they had to reveal that they had awarded Extant two million shares of stock and Qwest had received 5.2 million shares. In addition, Tellium also sold 333,333 shares of pre-IPO shares to several Qwest executives. Clearly, these arrangements make it appear as if Tellium used stock options to influence the decision makers at Extant and Qwest. An interesting element of the Qwest stock award was that the Tellium team tied the stock warrants to performance milestones of the Qwest contract. Hence, as Qwest purchases product from Tellium, it also ensures value of Tellium's stock. In a perfect world, Qwest would make vast purchases of Tellium equipment, which would drive up the value of Tellium's stock and Qwest would be able to recoup much of the capital spent on Tellium product by selling Tellium stock. It is not quite as perfect as a loan of two billion dollars, but it's not bad, especially when the deal is sweetened with stock personally awarded to key executives within your customer. Not only would Qwest the corporation do well with purchases of Tellium equipment, but the executives who made the decision will enjoy some personal reward for choosing Tellium as well. The contracts with Qwest, C&W, and Extant are important because they represent a validation of the ITO Revolution. Intellectuals who had extolled the virtues of the revolution used the commitments to Tellium as data points to size the market. *"As I said, Tellium's triumph helps validate the entire optical switching industry. Big contracts with big ISPs and carriers will be immensely important this year, setting the stage for significant growth in 2001,"* [see Scott Clavenna, President of PointEast Research and Director of research at Light Reading http://www.lightreading.com, September 26, 2000].

When Tellium was attempting to go public, the first signs of the Decline were emerging. Lucent made their first announcement regarding slower demand in mid 2000 and then warned of missed revenue expectations on October 10, 2000. Rich McGinn left Lucent on October 23, 2000. Lucent announced their first revenue recognition issues stemming from the WinStar situation on November 21, 2000. The internet element of the ITO Revolution had long since passed into the hands of the extremists. Intellectuals and revolutionaries were beginning to have doubts about the new economy. The revolution was not meeting their objectives. The new social order was not taking affect. The Tellium S-1 was an important sign to the revolutionaries and intellectuals. It was evidence that the new social infrastructure was still be deployed. The new economy was still replacing the old economy.

There was another event described in the Tellium S-1 that would have an important bearing on the final outcome of the Tellium story. Tellium had provided loans to its senior executives to procure restricted stock options granted by the company. The loans were not free as they did carry an annual interest rate, but this granting of loans would have a detrimental affect on the company's leadership team. Tellium provided loans of $17.6 million to eight executives and an additional $14 million dollar loan to Harry Carr, in total, $31.6 million, to purchase Tellium stock. It was expected that these loans would be easily repayable when the executives sold their sales public and exercise value plus interest was paid back to the corporation. During the ITO Revolution, there was nothing unusual about this practice. The stock options awarded to key employees were termed ISO stock options which carried the ability to be purchased and than held for more then one year. If ISO stock options are held for year, they provide an additional benefit of being subject to a lower tax rate than traditional non-qualified stock options, which must be sold immediately upon exercising. The loan provided by Tellium to these executives enabled the ISO stock options to be purchased and the clock started on reaching the important one year date. This is an excellent strategy as long as the public value of the stock continues to increase or does not fall below the exercise price of the stock option.

The Tellium IPO was priced in the $13-15 per share range in early November 2000. It was expected that this price range would provide the company with proceeds of approximately $250 million. The pricing of the proposed Tellium IPO came at an interesting time in the ITO Revolution. The extremists companies where gaining real market share. Tellium's business, which appeared healthy, was actually quite unhealthy. The business with Dynegy was not viable over the long term. Dynegy was a moderate ITO revolutionary. When the ITO market represented a significant opportunity with low market barriers, Dynegy was a revolutionary and wanted to invest in the market. When the ITO market conditions turned difficult and the Terror descended during the Decline stage, Dynegy realized that it was not as committed as the extremists and exited a challenging market. Qwest was another moderate ITO revolutionary. Although Qwest had purchased an old regime in the form of US West, the portion of the company that was purchasing the Tellium product was located in the revolutionary side of the company. Qwest was purchasing Tellium's product for their nationwide optical backbone as part of the unregulated business. As soon as market conditions changed and customers stopped purchasing services off this network or went out of business, the need to continue investing in their nationwide optical network ended. The vast majority of Qwest's cash flow is from the regulated side of the business.

By early 2001, Tellium had still not gone public. Market conditions had continued to worsen and the financial community had begun to question the market value of another optical systems company. In order to complete the IPO and raise much needed capital, Tellium decided to add intellectual leaders to their cause. In March 2001, Tellium revised the scope of the IPO ambitions downward to $8-10 per share, with the expectation of raising $150 million dollars. In addition, they added Morgan-Stanley to the IPO team. Even in the deteriorating market conditions, when the full extent of the power of the extremists was still unknown, Tellium, Morgan Stanley Dean Witter, Thomas Weisel Partners, UBS Warburg, CIBC World Markets, and Wit Soundview were going to muscle the Tellium IPO before the market window closed. At the time, although market conditions had worsened, many of the leading intellectuals of the ITO Revolution did not fully realize the scope of the changes occurring in the ITO markets. *"In June {2000} I revised my optical switch forecasts sharply downward. I didn't feel any differently about the viability of the market, but six months of listening to carriers convinced me reliability would be an overwhelming factor in purchase decisions, even though they remained overwhelmingly favorable toward optical switches. Combine that with the fact that vendors are taking a bit more time than anticipated to bring products to market, and forecasts shift noticeably to the right... By 2004, the market is forecast to reach a robust $7.5 billion, creating ample room for numerous successful vendors. This curve is in line with many emerging optical networking markets, which tend to be smaller in the near term than many hoped but larger over the long term, as the inexorable migration continues. In the end, the optical switch market remains very strong, with extremely aggressive,"* [see Scott Clavenna, President of PointEast Research and Director of research at Light Reading http://www. lightreading.com, September 26, 2000]. Rudy Baca, an analyst with the Precursor Group commented on the Tellium S-1 filing, *"There's a tremendous amount of competition. The past few years, however, have seen the development of markets in which smaller players can bring new technologies and have them adopted quickly. The providers themselves are not sure how the networks are going to develop or at what pace. We feel that it is likely to be a very solid growth market."* The Tellium S-1 filing acted as a self-fulfilling market prophecy. The technology was new, the markets were new, no one had a definitive idea of the market direction, Tellium has lined up customer commitments, therefore this must be an important marker direction and the Tellium S-1 confirms the existence of the market.

By May 2001, Tellium's executive team was on the road promoting their IPO. The size of the offering had been reduced for a third time and on May,

17, 2001 Tellium went public on the NASDAQ, raising $135 million. Lucent had already succumbed to the pressures of the Decline stage and Nortel had begun an inexorable spiral into the abyss. Tellium's closest competitor Ciena was still riding high because Ciena had won the last major optical backbone to be built in the United States. It was a network called Calpoint that was being built by Qwest. Even with overwhelming evidence that dramatic changes were occurring in the market, Tellium was able to raise money in the public markets by assembling a syndicate of powerful and influential underwriters. Shares of Tellium were publicly listed by an underwriting group managed by Morgan Stanley and Thomas Weisel Partners LLC, and co-managed by UBS Warburg, CIBC World Markets, and Wit SoundView. In addition to a powerful banking syndicate, Tellium hired a public relations firm to manage the perception of Tellium in the market. The firm Morrissey & Company stated that, *"Tellium faced its IPO at a time when the economy was slowing, IPOs were at a near standstill, and there was a general feeling of malaise in the business environment."* The solution offered by Morrisseey & Company was to begin a public campaign to raise awareness and shape the public perception of Tellium. *"For months prior to the IPO, Morrissey & Company and Tellium worked together to establish the company as an important industry player and position the company to move forward with its IPO in the spring of 2001. As the stock market became increasingly shaky in late 2000 and early 2001 and the telecommunications industry began to slide, Morrissey & Company took careful steps to position Tellium as a long-term player built on superior technology and some of the smartest minds in the industry. Morrissey & Company assessed the competitors, the markets and other*

IPOs, seeking to uncover Tellium's best assets. Tellium's strengths included leading optical networking scientists and their patents, the telecom experience of Tellium's leadership, and the company's focus on a single type of superior product. This story gave Tellium a pedigree in its industry, and awareness of Tellium swelled among telecommunications and major business media. Months prior to its IPO, Tellium was named by major business publications as a 'company to watch.' Major media outlets covered Tellium around its IPO and thereafter, indicating they had watched the company carefully throughout its extended quiet period and were ready to watch the company grow further." This is how revolutionaries and intellectuals [see *Essay One, Chapter Three for Thought Leadership Model*] use the forces of revolution to shape public perception.

The Terror of the Decline stage swirling around Tellium in 2001 and 2002 began to take its toll on Tellium's limited customer base. It also revealed the fragility of Tellium's business. On December 17, 2002 Tellium and Cable and Wireless announced a restructuring of their $350M contract that was signed in August 2000 and touted as one of the pillars of Tellium's business and foundation for their IPO. The net result was that C&W agreed to purchase an undisclosed amount of Tellium product and their remaining balance of the $350 million dollar commitment was forgiven. Deployment of the Tellium product was expected to start in early 2001, but the Terror of the Decline stage sweeping through the ITO Revolution had taken its toll on C&W. By 2002, C&W had announced massive layoffs and began closing more than half its data centers.

Of the three big contracts that Tellium touted as part of the IPO plan, all three were significantly revised or fulfilled. The Qwest contract had been reduced from $300 million to $100 million. The Dynegy contract (inherited from Extant) was nearly fulfilled by the end of 2002. In short, Tellium had run out of contracts and customers by the end of the 2002. Tellium's revenue fell from $46 million in Q1 2002, to $3 million, to $1.9 million, and $2.9 million for the remaining quarters of the 2002. In the first two quarters of 2003, revenues were $10 million each, which probably means the settlement with C&W called for them to purchase a total of $20 million over six months – which is considerable less than $350 million.

The net result of the Tellium IPO during the Decline stage was a series of shareholder lawsuits. In the span of few weeks since announcing the amended C&W contract, Tellium was sued five times by class action shareholder lawsuits. The primary allegation of the lawsuits was that the IPO was based on inflated estimates of the contract values that Tellium signed with Qwest and that Tellium's executives knowingly inflated these estimates to complete the IPO. As evidence of this assertion, the class action suit surmised that the Qwest executives were culpable because they knew the contract value was inflated, but supported the assertion because they had received shares in Tellium. In defense of Tellium, the ITO market was rapidly changing in 2001 and 2002. Few people realized the real size and extent at which the ITO markets had been overstated. *"While we continue to believe the worst quarters are behind us from a revenue perspective, we believe it is critical to continuously evaluate and realign our costs. We are committed to revenue growth and we remain focused on accelerating our path to profitability. We expect these difficult decisions will enhance our stability as a business, reduce our cash burn significantly, and allow us to remain a technology leader in optical switching,"* [see Harry Carr, CEO of Tellium, January 10, 2003]

As 2003 dawned, Tellium continued to make dramatic changes to their business model. In January of 2003, they announced a layoff of 130 employees or approximately 40% of their workforce. The prevailing mantra amongst startups and bubble era IPO companies at this time was: cash conservation. Reduce the burn rate and wait for the market to return to a growth period. Unfortunately this was an incorrect analysis of the evolution of the markets. In late July, 2003, Tellium announced that it was being acquired by a company called Zhone Technologies and that the new company would be called Zhone

Technologies and assume the public listing that Tellium held on the NASDAQ. In the end, the merger between Zhone and Tellium was motivated by several objectives. The loans provided by Tellium to its executives to acquire stock options in Tellium had an enormous tax burden associated with exercising of the options to combined value of $9.7 million. If Tellium's stock price had continued to rise or stay above the strike price of the option grants, then the executive team would have made money. Unfortunately, the value of Tellium stock fell below the value at which they purchased the stock options and the tax burden was assessed at the exercise rate. When the value of the stock fell, they could not sell the shares, they could not repay the loans, and they still had a tax burden to the U.S. government. The solution to this problem was for Tellium to merge with Zhone. Zhone forgave the executive loans (value of $21.6 million) and paid the tax liability (value $15.million), assumed Tellium's remaining cash, closed all of Tellium operations in New Jersey, and became a publicly listed company through an one for four reverse stock split.

Zhone Technologies was founded in 1999 by Mory Ejabat and Jeanette Symons. Mory and Jeanette were driving leaders within one of the biggest winners from the ITO Revolution, a company called Ascend Communications. In 1999, the Ascend leadership team sold the company to Lucent for $24 billion. Closing one of the biggest deals during the ITO Revolution did not satisfy the revolutionary desire of Mory Ejabat. Zhone Technologies was started in 1999 with a staggering first investment of $500 million from a variety of investment sources. About a year after founding, Zhone began to publicly speak about its corporate strategy. The company plan was to build what was fashionably termed in the Perigee stage of the ITO Revolution as a "God Box." Zhone's plan was to build a product that combined the functions of an edge switch, router, broadband access, DSLAM, and subscriber management functions into a single, cost effective product. When the Perigee stage ended and the Decline stage began, Zhone changed their corporate strategy and adopted a hybrid strategy from the bubble era, to be employed in post-bubble era; they started acquiring companies, products and distressed assets. The difference between Zhone's strategy and that of Cisco, Nortel, and Lucent during the peak of the ITO Revolution; Zhone was a buyer at the revolution bottom and the others were buyers during the rise of the ITO Revolution.

Date	Company	Transaction Value Announced	Currency
Jul-04	Sorrento Networks	$36.8 M	Stock
Feb-04	Gluon	$7M	Cash and Stock
Jul-03	Tellium	$181M	Stock
Jan-03	NEC Eluminant	$13.6M	Undisclosed
Jul-02	Vpacket	$19.2M	Undisclosed
Aug-01	Nortel AccessNode and UE	$37.7M	Undisclosed
Feb-01	Xybridge	$72.7M	Undisclosed
Feb-00	OptoPhone	$2.2M	Undisclosed
Feb-00	Roundview	$300k	Undisclosed
Nov-99	CAG Technologies	$8.8M	Undisclosed
Oct-99	Premisys	$296.8M	Undisclosed

Figure 35: Zhone Acquisitions
Source: Zhone's Web Page and SEC Filings

The total sum of the acquisitions made by Zhone total $675 million, which by the standards set during the Perigee stage of the ITO Revolution is quite modest. According to SEC filings by Zhone, the acquisitions of CAG Technologies, OptoPhone, and Xybridge have been written off. Even before the Tellium acquisition, it was clear that Zhone had an IPO as a corporate objective. Zhone filed to go public on October 2000. The lead underwriters for the filing were Credit Suisse First Boston, with Lehman Brothers, UBS Warburg, Thomas Weisel Partners, and U.S. Bancorp Piper Jaffray as co-underwriters. As the ITO markets continued to accelerate into the Decline stage, Zhone was forced to withdraw their IPO in May of 2001. At the time, Tim Donovan a Zhone spokesman said, *"This isn't any reflection of our core business or how we feel about the company. We now have a couple of new products we haven't announced yet that we're deriving revenue from. It made a lot of sense to just pull the filing because when you have that S-1 out there, you're in a quiet period. When we look at all these other companies that have gone public recently, such as Riverstone Networks, I mean, it's a forced play. What company in their right mind would go public in a market that's not settled yet?"* Two years later, as the market settled, Zhone acquired Tellium and completed their IPO through a backdoor strategy.

As the ITO Revolution accelerated into the Decline stage of the G3MM, the IPO window closed for Zhone. Tellium was the last company to go public and Zhone did not have the revenues or market expectations to support a public offering. At the time of the Tellium acquisition, Zhone had $1.9 million in cash on their balance sheet. The Tellium acquisition achieved two primary objectives for Zhone. The first was an infusion of needed cash; approximately $150 million in bank from Tellium's IPO, and second it was a vehicle for Zhone to become a publicly listed stock at a time when no ITO companies were going public.

Zhone Technologies is Mory Ejabat's company to stay invested in the ITO Revolution. A lifetime spent working and playing in the high stakes game of

ITO Revolution is not an easy life to give up. By mid-2005, Zhone is a stagnant company with revenues averaging about $30 million per quarter with cash of approximately $61 million and debts of $59 million. The prospects for extreme growth are limited in the near term. Perhaps ten to fifteen years of building their business and waiting for the next change event to occur will result in an opportunity to build the next AOL – but the present outlook is for a slow, measured management of the minor business in a market structure of large companies. Harry Carr departed Zhone shortly after the merger was completed and in late 2004 he was back in the game as CEO of a new company called Simpler Networks Corporation. Harry Carr and Mory Ejabat were not the only high-profile leaders that had tremendous success during the early stages of the ITO Revolution and could not stay out of the game.

Sycamore Networks was founded in 1998 by Gururaj Deshpande and Daniel Smith. Deshpande and Smith had already been successful ITO Revolutionaries when they were part of the team that started Cascade Networks. Cascade Networks was a raising start in the mid-1990s after being founded in 1992. Cascade went public in 1994 and was purchased by Ascend Communications in 1997 for $3.7 billion. Sycamore Networks was founded to take advantage of the continuing revolution in optics and telecommunications. Only a year after being founded, Sycamore went public in 1999 and still ranks among the top ten IPOs of all time in terms of value. Consider that Lucent Technologies spun out of AT&T in 1996 for a deal valued at $17 billion. When Lucent went public they had assets in the billions, over a hundred thousand employees and offices and customers around the world. When Sycamore went public on October 22, 1999, they had trailing quarterly revenues of $19 million, 228 employees, and approximately $21 million in cash. Sycamore's shares peaked on the first day of trading at $270 per share and closed at $184.75, giving the company an astounding market capitalization of $14.4 billion on the first day of trading, which was the largest market value ever achieved by an ITO related company on their first of day of trading. CEO Deshpande said of Sycamore's market position and valuation on the first day of trading that, *"The networked economy, I think it's going to be real and what's fundamental to that economy is bandwidth."* At the time of the IPO, Sycamore was generating revenues from a single customer, Williams Communications. Deshpande commented that this fact is an *"… indication that it's an early market."*

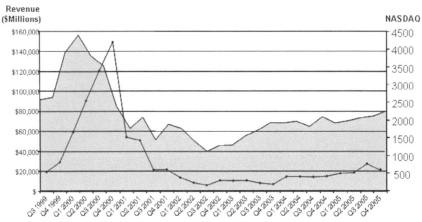

Figure 36: Sycamore Quarterly Revenues with NASDAQ Composite Index

At one time in 2000, Sycamore's stock traded as high as $189 per share. After the Apogee stage of the ITO Revolution, Sycamore's stock now routinely trades around $5, but with their large cash position, the company still has a market capitalization of around one billion dollars. The loss in share value is approximately 98%. Both Sycamore and Tellium provide an excellent model to illustrate the importance of timing in a revolution. Sycamore went public in 1999 and raised $236 million. They added additional capital as their stock appreciated. Tellium went public in 2001, raising $135 million. Both companies had major telecom provider wins worth hundreds of millions of dollars. Neither company was able to build a sustainable business beyond their initial customer wins. Yet, Tellium was acquired by Zhone for $180 million and Sycamore remains a public company in early 2005 with approximately $900 hundred million of cash and revenues of approximately $65 million per year.

The unfortunate reality for Sycamore is that it is a small company in an era of big companies – but it is not alone. Another company that was born during the Perigee stage of the ITO Revolution, and by a successful entrepreneur of the early years of the ITO Revolution, was Corvis. Corvis was founded by Dr. David Huber in June of 1997, just after Ciena's IPO. Prior to founding Corvis, Huber was one of the four founders of Ciena Corporation. Huber, Ejabat, and Deshpande were all serial entrepreneurs in the ITO Revolution. All three started new revolutionary companies near the peak of the Perigee Stage of the ITO Revolution and all three companies failed to gain significant and sustainable market share.

Unlike Ejabat and Deshpande, Huber's strategy for Corvis post the Decline stage was to turn Corvis into a service provider, rather than a network equipment supplier. Corvis acquired a company called Broadwing in 2003. Broadwing was a company that had evolved from its roots as Tower Communications in 1962, to

IXC Communications in 1994, merged with Cincinnati Bell in 1999 to become Broadwing. In 2000, Broadwing deployed an optical long-haul network across the United States. When the ITO Market exited the Perigee Stage, Broadwing found itself facing a contracting market, with limited market share to be a large company compared to the extremists of the ITO Revolution. Corvis found itself with an optical switch and no customers – but with cash in the bank, due to a wildly successful IPO in July 2000, and reaching a market capitalization of $25 billion. With over a billion dollars in the bank from the IPO and a vanishing market for its products, Corvis decided to become a service provider and purchased Broadwing for $129 million in 2003. In mid 2005, Broadwing has a market capitalization of around $350 million, revenues of $750 million per year, three hundred million of cash, and $140 million of debt. It is a nice business, but they are not changing the world and as market share has become fixed, they struggle to find a strategy to become a big company. They simply need to put another 10-20 years into the business, waiting for another revolution that changes the structure of their market and enables the migration from a small company to a large company.

A Viewpoint from 2005

As the ITO Revolution progresses into its last evolutionary stage called the Return, all three of its revolutionary markets have dominant companies. The innovative engine within the United States that produced the three markets that enabled the ITO Revolution still exists. This economic model combines several key elements that ensure that there will always be a cycle of technology and economic revolution. The first element is that government of the United States fosters research at the academic and commercial level by providing grants to universities, institutions, and corporations. From this comes the creation of intellectual capital. Ideas and new technologies are created within this system. The next element is the existence of private equity and venture capital. Venture capital and private equity exist to provide those with entrepreneurial desire access to financial capital to commercialize the intellectual ideas created from research within the academic community, government agencies, and the private sector. Private equity exists to satisfy the entrepreneurial spirit and to seek substantial reward in sectors of the economy wherein a discontinuity exists. The public markets reward sustained, predicable success in business – the public markets are not appreciative of volatility and unpredictable success. The leadership of a public company and the shareholders of that public company are comforted by visibility. When volatility is created in the market and visibility to success or failure of business becomes curtailed, that is the moment when public markets lose confidence in a company and the stock price declines. The segment of the economy wherein visibility is limited and volatility, change and discontinuity exist, is where value can be created and revolutionaries (i.e. researchers, entrepreneurs and visionaries) can be found. Markets on the verge of the Change stage of the G3MM are where private equity is invested. *"One's impression then...is that there were always sectors in economic life where high profits could be made but that these sectors varied. Every time one of these shifts occurred, under the pressure of economic developments, capital was quick to seek them out, to move into the new sector and prosper..."* [see Braudel, *The Wheels of Commerce*, page 432]. Venture capital is the birth place of new companies. Companies that commercialize new ideas are revolutionaries. The successful commercialization of intellectual property into intellectual capital creates companies, which is turn creates economic wealth and drives GDP. This cycle still exists post the ITO Revolution and this is the reason why another revolution is ahead of us, it is just a question of when and where.

As 2005 began, the companies still operating within the ITO Revolution were challenged by the structure of the market in which they were operating. The spending occurring in the telecom services market by the large service providers (i.e. wireline, wireless, and cable service providers are included in the term service providers) is being given to the largest networking equipment suppliers. This is the same state the market was in prior to the Telecom Act of 1996. Why?

The telecom services and technology equipment markets have returned to a market structure that resembles 1996 – rather than 2000. The names of companies are different. Companies own different businesses, but the customs and habits that the industry knew well prior to the Change stage of the ITO Revolution have come back in the Return stage of the ITO Revolution. This is why we find many of the large companies that survived the ITO Revolution are led by leaders who are experienced in the market conditions prior to the Telecom Act of 1996. There are a few new companies that are now part of the industry that in five, ten, or twenty years from now will be called old regimes, but it is clear that the structure of the telecom and technology industry in the U.S. and in many respects globally has returned to its structure during the Start phase of the ITO Revolution, circa 1996. Within this structure the business practices are well understood. Until the conditions required to create a revolution converge again, the business of the ITO markets will be the business of mending the disruption of the ITO Revolution. It is clearly possible that the ITO markets will enjoy a renaissance that will span many years and perhaps decades – but this will not be a return to fever pace and excitement of the Perigee stage of the ITO Revolution. It will be a good business, run within a well defined and predicable markets until the market structure is broken again by revolutionary forces.

CHAPTER SEVEN:
The Future in Now and it is Unevenly Distributed

Aggressive, offensive action deprives the enemy of time to think and act; while superior force at the time and place of battle is the guarantee of ultimate victory. - Jomini

The title of this chapter is derived from a quote from William Gibson. As the year 2005 progressed, the final obituaries for many of the ITO Revolutionaries were being written. SBC announced that it was acquiring AT&T for $16 billion and in early 2006, announced it would acquire BellSouth thus unifying the ownership of Cingular and creating a massive wireline and wireless service provider. In 2005 Verizon acquired MCI for $7.6 billion. When the BellSouth merger is complete, the telecom service provider market structure in the United States will be two mergers away from returning to state of market share concentration that would be more concentrated than before the breakup of AT&T in 1984. If Verizon and at&t (i.e. SBC) were to merge and then purchase Qwest, not only would the Bell System been reunited, but it would include GTE and MCI who were two of the few competitors in size to AT&T and the RBOCs in the 1980s and early 1990s. The market upheaval created by the Telecom Act of 1996 is almost non-quantifiable. It is highly unlikely that U.S. regulatory bodies would ever approve a merger between SBC-Verizon and Qwest – but the possibility is clearly financially viable and when examined in context of the market it appears to be a logical business strategy. In this chapter, the final stage of the G3 Market Model will be summarized, we will review some of the assumptions that were used to initiate and promote the ITO Revolution. In the final essay, the near term market structure of the ITO Markets will be reviewed and using the G3 Market Model, future revolutionary events that would cause the ITO markets to again cycle through the G3 Market Model will be identified.

By 2005, the structure of the Market Ecosystem began to reveal the challenges faced by many service providers as well as the companies that supply technology to service providers. They growth of bandwidth and proliferation of technology that can enable services over a broadband connection is the real conundrum for the service providers. The internet is the best transaction mechanism developed for the exchange of currency to facilitate global commerce. As such, companies that can leverage the infrastructure of the internet to complete transactions will be the dominant companies of the future. Transactions are defined as the end-user, consumer or business, with access to content which can be applications, games, entertainment, voice calls, etc. The 2005 Market Ecosystem is one of choices. End-users, whether they are consumers or enterprises have choices. The RBOCs have consolidated local loop market share – but consumers can find alternative providers of services from mobile and cable providers. There is a crossover convergence of services within the consumer market. Cable service providers are providing voice services, RBOCs are providing television services and mobile providers are seeking to deploy high-speed wireless broadband within a few years. Eventually, it is possible for the WinStar and Teligent business cases to be proved plausible, it simply requires a few more years of innovation to perfect the technology that can deliver the services at affordable infrastructure costs. See **Chart 7: 2005 Market Ecosystem** in the Chart and Model section.

The last stage of the G3 Market Model is called Return. Al Gore may have fashioned himself the father of the internet for being a leading political intellectual who was a proponent of the Telecom Act of 1996, but if current trends continue he might be able to add "new father of the Bell System" to his title as well. The last stage of the G3 Market Model is the era of big companies. The era of big companies is the market condition that produces Old Regimes. The last stage of the G3 Market Model is the stage that will eventually compel the revolutionary cycle to begin again and a return to the Start stage of the G3MM? The question is; what will be the events that will initiate the beginning of the next revolutionary change cycle of the G3MM for the telecom and technology markets? Until the revolutionary cycle begins, the market structure will reflect that of Old Regimes and be ruled by large companies. The era of big companies forms when a small number of companies control the vast majority of the market share. The Return stage of the G3MM is identified by market share consolidation and static state of market share. In the Change and Perigee stages, market share is increasingly dynamic and fluid amongst competitors. During the Return stage the opposite becomes true.

Return: Market conditions have become similar to the market conditions during the Start stage of the G3 Market Model. Market share fluidity has moved away from the point of maximum stationarity. There is still a significant market dichotomy in place, but the extremes of Perigee and Apogee have framed the boundaries for the market. Customers are willing to award business to companies that are not the largest, but the level of the business they award mirrors the strength of the supplier. Big companies win big deals and small companies win small deals. The ability for small companies to grow rapidly by assuming market share from competitors is minimal. It can be done, but rapid acceleration of top line revenues is not possible. This is the result of a confluence of two market conditions; (a) Large suppliers control the majority of the market share and as such they enact barriers to ensure that they maintain control of their market share, and (b) there is not enough new, organic market share being added to the overall market to provide new entrants with green field opportunities. In some cases, various market verticals within the overall market ecosystem can be contracting. This is why smaller companies struggle to find the market share acquisition velocity they require to achieve acquisition equity events and IPOs. During the Perigee stage, the metrics used to value companies and set the boundary conditions for IPO eligibility are much lower. Market share is fluid in the early stages of the revolution and that enables companies to achieve objectives early in the G3MM that are simply not possible in the later stages. See **Chart 14: G3MM Return Stage for ITO Revolution** in the Chart and Model section.

The Telecom Act of 1996 was a key legislative objective created by a new administration in their first term. There were high hopes placed on the Telecom Act of 1996 to be one of the three pillars of long term, economic growth through the creation of a technology and information based economy. People believed that it was major step towards unleashing the inherent value of a regulated market by creating a dynamic, unregulated market open to competition. Putting aside the shortcomings of the act, the Telecom Act of 1996 did foster major investment in the networking infrastructure of the United States. More investment is required, but the Act did function as an investment catalyst for the infrastructure of the ITO Revolution. The *"...boom was healthy too, even with its excesses. Because what this incredible valuation craze did was draw untold sums of billions of dollars into building the Internet infrastructure. The hundreds of billions of dollars that got invested in telecommunications, for example. You know, when the information highway was the craze, the question I would ask {then-Bell Atlantic CEO} Ray Smith and {then-TCI chair} John Malone was, Who the hell is going to spend the billions of dollars it will take to build this thing out? You guys? The federal government? It's not going to happen. And no one could give me an answer as to who was going to pay. Well, it turns out that the answer was the investing public, who rabidly ran and shoved the money into the hands of the infrastructure builders. It is probably true that the infrastructure would have gotten built anyway. But instead of it happening over 15 years, it happened over 5, because of the gold rush mentality and all these investors trying to get in on it. So the boom accelerated the deployment of the infrastructure, and I'm talking about the Amazons of the world as much as the JDS Uniphases. Amazon's database is a kind of infrastructure - commerce-related infrastructure. When {Merrill Lynch analyst} Henry Blodget projected Amazon would go to $400 and the investing* *public rushed in, they were funding the deployment of Amazon's infrastructure, which is part of the totality of the Internet infrastructure. And all I can think is, how would this all have happened any other way?"* [see Andy Grove, *Wired 9.06*, June 2001].

The challenge that service provides confront in the Return stage of the G3MM, is that market share has become concentrated, huge debts have been incurred, and the price levels for services have been reduced. In June 2005, the FCC released the annual *Trends in Telephone Service Report*. Chart 8-5 which is reproduced below, illustrates the market share split between ILEC/RBOCs and CLECs for local service revenues. Seven years after the passage of the Telecom Act of 1996, new competitors for local service have 15% market share. The ILECs/RBOCs own 85% of the revenue generated by the local service. Is this a competitive imbalance? If we use the intent of the Telecom Act of 1996, which was to allow for the sharing of the local loop as a method of measurement, then the conclusion is in the negative. Revenue from voice services is declining and leasing a local loop connection from an ILEC only to provide a similar service on a smaller profit margin is not a solid business plan. Hence the conclusion can be reached that 15% percent market share is probably a reasonable percentage for a challenging business model.

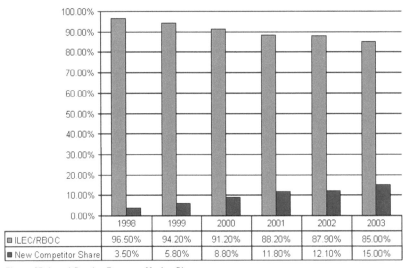

	1998	1999	2000	2001	2002	2003
ILEC/RBOC	96.50%	94.20%	91.20%	88.20%	87.90%	85.00%
New Competitor Share	3.50%	5.80%	8.80%	11.80%	12.10%	15.00%

Figure 37: Local Service Revenue Market Share
Source: Federal Communications Commission, *Trends in Telephone Service Report*, June 21, 2005. Chart 8-5

In short, high margin, high profit telecom services do not exist. They do not exist because the price wars initiated to secure market share in the prior stages of the G3MM for the ITO Revolution, combined with over-investment and regulatory challenges, have produced an environment in which investment in the infrastructure (i.e. CAPEX) is limited. If telecom service providers cannot provide profitable services, then investment in the network infrastructure will be slow. Andy Grove was correct in his assessment that the "…*boom was healthy…*" in that it spurred investment in a market segment that required billions, if not trillions of dollars in order to upgrade the network infrastructure of the United States. With the consolidation of service providers in the US market, the desire to create profitable data-centric services is increasingly being played out in the net neutrality debate. The crux of this debate is should service providers regard all data packets the same? If a user on a broadband circuit is accessing content on a network that is not served by their local service provider, then the local service provider wants the ability to charge an additional fee for our of network data packets. Whether this charge is direct to the end-user or a peering charge between service providers was not decided at the time that this manuscript was written. What is clear is that this is an attempt by service providers to find mechanisms to increase the profitability of broadband data services in order to maintain and improve profits as well as fund infrastructure investments.

The challenge facing the companies that survived the full G3MM cycle of the ITO Revolution is how to fix their business in the new market structure. The pace of change has slowed. Companies are not talking about initial public offerings in eighteen months. People do not talk about internet time anymore. They talk about the health of their business models and how to improve profit margins. More than ten years through the G3MM for the ITO Revolution, it is valuable to refresh the facts around a number of the metrics used to herald the dawn of the internet age and the new economy.

An early indication that something was occurring in the internet world was the phenomenal growth of subscribers to AOL's network. The growth rate of internet subscribers as well as the market potential for subscribers was cited as a proof point of the ITO Revolution in the *1996 Internet Report* by Mary Meeker and Chris DuPuy. The last graph of AOL subscriber growth stopped with 2002 [see *Essay One, Chapter One*]. Extrapolating another three years of subscriber data onto the graph reveals that AOL's subscriber count has deteriorated during the Decline and Apogee stages. This raises the question of whether AOL's dialup access business was really a paradigm shift or a short term consumer trend cycle. As AOL moves into the Return stage of the ITO Revolution, they are clearly the strongest on-line content provider, but they are challenged with the introduction of broadband services and evolving customer base.

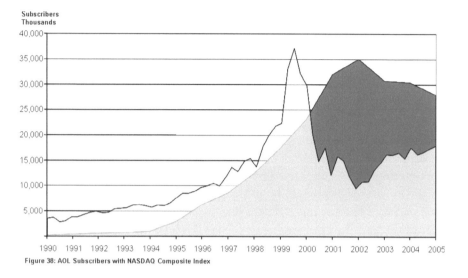

Figure 38: AOL Subscribers with NASDAQ Composite Index

The AT&T 1994 Annual Report highlighted the emergence of the internet and the linkage between global economic development and communications. AT&T communicated to their shareholders a focus on information services to meet the expanding demand of the global information industry that was estimated to be worth more than $1 trillion dollars annually and growing. During the Perigee stage of the ITO Revolution, AT&T acquired two cable service providers on the premise that these companies would replace the local loop void that was created when the RBOCs became independent companies in 1984. The two companies that AT&T acquired were TCI, for $48 billion in 1998, and MediaOne for $57 billion in 2000. For $105 billion, AT&T acquired approximately 13.5 million subscribers. AT&T realized that control of the local connection to the consumer is the critical element to a strong consumer based business. This single element is the compelling Holy Grail that attracts people and companies to the telecom business. The bond that ties telephony, cable, and mobile communications together is that every month, billions of people pay a monthly fee to telecom service providers, cable service providers, and mobile operators. This is the Holy Grail. The acquisition of monthly reoccurring revenue is the same mechanism that drove the value of AOL. It is the same mechanism that compelled Qwest to acquire US West. This is why venture capitalists and the public equity markets were eager to invest in companies that had the potential to create rich monthly, reoccurring revenue sources. Few industries in the world can match the allure of predicable reoccurring revenue streams that are deemed a necessity component of the pursuit of leisure time.

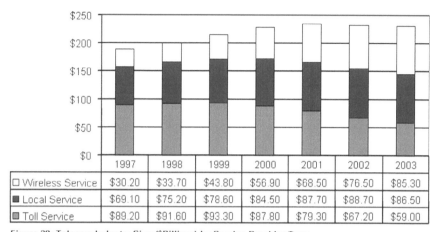

	1997	1998	1999	2000	2001	2002	2003
□ Wireless Service	$30.20	$33.70	$43.80	$56.90	$68.50	$76.50	$85.30
■ Local Service	$69.10	$75.20	$78.60	$84.50	$87.70	$88.70	$86.50
▨ Toll Service	$89.20	$91.60	$93.30	$87.80	$79.30	$67.20	$59.00

Figure 39: Telecom Industry Size ($Billions) by Service Provider Type

Source: Federal Communications Commission, Annual Telecommunications Revenue Report, March 1, 2005 Chart 1

The acquisition of two cable service providers by AT&T was the first step in rebuilding their local telephony business as well as the first move in fusing a cable franchise business, with internet access and telephony services. The challenge with the acquisitions that AT&T made was not in the soundness of the business plan; it was in the price they had to pay and the quality of the asset they were acquiring. AT&T simply overpaid for TCI and Mediaone during the Perigee stage of the ITO Revolution and did not have the additional capital required to complete the technology upgrades of the cable plant to support a broad range of services. Then the market shifted into the Decline stage. AT&T was faced with a huge debt load that was becoming increasingly difficult to service on a monthly basis. The result was that AT&T would be forced to sell their combined cable entity to Comcast for $47 billion in December of 2001. Comcast paid less than half of what AT&T paid for the same entity.

In November 1997, Jack Grubman commented that Worldcom was at the intersection of everything he liked and company had nothing to lose and everything to gain. On July 22, 2002, four years and eight months after Grubman's analysis, Worldcom declared chapter 11 setting a new bankruptcy record of $107 billion. No person saw the fate of Worldcom in November 1997, but after making ten of the largest telecom deals and proposing another blockbuster deal, Worldcom could not streamline the company to integrate the acquisitions and build a successful business model once the market conditions changed from the Perigee to the Decline stage. LDDS/Worldcom completed ten notable acquisition deals valued at more than $57 billion in addition to another forty smaller acquisitions. Add in the $115 billion offered for Sprint and the total rises to an astonishing $172 billion of acquisitions over a nine year period.

- 1989 Advantage Companies, (Advantage was a public company, thus eliminating the need for Worldcom to seek an IPO)
- 1992 Advanced Communications Corp. ($850 million)
- 1993 Metromedia Communication Corp and Reurgens Communications Group ($1.2 billion)
- 1994 IDB Communications Group, Inc ($936 million)
- 1995 Williams Technology Group, Inc. ($2.5 billion)
- 1996 MFS Communications Company ($12 billion)
- 1998 MCI ($30 billion + $5 billion in debt assumption)
- 1998 Brooks Fiber Properties Inc. ($1.2 billion)
- 1998 CompuServe Corp ($1.2 billion)
- 1999 Sprint ($115 billion bid blocked by Federal Regulators)
- 2001 Digex ($3 billion)

When the debt became too much for Worldcom to service, the market correction of the Decline stage set forth new metrics to measure the value of companies and the realization that the new economy was not as strong as expected, Worldcom was forced to admit to accounting errors. The result was a massive bankruptcy that, combined with Enron, changed forever the responsibilities and accountability standards for leaders of public companies. *"First, the big guys started consolidating. So, among the long-distance carriers and the Baby Bells, you came down from about 13 companies to seven. So, the number of potential buyers sharply contracted. And second, they borrowed more money to do this. Between 1997-2000, EBITDA in the big telecom companies grew by 65%, but interest costs grew by 85% and debt grew by 140%. The leveraging up by the old-line companies limited their ability to take on the debt that comes with acquiring a new economy company. So the business plans of 1996 that envisioned the old-line companies with pristine balance sheets swooping in to buy the new guys fell apart with each passing year. Then, in 2000, credit spreads really exploded for the big guys. Their credit quality started falling off a cliff, and their borrowing costs started going way up,"* [see Ravi Suria, interview with TheStreet.com, March 28, 2001]. Bernie Ebbers, Scott Sullivan, and other Worldcom executives were subpoenaed for appearance in front of tribunals by Congress and the courts to recount their actions and explain why they counted the number of coffee cups in the break room, but could not explain where they spent $100 billion of shareholder value.

As for the market structure for the network equipment suppliers, it is clear that ownership of enterprise market share was the end-game objective and the business plans for the many types of service providers that emerged after the passage of the Telecom Act of 1996 could not build businesses that were compelling to motivate a wholesale transition by private enterprises to outsource their networks. When the Decline stage began, CAPEX spending was drastically reduced by many service providers. Equipment suppliers, who relied on the service provider vertical market as their sole source of revenue, encountered dramatically different market conditions from the prior years. Time showed that John Roth's belief that enterprise networks would rotate towards dominance by service providers was false. It was precisely at the moment that the ITO Markets began to change that John Roth stated, "*I think the spread is opening up between the players. I think from my perspective that Nortel was the first from our cadre – Nortel, Cisco, and Lucent – to start doing acquisitions. And this group is now spreading out. Nortel has rapidly moved to the top of that, and that has corresponded to the rate at which we embraced the Web. Cisco is trying to follow the traffic. As corporations are saying, 'I don't want to build networks anymore,' Cisco is realizing that the business they have enjoyed from enterprises is really going to flip toward service providers,*" [see John Roth, InfoWorld, January 2000].

The result of the CAPEX decline was that Lucent and Nortel have returned to revenues that are within historical norms. Cisco's dominance of the enterprise network, coupled with their portion of the service provider market has resulted in a company that is larger in revenues than Nortel and Lucent combined. At the height of the ITO Revolution in mid-2000, Lucent and Nortel had combined quarterly revenues in excess of $16 billion. Cisco's quarterly revenues were just below $5 billion. From that perspective, it was clear that a vast majority of the CAPEX spending was occurring in the wireline and wireless service provider markets. Five years later the market structure is dramatically different.

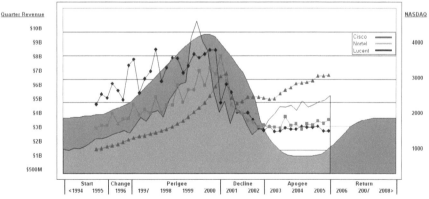

Figure 40: Cisco, Lucent, Nortel Quarterly Revenues with NASDAQ Composite Index and G3MM Market Share Model

In 2006 Cisco is the company enjoying quarterly revenues greater than seven billion. Nortel and Lucent are constrained to quarterly revenues averaging around two billion dollars. All three companies have employment levels of approximately 30,000-35,000 employees. Cisco is far more profitable and generates significantly more revenue from its customer base compared to Lucent and Nortel. There is no reason to believe that the market share structure between these three companies will dramatically change in the next few years unless there is a major regulatory change that enables static market share within the telecom services and technology market structure to become fluid. For those people who think the past six years of the Decline and Apogee Stages are the exception, as opposed to the norm, the question to be answered is; should we expect a sudden and sustained market opportunity that will enable new companies to rapidly grow revenues beyond the $1B annual level for suppliers of networking technology?

To answer this question, we can start with a model of total top line revenue for 34 publicly traded technology companies that primarily derive their revenue from networking equipment sales for voice, data or both. The quarterly revenue model was built from 1995 through the first quarter of 2006. It does not include all companies over the ten year period because not all companies were reporting revenues in 1995 – but the model is complete enough to draw conclusions. The model does include subtle quarterly adjustments for companies that have fiscal years that are not aligned to calendar quarters. The companies included in this model are listed below by stock symbol: LU, NT, CSCO, ALA, ERICY, JNPR, AV, TLAB, ADCT, COMS, ECIL, CIEN, ADTN, FDRY, CS (ETS), RBAK, SCMR, ADVA, AVCI, NWK, RSTN, FORE, XYLN, BAY, NN, TELM, EXTR, ATON, ARPT, CORV, ASND, CASC, AFCI and ONIS.

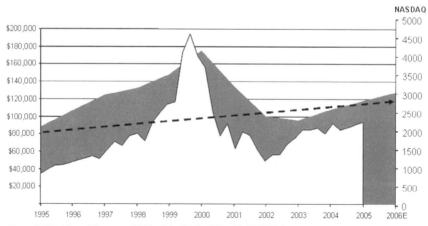

Figure 41: Total Annual Revenues ($Billions) for Public OEMs with NASDAQ Overlay

- The total top line revenue chart for the 34 companies included in the model looks similar the modified RHK North American Service Provider CAPEX model [see *Essay One, Chapter Five*]. At present there is no visibility to some great technology event that will alter spending and enable market share to become fluid. Market share may become dynamic and fluid if there is a regulatory change by the U.S. Government for the U.S. market or a change by the government of the People's Republic of China to the China. A regulatory change that provides a plausible basis for a speculative business plan will enable entrepreneurs and revolutionaries to gain access to capital and potentially build a business that acquires market share, thus creating value.

- The green trend line reveals that the overall market has been on a sustained growth curve from $87 billion in 2005 to greater then $127 billion in 2006 (estimated), which is excellent growth over a ten year period. Any market growing at a steady rate of over ten years is not a bad market. Often our perception of this market is framed by five years 1998-2002 [see *Essay One, Chapter Four*]. In 2002, total annual revenues topped $174 billion dollars, which is two times the market size in 1995.

- Although total top line revenue appears to have settled on its historical growth curve and the market size has grown 200% over a ten year period, the number of public companies participating in the overall market has <u>declined</u> from 1998.

As a follow-on step, the 34 companies reporting revenue were put into revenue bands. See **Chart 15: Annual Revenue for Public OEMs** in the Chart and Model section. These bands were:

- **Tier 1 Band**: Companies consistently achieving in excess of $2 billion a quarter
- **Tier 2 Band**: Companies achieving $300 to $1.5 billion a quarter
- **Tier 3 Band**: Companies achieving $75 to $275 million a quarter
- **Tier 4 Band**: Companies achieving less than $75 million a quarter

- 2004 through 2006 Tier 4 and Tier 1 companies have remained constant. In short, market share has remained static preventing new IPOs and restricting the ability of Tier 2 companies to move into Tier 1. The overall market of original equipment manufactures (OEMs) has been compressing since 2003.

- In 1995 the only companies in the Tier 1 band were Lucent, Nortel, Alcatel, and Ericsson. Cisco is the only company that used the technology shift of routing and switching to drive into the Tier 1 band. As service providers consolidate, market share becomes concentrated and the majority of the available CAPEX will go to Tier 1 companies as they are the only companies with internal infrastructure scale to compete for large contracts.

- Q1 1999: Five (5) companies controlled 88% of the reported revenues (i.e. market share)

- Q4 2000: Five (5) companies controlled 85% of the reported revenues (i.e. market share)

- Q3 2001: Five (5) companies controlled 83% of the reported revenues (i.e. market share).

- Q4 2005: Five (5) companies controlled 88% of the reported revenues (i.e. market share)

The contraction of telecom service provider market through mergers and bankruptcies has left a world in which big service providers are going to favor business with big technology equipment suppliers. This does not mean that there is no place for innovation and small companies – rather big companies are going to favor risk adverse strategies and prefer to award business in their core functions (i.e. most sensitive to risk and disruption) to suppliers who can provide a broader solution and scale to equivalent size. The challenge for small companies in this market structure is finding market share they can acquire. The consolidation within the service provider market has concentrated an enormous amount of CAPEX (i.e. market share) under the control of a few service providers. As the number of service providers who control market share declines, there are fewer overall purchasing decisions and less supplier diversity. As actual purchasing decisions within the market decline, it means few opportunities for new entrants to acquire existing or emerging market share.

It appears that movement from a Tier 4 company to a Tier 3 company is very difficult. The cost and complexities of company with sub $75 million quarters is dramatically different than a company achieving $150+ million dollar quarters. In addition, it appears that companies can achieve enough momentum in the present market to move from Tier 3 to Tier 2, but breaking into Tier 1 has not happened with the exception of Cisco. Another way to look at the market is that five (5) companies control 88% of the top line revenue in the networking equipment industry. These companies are Cisco, Nortel, Lucent, Ericsson, and Alcatel. That leaves 15 public companies contending for the remaining 12% of revenues – but this number is misleading because there are private startups in America (~20), several in EMEA (~10), and the Chinese suppliers (Huawei) who are trying to capture the remaining market share which is really more than 12% and estimated at around 20-25%.

As the global market for telecom services evolves through the Return stage and settles into a stage similar to that of the Old Regimes stage, several capabilities and characteristics become important decision drivers. During the frenzied stage of the ITO Revolution, business decision drivers focused on technology innovation, time to market, and speed of deployment. In the post frenzy period the business drivers have changed. Companies who compete for supplier contracts (i.e. market share) from the global service providers must have the ability to scale their business globally as well as possess integrated global operations. Small technology suppliers will be increasing forced to integrate their solutions with larger suppliers who act as a contract prime. Broader technology integration across the entire technology and market ecosystem will separate the largest companies from the second and third tier companies. Companies that confine their business to niche solutions (i.e. boutique suppliers) or specific market segments will not command the same competitive power as larger suppliers. Individual markets or niches will not possess enough organic market share (i.e. CAPEX spending) to drive enormous valuations for niche suppliers. Spending in the optical long haul market has returned to normalized rates, but spending in this specific market niche is unlikely to return to the levels of the frenzied period from 1997 to 2000. As such, companies that provide niche solutions will be unable to command dominant market share positions in the overall market ecosystem. This does not mean there will not be successful companies who provide specialization – it means that companies that specialize do not have unlimited growth potential as it is increasingly difficult to take market share from the large companies. Companies that are specialists will find that they need to partner and develop a consortium of companies to compete affectively in the market, as customers will look for an overall solution from a single source supplier.

In the Return stage of the G3 Market Model the terms of doing business have swung far away from frenzied days of the ITO Revolution. Today, business on a global scale is increasingly affected by regulation and capital constraints. The process of making technology investing decisions, investing capital, and providing technology is dramatically different from the 1990s. The vast majority of large technology companies are public companies. As such, the decision and negotiation process is dominated by these seven characteristics:

- Sarbanes-Oxley as a negotiation tool by both sides

- Revenue recognition as an incentive for concessions on price, technology commitments, and deliveries

- Public companies are increasingly risk adverse towards product futures, plans of record (POR), and any and all commitments that cannot be delivered in the near term

- No more asset swaps, stock options, quid pro quo, creative financial terms, or terms that can be considered a binding legal commitment

- Service providers not procuring on the "build it and they will come" business plan

- Network upgrades and new technology investments are increasing tied to rigorous cost studies or a specific customer commitment which means that service providers will issue the purchase order when their end-customer signs the contract. The unwillingness of service providers to offer binding purchase orders or binding equipment forecasts increasingly places pressure on global supply chains. Business is now inter-dependent through the entire supply chain. Few companies are willing to stock product or build in advance of demand. Companies must understand the market ecosystem in totality in order to manage endogenous and exogenous risks.

- Business trends are pressuring the supply chain – transition from Push to Pull

In closing this essay, we should review the words that President Clinton said at the signing of the Telecom Act of 1996. He said, "*This historic legislation in my way of thinking really embodies what we ought to be about as a country and what we ought to be about in this city. It clearly enables the age of possibility in America to expand to include more Americans. It will create many, many high-wage jobs. It will provide for more information and more entertainment to virtually every American home.*" There is no question that the Telecom Act of 1996 has provided far more entertainment in virtually every American home – but almost ten years later after the signing of the Act, there are not as many high-wage jobs. Thousands of companies have been destroyed. Trillions of dollars have been wasted. The United States invented the telecommunications industry. The result of the Telecom Act of 1996 is the Untied States is no longer the dominate supplier of telecommunication technology and is on the verge of being relegated to having a handful of boutique suppliers of telecom technology as the global innovators are now located in France, Sweden, Canada, Finland and China. As to the discussion of the future evolution of the ITO markets, this will be detailed in the final essay.

ESSAY TWO

Brinton, Boyd, Perez and Globalization

CHAPTER EIGHT
Brinton: The Anatomy of Revolution

Man is born free. No man has any natural authority over his peer; force alone confers no such right, the legislative power belongs to the people and can belong only to the people... - Martin de Marivaux, L'Ami des Lois

In 1966, Clarence Crane Brinton published a book derived from his research and lecture notes called *The Anatomy of Revolution*. This is an obscure book better known within scholarly political science circles than by the readers of books on the business best seller list. *The Anatomy of Revolution* is generally considered one of the foundations of revolutionary studies. Dr. Brinton studied four primary revolutions from western history and identified a sequence of events and a specific set of political and social conditions that were required within each nation-state to support a revolution. The revolutions he studied were the English, American, French, and Russian – which are widely considered the four important revolutions of western European history post the Enlightenment. Clearly, there were a series of important revolutions in 1848 that dramatically altered the history of Europe and in recent times we have seen many revolutions in the post-Second World War era – but the four western revolutions studied by Brinton were products of the Enlightenment and rejection of historical monarchies. Within each of these revolutions, Brinton identified shared elements, common stages, and similar conditions. From this he concluded that revolutions are not unique, spontaneous events – but predicable events. Revolutions occur when a specific set of conditions are attained, and revolutions undergo a predictable sequence of events. We tend to think of revolutions as a spontaneous uprising of an oppressed people against an unjust government. When we think of revolutions, we think of Liberty Trees, the Boston Tea Party, Bastille Day, and the rising of a united working class against the privileged class. The truth is that revolutions are really a stage in a cycle of change that is both political and social. Revolutions take years, not days, to complete their cycle. In some revolutions, as with the Russian Revolution, it can be argued that the cycle of change required years to play out and began the final stage in the post-Stalin era under the rule of Leonid Brezhnev. A conclusion can be drawn from Brinton's thesis that revolutions are merely an extreme form of political change. Using Aristotle's definition that humans are by definition political animals [see Aristotle, *Politics*], we can form a new thesis that the revolutionary process that Brinton defined is part of human nature and its iterative process can be identified in many aspects of the global human environment.

If one considers how the technology industry interacts with the financial markets, it can be argued that technology markets and financial markets are cyclical and revolutionary. Technology markets are the product of human creation. Each new technology that creates a market seeks to obsolete and replace existing technologies and their markets. There is opposition to the new technology until a few leaders or early adopters are bold enough to pioneer the use of the new technology. Once the new technology has been proven, there begins a process of market adoption. The suppliers of the old technology are forced from their markets and new companies or new technologies become dominant in the market. By that description, a technology market appears revolutionary. The corollary hypothesis to the G3 Market Model is: technology markets are a form of change, if the initial supposition is that business is a form of political change then it should be possible to apply Brinton's revolutionary thesis in order to improve the applicability of the G3 Market Model in order to identify the human element of market change, thus modeling the adoption of technology by markets and the interaction of technology companies with financial markets. In short, the hypothesis of this essay is to determine if Brinton's revolutionary cycle can be applied to markets and technologies to form a behavioral economic model.

In the first essay, a brief history of the personal computer, networking and the telecommunications industry were detailed. This history of these markets provides the foundation for our analysis of the ITO Revolution within the framework of Brinton's model of socio-political change, called revolution. The history of these three markets clearly demonstrates a repeatable pattern of (a) market existence, (b) market opposition (i.e. revolution), (c) new market creation, and (d) market decline (i.e. maturity). Companies grow and decline as new technologies enter the market championed by new entrants (i.e. companies). Investments of new capital flow from declining mature companies (i.e. old regimes) to new companies who contain a strong potential for growth, but possess greater risk. Growth is the engine that drives value and produces a positive return on capital resources. If you examine a revolution, the people (i.e. investors) of a nation-state withdraw their investment in the old regime (i.e. mature company) and invest in the revolutionaries (i.e. new entrants) who possess great promise but higher risk because they have never held political power. By this comparison, we can theorize that markets, revolutions, and value creation are bound by a common element that is human nature.

Financial markets exist as a product of human interaction. The basic definition of a stock market, in its purest form, is a definition of a revolution. Buyers and sellers appraise the value of companies on a daily basis. Their evaluation is a determination of whether a company will grow or decline; whether a company will increase in value or decline in value. The cycle of creation and destruction in the business world is the equivalent to an accelerated cycle of geo-political revolution amongst nation-states. Revolutions are not everyday events within the community of nation-states – but political change does occur and political change is a non-violent form of revolution. Within global markets, old companies are challenged by new markets, new technologies, and new entrants. The evaluation of whether these companies will grow or decline is the same evaluation in different terms as to whether the revolutionaries of France, Russia, or America would be successful. If investors were buying stock in the governments of nation-states and the political or revolutionary organizations within these nation-states, we would buy and sell based on our belief in the prospects for their success. On a global economic level, the evaluation of the strength of nation-states is a process that international currency traders undergo each day. Currencies are representative of each nation-state in terms of economic strength, prospects for economic growth or decline, and political stability.

To continue the correlation, imagine investing in governments and political organizations instead of companies. If the year was 1775 and we were living in the British Colonies in the New World, we would be making an investment decision between the Sons of Liberty in Boston versus investing in the British Government or perhaps its American subsidiary. The British Monarchy of 1775 is the old regime of its day. It is a vast empire spanning economic and business interests the world over – yet in 1775 people in Boston, New York, Philadelphia, Charleston, and southward had to decide if they wanted to remain part of the old regime or join the new entrant, the revolutionaries. If we were in St. Petersburg in 1917, we would be faced with a variety of investment decisions. We could invest in the Czar, Nicholas the Second and his government, or we could invest in a variety of political organizations such as the Mensheviks, Bolsheviks, Social Democrats, and long list of additional parties seeking control of Russia. Power is control of money and resources. Money and resources create value. The cycles of stability and instability are revolutionary by nature. The same principles should apply whether we are discussing capital markets or the course of nation-states. As our world evolves towards a global market, the geopolitical forces of nation-states are intertwined with the evolution of corporations and the creation and destruction of capital markets. Within this text, we will take the fundamental elements of Crane Brinton's theories and apply them to the ITO Revolution and the G3 Market Model that was derived in the first essay. The internet, telecom, and optical markets grew at extraordinary rates and then began to rapidly decline in the year 2000. The hypothesis studied in this essay is whether a model can be developed to examine technology and business markets using methods derived from the study of political change and the history of revolutions within nation-states. Can the principles used by Crane Brinton to study political change and revolution within nation-states be applied to technology adoption and the study of financial markets?

The Seeds of Revolution

Revolutions within nation-states are the product of three primary elements: financial crisis, structural weakness, and politics. These three elements combine to create conditions that enable the old regime to be overthrown. Brinton describes the history of the phrase "old regime" [see Brinton, page >26] as a product of France that was used to describe the way of life of the three or four generations that preceded the French Revolution of 1789. For our purposes in linking the study of revolutions within nation-states to financial markets and technology adoption, we will use the phrase old regimes to describe the companies, methods of business, technology, and the general structure of the telecom services and telecom equipment markets before 1995.

One of the important theorems that Brinton contributed was that revolutions do not occur during times of economic depression. In the four revolutions that he studied, the revolutions all occurred during periods of expanding economic wealth [see Brinton, page 29]. There was a burdening financial crisis in the four nations-states that he studied at the time of revolution, but it was the government that was in a financial crisis – not the social structure of the nation-state. Brinton writes, "...*yet in all of these societies, it is the government that is in financial difficulties, not the societies themselves,*" [see Brinton, page 29]. The theory holds that if the people of a society are suffering through economic hardship, their utmost priority will be survival and they will not have time for revolutionary activities. On the other hand, if the economy is expanding and they have access to the necessities of life, then they have time to commit to resolving issues of a greater scale. Leisure time, whether it is used for revolutionary purposes, social activities, or sport, is time obtained by securing the necessities of life. In short, it is hard to be a revolutionary when your primary priority is to find food for your family and pay your bills, but if you have a good job and your family is secure, then it is easier to be a revolutionary after work. Aristotle theorized that all of man's actions are the pursuit of leisure time. If that theory is correct, then man becomes a revolutionary when he believes that the opportunity to increase his security and leisure time is repressed. When given the opportunity to pursue the acquisition of leisure time unfretted from government rules, there comes a point where greed takes over. As we identified with the ITO Revolution, greed was an essential element that compromised rational business thinking.

Crane Brinton uses the phrase *"structural weakness"* to describe the state of the governments in his four revolutions. His research shows that within the four nation-states he studied, the financial crisis in which the government was undergoing produced an inability to govern. The term govern means the ability to control power. Fundamentally, governments on the verge of revolution are structurally weak. Most of the energies of the government are committed to resolving their financial crisis, which in turn fosters a structural weakness in the ability to govern. This weakness enables forces of change and revolution to build a foundation from which to operate. For our purposes, we will use the term *"structural weakness"* to describe the conditions of the markets in which our revolutions will occur. We are not analyzing the governing components of a nation-state, but rather the evolution of companies and the creation and decline of markets.

The component of politics as identified by Brinton in revolutions is similar to how it is used in describing markets and technologies. The telecom industry, as with many industries, is a regulated industry. To change the structure of market requires political capital. Politics, in time of revolution is the resolution of who will wield the power of the government. Politics is derived from the stricture that controls the distribution of wealth. Brinton describes this as, *"...we see that economic grievances – usually not in the form of economic distress, but rather a feeling on the part of some of the chief enterprising groups that the opportunities for getting on in this world are unduly limited by political arrangements – would seem to be one of the symptoms of revolution."* Politics in business is a reflection of who wields the power of regulation. When regulatory bodies change the laws that govern a market, they can have a profound affect on a market. In some cases, as in the Telecom Act of 1996, the politics of change were dramatic enough to launch a revolution.

Once the three foundations of the revolution are in place – (a) financial crisis, (b) structural weakness and (c) politics – the mantle of change has to be raised and championed. This task is undertaken by the intellectuals who provide thought leadership. The intellectuals are the industry analysts, consultants, pundits, politicians, leaders, and established thinkers with a reputation and respect within their industry. These people motivate change. They do this by influencing and creating a state of mind. This event is called the *"transfer of the allegiance of the intellectuals."* The phrase "transfer of the allegiance of the intellectuals" comes from Lyford P. Edwards in his book, *Natural History of Revolution* [see Brinton page >41]. In the first essay, the Thought Leadership Model was extracted from this concept and used to show how support of change progresses through the ecosystem of the *Thought Leadership Model* (i.e. TLM).

The intellectuals that espouse change are only willing to do so if they believe that change is necessary, possible, in the best interest of the majority of the people of a nation-state, and their personal risk is minimal. The later point is what separates the intellectuals from the hardcore revolutionary or extremists of the revolution. The hardcore revolutionaries are people who are committed to change regardless of their personal condition – but this is typically not the position of intellectuals of the revolutions. The intellectuals of the revolution become agents of change (i.e. revolutionaries) when they detect disorder and discontent. These two elements provide the intellectual with opportunity as well as security. If the government is weak, or the old regimes are weak, the intellectuals realize that conditions exist that will support a creation of a new order. They seek change because they view change as possible, but also because changes provides for their personal gain.

It is the state of mind that exploits the conditions of revolution. Change does not happen without leadership. People need to be told what the future will entail to become agents of change. This is the role of the intellectuals. The transfer of the allegiance of the intellectuals is the point at which the leaders of change show others the way to the new panacea that change will enable. This is the method in which a bill becomes law in the United States – but the process is typically conducted without a violent episode. Exceptions such as the Civil War and civil rights movements are noteworthy.

Once the intellectuals are committed to the revolutionary cause, they become the influencers of the state of mind. Change is rarely the product of the individual – but rather the product of the group. Brinton defines the agents of change as *"pressure groups."* In our contemporary world we think of pressure groups as lobbyists, consultants, or any type of organized group of people who have formed to promote change in favor of their position and this includes political action committees (PACs). Lobbyists are people who advocate change. They are the standard bearers of the revolution. Pressure groups are activists and can be classified as intellectuals who lobby and pressure for change. The intellectuals of the revolution are the planners and organizers of direct action. When the market is structurally weak and thus open to change and financial capital can be committed it is the intellectuals who lead the pressure groups to exploit the political process that enables change. They can achieve change, because as a group, they have a great ally and that ally is the abstract force of change. People rarely know the outcome of change – but the intellectuals are a fundamental force in driving the group consensus for change. When we examined the ITO Revolution, we found that it clearly had standard barriers of change that used their powerful intellectual positions to influence pressure groups, which in turn enabled change. It should be noted that ideas are not the agents of change. People are the agents of change, but the correct conditions must exist to enable a revolution. In his study of nation-states, Brinton states, *"We find that ideas are always part of the pre-revolutionary situation and we are quite content to let it go at that. No ideas, no revolution. This does not mean that ideas cause revolutions, or that the best way to prevent revolutions is to censor ideas. It merely means that ideas form part of the mutually dependent variables we are studying,"* [see Brinton, page 49].

The final element of the "old regimes" of which Brinton writes, is class antagonism. As he states, it is easy to think of this phrase in terms of a simple struggle such as proletariat versus bourgeois, or contending social classes – but this is not his intent. What he is describing is an underlining social tension that exists between contending classes. A component of the hypothesis of this essay is the application of his principals to modern market analysis. Brinton supposes that the class antagonism and their struggle is *"…usually carried on under rules, or at least without overt violence,"* [see Brinton, page 50]. It is within this definition, that we find an application to market analysis. When we refer to class antagonism, we are refereeing to the old market versus the new market, or the old regimes versus the intellectuals who are promoting themselves as agents of change and the desire to change the fundamental structure of the market dominated by the old regimes. Our class antagonism is a contention between old markets and emerging markets, between old regimes and new companies. The objective that creates this contention is market share. Old and new companies have the objective of controlling market share. The old regime as the incumbent is likely to defend their market and it is up to the new entrant to attack the old regime and create a new market. Brinton concludes his analysis of class antagonisms, by stating, *"…social antagonisms seem to be at their strongest when a class has attained wealth, but is, or feels itself, shut out from the highest social distinction, and from positions of evident political power…long before Marx, long before Harrington's Oceana, practical men knew that political power and social distinction are the handmaids of economic power,"* [see Brinton, page 64]. In our analysis of markets and change, this translates well to the old regimes that possess dominant market share and who have lost the allegiance of the intellectuals who are now seeking to create a new market and become loyal to new brands or new methods of operation.

The third chapter of *The Anatomy of Revolution* begins with a description of the third scene in the fifth act of Beaumarchais' play, *The Marriage of Figaro*. Captured in this scene is a long monologue by the protagonist Figaro that foreshadowed the anguish and resentment that the third estate (i.e. non privileged citizens of 19th century France) felt towards that of the second estate (i.e. royal and privileged class) in late 18th century France. In the spring of 1789, the Estates-General would be called to order for the first time since 1614 and France would begin an unstoppable slide into revolution. The Estates-General is a form of national assembly in which the three primary classes of society were represented – the nobility, the clergy, and the common people. These three classes of European society evolved when the feudal system was dismantled in the thirteenth century. Each estate represented an organized class of society that the King could call on for consultation as well as to revolve grievances. As the Estates-General came to order and began to address the pending financial crisis of the government, the nation-state of France began to slowly slip into the dark, deep, bottomless pit of revolution with the protagonists looking up at the fading light and struggling against the forces pulling them down. *"No, my lord Count, you shan't have her…you shan't have her! Because you are a great lord you think you are a great genius! Nobility, wealth, a station, emoluments: all that makes one so proud! What have you done to earn so many honors? You took the trouble to be born, that's all; apart from that, you're a rather ordinary man! Whereas I, by Heaven! Lost in the nameless herd, I had to exert more knowledge and skill merely to survive than has been spent in a hundred years in governing the Spanish Empire: and you want to joust!"* [see Beaumarchais, *The Marriage of Figaro*].

The first stages of a revolution are a time of great emotional extremes. The antagonism that the revolutionaries feel towards the old regime has been building for many years, as the nation-state approaches the inflexion point of revolution, the antagonism towards the old regime begins to peak. This antagonism is fueled by the Eternal Figaro. The Eternal Figaro is the underlying emotion that drives the revolutionaries. It consumes the thoughts of the revolutionaries and binds them in a common cause, that their view is noble in nature. The infallible dream of the revolution is what justifies all means to the end goal. The Eternal Figaro enables the revolutionaries to commit themselves entirely to their task. A revolution is an extreme event. People do not commit themselves to extreme activities without complete and total emotional commitment. The Eternal Figaro validates their commitment. The emotional commitment required by the revolutionaries eventually vents itself with the collapse of the old regime. The seeds of the revolution are planted by the economic crisis, the structural weakness of the government, and the politics of change. There must now be an event that builds on this foundation and channels the energies and emotions of the revolutionaries towards their cause.

You Say You Want a Revolution

Brinton describes the point at which the revolution begins as the *"point, or several points, where constituted authority is challenged."* There has always been a question concerning how revolutions begin. Do they begin as a child of spontaneity or are they a planned, choreographed event? Brinton believes that all revolutions have two common similarities at birth. The first belief is that revolutions begin when the government attempts to collect monies to resolve their financial crisis from the people of the nation-state who refuse to pay. There must also be a class distinction between what Brinton calls the *"party of the old regime and the party of the revolution."* The collection of monies that is viewed as unfair leads to the spark that starts the revolution. By this definition, revolutions are not spontaneous affairs – but they begin through a systematic building of emotional and intellectual frustration within society. There is an event that ignites the flames of the revolution, but this is not a spontaneous event. It occurs for a reason. In the case of France, the King called together the Estates General and empowered the people to take collective action because he had provided a defining moment in which people could choose to be part of the old regime or part of the revolutionaries and the new regime. In America, British troops marched from Boston to Lexington and Concord to seize arms and supplies that had been stockpiled by the local residents. This action by the British Army provided a point at which the colonists could choose to be loyal to the King or loyal to the local intellectual leaders, who were revolutionaries. In England, King Charles the First raised his standard to call for those who supported the King in his quarrel with Parliament. The result was that people of England were forced to choose sides. In Russia, the revolution that befell the Romanov Dynasty of three hundred and four years began when vast crowds of women filled the streets of Petrograd demanding bread. In all four revolutions that Brinton studied, there was an inflexion point at which the revolution was ignited – but the seeds of the revolution were planted well before this inflexion point was reached.

In terms of the ITO Revolution, it began when the government opened the telephony markets to competition with the passage of the Telecom Act of 1996. The actual revolution was visible when the old regimes attempted to continue business as usual. In relating business to revolutions, we do not have a central bank for businesses that is empowered by the government – therefore we must translate the collection of monies by the government to another act. The translation we will use is the act of collecting revenue, or the selling of products and services in the traditional manner by old regime. Revolutions are a break from the past and that break begins when the revolutionaries (i.e. companies) begin to offer goods and services in manner that radically challenges the existing market structure to include the cost and type of goods and services as well as the method in which business is transacted. Technology markets are not the only type of markets that endure this process.

The time at which authority is challenged, is the point at which a revolution is born. Whether that revolution will have a long life or a short life, is the question of the staying power of the old regime. If the old regime can successfully strike down this challenge, the revolution will not begin – but if this challenge is not met, it is a signal to the revolutionaries that the ruling class cannot respond to their challenges. The first stage of the revolution ends when the market structure controlled by the old regime collapses and power (i.e. business) is transferred to the revolutionaries. Brinton calls this stage "the Honeymoon." Suddenly, what had seemed impossible is now probable. There is a washing of sins from the soul. The build-up of angst within society is released and people can envision a prosperous future for themselves and the next generation. The future is bright and bountiful with hope. This is the euphoria of revolution.

As the old regime collapses, the people of the nation-state realize that the years of struggle and effort have brought about what, for many years, was only a fleeting dream. It is at this stage that the intellectuals, who had transferred their allegiance to the revolution, step forward to proclaim to the revolutionaries the expected fruits of their accomplishment [see *Essay One, Chapter Three for Thought Leadership Model*]. Wordsworth used these words to describe the French revolution, *"France standing on the top of golden hours, and human nature seeming born again."* Change is often a dramatic event that profoundly affects the human condition. Revolutions are an extreme form of change that motivates people to take extraordinary personal risks in seeking rewards – rewards that are not guaranteed. Revolutions are dramatic events that fuel the soul and breathe life into our imagination. Wordsworth's words are testament to our desires to dream the impossible dream. In many ways, the revolutionary nature of America is what creates a strong and vibrant life force in her society today. America has its periods of prosperity and recession, but the revolutionary cycle of her markets and economic structure forces America to consistently change and invent new strategies for success, which in turn maintains strength of forward progress. Amongst the four western revolutions, (i.e. America, England, France, and Russia) America has been the nation-state who has embraced the spirit of open markets and the cyclical nature of market change. Combine this characteristic with access to capital, the desire to innovate, and the foundation of America's entrepreneurial spirit and the result is an economic model that accepts a high level of risk to achieve a high level of rewards.

Great Expectations

The period of great expectations that follows the revolutionary event can be long or short, but it ends when the revolutionaries step forward and assume the task of governing. They must step into the place of the old regime and address the problems that still exist that the old regime was unable to solve. This is the great trap of the revolution. Revolutions do not solve problems; they simply affirm new leaders to be responsible for solving the same challenges that existed before the revolution. At an emotional level, the people of a nation-state may find the change of leadership to be worth the cost of revolution – but as the leaders of the revolution soon learn, the problems facing the nation-state are solved over time, not necessarily by a change in leadership.

The Honeymoon stage of the revolution is a time of optimism and joy. The old regime has been vanquished and suddenly the road most desired to be traveled – which has been blocked for so long – is open to all. Opportunities seem bountiful and the rewards and potential for success seem limitless. There is a measurably high level of optimism about the revolution because the future seems ripe with potential. People are positively engaged in the creation of a new government. In the four revolutions that Brinton studied, the Honeymoon period is best identified in the French Revolution. Brinton states that the Honeymoon stage of the revolution, *"…is most perfectly developed in France, where the revolution came in peacetime, and at the end of a great intellectual movement called the Enlightenment which had prepared men's minds for a new and practical miracle,"* [see Brinton, page 90]. Around the world, the news of the French Revolution was celebrated by poets and told in song and story to children and adults alike. Even the French national anthem that was composed by Claude-Joseph Rouget de Lisle in 1792, celebrated the spirit of the joyous moment of revolution.

> Arise, children of the nation!
> Our day of glory is here.
> For against us we see raised
> Tyranny's bloody banner!

The Honeymoon stage of the revolution is a time when hope abounds for the future with little concern for the complexities and challenges that lay ahead. Ignorance is bliss and the future is for those who dream. The internet and telecom deregulation were important events that foretold a bright future for the telecom service providers and networking equipment suppliers in 1996. Cisco Systems commented in their 1996 Annual Report, *"An important trend influencing demand for the Company's products is the worldwide phenomenon of the internet. The internet is a network of networks, consisting of thousands of sub-networks and computer resources linked together. The demand by companies, institutions and individuals for access to the internet is spurring demand for a wide variety of Cisco's remote access, switching, routing and software products, and the Company also benefits from the internet phenomenon through its relationships with numerous service providers. Another significant factor affecting internetworking is the global trend toward deregulated telecommunications and the resulting increase in use of higher-performance telecommunications services. Cisco has equipment installed with a majority of the world's major telecommunications carriers"* [See *1996 Cisco Systems Annual Report*, page 6-7].

In business and in the ITO Revolution, the Honeymoon period is normally longer than it is the cycle of revolutions within nation-states. It can be argued, that the Honeymoon period of the ITO Revolution lasted nearly a year, rather than a few days as in the case of the French Revolution. The creation of companies and the development of markets are processes that require time measured in months and quarters – not hours and days. We have declared that the signing of the Telecom Act of 1996 on February 8, was the Bastille day of the ITO Revolution, but our revolution is really three revolutions that combined to form the ITO Revolution. The internet component of our revolution can cite August 8, 1995 as their day of revolution, for it was on this day that Netscape went public. Revolutions need an event that captures the attention and imagination of the public. Revolutions need their fourteenth of July 1789 and their fifteenth of April 1775. Revolutions need an event that is dramatic and compelling enough to shake the bounds of complacency. People need to be told and shown that everything they had believed has changed. For the internet, Netscape's initial public offering was the event that captured the public's attention.

During the American Revolution, the march by the British Regulars on Concord and Lexington was a galvanizing event for the people of Boston and its surrounding communities – but it also was the event that drove all of the American Colonies to point of revolution. The Massachusetts intellectuals of the American Revolution, men such as John Hancock, Samuel Adams, Joseph Warren, John Adams, and Paul Revere, had planned for a preemptive move of aggression by the British Army. They knew any aggression by the British Army could be used to exploit the tensions in the colonies for separation from England. Through extensive planning, the Sons of Liberty had worked with the surrounding communities of Boston to perfect a system of alarms to call forth men and arms in defense of the outer towns surrounding Boston. This system is what enabled many men to be mustered in a short period of time in defense of Concord and the surrounding towns. What is not common knowledge is that within hours of the British Regulars' march on Lexington and Concord riders were dispatched to bring the news south to other American colonies.

News of the fighting at Lexington and Concord reached New York City within four days. Philadelphia received the news a day later and most of the southern colonies were informed within twenty days of the hostilities. By comparison, the news of the shot heard around the world did not reach London until May 27, forty days after the event. The American revolutionaries had planned well to exploit any aggressive move by British forces. American intellectuals knew the power of public opinion and had dispatched a fast ship called the Quero [see *Paul Revere's Ride*, Fischer, page 275] to bring the news and the American point of view to England, before ships loyal to the King would arrive. The revolutionaries had seen to their task well and were able to promote their version of events before the arrival of any official British military communication.

The dispatch riders, who carried the news from the colony of Massachusetts, were the IPO road show team of the American Revolution. It was their mission to sell the news of Lexington and Concord in order to convince the other colonists of the aggression of British regulars and the need for a revolution to separate from English rule. Companies going through the IPO road show process during the ITO Revolution were acting on a similar mission. IPO candidates were on the road to convince investors that a great event had occurred that justified their desire to stand on their own and conduct their own affairs. The mission of the American revolutionaries in 1775 was not much different. Personal fortunes, geo-political as well as the wealth of nation-states and multi-national corporations were all in play in 1775 and 1996 – the exception being that the stakes were higher in 1775 as life or death hung in the balance. The ITO Revolution would not reach this level until 2001.

The first government to form in a nation-state after a revolution is, in business terms representative of the first management team in a startup. It is rare to find a CEO who can start a company and successfully lead the company to the IPO stage and through the evolution into a large public company. Those who have successfully achieved at all three stages, startup, IPO, and public company often have a sizable ownership position in the company that requires them to be the agent of change. In the technology industry examples of CEOs who started the company and grew it into large corporations are: Bill Gates, Jeffrey Bezos, Ross Perot, Larry Ellison, Thomas Siebel, Michael Dell, and Terrance Matthews. There are many others, but the vast majority of management teams are skilled to match the phase of the company. Cisco Systems had one management team that lead the company during the startup phase, another management team that brought it through the IPO stage, and over time a third management team has emerged as Cisco became a large public company.

Perigee and the Rule of the Moderates

The Rule of the Moderates is the phase of a revolution that occurs after the old regime has collapsed and the spontaneous wave of change has broke upon the nation-state. Brinton believes that the Rule of the Moderates begins when the people of a nation-state and the revolutionaries realize they need to continue to govern the state. It is true that the old regime has fallen, but this does not dismiss the fact that the mechanisms of government must continue to serve the nation-state. Economic activities must be supported, services continued, and all the structures that support daily life in the nation-state must continue.

There are new people in positions of leadership within the government and there was a revolution – but this does not mean that the nation-state no longer needs the government that existed before the revolution. The reality is that the services that the government provided the nation-state still need to be conducted after the revolution. This means the trash needs to be collected, the mail processed, and money issued to banks. The government services that existed before the revolution must be continued after the revolution and the responsibility of maintaining services falls on the moderates who assume power after the revolutionary act.

Within the ITO Revolution, the government of the moderates is the collection of new companies that form to take advantage of the revolution (i.e. new market conditions). These companies have high expectations and position themselves as the intellectual leaders or role models of the revolution. They use public marketing campaigns to promote their products and access their markets. The challenges that these companies face are enormous. The new companies eventually realize that the old regimes still exist and the old regimes will fight to maintain market share. An interesting dynamic is that some elements of the old regimes emerge as extremists. New companies (i.e. revolutionary extremists) form from within the old regimes and from other revolutionary groups seeking access to the new market. Again, we can look at the Excite@Home history to find an example. When the cable service providers entered into agreements with @Home to provide cable modem services, they did so because the infrastructure of the internet was weak and their networks required sizable capital investments as well. Sharing the financial burden seemed like a logical and prudent business strategy. Then the unexpected happened. Service providers improved the capacity of the network elements supporting the internet and the cable service providers realized they could get more of the cable modem revenue as the network built by @Home was not as valuable or required as originally assumed. Hence, from within the partnership of Excite@Home emerged a group of extremists who wanted more from the ITO Revolution. This group was formed from within the @Home customer base and is known as the cable service providers.

The primary challenge facing the new leaders after a revolution is the need to reform the old system of government. When the intellectual leaders were in opposition to the old regime, it was easy to be critical of the government because they were not being held accountable for the actions of the government. Truth be told, it is simply easier to criticize when one is not held accountable. Now that the moderates are in control of the government, the task of reforming the existing institutions is daunting considering the complexities and confusion caused by the revolution. Perhaps the best example of this within the four revolutions that Brinton studied is the Russian Revolution.

The provisional government that emerged from the Russian Revolution of February 1917 was composed of Duma and various political groups that had opposed the Old Regime of Czar Nicolas the II. When Nicholas abdicated, the Duma assumed control of the state. A revolution had occurred and the Duma was a legitimate successor to Czar's government as it was empowered as the Parliament before the act of revolution. The provisional government realized the importance of maintaining their legitimacy as the ruling body. In doing so, they welcomed various revolutionary groups and organizations in an attempt to build a broad ruling coalition. Unfortunately, the siren call of power is to strong to draw all parties together and the actions taken by the moderates, in this case the provisional government, are not radical enough to satisfy the demands of the extremists of the revolution. It is doubtful that Alexander Kerensky, as leader of the provisional government post the February Revolution, realized that there were people in the old regime working against him as well as people organizing a second revolution. The actions of this later group resulted in what is known as at the October Revolution or the Bolshevik Revolution of 1917. The Bolsheviks were led by a man named Lenin.

For the ITO Revolution, the Rule of the Moderates occurred from 1997 through 1999. In what seemed to be a change that occurred overnight, America awoke and discovered the internet, new phone companies, computers at home, and online chat rooms. Pundits declared that a new economy was emerging. Thousands of web companies were formed in Boston, Silicon Valley, Silicon Ally, and many places in between. It seemed as if overnight every subtle element of the fabric of life had a web page. From pornography to religion, there was a web page on the subject. Every word in the English language was soon registered as a dotcom. Successful executives left promising careers to join the dotcom gold rush. Conference after industry conference heralded the changes that the ITO industries were invoking. Industry conferences became similar affairs to the marathon sessions held by the Duma after the Czar abdicated in February 1917. It seemed as if everyone was trying to find a way to capitalize on the new revolution. Revolution was in the air and no change was too great to theorize or predict. *"'The Internet as the Next Mass Medium,' and he's belting it out. 'We're gonna show all those people,' he says, 'the ones who say, 'Hey, the Internet's not gonna scale up,' or 'Gosh, there's gonna be bandwidth limitations.' It almost sounds like a taunt. 'We have the technical know-how, collectively. We have the resourcefulness and the commitment.' And the crescendo: 'You talk about the 15 hours a week that people spend listening to the radio, or 20 watching TV - four or five years from now we'll talk about the 10 or 15 hours a week that people spend experiencing audiovisual information over the Internet. It'll be just a standard part of the media fabric of people's lives. That's the kind of scale we're talking about here.'"* [see, Rob Glaser, *Wired Magazine*, 5.10 October Edition covering a speech by George Gilder].

In many ways, it was assumptions of change on an unimagined scale that drove the internet, telecom, and optical revolutions. Streaming mass media to users on an individual basis requires a massive amount of bandwidth. In the long term, George Gilder was correct. The internet or an evolution of the internet will be part of the medium of choice for the delivery of content, services, and many forms of human interaction. When we reach that point, television and the internet will simply be fused with many other types of content. Think of content as all forms of business applications, web sites, television, movies, music, books, art, and all forms of creative human endeavors designed to entertain, inform, interact, collaborate, and enable productivity. The internet can provide these capabilities to the individual user, but it can only achieve this state when it can exploit high capacity bandwidth to the individual user. In America, high capacity bandwidth on the individual level will not be possible until the copper local loop is removed and each user in each home and each business has access to fiber optics. Access to light via fiber optics is the critical element that has prevented the ITO Revolution from delivering on all its early promises. We may think that wiring America with individual conduits of fiber optics is a simple task – but George Gilder did frame the enormity of this challenge rather well; *"The ability to communicate – readily, at great distances, in robes of light – is so crucial and coveted that in the Bible it is embodied only in angels,"* [see George Gilder, *Telecosm*, page 4]. When we examine the old regimes and the revolutionaries of the ITO Revolution, we have been examining a time line that precedes the revolution by many years. The Telecom Act of 1996 was the single act that changed the laws that had prohibited the creation of a competitive local telephony market and it enabled access to the legacy telecom infrastructure of the United States.

The Accession of the Extremists Heralds the Decline

The inability of the moderates to reform and control the government empowers the extremists of the revolution. In all revolutions, there exists a group of radicals and extremists who insist that the revolution has not gone far enough [see Brinton, page 122]. These people take the position that the moderates are not revolutionaries – but rather saboteurs who have betrayed the revolution for their own personal gain. Rather than supporting the revolution, the moderates are accused of stopping the revolution. From an evolution perspective, consider that the old regime is conservative in nature, regardless of political sympathies. The moderates are revolutionaries, but they are not extremists. They seek change, but they also believe that power is inclusive – not exclusive. Brinton described a political scale [see Brinton, page 123] to illustrate this point. As power moves from the old regime to the moderates to the opposite end of the scale wherein the extremists are located, it goes from moderately concentrated, to less concentrated, to highly concentrated among a fewer group of people. The theory is that power under the old regime is concentrated within the old regime and a small number of political parties that are organized in opposition to the old regime within the protocols of the nation-state such as the parliament, Duma, or some recognized entity. During the time of the old regimes, political power is not concentrated by a few people, but rather within the old regime and political process. After the revolution, power becomes dispersed amongst many groups. This is the stage of the Rule of the Moderates. Power is less concentrated until it begins the process of concentration. Power within the nation-state becomes highly concentrated until it balances and returns to a level near that which existed during the old regime. In the G3 Market Model we used the assessment of market share as a corollary to political power. Brinton was not analyzing market share or the structure of markets – but he was analyzing the structure of political power within the nation-state. Political power is what creates the rule of law. In business, dominant market share is political power. The old regimes who dominate their markets have the ability to influence the political process and set the market price. The conduct of AT&T and the acceptance of the universal service is one of the few examples of this fusion of political and economic power. Adapting the G3 Market Model to Brinton's theories on the revolutionary process yields model for political change that could be adapted for behavioral economics:

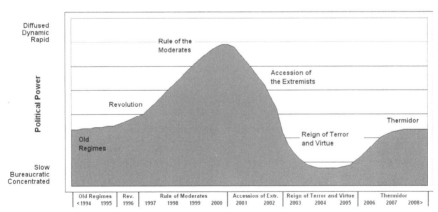

Figure 42: Adaptation of Brinton's Revolutionary Cycle to the G3 Market Model

The history of the baby bells from their birth is worthy of inclusion in Aeschylus. AT&T divested itself of the baby bells as a primary condition to settle the U.S. Government's assertion that it was a monopoly and exploited the market to derive unfair profits. There was also an element within AT&T's leadership that believed the local telephony divisions were their Achilles heel.

Technology was evolving at a pace that the vast amount of monies invested in the copper local loop would soon be bypassed by new technologies that would enable competitors to enter the market and offer highly competitive services within lower cost structures. The fear of new technologies obsolescing the investment in copper dated back to the Second World War, when AT&T convinced the U.S. Government to prevent the use of microwave technology to be used as a competitive technology [see *Essay One, Chapter One*]. At the time of divesture, the leadership of AT&T believed they had eliminated a huge capital risk to the company and that they were now free to invest in the future, which would be a global network wherein AT&T would provide connections from the many companies providing local telephony services regardless of technology. In 1984, long distance services were still an extremely profitable service.

It is an interesting observation that the strategy of AT&T post the 1984 breakup was similar to the original company strategy post the 1913 settlement with the Interstate Commerce Commission. Post-1984, the seven baby bells remained autonomous and focused on their local telephony service business. At the time, there was no major competitor to the services offered by the baby bells in their regions. This began to change as the revolutionaries began to convince the government of the need to deregulate. As technology and change collided in the early 1990s, only an event on the scale of a revolution could cause a structural change in the market that had remained static for a long period of time. During the initial year following the passage of the Telecom Act of 1996, the baby bells began merging, citing the need to be competitive against the many CLECs that were entering the market to compete for the local loop business. Before the Telecom Act of 1996, there were a handful of old regimes that controlled the local loop in America. The handful included the seven baby bells, GTE, Sprint, and about fifteen hundred rural or independent phone companies all of which existed in various markets with minimal competitive overlap. The power of the local loop in the major metropolitan areas of America was moderately concentrated within the baby bells and a handful of competitors. Post the Telecom Act of 1996, power became less concentrated as three hundred CLECs entered various local markets, offering competitive services on local loop infrastructure. The power of the local loop became less concentrated, but the market could not support all these suppliers. The baby bells responded by launching a crusade to consolidate power. Power is: territory, resources, and rights. By merging into larger companies, the baby bells were increasing their political power and market share by acquiring new geographic markets and adding resources and wealth. As the ITO Revolution evolved over time, power was becoming highly concentrated within a small set of companies. In Brinton's revolutionary cycle, when power becomes concentrated at the end of the Rule of the Moderates, the revolution is poised to enter a new phase.

The primary challenge the revolutionaries confront beyond the need to govern, is that elements of the old regime still exist after the revolution as well as other revolutionary parties. In the case of Russia, the Duma led the coalition of moderates until the October Revolution. Post the October Revolution forces loyal to the old regime used the extreme position of the Bolsheviks to unite moderate forces and launch a civil war against the Bolsheviks. Revolutions within nation-states and markets are multidimensional. Change is multidimensional. In the case of the ITO Revolution, the early revolutionaries entered the market with strong public awareness – but their power declined as they were unable to deliver on the promises of the revolution. In the background of the revolution during the Rule of Moderates stage, new extremists were uniting to exploit the multidimensional market changes in order to secure market share and enact barriers to change. In the case of the ITO Revolution, the baby bells used their dominance of the local loop to secure market position. From AT&T's perspective, the idea of eliminating the burden of the local loop now was viewed as a great market barrier. This is why AT&T CEO Michael Armstrong began to acquire cable service providers in his desire to posses a next generation local loop to the customer. In the end, the cost to upgrade the cable plant infrastructure was too great for AT&T and the company did not execute on the promise of offering a bundled service. Within seven years of the Bastille Day of ITO Revolution, the babies of AT&T have grown to become four of the largest telephony companies in the world. This power is derived from their dominance of the local loop, which is the end game to the customer.

Dual Sovereignty

When Brinton describes the existence of dual sovereignty, he is highlighting the process of the concentration of power and establishment of competing governments. For an historical example, we have been using the Russian Revolution and the role of the Duma, but we could easily use the English Revolution. Dual sovereignty is the first stage of the revolution within the revolution. It can be identified by the establishment of competing ruling groups. Dual sovereignty is the beginning of the breakdown of the government formed during the Rule of Moderates stage. As political groups, coalitions and elements within the nation-state realize that their goals will not be achieved; they begin to plot against the coalition of the moderate political parties. These groups each have a degree of legitimacy supported by a sizable portion of society. Sizable portion of society is a relative term. Think in terms of the competing groups we are discussing having enough people supporting their position, that it gives the group a legitimate claim to being representative of the people or some portion of the people. This is obviously more than a small or insignificant number of people – but rather enough people to be of a legitimate threat to the ruling coalition. When two or more governments within the nation-state reach this level, they begin to issue conflicting orders and directives. This is called dual sovereignty and it is at this point that the ruling government formed under the Rule of the Moderates becomes paralyzed [see Brinton, page 133].

An example of Dual Sovereignty within the ITO Revolution can be found in the story of the DSL providers. The three DSL providers that were highlighted in the first essay were quick to make technology decisions and begin deploying services to capture market share. The RBOCs were not as fast to make technology decisions and deploy new DSL services. The three DSL providers did have limited resources in which to service customer requests. In the case of Covad, they subcontracted with Bell Atlantic/Verizon to use their service people to install Covad DSL service. When a customer ordered a DSL circuit, the installation was a two part process. The first to arrive was a Bell Atlantic/Verizon service person to verify the circuit to the central office. The second service person to arrive was the Covad team, who installed the internal network connection. As Covad was pioneering the process of turning up DSL customers, the local RBOC had plenty of time to watch and evaluate. Covad had to purchase the local loop from the RBOC and they needed the help, including the field service teams of the RBOC to install and turn up the Covad service. This structure enabled Bell Atlantic/Verizon to focus on more important activities such as buying GTE and changing their name to Verizon, than worry about pioneering a new, unproven, and costly technology in the market place. Verizon could comfortably sit back, evaluate the technology, and measure the cost model of introducing DSL technology as well as evaluate the market take rates for DSL service. In short, the Dual Sovereignty that existed was two providers of the same service who were using the same infrastructure and one was much stronger than the other.

"To you who desires to cross this threshold, do you know what awaits you?"
"I know," replied the girl.
"Cold, hunger, abhorrence, derision, contempt, abuse, prison, disease and death!"
"I know. I am ready, I shall endure all blows."
"Not from enemies alone, but also from relatives and friends."
"Yes, even from them…"
"Are you ready to commit a crime?"
"I am ready for crime too."
"Do you know that you may be disillusioned in which you believe, that you may discover that you were mistaken, that you ruined you're your young life in vain?"
- Ivan Turgenev

The extremists of the revolution who emerge as a pressure group contending for control of the nation-state have two distinctive advantages over the government that assumed power from the old regime. The first advantage is that the ruling coalition must shoulder some responsibility for the ineffectiveness of government [see Brinton, page 134]. The ruling coalition of the moderates is not the old regime, but they did assume power with few, if any, of the challenges resolved that forced the revolution. By their position as the successor to the old regime, the ruling coalition of the moderates is blamed by the people when their expectations are not met. The second challenge they face is that the extremists are better organized with more efficient means of operations. The moderates assumed control from the old regime and with that the inefficient machinery of the state. The extremists have no need for the old regime and its ruling structure. Their objective is to eliminate all aspects of the old regimes and their ruling structures. The extremists are able to build efficient processes and machineries that serve only to achieve their objectives. In many ways, it is the ability of extremists to evaluate the political and operational structure of the government post the revolution that is their greatest asset. The extremists do not rush to power, but rather plot the collapse of their foes from within the nation-state, exploiting every weakness of the moderates. Considering the first few years of history for the three DSL providers, we see the DSL providers moving quickly to seize on the market opportunity. Their competitors did not move quickly but rather worked to align market conditions that would optimize their competitive positions.

When the government of a nation-state becomes paralyzed by the dual sovereignty, it requires violence to break the impasse. In almost all cases, the coalition of the moderates finds itself facing a rival government that is *"...better organized, better staffed {and} better obeyed."* The element that makes the rival government dangerous is it is illegal. It knows that it is illegal and the rival government is more predisposed to use violence to achieve their objectives. The rival government is the hardcore element of the revolution. These are the people who are the true believers. They have given themselves completely to the revolution and to its objectives, and no price is too high to pay.

In terms of ITO Revolution, the dual or multi-sovereignty period arrived in three identifiable forms. From a macro perspective, the first dual sovereignty was the perceived existence of a new economy versus the old economy. *"The belief that the real risk in such open-ended opportunities is not losing money, but missing big upside. The internet is a global mega trend, along the lines of the printing press, the telephone and the computer, that is changing the way companies and people communicate, research, buy, sell, and distribute goods and services, and spend leisure time,"* [see Henry Blodget, March 1999]. To highlight this contrast, we should briefly define what is inferred when the old economy is cited versus the new economy.

In the old economy pre-1996, e-commerce was limited to internal corporate functions or select, closed networks of companies that had the resources to integrate electronic exchange systems. Large networks were still primarily private networks. Companies conducted business through faxes and overnight mail and consumers accessed the economy in person through retail sales stores and the telephone sales. Networking was an expensive proposition and only companies with substantial resources could leverage their networks to realize cost benefits from EDI. The cost of implementing a network of computers could be segregated into two primary cost groups: equipment (i.e. CAPEX), people, and operational costs (i.e. OPEX). A large component of OPEX was the cost of private lines from the telecom service providers. It was purported by the intellectuals of the ITO Revolution that deregulation would foster competition, thus reducing service rates and making it easier for small companies to afford private networks. Companies imposing EDI capabilities targeted partner companies that were key supply chain partners in which the investment in EDI would yield substantial cost savings. In the old economy world, companies did not use networks as a means to interface with their customers and business partners. Interaction with customers and partners was a function that the company did on a day-to-day basis through its employees and physical locations (i.e. stores, offices).

In the new economy world, the leading intellectuals of the revolution envisioned a world wherein the bricks and mortar corporate presence would yield to a virtual, digital world created by computers. Companies would interface with its suppliers and customers via the internet. This was possible because the internet provided a low cost networking option for the world. Think of the evolution in networking that had occurred from the introduction of SNA through the dawn of the web. In the span of twenty years, the ability to network computers evolved from the domain of the Fortune 100, select universities and the government, to being accessible by all segments of the economy, including the home personal computer user. The ability to network computers became financially accessible by the individual user. Ironically, in the early days of the internet, home personal computer users were accessing the web via 28.8k modems and slowly downloading low quality content text and images. This is the same activity that corporate computer users were doing in the early days of networking. Twenty years of evolution brought the internet to the home user in the same format that early networking of corporate users experienced during the Carter Administration.

As the leading intellectuals of the ITO Revolution continued to prophesize a bifurcation of the economy, it created a need for companies not on the internet to get on the internet. One characteristic of revolutions is they have an undeniable force that draws the participants into their fold. People like revolutions – at least they like the part of being part of a group that is leading the momentum of revolution. There is an aspect of revolutions that empowers people and engenders a deep feeling of satisfaction that they are doing something important. Momentum plays a big role in revolutions as seen in Petrograd in 1917, Paris in 1789, and Boston in April 1775. Momentum played an important role in the ITO Revolution as well. There was a rush to the net. Companies that did not have a web strategy, suddenly had to get a web strategy. In a large part, the rush to the web was because leaders of companies were being told by credible intellectuals that a great shift was occurring in the economy. Companies had to adapt as soon as possible as a great divide was occurring between the old economy and new economy. That divide was being created by the internet. The internet provided a new low cost method for consumers and companies to conduct business. Aristotle believed that all our endeavors lead toward the pursuit of leisure time. If you believed in the total vision of the intellectuals who celebrated the ITO Revolution, then the internet would have been a panacea for Aristotle, for the internet enabled the global community of computer users to interact, engage in commerce, and increase their leisure time. Any phenomenon of this magnitude requires companies across all segments of the economy to become engaged.

An important segment within the intellectuals and revolutionaries who were promoting the new economy were the moneymen. Venture capitalists where the first to raise the banner of change, but there is no denying the influence that publicly visible financial analysts from established financial institutions had on the ITO Revolution. There was a rush to money. The barriers to public money were low and an opportunity existed for entrepreneurs to raise money as never before. The public was hungry for investment opportunities that revolved around the ITO Revolution. Investors wanted to be involved in the foundation of the new economy. The financial community was part of the power of the ITO Revolution. Equity events raised capital for investment in the new economy as well as generated a vast amount of banking fees. Deals were good for the companies in the ITO Revolution as well as good for the companies that provided the financial services that supported the ITO Revolution.

The banking industry has never been a career choice that brought with it the prospects of celebrity status. A banking career could provide substantial financial rewards, which could be used to promote oneself – but celebrity status because one was a banker was not a likely prospect. This changed with the ITO Revolution. Bankers and stock analysts became stars. The web promoted their opinions as well as traditional media mechanisms such as radio and televisions. One of great successes of the web and the ITO Revolution was the liberalization of financial information as well as access to financial information. Individual investors were major drivers of the stock market in the mid to late 1990s. The new found access to financial information created stars within the financial community. Examples of intellectuals who became important players in the ITO Revolution are Jack Grubman, Henry Blodget, Mary Meeker, Jim Cramer, and host of other analysts.

The second form of dual sovereignty arrived in the form of competing technologies. Not only were companies faced with the challenge of the new economy versus the old economy, but they were also faced with competing technologies in which to use to join the new economy. This is also the point where the belief in first mover advantage comes into play. Competing technologies provide a micro decision point to complement the macro decision point of the old economy versus the new economy. In short, these can be considered micro dual sovereignties within the overall macro dual sovereignty. Throughout the history of technology and the ITO Revolution, competing solutions for market acceptance is a recurring theme. Examples are:

- Alternating Current versus Direct Current
- VHS versus Betamax
- WINTEL Personal Computer versus the Apple Machintosh
- Windows versus OS/2
- Token Ring versus Ethernet
- Ethernet versus ATM
- Bridging versus Routing
- DSL versus Cable Modem

When there is a technology dual sovereignty, the best technology does not always win. More often, it is the technology that achieves a greater market growth rate, thus leading to market share dominance that wins the confrontation. It is in this regard that political revolutions and technology revolutions are comparable. The technology that wins in the market is the technology that is better organized and efficient with regard to capturing market share. When dual or multi sovereignty exists, one technology will emerge as a leader that dominates market share and becomes the de facto standard. The examples of this process are numerous:

- **Windows versus OS/2**: When the battle for operating system software was over, it was obvious that Microsoft had built a better product and executed faster than IBM. When OS/2 entered the market, it had a successful sales channel to exploit within the IBM customer family – but it was late and had ceded an unrecoverable amount of market share to Microsoft.

- **US Robotics 56K Modem versus Industry Standard 56K**: US Robotics beat the consortium of other modem suppliers to the market with 56k modem technology. The consortium of other suppliers was building an industry standard version of 56k technology, but USR beat them to the market by several months with a proprietary solution. In the end, the market demand for 56k technology was so great, that USR went on to dominate their market segment effectively pushing the other modem suppliers out of the market and into bankruptcy or consolidation.

- **Ethernet versus ATM**: In many ways, ATM was the perfect technology for the moderates. It was developed within multi-national working forums and was the product designed by a cross section of technologists to meet a myriad number of demands. For a period of time in the 1990s, it appeared as if ATM would equal or exceed expectations. ATM became widely deployed by most global telecom service providers as the technology that would provide the convergence between the traditional telephony (i.e. voice) world and fast growing enterprise data world. Unfortunately, for ATM, the enterprise market continued to grow and developed applications and services that required increasing amounts of bandwidth. The cost to deploy Ethernet continued to decline and the complexity and cost of ATM networks simply made it a loser when compared to Ethernet in the enterprise market. At the time of this writing, most global service providers own large ATM networks and are now faced with the problem of deploying new networks based on Ethernet that can provide a common handoff between the customer and service provider.

The third tier of dual sovereignty arrived in the form of the concentration of power within the telecom service providers. After the initial euphoria of revolution had passed, there existed two telecom structures in the United States. The first structure was the existing segment of regulated telecom companies such as the RBOCs and traditional long distance companies such as AT&T, MCI, and Sprint. The second structure was the concentration of new telecom companies that were unregulated. In this group, we find the collection of approximately three hundred CLECs, competitive access providers, and the new global telecom providers such as Level(3), Global Crossing, Qwest, 360 Networks, Touch America and Williams. Customers, whether they were consumers or commercial, were faced with multiple options from which to purchase services. If we found ourselves in Petrograd in late summer 1917, as a citizen of Russia we would be challenged with making a choice between two governments. Both governments have control of certain aspects of the governing structure – but they are clearly opposed to the existence of each other. The question, as a citizen, is which government to choose? In the ITO Revolution, it was the customers of the ITO Revolution who had to choose between competing services and technologies.

In the technology business, there is a belief that the first company to introduce a new technology or method of conducting business has what is termed a first mover advantage in the market. During the bubble days of the ITO Revolution, many internet and optical startups were founded with the mandate to get to market quickly. Even the new leading revolutionary telecom service providers, such as Global Crossing had the mandate of speed. Speed in the construction of their networks would enable new revolutionaries to capture customers and market share, thus enabling them to be the leading companies in the new economy. In March of 1997, Gary Winnick, co-chairman of Global Crossing, stated in a company press release, *"Due to the overwhelming demand for the internet and other new multimedia applications, coupled with market changes driven by deregulation and accounting rate decreases, we expect an explosive growth in telecommunications traffic worldwide, we expect the North Atlantic Region to be particularly dynamic due to the advanced economies that it services."* There is clearly some advantage to being a market first mover, but in reality, the advantage is minimal when compared to being the first supplier to market with a sustainable solution that generates revenue and profits. George Gilder remarked about Global Crossing in 2000, *"Just as MCI pioneered single-mode fiber in the U.S., TCI transformed cable, and McCaw launched a national wireless system, Global Crossing will pioneer the first integrated global fiber-optic network, fulfilling my decade-old predication of a 'worldwide web of glass and light,'"* [see Gilder, *Telecosm*, page 192]. Global Crossing declared Chapter 11 bankruptcy on January 28, 2002 with liabilities totaling $12 dollars and assets worth $22 dollars, five years after being founded. To their credit, Global Crossing emerged from chapter 11 bankruptcy on December 9, 2003 and has since enjoyed annual revenues of around $1.8 billion. For the balance of 2005 the company has maintained a market capitalization of between three hundred and four hundred million.

Brinton describes the weakness of the moderates as a *"paradox."* In the beginning, the moderates are given credit by the people for opposing and then disposing of the old regime – but as they are unable to control and improve the machinery of the government, they begin to lose credibility in the eyes of the people. Then the moderates are confronted by the radicals or extremists of the revolution. Eventually, the moderates realize that they have assumed power from the old regime and now find themselves subject to revolutionary forces applied by the extremists of the revolution who believe that the revolution has not gone far enough. The extremists seek radical and measurable change. The Rule of the Moderates ends with the *"...triumph of the extremists and the merging of the dual sovereignty into a single one."* In terms of the ITO Revolution and the DSL providers, the 1999 Annual Report for Northpoint foreshadowed this development. In that report, Northpoint stated, *"Traditional Telephone Companies With Greater Resources Than Ours May Directly Compete in Our Markets. The traditional telephone companies have an established brand name and reputation for high quality in their service areas, possess significant capital to deploy DSL equipment rapidly, have their own copper lines and can bundle digital data services with their existing analog voice services to achieve economies of scale in serving customers. In addition, most traditional telephone companies have established or are establishing their own Internet service provider businesses, and all of the largest traditional telephone companies that are present in our target markets are conducting market trials of or have commenced offering DSL-based access services. For example, Bell Atlantic, BellSouth, Cincinnati Bell, Pacific Bell and Southwestern Bell are offering commercial services in some territories in which we offer services, U S WEST is offering commercial DSL services and Ameritech has announced commercial DSL services in some areas of Michigan and Illinois. We recognize that the traditional telephone companies have the potential to quickly deploy DSL services and are in a position to offer service from central offices where we may be unable to secure space in traditional telephone companies' central offices."* This is a classic example of dual sovereignty and how companies can leverage their assets to force revolutionaries from the market.

In the plight of nation-states, Brinton stated that all revolutions were made in the name of freedom [see Brinton, page 138]. As such, the moderates believe in human rights and the freedoms of speech, press, and assembly. The extremists who oppose the moderates and want to continue the revolutionary process have no commitment to such freedoms. They are committed to the actions that bring about the accomplishment of their goals and they use the same tactics that the moderates used to bring about the collapse of the old regime.

When we examine why the Rule of the Moderates collapses and the Accession of the Extremists is successful, we find several reasons [see Brinton, page 145]. The first reason Brinton cites is that moderates who were leaders in the revolution were not fanatical revolutionaries. It is true that the Rule of the Moderates is dominated by intellectual leaders of the revolution, but these leaders and their government were not radical enough to satisfy the extreme core element of change within the society. Brinton describes the moderates as *"realists"* who are reasonably well adapted to the realities of government and common sense to support the radical extremes of change that would satisfy the extremists. The extremists view the moderates as people who betrayed the true potential of the revolution. In the view of the extremist, the moderates are people who used words and phrases to bring about revolution – but they reveal themselves to be uncommitted to the true cause of the revolution.

Brinton separates the moderates from the extremists by falling back on the belief that the moderates are practical people who seek practical solutions. He states that, *"In normal times, ordinary men are not capable of feeling for groups of their fellow men hatred as intense, continuous and uncomfortable as that preached by the extremists in revolution. Such hatred is a heroic emotion and heroic emotions are exhausting."* The moderates are people who want change and believe that the change they are seeking is quite dramatic and significant in nature, hence the need for a revolution to bring about the change they seek. The extremists view revolution as only partly about change. To the extremist, the revolution is about significant cultural change and power. Power is the real difference between the moderate and the extremist. The moderate wants power, but is unwilling to make supreme sacrifices to achieve and maintain power. The extremist suffers from no such restrictions. The extremist of any revolution easily and willing commits himself to the violent assumption and continuance of power.

When the moderates assume power, the majority of their objectives have been achieved, for the moderates are not true believers that they are in a position to change all of society and the ways of man. They are realists and realists are people who compromise to build broad coalitions to benefit the broadest segment of society. Briton states that these values give the moderates *"…part of their strength and give them hold over their fellow, who share at least their desire for comfort"* in normal society. Unfortunately, a revolution is not a normal time – but rather a time that enables those with radical ideas for change and fantastic visions for the future to find a stage upon which their message can be transferred into actions and deeds. This is Briton's *"Kingdom of the Blind"* wherein *"…the wisdom and common sense of the moderate are not wisdom and common sense, but folly."*

Why the Moderates of the ITO Revolution Failed

The failure of the moderates during the ITO Revolution occurred for the same reasons that the Rule of the Moderates collapsed during the French, English, and Russian Revolutions. There were six primary causes that forced the moderates from power and laid the foundation for the Accession of the Extremists of the ITO Revolution. These causes were:

- The moderates lost the support of the market (i.e. people)
- Technology dual sovereignty ended and one group was the clear winner

- The extremists controlled key parts of the infrastructure (i.e. governing apparatus)
- Barriers to market did not collapse fast enough for the moderates to solidify their foundation
- Financial capital withdrew its support of the moderates

The first sign that the moderates of the ITO Revolution were in danger occurred during 1997, for it was during this year that the first stock market correction occurred for internet stocks. The stock markets play an important role in the ITO Revolution for they provide a daily referendum on the progress of the revolution. The mobs in Paris might have a played a similar rule during the French Revolution, but in the case of the ITO Revolution, the mobs increase or decrease the value of the revolution – as opposed to a visit to the guillotine.

The 1997, stock market correction for internet stocks occurred because investors lost faith in many of the riskier internet ventures that were not showing signs of growth and profitability. When the aggressive financial goals for some internet companies were not achieved, it was the first evidence that there might not be an economic dual sovereignty. The old economy and the new economy did exist post the day of revolution, but as internet companies failed to realize their growth objectives, the strength and staying power of the old economy was validated and the riskiest internet ventures were eliminated. In our four revolutions, the government of the moderates loses the support of the people because their government cannot execute and deliver on the expectations that were set during the act of the revolution. The same action occurred during the ITO Revolution in 1997 when the expectations of investors were not met by many of the internet revolutionaries. When we look back on some of the more exotic internet ventures, we see their failure was part logistical and part social. From a logistical perspective, the early internet companies were building their business with emerging technology. Consumers were still learning to use the new technology and as we have identified, ingrained social habits are hard to change. People simply do not start buying furniture online because someone started an online furniture web site. *"Unlike with other famous bubbles...the Internet bubble is riding on rock-solid fundamentals, perhaps stronger than any the market has seen before. Underlying the crazy price increases are the foundations of what could become the early 21st century's leading growth companies, a group that in my opinion will include America Online, Yahoo and Amazon.com. So while the October-to-January run-ups have been crazy, the urge to invest in the companies that have seen the biggest pops is not. Just because the Internet stock phenomenon looks like a bubble, it isn't a given that the bubble will burst,"* [see Henry Blodget, *CNET News.com*, January 1999].

From a telecom perspective, the seeds of the collapse of the moderates were well laid. The RBOCs remained in control of the local loop. Post 1996, the RBOCs began their consolidation process and successfully remained in control of the local loop. From a revolutionary perspective, this is the existence of the dual sovereignty. In the telecom market, there existed two governments (i.e. companies) that each controlled key assets of the government (i.e. market). The RBOCs owned the local loop and the CLECs only had access to the local loop – but it was access they had to pay for. As the ITO Revolution pushed into 1998, the RBOCs were letting the revolutionaries spend vast sums of money to build network infrastructure, while they consolidated market share and resisted access to their infrastructure.

The failure of the market barriers to collapse quickly from the outset of the revolution was a primary reason that a dual sovereignty developed in the ITO Revolution. The extremists of the revolution fought access and fought to expand their markets. The RBOCs went from companies that had defined markets, regulated rates, and restricted service offerings to companies with the ability to expand and offer new services – such as long distance service – that were previously forbidden. The result of the Telecom Act of 1996 was an increase in the competitive offerings to the market, but it also enabled incumbents to leverage their market strengths and expand into new businesses. The result was the foundation for the collapse of the moderates and revolutionaries of the telecom component of the ITO Revolution. The telecom collapse would not occur for another two years – but the seeds were sowed during the Rule of the Moderates.

The moderates of any revolution are not the hardcore revolutionary that can endure long periods of disappointment and failure. As the extremists of the ITO Revolution began to gain power – the original panacea of the revolution seemed farther away. The moderates of any revolution simply do not have the will power to break through barriers when their initial vision that set their expectations is not realized.

The last force that began to force the moderates and revolutionaries from power was the elimination of financial capital. This leads back to the stock market and its role as the people's arbiter of success or failure. Expanding the stock market to include all forms of private capital, we create an important barometer as well as engine of the ITO Revolution. Working capital is the fuel that enables revolutionaries to create and sustain new business entities to compete in emerging markets. Financial capital began to leave the ITO Revolution because one fundamental metric was not performing at level to sustain confidence in these markets. The new entrants, who are the revolutionaries of our time, were not making money. They were not profitable. When companies and markets become non-profitable, capital leaves the market because value is not being created. No revolution in business can be successful without sustained profitability. As we pass through 2004 and into 2005, we find that the intellectuals that had led and called for the ITO Revolution are now being called before the peers who sit in judgment of the actions and question choices. In hindsight, we find their assessment of the opportunity at the time of revolution to be quite insightful.

The Accession of the Extremists

From a historical perspective, the Accession of the Extremists to power is marked by a series of violent escalating events. The initial overthrow of the old regime on the day of revolution is typically a bloodless event – in comparison to the Accession of the Extremists. When the old regime abdicates power, the process is more political than combative. Old regimes surrender power as part of the political process that respects the professionalism and protocols of the diplomatic process. If the old regime resists the revolutionaries, then open warfare will ensue as seen in the American and English revolutions. In the Russian Revolution, the Czar peacefully abdicated power. When power changes hands, the contending players for power do not kill each other on the day of revolution. They may kill each other in future days, but the transfer of power from the old regime to the moderates is a checkmate – not a period of intense violence. In the English Revolution, it took time for the lines of battle to be drawn.

Although the actual revolutionary event may shed blood as in the battles at Lexington and Concord, Paris, or in St. Petersburg, the initial collapse of the old regime is not a period of intense violence. When the revolution occurs, the old regime is vulnerable to change because it is structurally weak, thus the old regime is unable to control and govern power. The old regime's inability to maintain power results in their inability to vigorously oppose the revolution. In England, the King had to call for support from within the royal class. In America, the army of General Gage remained in Boston for nearly a year, until they were forced from Boston through a military checkmate on Dorchester Heights. When the collapse of the old regime occurs, the revolutionaries are usually startled with how easily the old regime capitulates or withdraws from their challenge to organize and count their supporters. The revolutionaries are surprised by the sudden change of power because they had labored at change for many years and the ease with which their objective was accomplished was unanticipated. When the Rule of the Moderates ends, the revolutionaries who were astounded with how easily the old regime collapsed are also surprised with the level violence associated with the Accession of the Extremists.

The violence that marks the historical transition from the period known as the Rule of the Moderates to the period called the Accession of the Extremists comes in many forms. Often it is identified by street fighting, bombings, open civil war, violent propaganda, forced seizures, and heated if not violent debates [see Brinton, page 148]. Brinton describes the state of society as a "...*universal state of tension*." As the tension increases within the society, reasonable men become unreasonable. In normal times, reasonable solutions that provide a compromise resolution to issues are unachievable in the time of the Accession of the Extremists. Progress in governing the nation-state by the post-revolution modernist government begins to slow. Governmental issues go unresolved as debate becomes preferred to governing. Across all levels of society there is a feeling that the revolution is entering a state of crisis. Some event or some group has to give in to break the impasse between the contending parties for power. When the breaking point is reached, the Accession of the Extremists is complete and the revolution will enter a term of intense violence. The Marquis de Lafayette, who was a moderate leader within the French Revolution, crossed the border to Switzerland to escape the deadly politics of the Terror. Kerensky went to the United States and Trotsky went to Mexico. During the English revolution, revolutionaries who were dissatisfied with the course of events and the policies of Oliver Cromwell left England for France and other continental nation-states. In the business world companies do not often have the choice of leaving revolutionary markets – but as the ITO Revolution showed, companies that entered ITO markets as a non-core business soon realized that they did not have the commitment to the market when the extremists made market conditions difficult.

Brinton comments that in his analysis, that the actual overthrow of the moderates is a quick and neat event [see Brinton, page 163]. The change of government usually occurs without the dramatic events that accompanied the overthrow of the Old Regime in the early days of the revolution. Power simply moves from those who cannot command it to those who can. At this point of the revolution, there is still a respect for politics and protocol. The government of the moderates is not an extremist group and as such, they yield power in a respectful manner. In the same predicament as the old regime was on the day of revolution, the inability of the moderates to maintain and wield power is the structural weakness of the ruling government. When the structural weakness of the moderates is confirmed by the extremists, the extremists act.

Why the Extremists Win

Alexander Kerensky and the Provisional Government that took control of Russia after the Czar abdicated realized all the problems that any government that follows an old regime assumes, with the addition of a war with Germany that was not going well. When Czar Nicholas abdicated on March 13th, 1917, he was replaced by a provisional government headed by Prince George Lvov.

Lvov was an interesting person to head the Provisional Government because he was born in Dresden and player in Russian national politics, but he was still an outsider to the core of Russian political power. Kerensky was appointed Minister of Justice and in this position he introduced a series of reforms abolishing capital punishment and guaranteeing civil liberties to include freedom of the press and abolishing discrimination based on ethic and religious differences. Prince Lvov's Provisional Government made no attempt to end the war with Germany. In May, 1917, Kerensky was appointed Minister of War and promptly announced a new offensive against the Germans on June 18th. The offensive made some gains, but eventually lost momentum and failed. Prince Lvov resigned in July and was replaced by Kerensky. Kerensky was still a popular figure within the government and he was now the leader of the Provisional Government and the first non-royal to lead the Russian Government.

After the February Revolution in 1917, the Bolsheviks met to decide their strategy. Some members of the party advocated supporting the post-revolution government as it was supported by a majority of Russians. Their view was that the revolution had occurred and a government of revolutionaries had taken control of the nation-state and this government was supported by the people. Lenin had the foresight to project through this disguise [see Brinton, page 158]. It did not matter that a majority of Russians supported the post-revolution government – what mattered was for the first time the structure of power had sufficiently changed to enable the possibility of the Bolsheviks accomplishing their objectives; the same objectives they had been toiling for years to achieve when the old regime was in control of the nation-state. To achieve their objectives in the ITO Revolution, the RBOCs used the same tactics as the extremists in the historical revolutions.

Within days of taking office, Kerensky announced yet another offensive by the Russian Army against the Germans. The soldiers of the Russian Army were unwilling to obey Kerensky's command and a couple million of them left for home. Kerensky's unwillingness to end the war, his continued call for new offensives and his failure to deal with the economic problems increasingly eroded his political support. This is the conundrum of the leaders who assume the power of the government post the revolutionary act. They are left with a set of high expectations to meet from the people and little ability to affect change in a reasonable period of time. Over time, the political power begins to erode as the people do not see tangible results from the revolutionary promises. On September 2nd, Kerensky proclaimed Russia a Democratic Republic in which he held the position of Minister-President.

The Bolsheviks and AOL share a history of means that resulted in a common end game. Lenin was not in Russia when the February Revolution occurred in 1917. He was in Switzerland. It was the Germans who transported him to Russia hoping that his destabilizing influence would work to their advantage. The conditions that enabled the Russian Revolution to occur were not a product of the Bolshevik Party. The Great War, the revolt by the workers in Petrograd and the collapse of the Czar's Government were not the result of efforts of the Bolsheviks – but it was the Bolsheviks who exploited these conditions to seize power and drive the moderates from the nation-state. AOL used the same tactic to drive others from the market and seize control of parts of the old economy.

Kerensky's government continued to weaken as conditions within the nation-state did not improve and the extremists led by Lenin systematically strengthened their position. On October 25th, the Provisional Government of Alexander Kerensky fell to the Bolsheviks. This was the October Revolution that the Communists would celebrate for another seventy four years. Kerensky escaped St. Petersburg on a Danish ship and spent the majority of his remaining life in the Untied States.

The easy answer to the question of why the extremists win and the moderates lose is that the moderates are weak and act indecisively and that the extremists grow strong and act decisively, but as Brinton highlights these generalizations are not a sufficient answer. Brinton states that the "...*extremists win out because thy secure control of the illegal government and turn it in a decisive coup d'etat against the legal government.*" The state of dual sovereignty is ended by the revolutionary acts of the extremists. Historically, the extremists of the revolutions that Brinton studied were the Independents, the Jacobins, and the Bolsheviks. Before detailing why the extremists are successful, it is important to remember the state of government post the revolution and who are the people who comprise the extremists. The government that succeeds the old regime is the moderates. They are a broad cross section of revolutionaries who unite to assume power based on noble ideals, but within the confines of the structure of society. The moderates are not people who seek to change the fundamental social structure of society, but rather they seek to change the people who wield ruling power in the nation-state. The power assumed by the moderates becomes less concentrated due to the broad social coalition of the government of the moderates. The extremists are the hardcore elements of the revolution. They have been organizing and working towards revolution for many years. Initially, the extremists are part of the ruling coalition of the moderates. Over time, the extremists become disillusioned with the coalition of the moderates as they believe that the revolution has not and will not reach their goals unless there is a continuation of the revolution. The application of power and the rule of government that was once a shared plurality amongst the post-revolution participants, collapses through a systematic process planned and executed by the extremists. It is the extremists who want the revolution to continue in order for them to assume power.

Organization and the efficient use of resources to oppose the moderates are fundamental to the success of the extremists. The extremists obtain their power by *"…ousting, usually in a series of conflicts, any and all active and effective opposition from these {government} organizations. The discipline, single mindedness and centralization of the authority which mark the rule of the triumphant extremists are first developed and brought to perfection in the revolutionary groups of the illegal government"* [see Brinton, page 149]. In the historical revolutions studied by Brinton, the existence of the extremists usually pre-date the revolution, as they have a history of being the hardcore revolutionists who have been seeking complete change of the nation-state during the years of the old regime. The confusion of the revolutionary environment enables the extremists to exploit their size and organization to become the decisive ruling force within the post-revolution society. They achieve this state by focusing on acquiring command of the key elements of the government that in turn control the nation-state. The key elements of the nation-state are the military, monetary supply, communications, and law enforcement resources. If these elements of the government can be controlled, then one would be in de facto control of the government.

The extremists who appropriate power in the revolutions that Brinton studied have a number of characteristics in common. The first characteristic is their size. They are few in number. Historically, Brinton cites the following examples of historical extremists [see Brinton, page >150]:

- Cromwell's New Model Army was created with a membership of 22,000 in a country with a population of three to five million
- The Jacobins numbered 500,000 in a country with a population of over twenty million
- Lenin's Bolshevik Party was well under 1% percent of the population in a nation-state of over one hundred million

The small size of the extremists is a pillar of their strength. They are a focused group that is capable of acting as a unified force focused on an overall objective that is macro by definition. This ability enables the extremists to concentrate their force on the vulnerable objectives that lead to the assumption of power. We defined vulnerable objectives as the military, monetary supply, communications, and law enforcement. Money, arms, communications, and law enforcement are the fundamental foundations of power within society. Governments wield power through these organizations. Controlling these governmental elements provides the foundation to power.

A characteristic of a revolution in a business market that is different from a revolution in a nation-state is that there exists a group of extremists who affect the revolution – but they are not revolutionaries in the traditional political model. Using the French Revolution as an example, we can align the three estates of French society prior to revolution in 1789 to elements of the business world prior to the ITO Revolution. The first estate in pre-revolutionary France was the clergy, the second estate was the nobility, and the third estate was everyone else who was not in the prior two estates. These estates provided French society with social division, as well as served to distinguish inequalities and rights that were enforced by law. If we assume that the second estate in the world of business is the old regimes and the third estate is the revolutionaries, the first estate in the world of business becomes the financiers. The financiers are the investment bankers, venture capitalists, stock analysts, and professional moneymen who run money and drive the valuations of companies. No discussion of the ITO Revolution is complete without examining the impact that the ITO Revolution had on the culture and traditional practices of the first estate of the ITO Revolution. The ITO Revolution provided the public with never before access, via the internet, to traditional financial, information, analysis and interaction with individuals in the first estate of the business world. The comparison of the financial community before the ITO Revolution to France's first estate prior to the revolution in 1789 reveals powerful similarities. In France, the clergy were a semi-secretive social order that relied on their ability to influence and draw spiritual, financial and political power from the other two estates. In the ITO Revolution, the financiers were a semi-secretive business order that relied on their ability to influence and draw financial and political power from the other two estates; the old regimes and the revolutionaries. This is the cyclic nature of creation and destruction that the first estate of the business world manipulates to create wealth, derived from the assessment and measurement of value.

The extremists that Brinton studied are fanatical. They have an intense devotion to their cause. Extremists are people who are willing to die for their cause. Typically, they are thoughtful intellectuals – but what separates the extremists from the intellectuals who lead the government of the moderates is their willingness to accept no compromise to achieve their objectives. The extremists do not have an attachment to the old regime and care little for the existing structures of society. In many ways, the extremist can be considered the dreamer of revolution. Their cause has a righteous nature of intensity that separates their motivations from the intellectuals and revolutionaries who played prominent roles during the events leading up to the revolution and within the government of the moderates. The extremist views change as a positive activity and the more change that can be inflicted on the nation-state will only serve to better the nation-state. Extremists would rather sweep away all elements of the old regime than live with anything less than the full achievement of their vision. This is why they perceive the government of the moderates as a weak byproduct of the old regime and as such, they are unwilling to accept its existence.

It is believed by Brinton that the historical age of the extremists provides to them an advantage over the moderates in the contention for power. The extremists are not newly converted revolutionaries. These are not people who flocked to the banner of revolution when the revolution became socially appealing. The extremists are the people who dedicated themselves to revolution in the dark days of the old regime. Actively suppressed by the old regime, the extremists have been plotting the downfall of the old regime for years during the darkest hours of their cause. When their goals seemed unattainable and they were actively suppressed, the extremists plotted their revolution. This is why they kept their membership small and their activities clandestine. The oppression of their cause taught the extremists to be a disciplined and secretive group. Within the ITO Revolution, the regional bell operating companies (RBOCs) that emerged from the break up of AT&T most easily fit this description, as well as AOL and Microsoft. The RBOCs played the unwanted step child who was cast out of the Ma Bell family and forced to live in a regulated world, without ability to go beyond their designated markets. For years, the RBOCs struggled against their former family member, biding their time until government controls on their business could be removed. Changing the policies of a ruling government, whether by legislation or by revolution, takes time. It does not happen easily and quickly without a compelling event. It takes a revolution to change the structure of a market and enable the revolutionaries to realize their goal. *"The Internet's pace of adoption eclipses all other technologies that preceded it. Radio was in existence 38 years before 50 million people tuned in; TV took 13 years to reach that benchmark. Sixteen years after the first PC kit came out 50 million people were using one. Once it was opened to the general public, the Internet crossed that line in four years,"* [see U.S. Department of Commerce, *The Emerging Digital Economy,* April 15, 1998].

The extremists in all the revolutions studied by Brinton had great leaders. These leaders were Oliver Cromwell, Lenin and Trotsky with contemporaries such as Mao, Fidel and Ho Chi Minh. The moderates have good leaders as well, but there is not a singleness of purpose. The leaders of the moderates are often champions of the revolution, but their personal objectives of wealth or recognition are more important then the revolution itself. The revolution is important, but the revolution is really a means to an end for the moderate revolutionary leader. When we look at the leaders of the moderates we identify many good leaders, but their numbers prevents them from be effective leaders. Power during the Rule of the Moderates becomes less concentrated. The leaders of the moderates cannot effectively concentrate their power to enforce the rule of the law. The extremists have no such liability. The extremists follow their leaders with devotion and unanimity. When the moderates are trying to consolidate power and build broad ruling coalitions, the extremists undermine their efforts and strike at the elements of society that control and project power.

The Reign of Terror is the beginning of a period of great social change within the four preeminent western revolutions. At this stage in the revolutionary cycle, each of the western revolutions had brought about a change in the structure of the government and the people who ruled the nation-state – but they had not greatly affected the lives of every citizen in meaningful way on a daily basis. The Reign of Terror begins with the assumption of power by the extremists and it provides the extremists with an unchallenged ability to wield power. For some period of time, ranging from several months to several years, the extremists have the ability to be as fanatical as they desire for no power exists within the nation-state to challenge their authority. The name extremist is given to the radical elements of the revolution because they seek change that dramatically affects the political and social structure of society. The extremists willing employ shock tactics to achieve their objectives. The term *"shock"* is used to highlight the secondary goal of the extremists, which is to traumatize the complacent nature of the society in order to highlight the magnitude of the change. The changes enacted by the extremists go far beyond the structure of the government. Their reign impacts the ordinary citizen and seeks to enact a permanent change in the social structure of the society. The change sought by the extremist attempts to undo the fabric of the social order, which was woven over many years. In some examples, the change wrought by the extremists is directed at revenge and retribution for crimes, real or perceived. When the people who wield power change, they are afforded an opportunity to exact revenge, small or large.

During the Reign of Terror, politics become real and serious for all citizens, as the punishment for being on the wrong side of the terror is death, pain, suffering, and imprisonment. Brinton states that the *"...terror touches great and small with the obsessive power of a fashion; it holds mean as little of the common weal ever holds them, unless they are professionally devoted to the study or practice of politics"* [see Brinton, page 177]. Politics become the daily obsession as unavoidable as our daily sustenance and the weather. Brinton examines the Reign of Terror from two perspectives. The first perspective is from the people who are not members of the revolutionary cult of the extremists. This group is called the outsiders. The second perspective is that of the insider; who is the true revolutionary believer, devoted to what they perceive is the real revolution. In this description we find one of the reasons why the terror occurs. The terror occurs at the hands of the extremist, because the extremist is a person unwilling to comprise and obsessed with achieving a higher order of existence for society.

Brinton describes the outsider as the person who makes up the majority of the society. He is the person who has a casual, passing interest in politics that peaks and wanes with the political season. The outsider is interested in politics during the political season – but politics does not consume their life. The outsider is not meeting clandestinely at night, plotting the overthrow of the state – but rather the outsider takes an interest in politics when it demands his interest. In short, the outsider is a bandwagon rider. He is inclined to join the bandwagon when revolutionary fever sweeps through the majority of the nation-state – but he will not be part of the bandwagon when the times are tough or contented. The attention span of the outsider is measured in months – while the attention span of the insider is measured in years and decades.

The Reign of Terror is difficult on the outsider because the fundamental elements of society that the outsider perceives as the foundation of their familiarity and comfort with society are changing. One of the early signs of the reign of terror is the phenomenon of renaming. In the four revolutions that Brinton studied, the extremists begin a renaming process that begins with people, processes and places. The extremists use the renaming process to confuse, misdirect and to signal an important break with the past. The target of the renaming process is the outsider. In each of the four western revolutions, renaming occurred at different levels of seriousness. In the English Revolution, the renaming process was confined to people and positions. In France, people and position renaming occurred, but it was also extended to street names, places, palaces, cities, daily conversation, and even the calendar [see Brinton page >178]. The daily greeting went from *monsieur* to *citizen*. The idea was to convey a new level of equal rights that all citizens of the revolution were now granted. The rallying call of the French Revolution was *"Liberté, Egalité, Fraternity."*

The Russians were especially fond of the renaming process, as cities such as St. Petersburg became Petrograd and eventually Leningrad. As the Russian Revolution completed the longest revolutionary cycle in terms of time, we witnessed a return to the names that had been familiar to the outsiders in 1917, nearly eighty years later. Leningrad was renamed St. Petersburg in 1991, seventy four years after the Bolshevik Revolution. The Supreme Soviet was replaced by the Duma after the collapse of the Soviet Union. The Duma was formed as a concession by the Czar as a result of the revolutions of 1905 in Russia. The Duma assumed control of the state in 1917 when the Czar abdicated. It was disbanded by the Bolsheviks (i.e. extremists) only to return when the Communist Party ceded power in 1991. Even the whole country was renamed Russia in 1991, as if the previous seventy-five years had never happened. This contemporary example witnessed in our own time, is testament to the strength and enduring power of the foundational pillars of embedded social fabric. Habits are hard to break and the extremists use name changing as one of many tactics designed to break social habits and create new habits and new familiarities. Even within the ITO Revolution, name changing was used to signify new beginnings for old companies as well as identification with the new economy that was emerging in the late 1990s. When Bell Atlantic and Nynex merged, they changed the name to Verizon to signify the joining of two companies as well as break from their AT&T roots. When IXC Communications merged with Cincinnati Bell, they changed the name of the company to Broadwing. A few years later when Cincinnati Bell sold off the assets they reverted to the Cincinnati Bell name and Broadwing remained Broadwing in name, but a separate company. After the bankruptcy of Worldcom in 2002, the company that emerged from bankruptcy in 2004 changed its name to MCI; a name that everyone knew and trusted. The name Worldcom was tarnished with the shame of bankruptcy and coffee cup counting. Some symbols of history are hard to change as the old Bell System logo can still be found on many central office buildings throughout the United States.

The difficulty in breaking social habits is a fact that is not lost on the extremists and it is the primary reason why they seek radical social change. Societies do not undergo revolutions as a common occurrence. Revolutions require a specific confluence of forces to occur. The old regimes are secure in the knowledge that social habits are difficult to change and over the long term, a society's comfort with the daily regime ensures the stability of power. The extremists are intimately familiar with the difficulties of changing social habits. Renaming is part of the process of demonstrating to the outsider that society has forever changed. The social pillars that had enabled the old regime and supported the moderates have now been stripped away. The extremists are also attempting to create new social pillars and habits that will provide the same stability to their extremist regime as was once provided to the old regime.

In all the revolutions studied by Brinton, there was also an attempt to address the virtues of society. The objective to create a new society based on higher standards of virtue is an attempt by the extremists to invoke a change within the society that enforces the seriousness of their intentions. The attempted elimination of vice and laziness are tactics used by the extremists to signal to the populace significant social change. To the extremist, who is the hard-core revolutionary, it is important to invade the lifestyle of the outsider and disrupt his habits. The life-style that existed during the old regime and continued into the early stages of the revolution is a barrier that restrains the society from reaching its potential. Eliminating vices such as gambling, prostitution, drinking, and other amusements are tactics designed to disrupt familiar patterns. Most extremists in revolutions view their actions as a means to a social utopia. The means justify the end and as such, it is believed that once a familiar pattern is broken, the seeds of a new social order can be sown.

Within the ITO Revolution, social change and virtue were promoted on many fronts. The internet held the promise of being a great equalizer in the field of education for the children of world. Email was replacing traditional mail services. Fewer trees would be cut down. Social isolation by political means would be broken by the internet. People around the world would be free to access and share information. For a revolution to be taken seriously, it must be perceived as having great social impact. This is why the telecom, the internet, and the optical revolutions where promoted as agents of profound social and economic change. New economies and new social orders are not tasks for the faint of heart – they are tasks for the dedicated revolutionary.

Opposed to the outsider is the insider. The insider is the extremist. He may not have been one of the leading intellectuals who transferred his allegiance during the last days of the old regime – but he is someone who has goals far beyond what was achieved in the earlier stages of the revolution. In Brinton's view, the insider is the true believer of the revolution. Brinton refers to the Reign of Terror and Virtue as the crisis period of the revolution. It is during this period that politics become lethal and the mere intellectual excitement and challenge of the revolution is eclipsed by the struggle for power. Before the Accession of the Extremists, violence was not overly prevalent in the revolutionary process. As the struggle of power begins to crystallize, conditions are created within the nation-state that support open conflict and civil war. To the insider, the strain of cleansing the nation-state of the enemies of the revolution begins to be too much. Brinton states that the insider "...*begins to have his hesitations and his doubts, to be bored with the endless ceremonies, deputations, committees, Stakhanovites competitions, tribunals, militia work and the other chores necessary to achieve the reign of virtue on earth*" [see Brinton, page 182]. Within the camp of the insider, a dichotomy begins to emerge. Some insiders break under the strain of the revolutionary process and evolve into outsiders – while a remaining group of insiders harden their resolve until the end. It is this resolve that increases the terror within the nation-state. The unwillingness to compromise is the path to violence.

On the same level as religious satisfaction, devotion to the extremist cause provides a sense of satisfaction to the insider. Many of the insiders have been devoted to their cause for many years and as the realization of their hopes, dreams, and plans begin to come true they experience a sense of satisfaction on a personal level similar to a religious awakening. The realization of the revolutionary dream provides a sense of deep satisfaction and this feeling becomes a substitute for religion devotion.

Throughout the Reign of Terror and Virtue, there is an important underlying motivation to the actions of the extremists. That motivation is the acquisition of economic power. In a subtle manner, Brinton has come full circle in the study of revolutions, as it was an acute economic crisis within the old regime that enabled the start of the revolutionary cycle. The extremists now stand as the arbiters of power within the nation-state. In order to maintain their power, they need to centralize power. Briton states that the centralization of power enables the extremists to *"...repel attacks from within and without."* To consolidate military and political power indicates that one has achieved control of the economic engines of the nation-state and thus must be in control of the dispensation of wealth. In the business world and the ITO Revolution, control of the economic engines means control of market share. The winners from the ITO Revolution were all companies that acted with extremist devotion to their businesses. Microsoft, AOL, Cisco, Verizon, Yahoo, eBay, Amazon, and SBC were the winners. Each of these companies fanatically devoted their energies towards the acquisition of market share and the elimination of competitors.

The true objective of the extremists is control of the economic engines of the nation-state. The tactics employed to this point of the revolution have been focused on controlling the apparatus of the nation-state that enforces power in order to seize control of the economic assets. The extremist connects the environment to the past, to the future, to the people, and the ideas and plans of their competitors. The extremist plays for the end-game. The moderate plays the game for the goal of playing the game. While the moderates are playing the game in the two dimensions of space and time, the extremists is playing the game with a third dimension and that is a projection of what their competitor is or will do. The extremist is not in the revolution for today, the extremist is in the revolution for tomorrow; a day when the extremist will control power and money – as money and power are linked. When companies have money, companies have power. When companies have power, companies can use that power to acquire money. *"The whole point, indeed, of the three revolutions we are about to analyze is that religious enthusiasms, organization, ritual and ideas appear inextricably bound up with economic and political aims, with a program to change things, institutions, laws, not just to convert people"* [See Brinton, page 185]. Revolutions within nation-states and within economic markets have entry and exit criteria that are one in the same. Revolutions find their beginnings in economic crises and reach their end when economic power is consolidated and once again controlled by the few. In short, that is the definition of a revolution. A revolution breaks the concentration of power, diffuses power amongst the many, and then returns to a state wherein power in once again controlled by the few – only a different few from the original state. When revolutions begin, the question is; who will be the controlling few at the end of the revolution? This is the question that the first estate asks everyday via the global financial markets.

By changing the laws, institutions, and social structure of the society, the extremists are in effect legitimizing their acquisition of power and enforcing their hold on power by being the final arbiters of economic wealth. If you remove the ideological element from the motivations of the extremists, they appear to conform to the contemporary definition of a Keynesian economist, such as Lyndon Johnson, believing that only the governing body of the nation-state can act as a mechanism to maintain full employment, steady production, and economic stability through activist monetary and fiscal policies. Control of the economy and the people of the nation-state are required elements to ensure that the ideological objectives of the extremists are achieved.

As the extremists assume power and induce the Reign of Terror and Virtue, they do not restrict their actions to their nation-state. In all cases, each revolution seeks to export their beliefs and revolutionary changes as well as the revolutionary process. Brinton identifies this action as nationalism. In each revolution, the nationalistic fervor to be exported differed – but in all the revolutions, the exportation of the revolution is clearly identifiable. In the 20th century, the Communist Party of the Soviet Union was an ardent believer in a global Marxist revolution and openly encouraged a bi-polar alignment against the western nation-states. The ironic aspect of this alignment is that the western nation-states of France, England, and America were all experienced revolutionaries who had used the revolutionary process to evolve from their monarchies. By the mid-twentieth century, all four revolutionary nation-states studied by Brinton were actively engaged in the nationalistic exportation of their revolutionary beliefs. Revolution, colonialism, and nationalism are terms for the same activity, which is the exportation of ideological and political systems in order to secure economic wealth.

It is at this point that Brinton ties nationalism and religion together. The exportation of the revolution by the extremists is a strategy to keep the insiders engaged in the revolution. Nationalism presents new opportunities to motivate the hard-core revolutionary. The success they achieved within their own nation-state provides motivation and hope that equal success can be achieved in other nation-states. This is why the extremists need to consolidate power. The exportation of their ideas is a threat to the bordering nation-states. The old regimes that border the nation-state undergoing a revolution fear that the forces of change will be exported to their nation-state. Brinton again highlights the parallel between the revolution and religion. He states, *"Our revolutionists are convinced they are the elect, destined to carry out the will of God, nature or science"* [see

Brinton, page 194]. This belief becomes an enabling aspect of the terror. The extremists use the fanatical belief in their position to justify the guillotine, the firing squad, and the hangman's noose. The result is a binary solution for the extremist. Either you are an ardent believer in the revolution or you are not. *"If there is but one truth, and you have that truth completely, toleration of differences means an encouragement to error, crime, evil and sin"* [see Brinton, page 194]. The determination of the extremists is easily identifiable in words of the great leaders who have been the winners in their revolutions. Mao Zedong stated *"this army has an indomitable spirit and it is determined to vanquish all enemies and never to yield. No matter what the difficulties and hardships, so long as a single man remains, he will fight on."* Ho Chi Minh stated, *"You will kill 10 of our men, and we will kill 1 of yours, and in the end it will be you who tire of it."* Ernesto Che Guevara, the Argentine revolutionary said, *"Whenever death may surprise us, let it be welcome if our battle cry has reached even one receptive ear and another hand reaches out to take up our arms."* Revolutions are full of extremists and their dedication to their cause does not change if the fate of a nation-state or business hangs in the balance.

Having come back to the religious parallel, Brinton eloquently defines the difference between the extremist and traditional religion. The extremist seeks to find their heaven on Earth in span of their lifetime. Organized religion creates an afterlife to bridge the gap between what man has now and what man wants. To the revolutionary, this is a foolish notion, as the revolutionary proposes to fill the gap in the present. It is at this point that we can realize another important component that supported the revolution in its early stages. Man has the ability to envision the future and that future is nearly always better – not worse. The leaders, who are doers, envision a better world. Their vision may be misguided, but they believe it is noble in nature. The actions of the revolutionaries, whether in business or in politics are not governed by an objection or a vision of future that is less than present. Revolutionary leaders do not start a company to change the world because they believe that the net result will be tragedy and despair. Those who envision tragedy and despair are typically those who are not doers. Brinton states that *"Even if you assume, as the positivist, the materialist, does, that man is an animal and nothing more, a part of nature – and that nature is all there is – it seems reasonably clear that man is unique in nature and among animals in being able to conceive a future"* [see Brinton, page 197]. The ability to conceive a future is part of the underlying foundation of revolution and change. People can envision a future and they can create that model of the future based on an extrapolation of present day facts. Those who can do that the best, obtain the most amount of money. This is the art of the venture capitalist, the revolutionaries, the entrepreneurs, and futurist of our time. They have a vision, a hypothesis of the future, and each day they are seeking to find the path that leads to their vision.

The two objectives of the extremist are the desire to wield power and to achieve their vision of heaven on Earth – but the extremist realizes that these goals are achieved within society. As such, the pillars of society that enable the old regime to be stable must be instilled within the post-revolutionary society by the new regime created by the extremists. People are creatures of habit and the old habits that served the old regime need to be replaced with new habits that serve the new regime. Brinton concludes that the extremists have had to "...*invent abstract gods, tribal gods, jealous gods. Their new faiths have not the maturity of the old. The have not, despite their aspirations, the universalism of the old. They have not for the weary and the disappointed the consoling power of the old. They have not yet gained the power of successful syncretism, the wisdom of the ages. They are still, in short, revolutionary faiths, more effective goads or prods than as pacifiers*" [see Brinton, page 197]. The terror that occurs as part of the accession of power by the extremists is the product of the extremist's attempts to consolidate power and change the social order.

Why the Terror Occurs

Changing societies and the habits of people are not easy tasks. They do not occur with a decree of a new law. The terror that grips all four of the revolutions during the crisis period is the product of seven forces that converge on the revolution in a complicated form. As we examine the seven forces that converge to create the terror, it is important to note their linkage to the old regimes. This is where man's habits of the familiar come into play. Voltaire said, "*As long as people believe in absurdities they will continue to commit atrocities.*" In the revolutions that Brinton studied, as well as in our ITO Revolution, we can clearly identify linkages from the terror to the old regime. This does not mean that the old regime is responsible for the terror, but rather that elements of the terror can be linked to the old regime. The history of the old regime and life within the society of the old regime shaped and influenced the outsider as well as the insider. These experiences affect the out come of events during the terror because people are shaped by the experiences of their past and their actions in the present often reflect some form of linkage to the past. This is the linkage between the terror and the old regime.

The first characteristic of the Reign of Terror that Brinton identifies is the habit of violence [see Brinton, page 198]. In all the revolutions, the habitual employment of violence does not begin for sometime. In most of the revolutions that Brinton studied, it occurred months or years after the initial revolutionary act. The reason for this seems to be that it takes time to reach a social and political state in which the employment of violent means is necessary. Even the extremists who are the most radical of the revolutionaries do not wake up the day after the revolution and start killing people. Violence requires people to be pushed into extreme conditions wherein the liberal application of violence becomes not only accepted, but also comfortable and necessary as a course of survival or perceived progress. When undergoing revolutions, perception is reality.

The second characteristic of the terror is the pressure of a foreign and civil war. This pressure is a galvanizing force within the nation-state as it clearly sets forth an immediate need for a call to action. War legitimizes the extremist's need to centralize power. In war, people choose sides. The extremists realize that civil and foreign wars against opposing nation-states provide a litmus test for loyalty to the revolution. They also realize that a foreign or opposing army is a threat they cannot influence. Armies are organizations of men who have accepted the need for prolonged and sustained violence. As we discussed with the first characteristic, when people reach a state at which they are comfortable with violence, they are no longer rational and open to dialogue and peaceful methods of change.

Further complicating the crisis that has engulfed the revolutionary nation-state is the newness of the government [see Brinton, page 200]. The prior government that was composed of the moderates who had assumed power from the old regime was a hybrid of new ways within the structures left by the old regime. The extremists are no such hybrid. They are experienced revolutionaries – but they are not experienced leaders of government [see Brinton, page 200]. The new centralized government created by the extremist uses some of the structures of the government left by the old regime and the Rule of the Moderates – but they are new and as such, they do not have well defined channels of operations. The extremists are simply administratively inexperienced in comparison to the old regime. Brinton declares that the "… *machinery of the Terror works in fits and starts and frequently jams baldly*" [see Brinton, page 200]. Conflicts within the new governing administration occur and these conflicts are typically resolved through violence. As the leaders of the extremists attempt to enforce the creation of their heaven on Earth, they find that the unexpected occurs and their plans are not implemented as smoothly as expected. Unforeseen challenges occur as people naturally resist change. The result of these breakdowns and missed objectives is violence. The extremists are comfortable with violence as their method of conflict resolution.

Each revolution found its roots in a financial crisis for the government – but it was not the nation-state that was undergoing the crisis, but rather the government of the old regime. As the terror takes hold in the revolution, a real economic crisis begins to affect the nation-state. The revolutionary process has systematical disrupted the economic machinery of the nation-state. As the struggle to consolidate power turns violent and the threat of civil and foreign war announces it presence, capital leaves the nation-state. Businesses are shutdown and people begin to horde and hide items of economic value. A slow steady decline in national resources begins. The basic supplies of food, money, goods, and services begin to disappear. This real economic crisis puts pressure on the extremists to deliver their new panacea – but it is not a revolutionary threat. Remember the Reagan from the period of the old regimes that revolutions occur when the people of the nation-state are economically prosperous and have time to devote to revolutions. At this stage of the revolution, the masses within the society begin to enter into survival mode and their actions on a daily basis are very non-revolutionary.

The sixth force that is a component of the terror is class struggle. This might be perceived as an obvious element of revolution – but Brinton's studies show that class struggles between the old regime and the revolutionaries are one form of class struggle found in the formative stages of the revolution. The class struggle that forms during the terror is not the same as the class struggle that precedes the revolution. In the beginning, the class struggle is the revolutionary element versus the old regime. The early class struggles can have several variations such as a proletariat versus bourgeois element, religious differences, or a division within the ruling branches of the government. The early class struggles are strong enough to be a driver of the revolution, but they do not approach the scale and scope of the class struggles that occur during the terror.

The class struggles that occur during the terror are between the multiple contenders for power within the nation-state. In the Russian Revolution, the struggle was between the Bolsheviks, Kadets, and Whites. In the American Revolution, it was the Whigs versus the Tories. In the English Revolution, it was Cromwell versus the King and the moderate members of Parliament who were willing to compromise with the King. In all revolutions, the extremists are initiating class warfare against the elements of the society that seek a compromise to share power. Those organizations that were part of the Rule of the Moderates are the enemy. The class struggle during the terror is also marked by extreme violence and the binary resolution of the problem. During the early stages of the revolution, the class struggle is marked by social change. In the terror stage of the revolution, the class struggle is marked by death and the departure of those on the losing side. As we look at our world in 2004, we find the ancestors of American Tories still living in Canada and swearing allegiance to the King. Only with the collapse of the Soviet Union did we find many expatriates from the Russian aristocracy return to their homeland. Revolutions change society, but the fabric of society that has taken years, decades, and in some societies, centuries to weave is difficult to unravel. This is why the class struggle during the terror is lethal. If you cannot change it, the extremists think you must kill it.

There seems to be a seventh force that affects the terror and that force is the determination of the extremists not to compromise. Politics in a stable society is the art of compromise practiced at a dull and thoughtful pace. Politics during the terror is decisive, fast, and results not creation of law, but the elimination of opponents. The extremists who ascend to power are skilled in survival and political intrigue – but they are not skilled in compromising. This characteristic of the terror forces an unusual set of events to occur in order to force change. The unwillingness of the leaders of the extremists to compromise will run its course until a large number of insiders defect to the outsiders. Eventually, the strain of the terror creates within the society a loss of power and support for the extremists. This may take weeks, months, or years, but the unwillingness to compromise and revert back to politics as usual puts the hardcore extremists at long-term risk.

Crane Brinton closes his discussion of the forces found in the terror by returning to the discussion of religious faith. In many ways, religion, religious faith, or mankind's need for faith is a foundation for revolution. Faith, whether it is religious or agnostic, is a driving force within society and mankind. Faith is what enables mankind to dream. Brinton states that *"religious aims and emotions help differentiate the crises of our revolutions from the ordinary military or economic crises and give to the reigns of terror and virtue their extraordinary mixture of spiritual fury, of exultation, of devotion and self-sacrifice, of cruelty, madness and high grade humbug"* [see Brinton, page 202]. As the forces we have outlined converge during the terror, it creates a cumulative effect on the society. The economic strains, the class struggles, the open warfare, and the requirement to meet unnatural levels of virtuous behavior, wear on and weigh down the society. Each break with the past, and the traditions and social order of the past disrupts the social system that had been set. Brinton states that *"...it would seem to be an observable fact of human behavior that large numbers of men can stand only so much interference with the routines and rituals of their daily existence. It would seem that most men cannot stand the strain of prolonged effort to live in accordance of high ideals"* [see Brinton, page 203]. The result of the accumulated strain of the terror is the final stage called Thermidor. Again we turn to Brinton, *"Thermidor comes as naturally to societies in revolution as an ebbing tide, as calm after a storm, as convalesce after a fever, as the snapping back of a stretched elastic band"* [see Brinton, page 203]. As we will see in the final phase of revolution, there has been a great upheaval caused by a revolution – but little has been permanently affected as the societies that underwent a revolution return to the social order familiar under the old regime.

Thermidor

The final stage of Brinton's revolutionary cycle is called the Thermidor Reaction. Brinton describes the period he calls Thermidor as a "...*convalescence from the fever of revolution*" [see Brinton, page 205]. In the four western revolutions studied by Brinton, the final stage of Thermidor arrived differently within each revolution. The exactness of timeline and the transition elements were not consistent across the English, American, French, and Russian revolutions – yet within each revolution a period of Thermidor is clearly identifiable. Each revolution entered the final stage of revolution on its own timeline, in its own way. Brinton named the final stage of his revolution model after the final stage of the French Revolution. It was during the French Revolution that the clearest transition to the final stage of the revolutionary cycle could be identified. The stage of Thermidor is a reference to the death of Robespierre in France, which occurred on July 27, 1794 or on 9 Thermidor Year II of the new French calendar.

In the early days of the French Revolution, Maximilien Francois Isidore Marie de Robespierre who was a lawyer in Paris prior to the French Revolution, was elected as a deputy of the Third Estate. Within the community of French revolutionaries, he gained notoriety for promoting progressive revolutionary polices and his vehement resistance to corruption. The old regimes of every revolution are guilty of corruption in the eyes of the revolutionaries. The corruption of the old regimes within each revolution varies in size and scope, yet the revolutionaries are successful in creating a comparison that the old regime is corrupt or not fair and a revolution would bring about a new social order that would be less corrupt and more just. The revolutionaries are successful in playing to the ebb and flow of feelings of social injustice. There are times when the social undercurrents are acutely aware of social injustice or inequalities and there are times when little attention is paid to these concerns. Revolutions always bring about a heightening of the awareness of social inequalities. The same is true in the business world. This is exactly what happened post the Second World War in the Britain when the population voted to assume state ownership of economic assets to ensure an equitable distribution of wealth. The same can be argued that the control of the commanding heights of the economy are what drove people to revolt against this economic structure in the late twentieth century. The evolution from owning the commanding heights of the revolution to viewing the ownership as a limiting factor in economic independence required thirty years.

Robespierre earned the nickname *"the Incorruptible."* His real rise to fame came as the spokesperson for the Jacobin Club. The Jacobin Club rose out of the Rule of the Moderates to terrorize France. It was the members of the Jacobin Club who embodied and enforced the extreme policies of the French Revolution as it entered the Reign of Terror and Virtue. Robespierre was the puritanical spokesperson who was lauded as the oracle of political wisdom during the tribunals and executions presided over by the Jacobin Club during the Terror. This small group of extremists called the Jacobins used their organizational discipline to appear larger and in control of the nation-state. When the Jacobins ascended to power, the ruling power of the moderates was diffused amongst many people and organizations. The nation-state was engaged in a foreign war and these conditions combined to enable the Jacobins to wield, first, influence over the revolutionary public and eventually ruling power. Robespierre's eventual arrest and execution was an ironic fate because it was a product of a conspiracy by fellow Jacobins who were engaged in corrupt politics and war profiteering. They feared that the incorruptible Robespierre, who was the champion of the Reign of Virtue and Terror, would use his power to institute social purity within French society. The conspirators where successful in having Robespierre arrested and his place secured on the guillotine as a traitor to the French Revolution. The unintended result of Robespierre's death was that it galvanized the French population and acted as a signal to begin social healing and a return to normalcy. Revolutions often begin their inevitable decline when an event of great social notoriety sobers the revolutionary masses. This is what happened in France, England, and the Soviet Union.

The transition to the period of Thermidor is marked by several important events within the society. The most important of these events is the sense on a personal conscious level that the terror that has griped the society is over. In France, this occurred with the death Robespierre and in Russia it was marked by Khrushchev's speech to the party denouncing Stalin. The society within each nation-state begins to recede from the furor unleashed by the extremists during the Reign of Terror and Virtue. This does not mean that the nation-state is suddenly ruled by leaders who are kind, full of wisdom, and virtuous – but it does mean that the disruption of the social fabric that has been a core activity of the extremists has ended. In France, the fall of Robespierre was met with dance halls opening and prostitutes practicing their trade. This is the beginning of a return to a social balance understood by a majority of the society. The revolution did not fulfill the early romantic dreams, but it did change the structure of power and disrupted the social fabric.

Within the ITO Revolution, the period of Thermidor was reached in late 2005. It was not marked by an event as dramatic and stunning as the beheading of Robespierre, but rather by a series of events in 2005 that signaled to the world that business was in recovery from its revolutionary hangover. Bernie Ebbers was convicted in 2005. The last chapter in the long story of AT&T was being written. The last chapter in the history of MCI was also being written. It is fitting that the year 2005 will be known as the year that AT&T and MCI were acquired and that Bernie Ebbers, a high-school physical education teacher and hotel owner, was convicted for his role in the Worldcom bankruptcy. The world was returning to normal. The telecom services and telecom equipment markets may not be booming, but the market began to return to predicable growth within traditional industry norms. The survivors were identifiable and there was still a long and prosperous future to the ITO Revolution for those companies that had emerged from the Reign of Terror and Virtue with credible business and reasonable balance sheet.

The Three Components of the Thermidor Reaction

Brinton outlines three important components that identify the period known as Thermidor. These components are (a) amnesty and repression, (b) return of the church, and (c) the search for pleasure. Brinton begins the discussion by noting that in all four revolutions the identification of a tyrant was fundamental to the beginning of the Thermidor stage. The establishment of the dictator is the attainment of the extreme range of power concentration with a nation-state and market. Brinton highlights Cromwell, Bonaparte, and Stalin as the dictators who assumed complete and total power over their post-revolutionary nation-states. Power within the nation-state moves to a dictator because after the *"...centralization of power, some strong leader must handle that centralized power when the mad religious energy of the crisis period has burned itself out"* [see Brinton, page 208]. The Reign of Terror and Virtue has centralized power, but the extreme state of tension cannot be maintained for an indefinite period of time. *"As time goes on, the pressures the Terror applied to ordinary men are relaxed: the special tribunals give way to more regular ones, the revolutionary police are absorbed into the regular police – which are not necessarily the equivalent of London Bobbies; they man be agents of the NKVD – and the block, guillotine or firing squad are reserved for more dramatic criminals"* [see Brinton, page 208]. In France, the death of Robespierre left the nation-state to be ruled by small group, who were eventually supplanted by Napoleon. Cromwell and Stalin both emerged from ruling committees to assume complete and total power within the nation-state. Only after the death of these dictators, would the nation-states of France, Russia, and England return to a state of a plurality of power. This is the beginning to a return to a state of power concentration in line with power balance during the old regime.

In the revolutions that Brinton studied, the period of Thermidor bore witness to the return to a position of prominence the church that was dominant during the period of the old regime. In nearly every western revolution, the role of the church within society was attacked during the revolution. No institution comparable to organized religion exists in the business world to equate the role that religion played in the historical revolutions. Organized religion provides spiritual fulfillment and moral guidance and acts as a mechanism to foster social unity. Business markets have trade organizations, unions, and societies that through affiliation provide some of the aspects of the religion, but these groups do not wield the power or play the role of the First Estate in the western revolutions. Therefore, we must identify a similar component in the ITO Revolution that matches the role of the church in the historical revolutions.

The closest alignment in the ITO Revolution to the role of the church in the historical revolution is not found in a single institution – but rather in the conduct, method, and confidence of doing business. The role of the church in the ITO Revolution was played by the old economy and the extremists companies that existed prior to the revolution. The same companies that emerged as the powerful companies post the revolution. At the time of writing of this essay, the ITO Revolution was still working through the period of Thermidor. Perhaps in a few years, all the elements of the Thermidor stage can be identified – but it appears that the return of investor faith in the quality of the companies, the soundness of the business models, and the legitimacy of markets is the logical analogy between the return of the church and the ITO Revolution. Cleary the actions taken by the government to enact the Sarbanes-Oxley law, the legal actions championed by Eliott Spitzer and the successful prosecution of key executives who were part of the ITO Revolution scandals are key elements of the return of organized religion to the ITO Revolution. Companies are valued by the metrics of earning money for their shareholders, success in real markets, and their ability to have and maintain internal controls.

The period of Thermidor also bears witness to the return of the moderates, members of the old regime, and the intellectuals who fled the revolution during the Terror. As the nation-state moves away from the polarization identified during the Reign of Terror and Virtue, the politically savvy moderates deem it safe to return. In some cases, they begin to take an active role in politics once again. The signal to return to the nation-state is the elimination of the most violent and extreme revolutionaries. Predictability and politics, process, and protocols familiar to the old regime return once again. Brinton writes that the "...*more active and violent leaders of the original Terror, they are of course eliminated, either by exile or by death. They are now declared to have been fanatics, villains, bloodthirsty tyrants, scoundrels. They become very convenient scapegoats, explanations of the difficulties the new regime has getting things settled*" [see Brinton, page 211]. During the ITO Revolution, we find evidence of Thermidor with the movements of value investing, technical analysis, and fundamentals. Investors did not think of how big the market was going to be in five years when the new economy took hold – but rather thought in terms of profitability, earnings, and multiples.

A key identifier of the Thermidor period is the settling of the ruling class. The new leaders may have been fanatical extremists when it suited their needs, but now that the revolution is beginning to settle and the hot fires of revolution are on the wane, we find that the new ruling class clearly intends to enjoy the privileges of their position and focus on the tasks at hand. Power still needs to be managed and power is usually concentrated in form of a dictator. What is not in question is the establishment of a strong ruling organization that is not vulnerable to another revolution or loss of power. Political power within the nation-state becomes permanent during Thermidor. The infrastructure of the nation-state is in need of massive repair and the new rulers begin the process of rebuilding the nation-state because this is a mechanism to secure power. The objective of the new ruling class is not to achieve any of the high ideals of the revolution, but rather to avoid further revolution by stabilizing society around familiar traditions and customs. Brinton states that *"There will be none of the dangerous direct appeals to the people, no risks of great popular uprisings"* [see Brinton, page 212].

The role of established religions in the old regimes positioned them as targets for the extremists of the western revolutions. The religious orders that were strong during the period of the old regimes had become targets for the extremists when they assumed power. This was primarily due to the fact that the extremists viewed strong organized religions of the old regime to be enablers of the power of the old regime. In Russian, the Bolsheviks possessed an absolute hated of the Greek Orthodox Church. In France, the extremists attacked Catholics loyal to the Pope in Rome; loyalty to God was one thing; loyalty to a foreign Pope was another. The result of the extremists attack on established religions that they viewed as enablers of the old regime is the return of these religions during the period of Thermidor.

A true identifier of the Thermidor period is the return of the search for pleasure. The nation-state begins to move away from the Reign of Virtue. Social standards and high ideals are abandoned. People are not persecuted at tribunals wherein they are held accountable to standards that few, if any, persons could meet. The quest to achieve noble standards of a Calvinistic, Robespierrean or Communist social order comes to an end. The revolution has run its course and it has left many changes to society. It is now the responsibility of the leadership that emerges from the Thermidor stage to set about fixing the nation-state. Improving what is imperfect, repairing the damage and setting an acceptable pace and cadence to government.

Conclusion

Two of the great contributions that revolutions provide are hope and opportunity. In the telecom services and telecom equipment industries, the ITO Revolution broke apart static market structures and provided opportunity where no opportunity for new players had existed before. As the Rule of the Moderates transitioned into the Accession of the Extremists and eventually the Reign of Terror and Virtue, the market conditions turned violently against the large companies and even more severely against the startups and small companies that where spawned when market conditions were optimistic.

In many ways the startups are the citizens of the ITO Revolution. They are not established companies; they are not the large institutions that have enormous resources to deploy. The startups are the small participants in revolution. They are the people who gather in the squares and cafes to talk with excitement about the revolution. During the ITO Revolution, the citizens were more likely to gather in the local Starbucks or microbrewery or trendy bistro. The opportunity to create new companies occurred during the ITO Revolution as never before. Thousands of networking equipment, telecom service providers, and internet companies of various types were created during the ITO Revolution. Many of these companies were opportunistically looking forward to a prolonged period of time, named the new economy, to build their companies when the revolution changed.

When the extremists come to power, market share rapidly moves under control of the extremists. It moves to the extremists for several reasons. The most significant reason is fear. Fear is a great motivator and as the Terror moves through the market, the decision making process for customers becomes driven by fear. Fear of weak companies. Fear of a loss of services from a supplier. Fear of failure. Fear of making a mistake and losing their job if they make the wrong decision. Fear becomes a significant driver in the decision making process and the extremists begin to capitalize on this fear to gain and control market share. Fear is a coercive force that enables the extremists to kill the startups and wrest control of the revolution. Analysts call this phenomenon market consolidation. It is only a consolidation if the startup or small company is being acquired. If the startup, the citizen of the revolution, is killed (i.e. bankrupted and shutdown) during this phase of the revolution, consolidation is a very kind term.

The business model for a technology startup building a hardware based system level product is quite simple to model. Assuming the company has a plan and is well down the path of product development, the company probably has about one hundred employees. A fair estimate that the cost to run this company is about $18 million a year. If they actually can sell their product and make a reasonable margin of 45-55 points, then the company needs annual sales of around $72 million – but this is a trap. To scale the business to support $72 million in annual sales will require a much higher level of expenditures. The company really needs much more capital to support the life-cycle costs, the large amount of R&D and the general operating expenses to grow the business. The startup must either take more venture capital or go public in order to raise the required funds. During the Rule of the Moderates, raising venture capital and going public were options available to many startups. The market barriers had declined. The large public companies were rapidly acquiring companies. From a venture capital perspective, there were many exit strategies for their investment to be successful. Once the Reign of Terror began, exit strategies for startups became nonexistent. Venture capitalists and revolutionaries who wanted to start new companies did not have a plausible path to exit the investment. The days of starting a company simply to build a product were over. The business of venture capital was returning to the historical objectives of using venture capital to build a business. There was simply no real return on investment (i.e. ROI) plan that seemed plausible and likely during the Reign of Terror. This is why many startups were shut down during the Reign of Terror [see *Foundations*].

As with our four western revolutions, the ITO Revolution had clear and distinctive linkage to the legacy methods of the business during the old regime. For the moderates of the ITO Revolution, the new economy and new methods of business did develop – they simply did not develop quickly enough to make their business plans with high upfront costs sustainable. The failure of many of the revolutionary companies to be successful opened the door for the extremists to close the market window and raise the market barriers. To close the market window and protect market share, the extremists attacked the moderates by lowering prices, slowing business, and bundling services and business offers that the moderates could not match. The extremists of the ITO Revolution turned out to be revolutionaries who had spent years building their businesses and they were not about to let a new converts to the cause steal their success. Microsoft, AOL, the RBOCs, and Cisco all leveraged their resources to increase the level of difficulty for new companies to be successful in the market. As a result of their actions, companies failed, employees found themselves unemployed, and investors lost money. This is the violence of the Terror stage of the ITO Revolution. It may not seem as bad as the Terror during the French Revolution, but when people cannot find jobs, cannot make mortgage payments, cannot provide for their families, and fear for their future, it is very much a real terror.

There is, in every business, revolution winners and failures. The winners make money and the failures lose money. This dichotomy produces a class struggle based on economic wealth and it becomes a driving force for change during the end of the revolutionary cycle and at the beginning of the next cycle. A perfect example of class struggle in a business context is the RBOCs, who were cast off by AT&T. The RBOCs realized their revenge on AT&T; it just took the RBOCs about fourteen years to be successful. Sun Microsystems was arguably one of the most successful companies that capitalized on the ITO Revolution – but when extremists came to power, Microsoft was the winner and Sun was the loser. When the revolutionaries lose, they typically turn to other means to be successful. Sun was a vocal advocate against Microsoft and tried to use the legal system of the Untied States to slow Microsoft's success. As in historical revolutions, the moderates who are on the losing side in a business revolution often end up out of business or in another line of business.

The unwillingness of companies not to comprise during the Reign of Terror during the ITO Revolution was abundantly identifiable. When the extremists gain the advantage in the market, they share a common characteristic: they are unwilling to compromise and seek the total elimination of their competitors through final defeat or acquisition. Extremists do not care if their competitors are suffering during the Reign of Terror. Verizon did not care that Northpoint was going out of business. Microsoft did not care that Netscape had lost the browser war. The RBOCs would have been quite happy to see AT&T, MCI, and Sprint go out of business. AOL was happy to acquire Compuserve when market conditions were favorable because AOL was growing at rapid pace and Compuserve was not. Acquisition of market share was far more valuable to AOL, who was growing, than Compuserve who was stagnant.

CHAPTER NINE
Boyd: The Theorist Practitioner

Every maxim relating to war will be good if it indicated the employment of the greatest portion of the means of action at the decisive moment and place.
- Jomini

Business is the war of making money. That is all it is and all it will ever be. War between nation-states is fought over territory, resources, and rights. War between companies is fought over markets (i.e. territory), resources (i.e. assets, people and technology), and rights (i.e. money and intellectual property). When companies have money, they have the right. To have money is to have the right to conduct your business the way you want it conducted within the boundaries of the law and the governance of nation-states.

There have been, and will be, successful businesses that were noble in nature, but in the purest form, business is war. Businesses are not endowed to their employees. Businesses do not owe their employees any form of compensation greater than that agreed upon for the specified amount of work. This might be viewed as laissez-faire – but each employee must make his or her choice and keep their personal interests as their primary responsibility. Companies do provide financial rewards to their employees, who in turn use these rewards to purchase goods, raise families, and put children through school. Business people run companies to make money. Some people are more successful than others and should be duly rewarded. It is the responsibility of the company leaders to position their company to be successful in their target markets, defeating their enemies by gaining market share and making the most money. Since the 1980s, numerous books on war from great military theorists have been popular reading in business circles. The reason these books have been successful is many people in business view the art of business to be the art of war without mortal combat. Perhaps more than any nation-state the society and business culture of America has fond an affinity for books on military strategy and their applicability to business. This affinity is most likely a product of America's nurturing.

As a nation-state, America is quite young in age, yet the competitive aspect of American culture and business has turned America into a powerful global force. America was not always considered a respectable global power. In 1775, Edmund Burke said of the Parliamentarians mocking America, "*Young man, there is America – which at this day serves for little more than to amuse you with stories of savage men, and uncouth manners; yet shall, before you taste death, show itself, equal to the whole of commerce which now attracts the envy of the world.*" The ascendance of America as a global power began in the years prior to the Second World War. The effects of the First World War and the recession that followed the 1929 stock market crash created a deeply troubled and unconfident American nation-state. Our military was weak, our businesses were weak from a global perspective and events in Europe and Asia were a driving force behind a strong isolationist and pacifist movement. In 1941, as Europe was engulfed in the first years of the Second World War, Henry Luce called on America to reject its isolationist position and assume a role of global leadership. "*In the field of national policy, the fundamental trouble with America has been, and is, that whereas their nation became in the 20th Century the most powerful and the most vital nation in the world, nevertheless Americans were unable to accommodate themselves spiritually and practically to that fact. Hence they have failed to play their part as a world power – a failure which has had disastrous consequences for themselves and all mankind. And the cure is this: to accept wholeheartedly our duty and our opportunity as the most powerful and vital nation in the world and in consequence to exert upon the world the full impact of our influence, for such purposes as we see fit and much means as we see fit,*" [see Luce, *The American Century,* 1941, page >22]. This was the first public call to oppose the isolationist mood of America. The dawn of new era in which America would accept and actively engage in a world leadership position was still a few months away. "*Ours cannot come out of the vision of any one man. It must be the product of the imaginations of many men. It must be sharing with the all the peoples of our Bill of Rights, our Declaration of Independence, our Constitution, our magnificent industrial products, our technical skills. It must be an internationalism of the people, by the people for the people,*" [see Luce, page <32]. Six months later Pearl Harbor would be attacked and American entered the Second World War. From Luce's essay we find one of the first calls for a century dominated by American leadership the world over. We hear the call for technical, industrial, and economic leadership. Within this essay are the seeds of globalization, the Arsenal of Democracy, and the ascendancy of America over her European forebears. Thirty years on, America would face the economic malaise of the 1970s. Mired in the Cold War, stagnation, and inflation, America again turned to its industrial and technological ecosystem. As the golden age of the American automobile industry began its decline in the 1970s under the weight of global competition, the seeds of a new industry were germinating. This new industry would be built around the computer and be aptly called the Age of Information and Telecom. "*Consider where the country has come from and where it is undoubtedly going. America was all but written off in the*

1980s because of its apparently uncontrollable fiscal deficit and its products' steady loss of competitiveness in the global economy. Downsizing and restructuring depressed everyone, but that valley is now largely traversed. In a literal application of Schumpeter's notion of creative destruction, the United States lost some 44 million jobs in the process of adjusting its economy but simultaneously created 73 million private sector jobs – a net gain of over 29 million jobs since 1980. A stunning 55 percent of the total work force today is in a new job, some two thirds of them in industries that pay more than the average wage," see *A Second American Century*, Foreign Affairs, May/June 1998, Mortimer B. Zuckerman, page 19].

In the eighties, America was losing the business war in many global markets. Part of our introspective search for a solution was to seek out what was successful and study its methods. The successful companies seemed to be from the Asia-Pacific region and thus the search led us to study the works of Sun Tzu and Mushashi, which are the pre-dominant Asian literary works on military theory. Alexis de Tocqueville once stated, *"Consider any individual at any period of his life, and you will always find him preoccupied with fresh plans to increase his comfort."* The comfort of our industries and the comfort of those employed within those industries were threatened in the eighties. In our relentless competitive drive, we turned to studying the structures and processes of successful companies, including their cultural environments. To understand the competitive strategies of Asia-Pacific based companies, we turned to studying their great military thinkers because business is a form of warfare. Business and warfare are inseparably linked.

During the 1980s, two books were popular within the financial, banking, technology, and stock market communities. These books were Sun Tzu's *The Art of War* and Musashi's *The Book of Five Rings*. The rise of the Asian-Pacific economy during the 1980s was an important event in American history. The success of Asian-Pacific companies in the field of automobiles, electronics, and technology was a call to action for America. The foundation of America's domination of the computer, networking technology, optical, and communication markets can be directly linked to the competitive threat that Japan presented to America. The American economy created dominant companies such as Intel, Microsoft, Motorola, Compaq, Dell, HP, Sun, Cisco, and others because we willingly accept a worthy challenge and the business environment was conducive to the creation of these companies. American companies embrace the call to arms and welcome the sound of battle – but they would not be successful if the social, economic, regulatory, and financial and macro economic forces were not aligned to encourage the creation of new companies. American companies thrive on the competitive nature of her industries and the environment that enables fosters and rewards entrepreneurial initiatives.

Of all the great military theorists, Jomini has broad applicability to business – but probably the most obscure in breadth of common knowledge. Antoine-Henri Jomini was a product of the French Revolution and a disciple of Napoleon. He lived during a most interesting time when the intellectual concepts of individual freedom and self-determination developed in America were exported to France and Europe. It is possible that concepts embodied and championed by the American Revolution were the first great export from American and the first threads of globalization that came to the fore in the late twentieth century. France in the late 1700s was influenced by ideas from America in the same way America was being influenced by ideas from Asia-Pacific in the 1980s. Jomini's first career choice was to be a banker, which is not an uncommon career choice for a Swiss citizen. Following the French Revolution of 1789, the Swiss staged their own revolution in 1798. When French troops entered the fray, a young Jomini gave up his career in banking and spent the next seventy years of his life waging war and studying its machinations.

Jomini stated that, *"War having been determined upon, the first point to be decided is whether it shall be offensive or defensive."* In business terms, this means a company has a choice between protecting their market share – or attacking their competitor's market share. Either path is acceptable depending on the strengths of the company. Some companies attack in new markets, while others attack on a narrow front within an existing market segment. Other companies decide to defend their markets until they can improve their quality of their products (i.e. troops) and mass their forces (i.e. soldiers) at decisive points of attack. Regulated markets are by definition artificial market structures. When legislative bodies impose controls on markets it creates a natural tension with the human spirit. People want to have the ability to compete and realize value for their efforts. In 1775, Martin de Marivaux, L'Ami des Lois said, *"Man is born free. No man has any natural authority over his peer; force alone confers no such right, the legislative power belongs to the people and can belong only to the people..."* Regulating markets and restricting the self-determining rights of people result in the same. In the case of markets, those who are not part of the regulated market structure desire an opportunity to compete in the market and be the sole arbiter of their success or failure. In the case of nation-states, the individual rights of man and the collective right of self-determination are fundamental to a free and open society. When markets are artificially restricted and the rights of people are artificially restricted, the end-result is the creation of a desire for change. In the time of Jomini, the concept of freedom was the driving force in politics and war. Thomas Paine eloquently captured the concept of the spirit of freedom in the opening lines of *The American Crisis* in 1775, *"THESE are the times that try men's souls. The summer soldier and the sunshine patriot will, in this crisis, shrink from the service of their country; but he that stands it now, deserves the love and thanks of man and woman. Tyranny, like hell, is not easily conquered; yet we have this consolation with us, that the harder the conflict, the more glorious the triumph. What we obtain too cheap, we esteem too lightly: it is dearness only that gives every thing its value. Heaven knows how to put a proper price upon its goods; and it would be strange indeed if so celestial an article as freedom should not be highly rated."*

As America emerged from the dreary decade of the 1970s, technology was being developed that was going to change the world of computing and networking. An industry that was relegated to the glass house and the domain of specialized, university educated people was about to begin a great metamorphosis that would see it reach out and touch billions of people the world over and change the way people interacted, exchanged information, and communicated. Before this could happen, a sleepy industry had to change to launch a great revolution. *"All things entail rising and falling timing. You must be able to discern this,"* [see Miyamoto Musashi, *A Book of Five Rings, The Ground Book*].

Previously, the contributions of Sun Tzu, Mushashi and Jomini to contemporary business theories were discussed. A common characteristic shared by these military theorists is that they have no contemporary knowledge of our time. Our adaptation of their theories to business is purely the product of our own perception of their theories and ideas. We could be correct, or our adaptation and interpretation of their ideas could be incorrect. Jomini is the closest contemporary of the three and he lived in a time before the European revolutions of 1848 and Europe's full evolution from the monarchies that pre-dated the First World War. What would Jomini say if he lived today to see a European Union and North American Treaty Organization? It is quite possible that the history of the twentieth century would have influenced, if not changed the thinking of Sun Tzu, Mushashi, and Jomini. In our time, there was a military theorist who has greatly influenced the evolution of military theory. His theories are eminently applicable to business, yet his contributions toil in relative obscurity to Clausewitz, Sun Tzu, Mushashi, and Jomini. He is still considered a controversial figure inside the United States military community. His name was John R. Boyd. Above all military theorists to come to the fore post the Treaty of Paris, May 30, 1814, Colonel Boyd's concepts of warfare as a rapid succession of decision making cycles has dramatically affected the strategies of the United States military in the post Vietnam era. His theories are not widely published and yet they were the foundation of U.S. strategy during Gulf War One, Afghanistan, and Gulf War Two.

Colonel Boyd had a long, distinguished and controversial career in the United States Air Force. At one time he was considered one of finest pilots in the United States Air Force; some people would argue that he was best the pilot ever to fly in the U.S. Air Force. After his flying days, he spent the remaining years of his career in a variety of postings that eventually led to positions in the Pentagon. He is credited as the father the of the F-16 airplane concept, which for a twenty-year plus period has been the finest multi-mission aircraft in the world and the backbone aircraft for the air forces of twenty-four nation-states. During the later years of Colonel Boyd's career, he began to develop a synthesized model for understanding modern combat based on his own studies of military history from the age of Alexander the Great through Vietnam. The result of Boyd's studies are too numerous to detail in this essay, but we can extract several important tenants from his model and theories. These tenants can be adapted to the G3 Market Model and used as a tool to define business strategy as markets evolve through change cycles. When we synthesize Boyd's theories with the revolutionary process of Crane Brinton and the G3 Market Model, it is conceptually possible to create a model that provides a multi-dimensional view of market evolution. The three views this model would provide are (a) the change or revolution of the market, (b) the socio-human element from Brinton, and (c) the structure to understand cause and effect of deliberate market strategies from Boyd. The unification of these three creates a tool for understanding market, human and company dimensions. This model can be utilized for the employment of business strategies in targeted markets.

Understanding the essential elements of Boyd's theories begins with the eight fundamental tenants that he used to develop his model for understanding human warfare. An interesting component of Boyd's model is that it can be used to understand any form of competitive human endeavor. It can be applied to business as well as the ultimate human competition – warfare. Boyd's model is important to our analysis because we defined business as warfare by other means. The basis of Boyd's model is based on eight important tenants that he developed from his study of military history. These tenants are:

- **Knowledge of the strategic environment** is important and this is achieved by being observant and aware of the environment in which operations (i.e. business) are conducted [see *The Essential Boyd*, Hammond]. This is Boyd's way of describing the need for market intelligence. Market intelligence is not a one time event. Market intelligence is a constant activity. To guard against stationarity, strategies, and tactics must be updated continuously. Never lose sight of the ultimate objective by allowing tactics and strategies to be governed by a false analysis of the environment and the impact of actions on the outcome. In the evolution of our market model, we use the G3 Market Model to understand the ebb and flow of market share as a market progresses through a change cycle and consumes capital to prove in the new market model. Information does have a negative value [see *Price, Value and Risk*]. When companies or people disclose information, it is typically the information they want you to know. The more sophisticated competitors seek the information that their competitors do not want them to know.

- **Appropriately, interact with your environment** through a combination of rapidity, variety, harmony, and initiative [see *The Essential Boyd*, Hammond]. One must be able to act in a manner that fosters the ability to survive, prosper, and succeed by shaping the environment where possible to suit your objectives. Businesses must be profitable and sustainable. An example of this Reagan is described in the Price, Value, and Risk lead-in essay. A cultural shift occurring as a product of the ITO Revolution is the ability to increasingly calculate risk through real-time analysis of market data points. Rapid decision making based in near real time is becoming possible through technology.

- **Mind-Space-Time** [see *The Essential Boyd*, Hammond]. We typically think of our opponents in two dimensions. These dimensions are space and time. To paraphrase, the market or environment in space and time is what our competitors have done (i.e. market share) and are doing (i.e. actions they are undertaking). Boyd expanded this model to include the concept of mind. Mind is the forward looking element of Boyd's model. He believed that no effective strategy can be successfully executed without an assumption of what the competitive forces (i.e. companies) are planning to do and how our actions can intercept their planned actions and put them at a disadvantage. An enemy is only defeated in their mind – not your mind.

- **Embrace Ambiguity** [see *The Essential Boyd*, Hammond]. We are never sure of the future and we can never have complete and perfect information. We should welcome ambiguity and turn ambiguity to our advantage. We can do this by adapting to our environment and perfecting our ability to deal with incomplete information, thus remaining fluid in our actions. Again, this is the emerging ability to work in near real time as the global market evolves from a push model to a pull model.

- **Entropy.** *"Confusion and disorder are also related to the notion of entropy and the Second Law of Thermodynamics Entropy is a concept that represents the potential for doing work, the capacity for taking action, or the degree of* *confusion and disorder associated with any physical or information activity. High entropy implies a low potential for doing work, a low capacity for taking action or a high degree of confusion and disorder. Low entropy implies just the opposite. Viewed in this context, the Second Law of Thermodynamics states that all observed natural processes generate entropy. From this law it follows that entropy must increase in any closed system—or, for that matter, in any system that cannot communicate in an ordered fashion with other systems or environments external to itself. Accordingly, whenever we attempt to do work or take action inside such a system—a concept and its match-up with reality—we should anticipate an increase in entropy hence an increase in confusion and disorder. Naturally, this means we cannot determine the character or nature (consistency) of such a system within itself, since the system is moving irreversibly toward a higher, yet unknown, state of confusion and disorder."* [see Boyd, *Destruction and Creation*]. The concept of entropy is adaptable to business. Using this concept and applying it to market share and productivity, we can create a method for assessing the ability of companies to executive within markets and the change cycle. If we understand how markets are changing and we can understand a company's ability to successfully execute within the market change cycle, we have then created a model for a two-dimensional analysis.

- **It is a matter of connections and choices** [see *The Essential Boyd*, Hammond]. The more we know the more we connect to the environment, to the past, to the future, to the people, to ideas and to our competitors. Brinton's analysis of revolutions provides a structure for understanding the socio-human element. People act on what is familiar, and social and cultural habits are difficult to change. Fusing Brinton's understanding of the human change process with the market analysis and Boyd's entropy concept the two dimensional model can be modified to create a three dimensional model: market-companies-human behavior.

- **Real target is your enemy's perception** [see *The Essential Boyd*, Hammond]. You must know and understand the enemy's values and aspirations. The enemy decides when they are defeated – not you.

- Moral-Mental-Physical [see *The Essential Boyd*, Hammond]. Effective strategy works on three levels. The easiest way to lose is to lose the trust that is the basis for social cohesion within and a group, team, company, or army.

Let us begin our quick summary of Boyd with a quote from his paper entitled *Destruction and Creation*. Boyd stated that, *"Studies of human behavior reveal that the actions we undertake as individuals are closely related to survival, more importantly, survival on our own terms. Naturally, such a notion implies that we should be able to act relatively free or independent of any debilitating external influences— otherwise that very survival might be in jeopardy. In viewing the instinct for survival in this manner we imply that a basic aim or goal, as individuals, is to improve our capacity for independent action. The degree to which we cooperate, or compete, with others is driven by the need to satisfy this basic goal. If we believe that it is not possible to satisfy it alone, without help from others, history shows us that we will agree to constraints upon our independent action—in order to collectively pool skills and talents in the form of nations, corporations, labor unions, mafias, etc.—so that obstacles standing in the way of the basic goal can either be removed or overcome. On the other hand, if the group cannot or does not attempt to overcome obstacles deemed important to many (or possibly any) of its individual members, the group must risk losing these alienated members. Under these circumstances, the alienated members may dissolve their relationship and remain independent, form a group of their own, or join another collective body in order to improve their capacity for independent action"* [see Boyd, *Destruction and Creation*]. This quote provides good linkage to our understanding of the revolutionary process and why people become revolutionaries. As we will find, within large corporations or within nation-states, revolutionaries are formed from the process of alienation. The strongest companies are the companies that foster a strong internal bond of teamwork based on a fulfillment of objectives (i.e. victory). When companies begin to lose their ability to control and influence market share, a structural weakness is occurring and the one of three boundary conditions required for change (i.e. revolution) has been achieved.

In order to understand Boyd's model for operations, we must understand his premise that there is a fundamental need for decisions. He states, *"Against such a background, actions and decisions become critically important. Actions must be taken over and over again and in many different ways. Decisions must be rendered to monitor and determine the precise nature of the actions needed that will be compatible with the goal. To make these timely decisions implies that we must be able to form mental concepts of observed reality, as we perceive it, and be able to change these concepts as reality itself appears to change. The concepts can then be used as decision-models for improving our capacity for independent action. Such a demand for decisions that literally impact our survival causes one to wonder: How do we generate or create the mental concepts to support this decision-making activity?"* [see Boyd, *Destruction and Creation*]. This quote highlights the basic contribution that Boyd provided. He developed a model that can be extrapolated into a process for decision making.

Boyd called the model he developed the O-O-D-A loop. The O-O-D-A loop is a complex model of the decision making process that Boyd developed based on the above mentioned concepts. O-O-D-A is an acronym for Observe-Orient-Decide-Act. Within this model, or loop, decisions are generated. The true value of the cycle is that it is not a binary process. Boyd believed that this decision making process must be continuous and rapid in nature. When an organization has mastered the ability to cycle through the O-O-D-A Loop, Boyd added a second element to consider; understanding your opponent's O-O-D-A Loop and having the ability to move inside their O-O-D-A Loop. Once you are inside your opponent's O-O-D-A Loop, interesting events can be created. This is the application of his principal that the real target is your enemy's perception. See **Chart 16: O-O-D-A Loop** in the Chart and Model section for an illustration of Boyd's O-O-D-A Loop.

From a historical perspective, we can find applications of the O-O-D-A Loop within the ITO Revolution. When the large network equipment suppliers started using their balance sheets to provide vendor financing to emerging service provides, the startups and private companies responded by using stock options as a counter incentive. When Nortel bypassed the 2.5G solution for a 10G solution, they priced the product at 2.5G prices to acquire market share. Competitors such as Lucent, Fujitsu, and Ciena had to respond to the 10G market. On the service provider side of the ecosystem, the deployment of a 10G network by Qwest forced competitors to upgrade their 2.5G networks to 10G. The RBOCs cycled through the O-O-D-A Loop quickly and determined that market share and concentrated ownership of the local loop was critical for survival and success as the ITO Revolution played out. AOL realized that at some point in the future broadband services was going to affect their business model and as such decided that ownership of content was a defensible market position. Qwest came to the realization that obtaining a steady flow of monthly revenue from local telephony services would elevate Qwest above its rivals of AT&T, Level(3), Williams, 360Networks, and others. In the end, Boyd believed that decision making is a matter of connections and choices throughout the ecosystem of connected markets. The purpose of introducing Boyd was not to provide an analysis of the O-O-D-A Loop – but rather to apply his principals of decision making within a connected ecosystem of markets as a foundation of the G3 Market Model.

New Application of Boyd's Concepts

By adapting Boyd's use of the Second Law of Thermodynamics and the concept of entropy to companies within a market, a dichotomy model can be created to determine which companies are efficiently executing within evolving market structure. Whether a company is an old regime, a moderate, an extremist, or a revolutionary (i.e. new entrant the concept of executing efficiently, decisively, internally, and externally within the market structure to intercept a point in the future with a discernable and sustainable competitive advantage is how value is created. The three objectives of a company are (a) to acquire market share and (b) protect market share and great companies then separate themselves from competitors by (c) defending their market share from erosion. Companies new and old want to have competitive advantages in stable market structures. As markets go through a change process, the extremists companies will be identified by the companies to capture market share and have defensible barriers against market share erosion. To assess a company's internal efficiencies or ability to execute through actions within their market, we will use income, GPM, and internal and external market drive on the X axis and the company size based on quarterly revenues on the Y axis. Quarterly revenues can be viewed as a top down measurement of market share. The model created by these data points is called the Entropy Base Model or EBM. The EBM is suited to technology markets because it assesses the ability of a company to control and acquire market share through the creation of intellectual property, channels to market, and existing relationships. See **Chart 17: Entropy Base Model (EBM)** in the Chart and Model section.

The EBM model places companies into four quadrants. As markets cycle through the progression of the G3 Market Model, companies can move from quadrant to quadrant based on the acquisition or loss of market share. Each phase of the G3MM has characteristics which enable or prevent the acquisition of market share. In markets in which market share is static the large companies reside in quadrants 3 and 4. The smaller companies or niche players reside in quadrants 1 and 2. Value is created or destroyed as companies move within the EBM from quadrant to quadrant. Market barriers enable or prevent companies from creating value by impending or restricting the flow of market share. The market conditions in the 1980s severely limited the ability of AOL to become a big company. AOL was a company that lived in quadrant 1. AOL did not have the ability to move into the other quadrants until the personal computer, internet, and telecom deregulation collided to form a fluid, expanding, and dynamic market. AOL had the opportunity to move from a quadrant 1 to a quadrant 3 once market share began to be organically created in a vast quantity in the form of new PC users who were gaining access to the internet and market share was allowed to flow between companies. As AOL secured market share and became a multi-national company, they acquired the ability to purchase a multi-national company from quadrant 4 in the form of Time-Warner. Time-Warner was a media company in an adjacent market that was connected to the overall ecosystem of ITO markets. AOL used the ITO Revolution to grow into an extremist within the ITO markets and then cross markets and purchase a quadrant 4 company in a different market.

Using the EBM in relation to the G3 Market Model enables an assessment of a company's ability to move from one quadrant to another quadrant, thus creating or destroying value. In static market conditions in which a regulated pricing structure exists, it is unlikely that companies will be able to move without a dynamic change event (i.e. revolution). To place the EBM into perspective with the ITO Revolution, we can examine the evolution of the service providers and the network equipment providers (i.e. OEMs) as the market structure changed due to technology and regulation, thus enabling the creation and destruction of value.

As 1996 came to a close, the telecom service provider industry in the United States looked reasonably unchanged from previous few years. AT&T was the only service provider with revenues in excess of $12 billion per quarter. MFS Communications would be acquired by Worldcom in 1996 and with it UUNet, which was acquired by MFS in early 1996. The RBOCs all had quarterly revenues in the range of $2 to 5 billion dollars. MCI and Sprint were the only real IXC competitors to AT&T. GTE was a strong player in the local telephony market against the RBOCs. Worldcom was the other notable company, but they were still a quadrant 1 company in 1996. MFS a strong niche player, but with their acquisition of UUNet, MFS appeared to be a strong revolutionary company with the ability to acquire market share. MFS had a growing CLEC business and with UUNet became the leading provider of commercial internet access. See **Chart 18: EBM for Service Providers, Change Stage** in the Chart and Model section.

Two years into the ITO Revolution and the EBM is clearly reflective of market conditions of the Perigee stage of the G3 Market Model. AT&T is still the largest service provider in terms of quarterly revenue, but SBC and Verizon have been using telecom deregulation to merge with other RBOCs to form larger companies. Market share was being consolidated through the merger and acquisition process. Telecom deregulation lowered market barriers and enabled market share fluidity. In 1996, Worldcom was in the early stages of using telecom deregulation to embark on an aggressive acquisition strategy to increase market share. A host of new CLEC, IXC and DLEC companies had been started and they are listed in quadrant 1. For simplicity, only five of the largest CLECs have been included in the ITO Revolution Service Provider Entropy Base Model: McLeod, XO, Time-Warner Telecom, eSpire and Allegiance Telecom. The three xDSL companies (i.e. DLECs) had been included as well: Covad, Northpoint and Rhythms. It is interesting to note that Bellsouth, Sprint and US West had opted to forego the merger and acquisition business strategy option and their revenues remained strong, but not overly different from the end of 1996. Three of the prominent IXCs competitors that would fuel the optical bubble of the late 1990s appear on the EBM for the first time at the end of 1999: Global

Crossing, Level(3), and Qwest. See **Chart 19: EBM for Service Providers, Perigee Stage** in the Chart and Model section.

As the ITO Revolution entered the Decline stage of the G3MM, a clear market separation became visible. Two of the three DSL providers were eliminated. VZ and SBC had eclipsed their former parent, AT&T, in terms of quarterly revenues. Qwest had made the jump from quadrant 1 to quadrant 4 through the acquisition of US West and access to the billions in recurring local telephony revenue. Qwest used the ITO Revolution and the valuation placed on their stock price as a currency to acquire an old regime of the ITO market. AOL used their currency to cross markets and acquire Time-Warner; Qwest used their currency to do the unthinkable. They purchased an old regime. Why? Qwest purchased an old regime because their leaders knew that owning the local loops in the US West region was a once in a life time opportunity. How many times does an opportunity present itself to buy into a regulated industry that still appears to act like a monopoly despite telecom deregulation? Every month US West has customers that pay their local telephone bills. This reoccurring revenue stream (i.e. market share) was too hard to pass, for the Qwest leadership team. US West presented the Qwest team with the cash flow and balance sheet to fund their debt payments. See **Chart 20: EBM for Service Providers, Decline Stage** in the Chart and Model section.

Two years on from 2002, the ITO Revolution was in the middle of the Apogee stage. Apogee is the stage that companies find obtaining market share is at the most difficult level. The companies located in quadrants 1 and 2 soon realize that end-users are unwilling to award them business because revolutionaries are viewed as high risk. Quadrant 2 companies find that they can only win niche business in which they possess some technical or commercial advantage. Both quadrant 1 and quadrant 2 companies recognize that winning large deals that alter the strategic value of their company is an impossible dream during the Apogee stage. The effects of the market correction, layoffs, and general disappointment in the failure of the revolution alter the decision making processes of the end customers (i.e. market share). The period is often described as a period of uncertainty. Few of the thought leaders who advocated the revolution in prior years have clear thoughts on the future. Across all three levels of the thought leadership model, the Decline and transition into the Apogee stage have a negative affect on the revolutionaries, intellectuals, and operating leaders who were proponents of the revolution during the Perigee stage. This is the beginning of the era of big companies, for it is the big companies that can undertake large scale projects and command the financial resources to consolidate and defend market share.

By the end of 2004, the telecom market structure was clear to everyone. SBC and Verizon were the winners. AT&T was the ultimate loser. From mid-

2000 onward, AT&T's quarterly revenues have been in steady decline. At the height of the ITO Revolution in 2000, AT&T had a $14 billion quarter. By the end of 2004, AT&T quarter revenues had declined to half that amount. MCI would emerge from bankruptcy with $4 billion in debt. Qwest had $17 billion of debt. Sprint and BellSouth round out this group of quadrant 4 companies with good revenues, but challenging business models with limited prospects for growth. The few revolutionary survivors from the Perigee stage of the ITO Revolution have all become quadrant 2 companies. They have challenging business models with various levels of debt, limited revenues, and the market structure limits their ability to significantly grow revenues through the acquisition of market share. Most of these companies are left to compete on price, which reduces the overall ability of all companies in the market to maintain business models that generate margin dollars. The result of this market structure was another round of mergers and acquisitions. In comparison to the mergers and acquisitions during the Change and Perigee stages of the ITO Revolution, these deals would not be closed at premium prices – most deal sizes could be classified as massive decline in value from the previous stages of the revolution. In this round of consolidation, the extremist companies were presented with an opportunity to acquire market share through acquisition at deeply discounted prices.

In all revolutions, there are people who arrive after the Terror has subsided and use the beginnings of the return to normalcy to become involved in society, business, and government. This is the return of the moderates. In business, new revolutionaries do form at the end of Decline stage and into the Apogee stage. These are companies who have analyzed the market conditions or have developed a technological advantage that enables them to attack the marketshare of the quadrant 1 companies. The threat poised by these companies is not as grand or apocalyptic as during the Change and Perigee stages, but the threat is real enough and these companies act as road signs to the future. During the Apogee stage of the ITO Revolution, two companies emerged who promoted a business model that had the potential to have a profound impact on the structure of the telecom services market. See **Chart 21: EBM for Service Providers, Apogee Stage** in the Chart and Model section.

Two of these companies were Vonage and Skype. The business model offered by these companies was telephony services over the internet using VoIP (voice over IP) and a broadband internet connection. For the first time, it was effectively possible to be a service provider without owning a network. The implication of this ability is quite profound and will be explored in the final essay. As for the market structure evolution in the Return Stage of the G3MM, what occurred was a vast amount of revenue concentration under the ownership of two companies. Verizon/MCI and the SBC/AT&T with the acquisition of BellSouth creates a market structure with two companies with quarterly revenue around or above $19 billion a quarter and the remaining competitors are $2 billion or below in quarterly revenues. In comparison to the largest cable service provider, which is Comcast in 2006; quarterly revenues for Comcast are just below $6 billion a quarter. In 2006, Vonage filed their long awaited S-1, signaling their intention for a public listing. In this document they revealed their quarterly revenues. From 2003 through the end of 2005, Vonage had revenues of $5.2 million growing to $73 million in September 2005 and presumably $100 million a quarter by March 2006. In May 2006, Vonage priced their initial public offer of 31.25 million shares at $16-18 dollars per share. This price range would give Vonage a market capitalization $2.6 billion dollars on the offering day. To build the company's value, Vonage required nearly $390 million of private equity and five years. In comparison the new at&t and Verizon have quarterly revenues of $19 billion dollars and market capitalizations of around $100 billion dollars. See **Chart 22: EBM for Service Providers, Return Stage** in the Chart and Model section.

The market structure for service providers in early 2006 is clearly a story of two groups. The new AT&T and Verizon are the dominant companies, they are not without challenges from cable service providers, but both companies are integrated long distance, local, and mobile service providers. Sprint/Nextel is emerging as a full on wireless provider. The remaining long distance providers are confined to a market structure that is better served by a twenty-year business plan than potential exit option in three to five years. The real battle going forward in the U.S. service provider market will be between cable providers and integrated service providers such as AT&T and Verizon.

Entropy Base Model for ITO Equipment Suppliers

As 1996 came to the close, the Change stage of the ITO Revolution was well underway. The new service providers who were forming were laying the foundation for the bubble era CAPEX overspend that was on the horizon from 1997-2000. The CAPEX overspend was intended to provide the new competitive carriers entering the market with a next generation technology network from which to offer services that was unencumbered when compared to the legacy technology networks owned by the RBOCS, AT&T, MCI, and Sprint. In early 1996, the service provider CAPEX overspend had yet to begin, hence the structure of the network equipment suppliers was still relatively stable and reflective of a market structure that was on the verge of change. The barriers to entry were still high because competitive service provides were just beginning to plan for the massive building of local, regional, and global networks. Lucent and Nortel were dominant North American suppliers for telecom equipment. Cisco, 3Com, Bay, and Cabletron were companies that had grown during the enterprise hub, bridge and router wars of the 1980s and early 1990s. At this stage of the ITO Revolution, the flow and exchanges of market share is relatively stable. Within the enterprise markets a fierce battle is still waging for control of networks and information technology (IT) spending market share – but the service provider market had yet to begin spending. For companies focusing on providing equipment to the service provider market, dynamic growth of market share is not possible until market barriers that have kept market share static are changed. This would occur with the passage of the Telecom Act of 1996.

It is interesting to observe that Ascend, Cascade, and Ciena are small companies compared to Lucent and Nortel. This is evidence of the market structure still existing from the period known as the Old Regimes. Lucent and Nortel are established suppliers of technology to the service provider market. Cisco, 3Com, Bay, and Cabletron had all secured significant market share within the enterprise end-user market. The consumption of technology by the service provider market has not grown large enough to lift companies such as Ascend, Ciena, ADC, and Tellabs beyond the size of Cisco and 3Com, who primarily derive their revenues from the enterprise market segment. None of the companies listed on the EBM have strong consumer business models. See **Chart 23: EBM for Equipment Suppliers, Change Stage** in the Chart and Model section.

The Telecom Act of 1996 and emerging technologies being developed and deployed began to lower market barriers in 1996 as the ITO Revolution entered the Perigee stage. When the market barriers were lowered within the service provider market, through the creation of new service providers, the technology equipment companies had the ability to create value by securing new market share (i.e. CAPEX overspend) being spent by the emerging service providers as well as the old regimes. The old regimes were clearly motivated to accelerate technology deployment by shortening technology selection cycles in order to match the threat from emerging service providers. The Telecom Act of 1996 deregulated the telecom services market, lowered market barriers, and enabled the dynamic exchange of market share by enabling more market share to be organically created. The new market share was created by the new telecom service providers who planned to spend CAPEX on new networks. This is the point of the ITO Revolution when private and public capital was committed to the ITO Revolution. By the end of the 1999, the market structure for the equipment suppliers of the ITO Revolution had changed. Revenues had increased for all of the equipment suppliers, as this is reflective of the increase in CAPEX spending within the service provider market. Nortel was still second to Lucent, but Lucent's missed technology cycle of the 10G optical long haul product would soon force Lucent to lose significant market share. Ciena, Tellabs, and ADC Telecom were able to leverage their positions as early revolutionaries to capture significant market share of the spending occurring. As the market for network equipment expanded, opportunities increased. Bay, Cascade, and Ascend would be swept up in the merger and acquisition frenzy of the late 1990s. This is the rising tide raises all boats theory. The companies who are executing most efficiently within this stage of the ITO Revolution are working to secure market share as well as a competitive advantage to sustain their business (i.e. value created) when the market conditions change. Cisco Systems is the clearest example of a company thinking through the evolutionary future and the interaction between enterprise, service provider, and consumer markets.

It is interesting to note that there is a group of companies who are in the *"revolutionaries"* quadrant of the EBM. These are companies who have been formed to leverage their ability to create an advantage through technology innovation or to acquire market share due to the lowering of market barriers. Companies who were able to use the market conditions to complete an IPO without owning a significant market share and sustainable competitive advantage (i.e. IPR advantage) to build a large multi-national business are: Sycamore Networks, ArrowPoint, Alteon Web Systems, Foundry, and Extreme. As the market conditions changed during the Decline period of the ITO Revolution, each of these companies simply did not have a large market share position to be considered a multinational corporation such as Lucent, Nortel, and Cisco. In some cases they have built a commendable business, but unless there is another event (i.e. regulatory or technological) that dynamically changes the structure of the network equipment market; it is unlikely that these companies will be able to significantly create new value beyond their current value. This is not a criticism of these companies, but rather a statement of fact concerning market conditions and the ability for these companies to create an event that enables then to significantly grow revenues and market share. Of the mid-tier companies Tellabs, ADC Telecom, and Newbridge Networks, it was Newbridge who decided that the time had come to become part of a larger company and thus was acquired by Alcatel. See **Chart 24: EBM for Equipment Suppliers, Perigee Stage** in the Chart and Model section.

Post the Perigee stage of the ITO Revolution is when the rapidly contracting market size for networking equipment revealed which companies had built valuable business models and which companies had not. Within the service provider market segment, many of the new CLECs and IXCs that had been formed in the late 1990s were unable to reach levels of profitability that enabled these revolutionaries to continue to invest in their networks. Overall CAPEX by service providers rapidly declined [see *Essay One, Chapter Five*] and with the shrinking market, the barriers to entry began to rise again for companies seeking to sell products into the telecom equipment market. The enterprise markets also witnessed a reduction in overall CAPEX (i.e. market share or market size), but this reduction was more graceful, as enterprises reduced IT budgets to assess the new market conditions. Over time, large corporations still had to spend hundreds of millions of dollars and in many cases a billion or two a year to maintain their IT infrastructure because they had sustainable business. Many of the new service providers created after the Telecom Act of 1996 had unsustainable business plans – but the fortune 5000 companies in the U.S. were not affected by the inability of new service providers to become profitable. Citibank did not go out of business because they had purchased bandwidth from Global Crossing, MFN, and Qwest. The economy became unhealthy post the stock market crash in 2000 – but that did not mean that traditional old economy business became unhealthy. The consumer market still required goods and services from banks, retailers, manufactures, and entertainment. As the ITO markets began to recede from the fervor of revolution, the dynamic exchange of market share between equipment suppliers was on the ebb. As markets contract, the barriers to entry rise and market share becomes static. See **Chart 25: EBM for Equipment Suppliers, Decline Stage** in the Chart and Model section.

As the ITO Revolution reached the end of the Decline stage of the G3 Market Model, the segmentation of the network equipment suppliers was a cruel reality for companies that once had valuations in the billions. Nortel and Lucent had receded to companies with quarterly revenues in the $2 to $3 billion level. 3Com and Cabletron continued to decline from their revenue highs in the year 2000. Foundry, Extreme, and Ciena are all companies with loyal customers, but an inability to dramatically increase their company value through the acquisition of meaningful market share. Tellium, Corvis, and Sycamore never built a sustainable business and by the end of 2002, were in a position of irrelevancy. A host of small companies such as Tellium, Corvis, and Riverstone succumbed to the market structure and resolved their business model challenges through disappointing mergers billions less than their valuation during the glory days of the ITO Revolution. See **Chart 26: EBM for Equipment Suppliers, Apogee Stage** in the Chart and Model section.

By the end of 2004, the market dichotomy that was forming at the end of 2002 had become more pronounced. Cisco has quarterly revenues in excess of $6 billion. Foundry is a profitable competitor to Cisco because they focus on internal efficiencies to ensure profitability and maintaining a technology advantage against Cisco – but lack the capacity as a company to significantly acquire market share. Foundry does not have a sustainable intellectual competitive advantage, but they do execute product development cycles faster than Cisco and use this ability to maintain a market share position. The challenge Foundry faces is the inability to deploy enough global resources to attract new market share. Cisco is a larger company and they have more resources at the point of attack in the market. Cisco wins deals that Foundry never even sees. Extreme has not been able to execute as efficiently as Foundry and as such they are not a profitable. 3Com and Enterasys (formerly Cabletron) are sinking into the abyss and will go the way of DEC and Wang. Sycamore will soon go out of business and Ciena is in the same position as Extreme and Foundry. Nortel and Lucent have returned to their roots as core telecom equipment suppliers. The difference from 1985 is that wireless – not wireline, is the core business driver of the two companies. The company that is executing most efficiently in this market segment is Juniper Networks. Juniper has focused on winning against Cisco for specific applications while broadening their business into emerging technology market silos. As a result, Juniper is growing revenues, building an alternative Cisco solution, and has a legitimate opportunity to be the second router supplier over the long term, which was a position once held by Wellfleet/ Bay, but was lost under the leadership of Nortel Networks. It is a cruel irony for John Roth that he spent $9 billion on a company because he believed that the IP revolution was an inevitable force – yet it was his leadership team that did not capitalize on the market share and technology owned by Bay to be the alternative to Cisco. It was Cisco who used the IP revolution to be the only company to rise from a startup to challenge the old regimes of Lucent, Nortel, Alcatel, and Ericsson. See **Chart 27: EBM for Equipment Suppliers, Return Stage** in the Chart and Model section.

As the ITO Revolution exits the Apogee stage and enters the Return stage, the questions facing the companies that survived the Decline and Apogee stages of the ITO Revolution is focused on the future course of the ITO Revolution. What does the future hold? Will the market frenzy of the 1990s return? Will the dynamic market conditions that enabled small companies to become big companies and big companies to collapse, return? To understand the stage of the Return/Thermidor stage of the ITO Revolution we need to place the ITO revolution into a broader context. This context is provided by Carlota Perez.

In 2003 Carlota Perez completed a book entitled *Technological Revolutions and Financial Capital*. Perez introduced a macro model developed from studying cycles of technological change in western society. These five revolutions or technological waves are:

	IRRUPTION	FRENZY	TURNING POINT	SYNERGY	MATURITY
Industrial Revolution	1771 - 1780	1780s - 1790s	1793-97	1798 - 1812	1813 - 1829
Age of Steam and Railways	1830s	1840s	1848-50	1850 - 1857	1857 - 1873
Age of Steel Heavy Industry	1875 - 1884	1884 - 1893	1895-07	1895 - 1907	1908 - 1918
Age of Oil And Auto	1908 - 1920	1920 - 1929	1929-45	1943 - 1959	1960 - 1974
Age of Info and Telecom	1971 - 1987	1987 - 2001	2001-04	2005 - ?	

BIG BANG   CRASH   INSTITUTIONAL RECOMPOSITION

Figure 43: Perez Model of Five Great Disruptions
Source: Author's Reproduction, *Technological Revolutions and Financial Capital*, Perez

By studying these five successive revolutions, Perez developed a model that reveled that the first four revolutions all experienced a similar set of phases and time lines. The fifth revolution, or Age of Information and Telecom, is following the same pattern as the first four revolutionary events. Perez's model for technological change aligns closely with the G3 Market Model for the ITO Revolution. This discourse viewed the ITO Revolution as a singular event, but if it is placed in the context of Perez's mode it assumes greater significance. The ITO Revolution and the G3 Market Model that was developed in the first essay, was created within the period that Perez describes as the *"frenzy"* and the *"turning point."* Perez's models all begin with the creation of a significant technology that spawns a subset of related markets and adjacent technologies that can be collectively called an industry or ecosystem of related markets. Each of the five revolutions she defined progressed through a period of extreme growth, which this discourse termed a revolution. As the revolution peaks and then declines, there is an economic correction. All of the technology revolutions she studied had an interim economic recession that divided each revolution into the work of two generations. The recession is pause between two periods in which there is a reset of expectations and financial commitments. After a period of time called the *turning point*, the revolution emerges from the turning point and enters the stages of synergy and maturity. This is the time of healing and institutional recomposition. It is the age of big companies and in all the prior revolutions studied by Perez, viewed as a second renaissance and the work of a successive generation.

For the purpose of this essay, we will focus on the Synergy stage, of Perez's model as this will lead the essay into a unified market model and discussion of the future evolution of the ITO Markets. Perez states that, *"Perhaps because it comes after the collapse of an unregulated world, Synergy is a time of orderly and ordered behavior. If regulation of the economic world was put in place during the turning point recession, it is generally accepted; if it was not, it is consistently sought by social and political forces,"* [see Perez, page 128]. This is easily identifiable in the ITO Revolution by way of the Sarbanes-Oxley Act, executive compensation guidelines, accounting treatment of stock options, and the division of research and brokerage functions. *"Accounting and disclosure legislation is usually enacted to avoid the specific abuses revealed during the previous Frenzy,"* [see Perez, page 129]. As each cycle of change clears through the Turning Point, the enactment of regulation to prevent future abuses from the Frenzy period are required for progression into the Synergy phase.

The ITO markets are on the verge of Perez's Synergy phase. *"What makes the Synergy prosperity an era of good feeling is its tendency to encompass greater and greater parts of the economy and larger and larger parts of society in the benefits of growth. After a period of acute polarization on several fronts, when prosperity was extremely lopsided, the system searches for coherence through widespread application of the now established paradigm, as the logic of both production and consumption"* [see Perez, page 133]. This is the point at which we are at in the ITO Revolution. Perez identifies two important characteristics of the Synergy phase that are essential to understanding the future evolution of the ITO Revolution. In the first essay the Return stage of the G3 Market Model is defined to have attributes of (a) large suppliers controlling the majority of the market share and as such they enact barriers to ensure that they maintain control of their market share and (b) there is not enough new, organic market share being added to the overall market size. In some cases, various market verticals within the overall market ecosystem can be contracting. This is why smaller companies struggle to find the market share acquisition velocity they require to achieve acquisition equity events and IPOs. Perez notes that the fixed structure of market share is a reflection of *"...the main industries of the revolution reaching their basic structures in terms of leadership, forms of competition, relative size and production facilities and other defining features,"* [see Perez, pages 124-135].

The first essay was concluded with a quote from Andy Groove in which he surmised that the *"...boom was healthy too, even with its excesses. Because what this incredible valuation craze did was draw untold sums of billions of dollars into building the Internet infrastructure. The hundreds of billions of dollars that got invested in telecommunications, for example. You know, when the information highway was the craze, the question I would ask {then-Bell Atlantic CEO} Ray Smith and {then-TCI chair} John Malone was, Who the hell is going to spend the billions of dollars it will take to build this thing out? You guys? The federal government? It's not going to happen."* Perez makes the same observation of the Synergy stage in her study of technology revolutions and financial markets. *"Growth during Synergy, in the first phase of full deployment period, takes place in the midst of increasing externalities. One of the effects of the bubble economy is to have enough to enable massive use at decreasing costs. During the whole installation period, the diffusion of the technology revolution was wide and deep enough to have allowed the paradigm to become fully visible. Consequently, when Deployment arrives, growth takes place provided with a set of widely shared principles for most effective and profitable practice as well as an implicit understanding of the various technological trajectories to exploit,"* [see Perez, page 134.] The future evolution of the ITO Revolution is predicated on the several market conditions that exist. These conditions are:

- Infrastructure has been deployed such that pockets of concentration exists, interspersed with pockets of need

- The dense pockets of deployed infrastructure coupled with the number of companies attempting to acquire market share have driven the price of goods and services to minimal levels

- Profitability is insufficient to support a continuation of deploying and upgrading infrastructure on a massive scale

- Market share, market structure, and supplier positions are relatively static with the large companies owning such a large amount of market share that is it produces a market discontinuity that in a prolonged state will result in the formation of old regimes as it minimizes the competitive drive for innovation.

CHAPTER TEN:
Foreign Policy, Market Policy and Globalization

Our moral criticism of past ages can easily be mistaken. It transfers present-day desiderata to the past. It views personalities according to set principles and makes too little allowance for the urgencies of the moment.
- Burckhardt, *Judgments on History*

The end of the bi-polar alignment of the Cold War enabled global revolutionary forces to emerge and become leaders in a secular revolution against the real or perceived American led globalization movement. When we examine the foundation of this revolution against American led social globalization, we find there is a linkage between the (a) foreign policy of dominant nation-states, (b) the pursuit of economic certainty and stability, (c) the manifest destiny of people along ethnic and religious lines of unity, and (d) how these lines of unity have fostered regional, ethnic and religious nationalism. These four forces form the core elements of a revolution against American led globalization. We are in an international revolution and the foreign policy tenants of the United States must adapt to counter the global revolutionary forces in order to end this cycle of revolution and its direct impact on the United States. A corollary for consideration is the relationship of the ITO Revolution to the global revolution against American globalization. Can linkage be found between this revolution and the spread of American culture through media and the emergence of the internet as a global means of communication? *"Americans have always had a genius for communications. The powers of our Founding Fathers' words reverberated across the world from the moment they were said down to the present day. From the Pony Express to the miracle of a human voice over the phone line, American innovations and communications have broken the barriers of time and space to make it easier for us to stay in touch, to learn from each other, to reach for a highest aspirations. Today our world is being remade yet again by an information revolution, changing the way we work, the way we live, the way we relate to each other. Already the revolution is so profound that it is changing the dominant economic model of the age. And already, thanks to the scientific and entrepreneurial genius of American workers in this country, it has created vast, vast opportunities for us to grow and learn and enrich ourselves in body and in spirit,"* [see President Bill Clinton, remarks as the signing of the Telecom Act of 1996, February 8, 1996].

The globalization revolution is not a clash of civilizations, but rather a revolution of ideas, economics, and self-determination. This revolution is unique because of the global scale of the event. We are experiencing a revolution that is not contained within a single nation-state or a region of our world. It is a revolution that is being played out on a global stage with an impact that all Americans can sense in their homeland and abroad. Traditionally, revolutions have been viewed as self-contained political events that occur within their individual nation-state and occasionally disrupt regional stability. We know that revolutions have affected regional stability such as those around Europe in 1848 – but it is rare that the forces unleashed during the revolutionary cycle have been exported to nation-states out of region to affect the course of nation-states on a global scale. The globalization revolution we are facing today is a result of several forces unleashed during the closing years of the Cold War. These forces are:

- The ideological collapse of the former Soviet Union (FSU) and pro-Soviet Union bloc of nation-states. This collapse freed nationalistic, cultural, and religious forces that had been contained by dominant nation-states since the time of the colonial empires pre-dating the twentieth century. Colonialism, imperialism, and the struggle between East and West that formed after the Second World War did isolate conflicts at the regional level. The power struggle between the United States and the Soviet Union was contained to specific nation-states within regions. The interests of the people within the nation-states that were aligned with the United States or Soviet Union were subservient to the struggle between the United States and the Soviet Union. The rapid collapse of the Soviet Union and its withdrawal from global ideological pursuits, unleashed opportunities for oppressed people the world over to pursue their Manifest Destiny. The withdrawal of Soviet economic support also unleashed inherent economic value in these nation-states. Infrastructure required modernization and state owned assets were privatized.

- A policy shift by western nation-states from state ownership of industries and regulation to privatization and deregulation. The push towards a global, market-based economy has drawn deep divisions between the wealthy and poor nation-states. The collapse of the Cold War eliminated the insulated, economic alignments of the western world and the pro-Soviet Bloc. New and old nation-states were free to seek their own economic destiny and security. The laissez faire economic polices of the 1990s created a massive economic inequality between nation-states that set the foundation for alienation and resentment between nation-states and people. The revolutionary leaders view the global economic disparity as evidence of American power, which prevents them from achieving their own destiny. This is why the revolutionaries attacked the World Trade Center. They believed that the World Trade Center was a symbol and source of American domination of global economics with the end-goal being globalization to the benefit of America.

• The rapidity of communication and the global interaction of ideas have expanded the impact that people acting as a group can have on the global family of nation-states. Our world is closer than at any time in our history. The insulating barriers of distance, travel and cultural have been diminished by the ability of people from many cultures to communicate and share ideas. *"But by 1830 a different type of machine came into being that changed the life and minds of all peoples. The memory of it is nearly gone, but it was the completest change in human experience since the nomadic tribes became rooted in one spot to grow grain and raise cattle; it was in effect a reversal of that settling down. Locomotion by the force of steam, the railroad, uprooted mankind and made of it individual nomads again,"* [see Jacques Barzun, From *Dawn to Decadence*, 2000, page 539]. The geographic distances have not changed, but the speed and thoroughness with which we communicate, share ideas, and become influenced by others has never been greater. We are influenced by the ideas and actions of others and the leaders of the anti-globalization revolution realize that they possess an ability to influence global opinion by acting on a global scale. The proliferation of communication methods has had a profound ability to enable ideas. People can look beyond their individual plight and believe there is a greater force that is affecting their lives. This is a sine qua non of revolutionary thought and deed and the ITO Revolution had a profound affect on the world by acting as an enabler of communication.

• The alienation perceived by the people of other cultures by the unrelenting export of American culture and innovation. There is no question that America is an exporter of culture, ideas, and beliefs. We are a young nation-state of immense power and influence and the people of other nation-states can feel alienated and threatened by our culture. The word "innovation" was chosen carefully instead of the word "technology." Computer and biotechnologies are components of the overall innovative drive of the United States. As a nation-state, we are innovators in technologies such as biotechnology, computers, food, transportation, energy, military, and many other smaller categories. We are also innovators in cultural elements such as media, entertainment, and film. We export our culture and innovations through technology and the ITO Revolution rapidly enabled a means for other people to be influenced by American culture.

The revolution that is underway is a reaction to the creation of a global economy and the global nation-state. All the foundational elements were in place at the end of the Cold War to support the early stages of the revolution [see Brinton, page >27]. The old Soviet regime and the governments supported by the Soviet Union were structurally weak and could not maintain leadership, control, and influence over their nation-states. The economies of the pro-Soviet bloc nation-states, the emerging nation-state economies, and the regional nation-states in conflict (e.g. Lebanon, Palestine, Kashmir, Afghanistan, Balkans, etc.) were under enormous economic pressure. The economies of these nation-states were failing or had become an acute crisis on the verge of outright economic collapse.

Within the nation-states that were beginning to cycle towards revolution, the intellectual influences were more than local – they were global. The collapse of the bi-polar alignment freed people to explore new ideas and react to the elements of their nation-states that were failing. In some cases, the solutions or reaction of the people were along religious lines and in other nation-states, the solutions were militaristic. The pursuit of the new ideas was an important step, as it signaled that the intellectual leaders of these societies had transferred their allegiance [see Brinton, page >39] from the old order and were willing to seek new solutions. The influence of the intellectuals had begun to permeate all levels of society within the revolutionary nation-states. The difference between the traditional revolutions of history and those of our contemporary time is the opposition of revolutionaries. Social distinction and the rights of man are secondary objectives to the global revolutionary. The new revolutionaries view their struggle on a global scale. From their viewpoint, their cause is the product of a class struggle on a global scale. Local class struggles, which had been a foundational element of historical revolutions, have been transposed to class struggles between nation-states. Even by mid-2005 this struggle is clearly visible on the global scale. The G8 nation-states are pushing a plan to cancel $40 billion of developing world debt as well find investments to foster economic development. The investment plan has been termed a Marshall Plan for the developing world. Tony Blair, Prime Minister of England, was advocating a global aid package of $25 billion for Africa and he realizes that his plan will not be successful without the United States playing a prominent if not leadership role. *"The brutal truth is, without America in a process of dialogue and action in the international community, we are not going to make progress on it,"* [see Tony Blair, June 8 2005]. For American foreign and economic policy, the interdependencies between foreign policy, economic policy, technology markets, and globalization must be considered in totality because global forces do affect markets on a global scale.

The Eternal Figaro on the Grand Global Stage

In 18th Century France, the revolution by the people was directed at the royal class and the government that served the royal class. In the 21st century, the vast distances between people no longer separate and insulate. The Eternal Figaro no longer stands to admonish the second estate – but rather to admonish the wealthy nation-states, the ruling nation-states, and their values and culture. The struggle of the revolutionary is a struggle on a global stage. This is not a revolution within a nation-state, such as those that occurred in America (1775), France (1789), Germany (1848), and Russia (1917), but a rather a global revolution wherein the policies and rule of the individual nation-state are played out on the global scale because of the dominance of American economic, cultural, and military power. The events of September 11, 2001 are the actions found in the Accession of the Extremists. Our position in the world and our foreign polices have driven the revolutionaries who embody the Eternal Figaro, to seek an argumentum ad hominen from the social classes. The intellectual leaders appeal to nationalistic fervor to insight their revolution and pursue their ultimate goal of independence.

There is a clash of civilizations in our world, but this clash is really occurring within the context of the overall revolution or evolution. The elements that nation-states seek are universally the same. People seek self-determination, autonomous rule, religious freedom, economic stability, military security, and the prospect of a prosperous future. From the perspective of America, these changes are revolutionary – but from the perspective of the revolutionary, these changes are simply evolutionary. American foreign policy must address the challenges from both perspectives.

The United States is the biggest exporter of culture in the world; we endure most of the criticism from those who resist change regardless of whether we deserve said criticism. America is a relentless machine driven by innovation, growth, and success. Other nation-states share similar characteristics with the United States, but no other nation-state can compete with the United States in terms of economic and military power. Our global power, global reach, and unrelenting drive is unmatched in the global market and it often has adverse cultural affects. The unfortunate result of American innovation is that people feel alienated and threatened by our actions. They view our innovation as a challenge to their way of life. By nature, people resist change and American innovation is often viewed as a catalyst to a changing way of life. The intellectuals, the older generation of revolutionary leaders, use the position of the United States to exploit the feelings of non-fulfillment within the younger generation of their nation-states. The gap between generations is bridged by the four core elements of the revolution. The events of the past ten years sequence well into Crane Brinton's model of revolutions and we should be able to anticipate the course of events and adjust the foreign policy of the United States to counter the forces aligned against us.

It is important to value that the people of stable nation-states possess hope. Hope comes in many forms and addresses many needs. People take extreme and radical courses of action because they have lost hope. People must have hope that the future can and will be better. Nation-states must have hope that they can achieve economic stability and certainty. Self-determination and the fulfillment of their nationalistic drive must be realized by all people and cultures bound within their nation-states.

Throughout most of our first 170 years, America has had a foreign policy that was isolationist and reactionary in principle. In the mid twentieth century, that policy changed. Our foreign policy became one of intervention and active containment concerning the Cold War. Our business practices and innovative drive became intervention based as well. The United States has put itself in a position of supreme military and economic power. The forces unleashed by the end of the Cold War represent very well a revolution on a global scale against the power of America, and her leadership of the globalization forces.

We have begun a new century and a new millennium in a turbulent time. We are very much in the period known as the Reign of Terror [see Brinton, page >176]. What we do not know is how long this period will last. What we do know, is that in order to end this revolution we must address the immediate causes of this stage of the revolution and over the long-term put forth a set of foreign policy principles that eliminate the forces of revolution on a global scale.

Brinton defined seven characteristics that embody the Reign of Terror. We can examine each of these characteristics and apply them to the actions of the revolutionaries that have affected our world in recent years. The first of these characteristics is the habit of violence. From the end of the Six-Day War on June 10, 1967, a generation in the Middle East has been raised with violence as a common occurrence in their lives. Regions of the world have gone through tremendous political change over the past twenty years. The breakdown of government, education, law, and social dignity has mothered a generation that knows no other option than violence in their lives. The Reign of Terror is only broken when the people of a nation-state tire of the cycle of violence. Brinton observed that societies cannot go on forever with the intense scrutiny and heightened tensions of the Reign of Terror and Virtue. Eventually, society breaks under the weight of the violence and expectations of heaven on Earth. This is what happened in Lebanon as the new millennium emerged. After years of civil war and violence, leaders emerged and outsiders of the extremists began to exert power. In time, Israel and Syria left Lebanon and the people began to rebuild the nation-state.

In nearly all of the nation-states in which we find revolutionary forces aligned against the United States, we find a nation-state or region torn apart by continuous or sporadic civil war over the past fifteen or more years. The list is lengthy: Afghanistan, Lebanon, Balkans, Somalia, Pakistan, Palestine, central Africa, and more. The pressure of internal civil wars forces people to take extreme measures. In a world in which revolutionary forces cannot conclude their internal civil wars, they begin to focus on what they believe to be the foundation of the government they oppose. In the Middle East, the United States is viewed as the guarantor of Israeli power and security. If the revolutionary forces aligned against Israel cannot defeat the forces of Israel on the battlefield, then they will strike at the foundation of Israeli power, which in their perception is the United States.

The end of the Cold War brought forth a new era in which the United States is viewed as the new central government of the world. Perception is reality. The United Nations is viewed as a vehicle by which the United States uses its economic power to govern the weak nation-states. The IMF is merely an extension of the United States Federal Reserve. There is enough evidence to support the perception that the G8 multinational corporations exploit the poorer nations and dominate the lesser corporations from weaker nation-states for the sole purpose of increasing the wealth of the dominant nation-states. These are not truthful statements, but there is enough circumstantial evidence to promote a perception that they are true. As a leader within the G8, the United States is without question the most powerful military force. To the person who perceives himself a revolutionary struggling against a central power, the elements are in place to expand their perception of their opposition beyond local and regional governments of their nation-state and question the role that the United States plays in their lives and the world.

The post-Cold War alignment witnessed opposing extremes of economic success and depression. For the active revolutionary regions of the world, (e.g. Middle East, Central Asia, Balkans, Africa) the past ten or more years have been a time of extreme economic depression. People have existed in cultures with little hope of economic progress. Economic stability is a mere dream. At some point, people become desperate and lose hope. They become desperate for jobs, for money, for stability, and for the future of their families and lives. When this happens, revolutionaries are born.

It can be argued that at no other time in human history has there been such a large gap between the wealthy and poor nation-states. The rapidity of communication and greater global awareness enabled by the ITO Revolution has created an environment wherein the poorer nation-states do not view their weakness as individual challenges – but rather view their weaknesses as a part of a global struggle. The class struggles that Brinton identified as a core element of the reign of terror within individual nation-states, is in our time a class struggle between nation-states.

The leaders of the class struggle have concluded that their actions must be taken to the heart of the nation-states that support the policies that they oppose. To achieve their goals, the revolutionary leaders of our time have begun to push the extreme of boundaries of their actions to highlight their cause and make their point. High visibility terrorist actions such as the events of September 11, 2001 are examples of pushing their revolutionary extremes with their actions. The unanswered question is whether the revolutionary leaders will be able to gain weapons of mass destruction and use these weapons to continue their Reign of Terror.

The Reign of Terror will end when the Reign of Virtue begins. The Reign of Virtue begins when the gap between human nature and human aspirations is closed [see Brinton, page >202]. This is what happened in Lebanon. The extremists realized that they had lost support from the majority of the people, or groups within the structure of the nation-state had grown stronger politically. At some point in the revolutionary process, the cycle of violence that has dominated the Reign of Terror will decline. When the madness and cruelty of the Reign of Terror reach an extreme level, it will drive forces that will break the cycle of violence. The leaders of the revolution use extreme violence to advance their cause. As the violence escalates in the Reign of Terror, it triggers a response in the people of the nation-state and leaders of the opposing forces. The cycle of violence can be broken by spiritual renewal, devotion, and self-sacrifice of the forces opposing the revolution. Extreme actions trigger extreme actions in response. Hope and personal courage lead to the end of the revolutionary cycle. The people of the nation-state realize that the revolutionaries are not the answer to their problems. Commitment to their own nation-state and the leap of faith required to have hope in the future comes from the leaders who emerge after the revolutionaries have failed. The hardest lesson to learn is the least complicated. The United States can facilitate this process by sowing the seeds of hope through economic assistance.

Tenants of a New American Foreign Policy

When George Kennan defined the foreign policy of the United States as a policy of containment in an article published in *Foreign Affairs* in July 1947, few people envisioned that it would take this policy Reagan forty years to succeed. The structure of government that the United States employs enables our nation-state to enjoy many freedoms – rarely does this structure allow our nation-state to have a sustained, long-term foreign policy. To succeed against this new globalization revolution, United States foreign policy must address the revolution as well as the foundational elements of the revolution's power. As with our policy of containment, we must confront the revolutionaries through a sustained, long-term foreign policy initiative. Our history of two hundred and fifteen years is quite small compared to most nation-states, yet in that time we have risen to unparalleled heights of power. We must now respect our achievements and accept that we must change the tenants of our foreign policy to reflect the long-term commitment required to end the global revolution.

The long-term foreign policy tenants of the United States must go beyond the security and prosperity of the homeland. We cannot be isolationists. Our businesses, our prosperity, and our future are found in the community nation-states – not in the community of self. We cannot have a policy of appeasement, for this is a policy of failure and weakness. We must have a policy of containment of the revolutionary forces that oppose our nation-state and a willingness to address the fundamental elements of change and revolution that drive the global revolution.

- *Class Struggle between Nation-States*: The foreign policy of the United States must be aligned and linked with our economic polices and our business practices. We must close the gap between wealthy nation-states and poor nation-states. We cannot have nation-states living in abject poverty and possess an economic infrastructure equitable to a pre-industrialized society. The wealthy nation-states and the private sector must develop strategies for joint investment to build the economic markets of the future. The development of economic stability and prosperity amongst all nation-states is the foundation that builds trust, security, and peace. This is the policy that creates hope. This is not a goal that will be realized overnight. It is goal that will take many years to achieve and perhaps longer to succeed than Kennan's policy of containment.

- *Elimination of Social Injustice and Promotion of Social Equality*: The

Eternal Figaro can only be quelled through the elimination of social injustice and the promotion of social equality within the individual nation-state and the community of nation-states. We cannot have a foreign policy that promotes co-existence with nation-states that support disharmony amongst nation-states. Social inequality is the product of inadequate education, poor infrastructure, and economic instability. The United States must lead other nation-states and multinational corporations to develop flexible programs of investment that strengthen the internal infrastructure, promotes economic stability, and improves education and human services within the poorer nation-states. The summum bonum for any nation-state is to display the courage and wisdom to assist those nation-states who are less than us.

• *Promote Regional Stability and Self-Determination*: The United States must seek strategies within the United Nations to promote regional security and cooperation. This policy will only be successful within a framework that is inclusive to all regional nation-states. The United States should seek to build regional coalitions to resolve disputes, contain moderate regional conflicts, and seek consensus solutions. The jus gentium must be enforced by alliances amongst regional nation-states.

• *Active Containment of Revolutionary Forces*: The revolutionaries, who seek to disrupt the global order, must be actively opposed and brought to justice. The Reign of Terror will end when the revolutionaries who employ the practices of extreme violence are eliminated. This will act as a signal to the moderate leaders of nation-states to return to the practical polices of change that are accepted within the community of nation-states.

• The anti-globalization and anti-United States movement are symbolic of the alienation felt by people who oppose American foreign policy, American culture, and American business practices. Their perception is real. People of other nation-states are dissatisfied with their plight and like Figaro, they assign blame to the ruling class whom they view are the privileged nation-states.

During the Great Depression, Franklin D. Roosevelt positioned the government of the Untied States to be the provider of hope. He did this through investments in the infrastructure of the United States and by creating safety nets to prevent people from falling so far behind that their personal situation was unrecoverable. In this new century, the United States needs to be a leader, a leader that can marshal the wealthy nation-states and multi-national corporations to be the investors in the infrastructure of nation-states and provider of hope. We cannot let nation-states fall so far behind that their only recourse of action emboldens them to take desperate actions.

The United States must be in the business of building the business market of the future. We cannot assume that our industries and technology have universal application the world over. Foreign polity, market regulation, and technology investments must be linked to form a global framework for policy and action. In terms of telecom infrastructure investment, the United States has already fallen behind other nation-states. When President Clinton signed the Telecom Act of 1996, he hailed America's leadership of innovation in the field on communications and hailed the Act as our commitment to the new information based economy. Ten years later, our information based economy is struggling to find ways to be meaningful. We see the rise of global competitors from Asia and Europe. Investment in the infrastructure of the American communications infrastructure is on the wane. It should be the policy of the United States to ensure that competitive, meaningful, and vibrant information industry exists and is tied to the global competitive nature of American companies and the foreign policy of the United States.

In closing this section on the impact of the globalization revolution against American, we should look back at the inaugural address of John F. Kennedy given on January 20, 1960. Forty-five years later, his words spoken on that day, have meaning for our generation, during our time. *"We dare not forget today that we are the heirs of that first revolution. Let the word go forth from this time and place, to friend and foe alike, that the torch has been passed to a new generation of Americans... unwilling to witness or permit the slow undoing of those human rights to which this nation has always been committed, and to which we are committed today at home and around the world. Let every nation know, whether it wishes us well or ill, that we shall pay any price, bear any burden, meet any hardship, support any friend, oppose any foe to assure the survival and the success of liberty. This much we pledge – and more. To those old allies whose cultural and spiritual origins we share, we pledge the loyalty of faithful friends. United there is little we cannot do in a host of cooperative ventures. Divided there is little we can do--for we dare not meet a powerful challenge at odds and split asunder. To those new states whom we welcome to the ranks of the free, we pledge our word that one form of colonial control shall not have passed away merely to be replaced by a far more iron tyranny. We shall not always expect to find them supporting our view. But we shall always hope to find them strongly supporting their own freedom – and to remember that, in the past, those who foolishly sought power by riding the back of the tiger ended up inside. To those people in the huts and villages of half the globe struggling to break the bonds of mass misery, we pledge our best efforts to help them help themselves, for whatever period is required – not because the communists may be doing it, not because we seek their votes, but because it is right. If a free society cannot help the many who are poor, it cannot save the few who are rich...to assist free men and free governments in casting off the chains of poverty. But this peaceful revolution of hope cannot become the prey of hostile powers...To that world assembly of sovereign states, the United Nations, our last best hope in an age where the instruments of war have far outpaced the instruments of peace, we renew our pledge of support – to prevent it from becoming merely a forum for invective- -to strengthen its shield of the new and the weak – and to enlarge the area in which its writ may run. Finally, to those nations who would make themselves our adversary, we offer not a pledge but a request: that both sides begin anew the quest for peace, before the dark powers of destruction unleashed by science engulf all humanity in planned or accidental self-destruction....Now the trumpet summons us again--not as a call to bear arms, though arms we need – not as a call to battle, though embattled we are – but a call to bear the burden of a long twilight struggle, year in and year out, 'rejoicing in hope, patient in tribulation' – a struggle against the common enemies of man: tyranny, poverty, disease and war itself..."*

ESSAY THREE

A Market Model Hypothesis

CHAPTER ELEVEN:
From Pride and Foolish Confidence

The Golden Age, which a blind tradition has hitherto placed in the past, is ahead of us. - Claude Henri de Rouvroy, Comte de Saint-Simon, 1825

Revolutions are emotional and intellectually interesting events. When they are over, people look fondly upon the heady days when revolution was in the air and world was going to change as it had never changed before. This is the affect of a revolution. Revolutions have the power to change old regimes. Revolutions foster a heightening of the seriousness of the political process within the nation-state as well as within the competitive state of any business whose market is being affected by revolutionary forces. When markets go through a revolution – people and companies in the market experience a heightening of intensity and tension. This is the origin of the notion of competing on internet time. Revolutions transpose the perception of difficult problems. Challenging problems appear easily solved in time of revolution as the details are often overlooked. The rewards for the winners in any revolution are enormous. In July of 2004, Microsoft announced that it would pay a one time dividend to shareholders of $3 per share. This amounted to a one time distribution of $32 billion. Over the next four years, Microsoft was committing to returning $75 billion dollars of cash to its shareholders. None of the extremists of ITO Revolution did as well as Microsoft. For their own personal satisfaction, Microsoft could pay cash for Sun Microsystems, who was a revolutionary and ardent supporter of the government's investigation into Microsoft's trade practices during the ITO Revolution. It was Scott McNealy, CEO of Sun Microsystems who said, *"Only a monopolist could study a business and ruin it by giving away products,"* which is a reference to how Microsoft competed against Netscape during the browser wars. For all battles that Sun and Microsoft waged against each other, the result was one company became an extremist (i.e. quadrant 3 company) and the other became a moderate (i.e. quadrant 2 company).

Throughout 2004 and into 2005, Microsoft generates approximately one billion dollars of free cash flow per month. They dominate their markets and have vanquished all competitors to their core businesses. In time, Microsoft will become an old regime. It will evolve from being an extremist to an old regime in much the same way the Bolsheviks became the aged, ineffective, centralized ruling party that simply gave up ruling the Soviet Union in 1991. The structural weakness of the Soviet government was their inability to control the mechanisms that projected power in the nation-state. In the structure of markets, when the dominate companies fail to defend their market share, they are demonstrating to their competitors a form of structural weakness. Microsoft is the current defender of the established market share. For Microsoft the "... *successes of the early phases of the deployment period have strengthened the confidence of the defenders of establishment. For them, by the maturity phase, complacency has arrived, progress seems guaranteed and the great virtues of the system can be proclaimed with certainty,"* [see Perez, page 137].

When the extremists within Microsoft pass the mantel of leadership to successive generations, who by nature will not be as fanatical as the founders, Microsoft will begin the transformation from an extremist to an old regime. IBM went through the same evolution as their markets and leaders changed in the late 1980s and into the 1990s. IBM was savaged by competitors from all sides until new leaders took control, stabilized the business, and put IBM on the path of being a revolutionary in new markets. Success is measured by market share and market share is acquired through innovation which compels customers to purchase new technology. When companies stop innovating they stop exerting control over their market share. Lack of control of market share is a structural weakness. When companies are structurally weak, they feed the Figaro within other companies and revolutionaries. In time, the Eternal Figaro will grow inside Microsoft, Cisco, Yahoo, Verizon, SBC, Comcast, and the other victors of the ITO Revolution. Perez believes that the end of age of dominant companies will be preceded by a "...*growing social discontent followed by the economic decline of the established production structure. Another surge is about to emerge; another turbulent period of installation, with increasing control of financial capital, will spread the next paradigm, until it reaches a critical mass at the next turning point,"* [see Perez, page 137].

The victors in any revolution are the companies that are led by great leaders who understand the cycle of change and strategize not for victory on the day of revolution, but for victory in the Apogee stage of the G3 Market Model. When Microsoft becomes an old regime and the conditions required to support a new revolution materialize, revolutionaries will come forth. Even today there are revolutionaries who operate in fear of Microsoft. Similar to the formative years that shaped a young Bill Gates, the new revolutionaries might be students at Harvard, MIT, and Stanford or located in far away places such as Moscow, India, and China. They might even be employees of Microsoft. At night they clandestinely plot the downfall of Microsoft in darkened basements of their homes, fearing that Microsoft will not discover their treacherous plots for they know it will cost them their jobs. This is where revolutions begin. They begin with the revolutionary who is motivated by the quest for change, the desire for power, and the belief in a higher ideal, a better plane of existence that in the end will provide some form of social justice and personal satisfaction. Revolutions start when people create a solution to a complex problem. The people working inside Google are clearly revolutionaries who are planning to attack Microsoft from outside the computer operating system. Google's strategy looks very much like the new generation of service providers who want to offer a service without owning a network. Google is looking to create applications that reside in the web and do not require a specific operating system. If Google can find a way to bypass Microsoft's core advantage in their dominance of the personal computer operating system and productivity application markets, it will mean that Microsoft will have a major revolution to endure.

The Untied States is born from revolution. We have adopted an economic structure that is not perfect, but it fosters change. The United States changes its government every two to four years. We have a predicable timeline of points when change might occur, called elections. We have an economic system that rewards success and punishes failure. We have a private equity mechanism in place that encourages risk, supports revolutions, and rewards success. "...*in America you can drop out of college and start Microsoft, Oracle or Dell. You can get a "C" grade at the Yale School of Management and still launch FedEx. You can dropkick your Ph.D. pursuit and start Google,*" [see Rich Karlgaard, *Why we Need Startups*, Forbes, July 21, 2003]. The result is a nation-state that is far from perfect, but has an infrastructure in place that supports change and revolutions. The roots of this system can be traced back to the Sons of Liberty in Boston during the years leading up to the American Revolution. The people that confronted the government in London found their financial backing from private funds within the American colonies. Privately raised funds were not being used to start a new biotech startup on the banks of the Charles River in 1775, but they were being used to fund the active opposition to General Gage, his military forces in Boston, and the English Monarchy of King George the III. This is how wealth, revolution, and ideas are linked.

Where Do We Come From? What Are We? Where Are We Going?

The questions that Eugène Henri Paul Gauguin posed in 1897 are as relevant today as they were in the waning years of the 19th century. The internet, telecom, and optical markets within the United States are clearly in the midst of the last stage of the G3 Market Model. Beyond the ITO Revolution, there is still a question of whether a new economy is taking hold. Was the internet an over-hyped waste of money or the foundation for a new economy that will be a carrier for economic transactions over the millennium? The perfect storm of the Terror has passed and the survivors are battered, beaten – but alive. The surviving companies have stabilized their business and most have returned to profitability. There are several dominant companies and the remaining companies are niche survivors living in quadrant 2 or 4 of the Entropy Base Model. The survivors who are not the dominant companies know that it is time to continue to correct their business model as the pace of change accelerated by revolution within the internet, telecom, and optical markets has slowed, thus enabling the survivors to build their business based on realistic business plans and rational market metrics. It is doubtful that any of niche survivors will emerge as a large corporation, unless another change event occurs to enable fluidity of market share. The current market structure does not enable companies to rapidly acquire market share using traditional growth strategies. Explosive revenue growth and the valuations based on growth are not possible in the Return stage of the G3MM. *"...our business continues to be impacted by industry-related conditions,"* [see Dan Smith, CEO of Sycamore Networks, August 2004 Earnings Conference Call]. The industry conditions that are affecting the growth of a one time rising star of the ITO Revolution are the structure of market share and the barriers that prevent fluidity of market share. Sycamore Networks is too small a company to acquire market share from the large service providers who survived the ITO Revolution. These quadrant 3 companies prefer to award business to companies of equivalent size. Even though Sycamore is a well financed company (e.g. $900 million is cash in mid-2005), they have not demonstrated an ability to attract people who can create innovation that solves complex problems that in turn provides Sycamore with a competitive edge that compels the large service providers to invest in solutions from Sycamore and abandon their incumbent suppliers. Market share in the ITO markets is static and it is split between those that have market share and those who do not have market share. The result of this dichotomy is the companies with dominant market share do not have competitive forces that drive them to be innovators. The large companies know that the small companies cannot use innovation as a competitive weapon – therefore they slow their R&D expenditures. Innovation slows; it does not end in a market structure in which market share is dominated by a few firms.

As we move farther away from the heady days of ITO Revolution's initial five stages, companies in the ITO markets are still locked in battle for control of their markets. The difference between the final stage from the previous stages is rapid acceleration from a small company into a large company is simply not possible in the current market structure. Venture backed startups are not announcing that they have a goal of going public in eighteen months. Access to capital is constrained, even though there is arguably a large amount of idle, non-invested venture capital compared to the Start stage of the ITO Revolution [see *Essay One, Chapter Two*]. The entry market barriers are once again high, as they were during the Start stage of the ITO Revolution. The telecom service provider and network equipment markets are settling into the state that will eventually lead to the formation of old regimes from the extremists of today.

The survivors of the ITO Revolution are determined to strengthen their businesses and keep competitors out. A compelling feature that made the ITO Revolution possible was the lowering of traditional market barriers combined with access to financial capital. Whether this was a generational event will be answered in the future – but this rare event was a driver of significant investment in telecom and networking equipment by public companies and private investors. If the ITO Revolution is to continue to track to the model that Perez developed, we should expect a reasonably long period of sustained, but modest growth as concepts proven to be correct in the ITO Revolution are fully commercialized and institutionalized. It is the institutional process the leads to the creation of old regimes. *"When a disruptive new technology arrives, the greatest business opportunities often lie not in creating the disruption but in mending it — in figuring out a way to use an older, established technology as a bridge to carry customers to the benefits of the emerging technology,"* [see *Bridging the Breakthrough Gap*, Strategy & Business, Winter 2004]. This is the crux of Perez's model post the *"turning point."*

Despite the tremendous boom and bust cycle of the ITO Revolution, the winners of the ITO Revolution are now only at the dawn of this revolution's most significant battle. The upcoming battle for the convergence of several markets and a transition to a new economic order will result in a smaller number of dominant companies, but require that complex problems of computing and network integration be solved. The drivers that formed and shaped the conditions required to create the ITO Revolution are the same drivers that will create the next revolution in telecom services and networking. As we hypothesize on the impact of convergence, we will find that many of the winners (i.e. extremists) from the ITO Revolution are positioning themselves to be significant players in the next revolutionary cycle – but face daunting challenges on a global scale. The pre-turning point ITO markets were global in nature – but they were not globally connected and interdependent. As the ITO markets move further away from the turning point, the next long phase of the telecom and technology revolution appears to be less U.S. centric, with companies competing for market share on a global scale, with global competitors from many geographic markets. This emerging global market structure creates a level of complexity that few U.S. based technology companies have had to address. From a generational perspective, Perez's model reflecting pre and post turning point periods can be positioned as separate cycles. It is quite plausible that the generation that experienced the ITO markets during the years 1971 to 2001, would find the emerging market structure post-2005 to be unfamiliar and foreign.

Long Term Prospects for Service Provider Revenues

The ITO markets (i.e. internet, telecom, optical) are from distinct and different sources. Telecom has historically been about long distance voice and local telephony services. As we emerged into the broadband era, service providers no longer segment and share the revenues of a voice call into local and long distance portions. Service providers look at the challenge that will grow in the future as two-fold. End-users will have a broadband connection or what the FCC terms an Advanced Services Line. The broadband or high speed data connection to the internet might be a wireline connection of some type (e.g. bonded copper, fiber, other) or it can be a wireless connection (e.g. WiMAX, EVDO, OFDM, other). The technology used to provide the broadband connection is in question, but will evolve over time – what is not in question is that a broadband connection of some type will be required. Legacy circuit-switched telephony connections will be active in the market for a long time – but the future for service providers is a two-part problem concerning connectivity and content.

In 1955, a three minute international telephone call cost $55. Today, a three minute international telephony call costs less than $1 dollar [see, *The Future of Telecommunications: Connectivity through Alliances*, April 1998]. Since 1980 the billed per minute rate for an international call from the U.S. has been declining with an accelerated descent post 1996. In addition, the average total cost per call has declined from more than $8 per call to less than $2 per call.

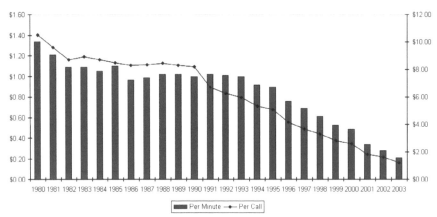

Figure 44: International Call Charges from the United States
Source: Author's Adaptation of Federal Communications Commission, *Trends in Telephone Service Report*, June 21, 2005 Chart 6-1

When AT&T divested the local telephony divisions in 1984, it enabled the measurement of revenues on a per call basis, based upon the local and long distance portion of the call. The FCC has been reporting these revenues in varying levels of totality since 1993. The chart below reflects the share of long distance (i.e. LD or Toll Revenues) by service provider or service provider grouping. The discerning trend reflected in the slide is the overall market contraction post 1999.

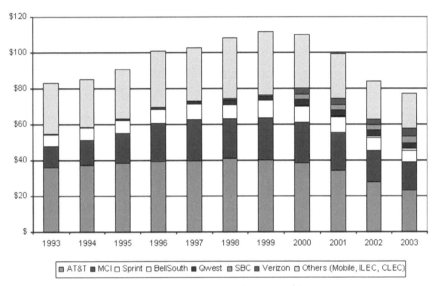

Figure 45: Total Long Distance (LDD) Revenues Reported ($Billions)
Source: Author's adaptation of statistics reported in June 21, 2005 FCC *Trends in Telephone Service Report*

To compound the decline of overall LD revenues, the emergence of the four RBOCs into the long distance market have begun to affect market share. The 2004 market share data will be critical to show how the market is evolving, but it appears that RBOCs are taking market share from AT&T as well as other ILEC and CLECs who provided LD services. LD market share for Sprint and MCI remained relatively constant from 1996 through 2003. The steady market share of MCI is somewhat surprising, due to the acquisition of MCI by Worldcom in 1998. It would have been logical to assume that MCI acquisition would have been reflected by a change of market share in the FCC report. Perhaps this is an indication that Worldcom's LD business was minimal compared to MCI or the reported numbers are inaccurate.

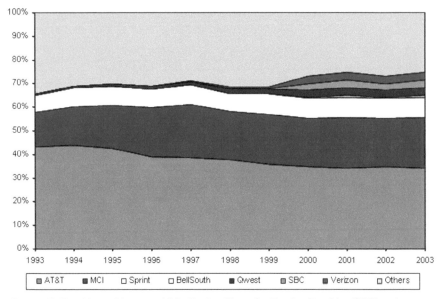

Figure 46: Total Long Distance (LDD) Market Share by Service Provider ($Billions)
Source: Author's adaptation of statistics reported in June 21, 2005 FCC *Trends in Telephone Service Report*

A clear objective of the breakup of AT&T was to foster competition and distribute AT&T's market share to other service providers – thus creating a healthier market construct. With the overall decline in long distance pricing and revenues, coupled with the distribution of market share to other service providers, the acquisitions of AT&T and MCI in 2005 were a logical conclusion to the process that started with the litigation between AT&T and MCI and the ruling of Judge Harold H. Greene in 1982. It was the Telecom Act of 1996 that produced the market and financial conditions that enabled alternative long haul optical networks to be built in a short period of time. Before the Telecom Act of 1996, the nationwide backbones that were built by AT&T, MCI, and Sprint were viewed to be difficult engineering, financial, and legal undertakings. In the regulated industry stage of the U.S. telecom market few companies contemplated building an alternative long haul fiber optic backbone. The emergence of many long haul networks post the Telecom Act of 1996 was based on the premise that there would be a healthy market of competitive local exchange carriers that would drive local telephony onto long distance networks. The long distance network that AT&T had used as a competitive advantage and positioned as a national asset for decades, was easily replicated post the Telecom Act of 1996 by technology innovation and financial capital.

The Telecom Act of 1996 unleashed capital, curtailed regulation, and created market conditions that enabled the deployment of large fiber optical backbones. A host of emerging IXCs and CAPs built national backbones and regional optical networks. Once the RBOCs secured regulatory approval to offer LD services, it was easy for them to find the capacity and networks to support out of region transport in the form of the new IXCs who were building or had completed long haul optical networks. As the ITO Revolution progressed into the Apogee stage, the decline of the LD market adversely affected the market capitalization of AT&T, MCI, and Sprint. The result was that the two largest RBOCs decided to purchase nationwide backbones via AT&T, and MCI and Sprint decided to bet their future on mobile networks and merged with Nextel.

The driver of erosion within the LD market was the inability of the Telecom Act of 1996 to affect market share within the local telephony market with the same effect as it did in the LD market. Statistics from the June 2005 FCC *Trends in Telephone Report* clearly indicate that overall local access lines in service have been in decline since 2000. This is a function of the market correction incurred by the ITO Markets during the Decline stage as well as a migration from dial-up internet access to broadband connections that the FCC terms Advanced Services lines.

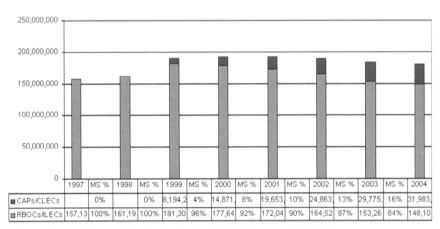

Figure 47: Local Access Lines in Service by RBOC/ILEC versus CELC/CAP
Source: Author's adaptation of statistics reported in June 21, 2005 FCC *Trends in Telephone Service Report*

The above chart not only shows that the market for legacy, circuit switched telephones has begun to decline, but it also highlights the erosion of market share achieved by the CLECs and CAPs post the Telecom Act of 1996. Eight years removed from the passage of the Act, competitive local exchange service providers have acquired 18% market share in the U.S. for local access service. The transfer of 18% market share from incumbents to new service providers within eight years can be used to argue that the Telecom Act of 1996 accomplished what was intended – but simply assessing success based on access line market share can be misleading. The following chart is a reflection of local access line revenues by service provider type. Several important trends are apparent. Although the overall market size for local service revenues grew from 1993 to 2001, with a decline in 2002 and 2003, the RBOCs have maintained more than 70% market share of local service revenues since 1993, with yearly fluctuations.

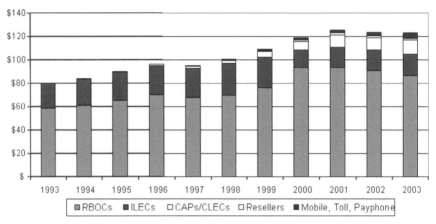

Figure 48: Local Access Revenues ($Billions) by Service Provider Type
Source: Author's adaptation of statistics reported in June 21, 2005 FCC *Trends in Telephone Service Report*

Another perspective to view the market trend for local access is to view local access lines and local service revenues as 100%, regardless of the fluctuations in total market size. In this view, the acquisition of market share by CAPs and CLECs post the Telecom Act of 1996 is visibly apparent, while the other two service provider segments report minor changes in market share from 1998 through 2003. Clearly, this chart is a vindication of ability of the Telecom Act of 1996 to foster local competition – but there is another dynamic to local access and that is the quality of the revenue generated by a local access line.

Voice has been the driving service and revenue generator for telecom service providers. Only in the past twenty-five years did touch tone dialing and * services (e.g. *69, callerID) impact the revenue lines of telecom service providers. As the ITO Revolution was raging through the Perigee stage in 1999, there were still people living with shared phone lines; called party lines. As Vermont was implementing the enhanced 911 service in 1999, the new system required the dismantling of the last ten party lines in the state. In 1995, there were 8,600 party lines in Vermont, down from 35,000 in 1979.

In the age of the digital revolution, some people simply did not care. This minor statistic is significant because it illustrates the pace of change across the telephony market spectrum. Telephony, whether local or long distance, digital or shared party line, has always been about voice and billing for voice services. Technology has a longer market tail than most intellectuals in the Thought Leadership Model realize. Social habits are customs that are deeply ingrained in society [see *Essay Two, Chapter Eight*]. This is why the internet did not change how people purchased groceries and pet food.

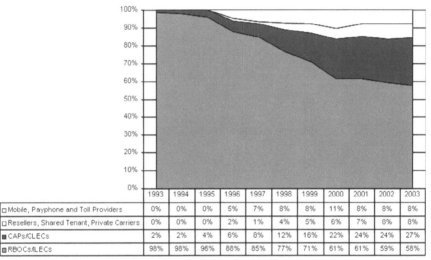

	1993	1994	1995	1996	1997	1998	1999	2000	2001	2002	2003
☐ Mobile, Payphone and Toll Providers	0%	0%	0%	5%	7%	8%	8%	11%	8%	8%	8%
☐ Resellers, Shared Tenant, Private Carriers	0%	0%	0%	2%	1%	4%	5%	6%	7%	8%	8%
■ CAPs/CLECs	2%	2%	4%	6%	8%	12%	16%	22%	24%	24%	27%
▣ RBOCs/ILECs	98%	98%	96%	88%	85%	77%	71%	61%	61%	59%	58%

Figure 49: Local Access Line Market Share by Service Provider Type
Source: Author's adaptation of statistics reported in June 21, 2005 FCC *Trends in Telephone Service Report*

A better method to measure the success of local competition is too measure market share based on revenues. Putting aside the fluctuations in overall market size measured by the number of local access lines in service, analyzing the structure of the market based on revenues reveals that the new service providers that emerged post the Telecom Act of 1996 have achieved market share gains. These market share gains have been at the expense of the ILECs – not the RBOCs that were spun out of AT&T in 1984. The statistics provided by the FCC clearly show that the RBOCs have successful maintained 70%+ market share of local service revenues through the cycle of the ITO Revolution. In that time they have also built a successful business by offering long distance services to their local telephony customers. What conclusions can be drawn from this?

It appears that the market share that the CLECs and CAPs are securing is being taken from the ILECs as well as new local access line business. A reasonable hypothesis is that although overall local access lines are declining and the RBOC market share of local access lines is declining, the ability of the RBOCs to defend market share in valuable markets indicates that the RBOCs can enact strong barriers to entry against competitors. The real battle for the local loop to the end-user appears to be between the RBOCs, mobile service providers, and the cable service providers. It is these companies that have the capital to wage war for control of market share in the markets that have high revenue take rates of value add services.

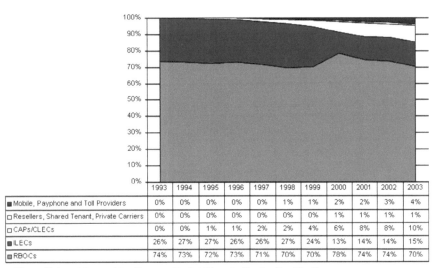

	1993	1994	1995	1996	1997	1998	1999	2000	2001	2002	2003
■ Mobile, Payphone and Toll Providers	0%	0%	0%	0%	0%	1%	1%	2%	2%	3%	4%
□ Resellers, Shared Tenant, Private Carriers	0%	0%	0%	0%	0%	0%	0%	1%	1%	1%	1%
□ CAPs/CLECs	0%	0%	1%	1%	2%	2%	4%	6%	8%	8%	10%
■ ILECs	26%	27%	27%	26%	26%	27%	24%	13%	14%	14%	15%
▨ RBOCs	74%	73%	72%	73%	71%	70%	70%	78%	74%	74%	70%

Figure 50: Local Access Line Revenue Market Share by Service Provider Type
Source: Author's adaptation of statistics reported in June 21, 2005 FCC *Trends in Telephone Service Report*

In the last data points provided regarding local access revenues, it appears that the RBOCs lost four market percentage points that were distributed amongst the other market segments. The strength of the RBOC hold on local access revenues can be attributed to the fact that they are a direct supplier of the local loop and they have market share in demographic areas that demand higher value services. A simple calculation of revenues secured, divided by access lines reported, shows that RBOCs drive an average annual contribution of $683 per year, per line, while CLECs and CAPs drive $416 per line, per year.

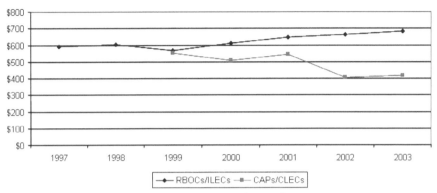

Figure 51: Annual Revenue Per Access Line by Service Provider Type
Source: Author's adaptation of statistics reported in June 21, 2005 FCC *Trends in Telephone Service Report*

As we move into 2006, two transformations are occurring within the deregulated telecom markets. The first transformation is that service providers do not need a network to offer a voice service. A network is needed to offer a data or packet based service via a broadband connection – but not a traditional circuit switched voice service. This means that voice revenues are subject to competitive pressure in the market because service providers of all classifications can attack traditional voice revenue streams without incurring the expense of building a circuit switched network. For the first time, services and providers of services can exist outside of the network. Services are still network dependent, but it is possible for service providers to innovate and offer services without the massive capital investments required to build a network on which to offer a service. The second transformation occurring is services are becoming data centric. Companies that offer VoIP (i.e. voice over IP) services can do so with minimal infrastructure investment. A VoIP service needs the network, but it does not need the traditional infrastructure of circuit switched telephony network. This leads us back to the net neutrality debate of 2006.

Forming a Pull Based Ecosystem from the Legacy Push Based Structure

The primary driver of economic development is productivity. When productivity rises it is the driver of economic investment and development. Capital was invested in computer networks after the deployment of the personal computer into the enterprise market in 1981. A computer on the desktop of workers had a finite potential to improve worker productivity. Networking the personal computer increased the productivity potential of the PC and the end-user (i.e. worker). In the post-ITO Revolution market, the driver of economic investment will be reducing the cost of transactions across the infrastructure of the technology ecosystem. The forces that drive transaction cost reductions can be broadly grouped in to two categories: (a) innovation through technology or technology specialization and (b) business model innovations. The deployment of broadband service connections to the internet is the foundation for both of these categories.

The proliferation of broadband and the expansion of the internet provide a network in which users can utilize the internet infrastructure to place voice calls using VoIP. Other companies are offering peer-to-peer applications that enable communication such as Skype, which was acquired by eBay in 2005 for $2.6 billion dollars. The use of peer-to-peer applications is a challenge for service providers as it does not generate service revenues for the service provider. There is revenue for the broadband connection that supports the data flow to and from the internet – but not for use of a voice application over a broadband connection. The internet as a transaction carrier has reduced the length and breadth of the chain of commerce that is supportable.

Technological innovations that replace, eliminate, or marginalize service revenues will lead to a market structure in which the service providers who control the majority of the market share will have wonderful top line cash flow, but minimal operating profits. Their inability to generate high operating margins may potentially lead to minimal infrastructure (i.e. network) investment. In September 2005, Skype was purchased by eBay for $2.6 billion. With 54 million registered users, Skype was valued at approximately $48 per subscriber. AT&T was acquired by SBC for $16 billion in January 2005. In comparison, Worldcom acquired MFS in 1996 for $12 billion and MCI in 1998 for $30 billion. These four valuations frame the service provider value curve for the frenzied period of the ITO Revolution.

In mid-2005 Vonage is offering unlimited telephony calling in the U.S. for $24.99 per month. If consumers and businesses begin bypassing voice services from traditional wireline service providers and start using peer-to-peer applications in larger numbers, it raises the question of who is going to pay for the network infrastructure. That is the challenge. As the supportable chain of commerce shrinks, it places enormous pricing pressure on entire market ecosystem. For the first time companies that do not own or invest in a network infrastructure can use the network (i.e. internet) to offer a service and generate revenue. The result of this technical innovation is that companies that own and invest in network infrastructure may not realize revenue for the use of an application over the network that eliminates service revenues. The large service providers want to sell more than just a broadband connection to the consumer or business. They want to sell a broadband connection and voice service and a video service. If competitors can provide voice and video services via the broadband connection then it leaves the service provider of the local loop with only the revenue for the broadband connection. In the world of networking, being a service provider that only offers value based on the cost of bits per second is a low margin business at best. If the service provider of the broadband connection (e.g. wireline or wireless) to the end-user cannot build a profitable business on only the broadband connection – then service providers will have minimal capital to invest in the network infrastructure that competitors are using to offer services. The net effect of this will be a slowing of the upgrade of the network infrastructure. Why would the companies who have dominant market share of the local loop to the end-user invest in a network infrastructure that others can use to steal their business? The current structure of the U.S. telecom market is a hybrid structure of regulation, franchise exclusivity for cable operators with little open competition for the local loop. The objective of the framers of the Telecom Act of 1996 was to encourage competition by providing access to assets of the regulated RBOCs. The result was an uncompetitive market with pseudo deregulation that has created a market structure which does not encourage investment and is certainly not unleashing a *"digital free for all"* in America.

The structure of the U.S. telecom services market can be reflected in a dichotomy that demonstrates where margin dollars are created. Historically, service providers generated profits from services. Over time, the proliferation of service providers and the commoditization of voice revenues have affected the value that end-users place on simple voice services. In the past when there was a single company offering voice services, customers had to pay a premium for that service. Today, there are many choices for voice services and the result has been a decline in the profitability of voice as a service. The clear macro-trend that has emerged post 2001 is that value or margin dollars are being created closer to the computer, which is the device that transmits content. The computer is not simply a personal computer, server, or mainframe. The computer is any device that computes and transmits content with content being defined as applications, entertainment, information, and service applications such as VoIP, video, gaming, and more. The ability to generate profits in and from the network for traditional services has declined. Revenues and margin dollars are being created by computing power that is transmitting content.

- **Content:** Applications that provide services, entertainment broadcasts, videos on demand, music on demand, interactive gaming, real time broadcasts, collaborative productivity applications, and information that results in the completion of an economic transaction in which value is exchanged.

This brings us to the question of the real value of the internet and what tangible value can be extracted from the capital invested in the ITO Revolution and the prior twenty-four years since the introduction of the PC. The internet is the low-cost and most powerful economic transaction carrier available to corporations with which an economic transaction can be completed. It can provide global reach, assuming network and computing infrastructure is present. Dell, eBay, Wal-Mart, and Amazon are proof points as to the transaction capabilities of the internet. The value of the internet as a transaction machine becomes apparent when it is put into the context of the chain of commerce. The internet provides the end-user (i.e. consumer and businesses) with the ability to have constant reach for information and continuous ability to execute transactions. Transactions can be any computing event that triggers an exchange of value for support of the transaction. A transaction can be an order for goods or services, a voice call, a video on demand purchase, a music purchase download, on line gaming participation, a stock trade, etc. A transaction can take many forms and the internet is an enabler of a low-cost transaction model that can be leverage to increase transactions through reach, transparency, and availability. Lowering the cost of transactions and improving productivity by leveraging the internet will drive economic development.

In October of 2004, Apple Computer announced a deal with ABC to distribute episodes of ABC shows through their iTunes Music Store for $1.99 per show. *"With that, Apple may have helped open a Pandora's box for the media business. The Cupertino, Calif., company and its first TV partner – Walt Disney Co., the parent of ABC – have taken a potentially significant step in the dismantling of a decades-old system for distributing TV programming to viewers, a move that could have profound long-term consequences for broadcasters, cable systems and satellite companies if more users download shows instead of watching them the old-fashioned way,"* [see *TV Downloads May Undercut ABC Stations*, Nick Wingfield, Joe Flint and Ethan Smith, The Wall Street Journal, October 17, 2005, page B1]. The response from ABC affiliates was a statement of disappointment and concern over an emerging competitive threat to their ability to generate advertising revenue if there are other distribution outlets of content.

Economic development and investment will occur in markets wherein the innovation is realized that leverages the internet as a commerce carrier. What the ITO Revolution proved is that the panacea of a new economy does not exist in the near term – but the proof points have been identified and working models have been created around these proof points that can lead to an economic transformation on a global basis. This is the real result of the ITO Revolution. We have merely glimpsed the early light of a sunrise that will, in time, change how we work and live on a daily basis. With each passing week, month, and year, we gain visibility to the future and realize that the early promises of the internet revolution were indeed true – what was incorrect was our expectation level as to the timing of this global transformational event. We are still at the early phases of the economic and social changes that will in time have a profound affect on all societies.

From a business perspective, consider viewing the service provider business from the perspective of what is easy and what is difficult and how this affects profit margin at each level. Post the Telecom Act of 1996, the number of service providers offering traditional telephony services has increased.

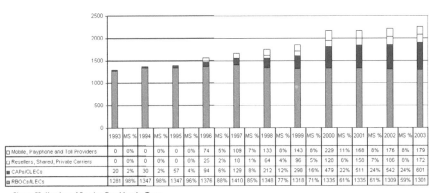

	1993	MS %	1994	MS %	1995	MS %	1996	MS %	1997	MS %	1998	MS %	1999	MS %	2000	MS %	2001	MS %	2002	MS %	2003
□ Mobile, Payphone and Toll Providers	0	0%	0	0%	0	0%	74	5%	109	7%	133	8%	143	6%	229	11%	168	8%	176	8%	179
□ Resellers, Shared, Private Carriers	0	0%	0	0%	0	0%	25	2%	10	1%	64	4%	96	5%	120	6%	150	7%	106	0%	172
■ CAPs/CLECs	20	2%	30	2%	57	4%	94	6%	129	8%	212	12%	298	16%	479	22%	511	24%	542	24%	601
■ RBOCs/ILECs	1281	98%	1347	98%	1347	96%	1376	88%	1410	85%	1348	77%	1318	71%	1335	61%	1335	61%	1309	59%	1301

Figure 52: Number of Service Providers by Type
Source: Author's adaptation of statistics reported in June 21, 2005 FCC *Trends in Telephone Service Report*

The statistics reported by the FCC reveal that the number of RBOC and ILEC service providers in the U.S. market has returned to historical levels of approximately ~1300 after rising to 1410 in 1997.

Mergers and acquisitions have returned the number of ILEC/RBOC classified service providers to 1301 in 2003. The noticeable change has been the addition of 579 CAPs and CLECs, 172 resellers, private carriers, and 179 mobile service providers. The market effect of 930 new service providers has been a decline in the cost of voice services. Post the telecom crash of 2001 enough network infrastructure had been deployed to sufficiently support the migration to data centric voice services such as VoIP and peer to peer applications. The result is that it is difficult for a traditional wireline service provider to exist solely on voice revenues. Two major forces in the market are moving against voice as a revenue generating source. There seems to be a systematic march towards the computer as the transmitter of content. Content is where high margin dollars can be realized. The closer a company is to owning content (i.e. IPR), or in other terms the originating source of an economic transaction, the higher the potential for profits. The further away a company is from content and the transaction source, the lower the profits. The bandwidth connection between computer user A and computer user B is worth a set value. Those two users can conduct transaction with each other using the set value of the connection. In traditional telephony markets, the service provider profited from the connection between two users making a phone call. The length of call was proportional to cost and profit. Fixed, always on broadband connections, in which the application replaces the service, alters the traditional business model of service providers.

There is a work in progress within the software community that is going to affect service providers who rely upon services such as voice and television as a primary revenue streams. Software technology is constantly evolving and in time systems will emerge that leverage the cost advantages of the internet. The new software systems that will emerge will harness the reach of the internet to transparently support on demand services. The transparent portion of the transaction will be realized in the connectivity and geographic component of the transaction. As internet access becomes ubiquitous, end-users are no longer limited to geographic based service providers and pricing structures. For service providers of all types, delivering a service is changing. End-users will no longer have limited choices of structured plans, but rather unlimited choices that will enable them to pay only for what they use.

In time, end-users will form collaborative work teams that utilize adaptive systems that transparently negate location, closed systems, and service specific definitions to serve demand where demand is occurring in the network. In this model, service providers will be challenged to find mechanisms to generate revenue not based on bandwidth or service usage, but for adaptable transactions and transparency. It is clear that software is emerging that decouples the workflow for the user. Eventually this software will find its way into service provider networks of all types and accelerate the effects of VoIP and peer to peer applications. When this occurs, it will have a profound effect on the network and where economic value (i.e. profit margins) is generated.

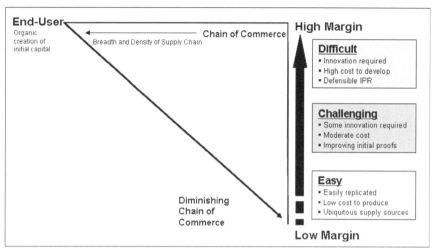

Figure 53: Problem Solving Chain of Commerce

Solving hard and difficult problems will result in a business that generates higher margin (i.e. value) dollars. Competitive differentiation based on cost is generally a lower margin business that rewards the company with the most efficient cost model and business structure. A net result of the ITO Revolution was a concentration of companies at the lower level of the margin model within all three of the ITO markets. There were many companies who were successful at deploying infrastructure and competing on cost. There are many companies who were successful at building networking equipment and hosting web pages. There are few companies that are successful at producing value differentiation via the internet that enables their business model to command higher margins for the value they provide. Value (i.e. margin) is a derivative of innovation.

The internet finds its origins in the world of data and computers. The computer and networking industries have traditionally had a faster pace of technology adoption in comparison to telephony markets. The personal computer had a faster rate of adoption by American households than the telephone and television. The internet is a global unifying network of computer networks. As computer networks evolve, they are fast becoming the carrier of digital communications. Data, voice, and video are now digital services capable of being carried by computer networks globally.

The internet as a transaction mechanism has altered the economic chain of commerce facilitating the emergence of a pull economic model. A pull economic model is radically different from the economic model that the world has been perfecting for the past few centuries based on the laws of supply and demand. As a social-economic engine, the global economy pushes resources from sectors of high supply to areas of high anticipated demand. Examples are oil, energy, automotive, food, and nearly every good and service that is consumed on a daily basis in a variety of markets. This is accomplished by perfecting automated supply chains, process standardization, logistical planning, infrastructure, and the associated costs required to scale the capacity of chain of commerce to meet anticipated demand. The vast majority of the infrastructure of the western world has been scaled to support the push economic model. The downside of a push economic model was acutely identified in the ITO Revolution.

Through the first three stages of the ITO Revolution, companies throughout the ITO ecosystem invested in scaling their businesses to meet the anticipated demand of the new economy that the internet was projected to create. Financial capital, infrastructure, equipment, and even companies were pushed to meet the anticipated demand shift that was going to occur with the new economy. When the demand failed to materialize, the massive capitalization bubble that had formed in anticipation of demand collapsed. The result of the failed achievement of expectations of the ITO markets has been twofold. The first development was that the majority of companies executing a traditional push based model instituted tighter controls on inventories, supply chains, revenue recognition, fiscal budgets, and decision making. When economic conditions turn unfavorable and companies falter in their execution model, decision making contracts to the very highest level of authority within companies utilizing push economic models. The government of the U.S. responded to the collapse of the ITO markets by dictating internal control standards intended to prevent abuse of power and ensure leadership checks and balances. These controls were outlined in the Sarbanes-Oxley Act and as time will show, they are designed for a push economic model that will fade away as a new economic model is emerging and taking hold on a global basis.

The emergence of the pull economic model is driven from the desire to leverage the internet to manage growing uncertainty in the chain of commerce. The conceptual objectives of the pull economic model is focused on exploiting uncertainty by enabling collaboration between the participants involved in an economic transaction to complete the transaction immediately. The resulting structure of increased controls placed upon companies executing push models has been to constrain resources, dictate process, lengthen decision making, and delay economic transactions. In the push model, the demands of the end-user is analyzed and anticipated by a central decision making process who by definition is at the furthest point of immediate knowledge from the end-user conducting the economic transaction. This is the process by which old regimes are formed from revolutionary companies. Old regimes are formed when they lose control and knowledge of market share.

Pull economic models place the initiative to complete the economic transaction within the dictates of the end-user through collaboration. By rapidly and collaboratively placing the power to complete a transaction at the point in the market wherein transactions occur, it obsolesces the need to anticipate demand by central planning. Braudel observed that long distance trade produced enormous profits because the chain of commerce supported a long chain of commerce in terms of time and density in the number of people required to deliver the goods to the end-user. Long-distance trade provides an interesting base for contrasting the evolution from a push to a pull economic model. *"Long distance trade certainly made super profits: it was after all based on the price difference between two markets very far apart, with supply and demand in complete ignorance of each other and brought into contact only by the activities of middleman. There could only have been a competitive market if there had been plenty of separate and independent middlemen. If, in the fullness of time competition did appear, if super-profits vanished from one line, it was always possible to find them again on another route with different commodities."* [see Braudel, *The Wheels of Commerce*, page 405]. Braudel's observation that super profits between supply and demand occurring over a great distance was the product of information ignorance, implies that the internet and emerging pull model will couple geographic markets and thus shorten the information gap. Supply and demand will be closely linked and large variations of price will be limited as global consumers will have relevant, if not near real time, market data.

How will this affect the creation and destruction of markets on a global basis? Again we look to an observation made by Braudel. *"One's impression then (since in view of paucity of evidence, impressions are all we have) is that there were always sectors in economic life where high profits could be made but that these sectors varied. Every time one of these shifts occurred, under the pressure of economic developments, capital was quick to seek them out, to move into the new sector and prosper. Note as a rule it had not precipitated such shifts, This differential geography of profit is key to short-term fluctuations of capitalism, as it veered between the Levant, America, the East Indes, China the slave trade, etc., or between trade, banking, industry or land."* [see Braudel, *The Wheels of Commerce*, page 432]. The shifting and variation of profitable economic sectors is the essence of globalization. Instead of the shifts occurring over time, they will occur rapidly in a pull economic model. The shifts will not be in ignorance of the market – but rather they will define the market. The companies building businesses for the emerging pull economic model must have infrastructure, real time market data. and the capability to shift their business with the rapidity of the sectorial economic shifts.

Pull economic models are intended to accelerate the pace of transactions by matching the participants to a closely defined set of transaction criteria. For service providers, this is an evolution from packaged service plans to on-demand service plans. An example of this evolution can be prophesied for both cable and wireline service providers who are feverishly competing to enter each other's core markets. Cable providers offer to their customers a flat rate package of selected channels. The more money the end-user wishes to spend, the more television programming they are offered. The premium channels are offered as part of the high-end package. This is a push economic model of service pricing by a cable company. They determine the market barring price for basic service packages and then build higher priced packages that include premium content. This model works well in a market structure in which demand can be planned for and there is no competition or competition is minimized through market share control. The evolution to a pull economic model will affect the ability of a cable provider to rely upon programming packages. How many channels do the end-users really watch of the 200 channels available? This is where a pull model affects the market structure. End-users will access the specific channels and content they desire, when the want it, to view the content or they will download the content and store it locally for future viewing. End-users will not pay for 200 channels, of which 35 they watch occasionally.

The evolution from push to pull is already visible in the telecom services industry. VoIP service providers are utilizing low cost flat fee pricing or call (i.e. per transaction) based pricing. Historically we are familiar with paying a flat fee per calling plan type for local telephony with additional long distance service charges. If we do not make any calls during any one month, we still have to pay the monthly service charge. Why? The answer is the phone company deployed a push model and built a predetermined amount of anticipated demand or usage into their network. If we do not use it, that is our problem not their problem. The price structure of the push telephony model goes far beyond the bill for local telephony. The cost structure of a large telecom service provider is enormous. They have organized labor contracts, health care, pension programs, facilities, assets, and hundreds of thousands of employees. This was the cost structure associated with the deployment of universal service. In order to fund the deployment of telecom infrastructure in unprofitable markets, the entire consumer base of telecom subscribers had to bear the cost for universal service. The deployment of networks require physical installation, which requires construction teams, maintenance teams, as well as lobbyists and legal representation to ensure the proper laws are complied with during construction of aerial or in ground wiring. Digging up the streets of New York City or small town America has an equally unappealing reaction within the local populace. If the internet can provide on demand services tailored to the desires of the end-user, then it would be fair to reason that the cost structure of traditional service providers who push untailored content (i.e. pricing packages) to their end-users will be adversely affected.

An important conclusion learned from the ITO Revolution is that demand is often uncertain and shifts rapidly. Examining the revenue profiles of Sycamore Networks, Ciena, Tellium, Nortel, and Lucent provide examples to this lesson. It had been reasoned within *The Internet Report* by Meeker and DePuy that the equipment or infrastructure suppliers for the internet were an important meter as to the expansion and growth prospects for the internet. Meeker and DePuy first selected Cisco Systems, Ascend Communications, and Cascade Communications as recommend investments because these companies were viewed as leaders in supplying networking equipment to emerging service providers [see, *The Internet Report*, Mary Meeker and Chris DuPuy, February 1996, page 1-3]. This is one of the reasons why examining the growth, decline, and fluctuations of the revenues of networking equipment suppliers is important. The deployment of the internet infrastructure can be measured by tracking the revenues of companies who supply internet infrastructure. It can be reasoned that if the internet is the basis for the development of a pull economic model, then several macro drivers will become apparent:

- The internet drives the cost of sale lower by extending reach and rewarding specialization. Companies who leverage the cost advantages of the internet will be successful, compared to those companies who subscribe to a push economic model.

- Globalization is accelerated through information flow enabled by the internet

- If goods and services can be offered through the internet, then market barriers are lowered and competitors have the ability to enter markets that were previously unreachable due to geography, incumbent market share control, or regulatory barriers. In reference to service providers, whether telecom or cable, if a provider has content and a user has a broadband connection to the internet, there is no restrictions to service providers outside of a geographic region offering access to content. This is an assumption that the internet can and will enable specialization of content, goods, and services.

- If high-speed, high-capacity access becomes ubiquitous, it stands to reason that more margin dollars will flow to those who own content, rather than those companies that simply provide access to content.

- A pull model requires companies to embrace adaptation and flexibility to be successful. Business constructs (i.e. teams) built to leverage market opportunities will be fleeting in nature as spending cycles by end-users in the market come and go rapidly. Push models cannot adapt to spending cycles that begin and end rapidly. To be successful in a pull economic market structure, companies must be modular in nature to enable customization of goods and services to meet specialized market demands on a global basis.

The evolution from a push economic structure to a pull economic model will happen. Companies unwilling or unable to make the transformation will be become uncompetitive in the global economy. The ITO Revolution did alter the old economy – but in ways few people envisioned in 1996. The old economy based on regulated, stable market structures in which demand can be anticipated and planned for is disappearing. Even in the commanding heights of the economy in 2005 we see the affect of globalization, war, and Hurricane Katrina. Few people in the spring of 2005 envisioned $3-4 dollar a gallon price for gasoline. As transaction or demand uncertainty increases, push economic structures compensate by deploying hedging strategies, workflow planning, and cost reductions. The net result is an inability to meet demand when demand returns, thus providing diminishing returns, creating a structural weakness inside the company, and providing an opportunity for competitors to acquire market share. The old economy push model worked well in less complicated market structures in which there were limited customer diversity or a limited set of options for good and services. The ITO Revolution provided the mechanism for information flow and has begun to deliver on the promise of a diversity of choice for end-users.

The essence of the internet as a pull economic engine has been put forward by a number of intellectuals providing thought leadership including Ester Dyson and John Hagel III. Esther prophesizes the internet as a cloud of metadata that provides information on the structure of content, version control of content, access control to content, identification management, and content itself. It is important to remember the definition of content data in the form of transactions: applications that provide services, entertainment broadcasts, videos on demand, music on demand, interactive gaming, real time broadcasts, collaborative productivity applications, and information that results in the completion of an economic transaction in which value is exchanged. Inside the cloud users have messages, links, applications, documents, contacts, expenses, in short all the content that they interact with a daily basis to be productive. As part of collaborative work teams, called corporations, the internet provides the umbrella specific to a users needs to participate in the chain of commerce specific to their work team (i.e. corporation).

Looking closely at several of the successful internet proofs that emerged from the ITO Revolution, it is apparent that they are all examples of pull economic models leveraging the internet as a low cost transaction mechanism.

The key examples mentioned previously were Dell, eBay, Yahoo, Amazon, and Google. All of these companies are leveraging the strengths of the internet to (a) increase global reach for their goods and services, (b) provide real time transaction closing capability, and (c) and real time transaction status updates and customer care. The result is an adaptive business model that increases the number of potential customers, increases productivity, and lowers the cost structure of the business model.

Impact of Adjacent Markets

Globalization is a trendy word that describes the effect of adjacent markets that are in the process of colliding. A pull economic model facilitates globalization, the opening of previously closed markets, and accelerates the coupling of geographically dispersed markets. To prophesize about the future of the ITO markets, we need to consider globalization and the affect that two adjacent technology markets will have on the ITO markets on a global basis. The adjacent technology markets that are becoming increasingly important markets within the ITO market ecosystem are mobile or wireless services and the cable service providers that offer a television broadcast (i.e. push) service in addition to internet access and voice services. Mobile networks are a method of accessing content and peer to peer services, such as voice and data. A voice phone call is a peer to peer transaction whether that transaction is transmitted over a traditional wireline infrastructure, wireless network, or VoIP connection via a broadband internet connection. The evolution occurring in the market ecosystem is two-fold: (a) the commoditization power of peer to peer services leveraging the cost points of the internet as an alternative to traditional service revenues and (b) the need to provide access to other forms of content. Content defined to include a broad set of applications that provide services. Consumers define content in terms of entertainment such as movies, sporting events, real time broadcasting, web content and gaming applications as well as productivity applications for business or consumer usage [see Ester Dyson]. All computing that provides content becomes an on demand driven activity in which end users access computing power via a broad range of devices, for many types of content in many locations to complete transactions.

The common characteristic that the internet, telephony, television, and mobile markets have in common is the evolution to an on demand model that requires the fusion of computing power and the network. Traditional telephony markets were service orientated markets. Customers placed phone calls, but the billing and structure of the calls were based on the service plan purchased. The industry had many various service plans such as "nights and weekend" or "friends and family." The billing structure of the plan was dependent on whether customers were making local calls, in region area code calls, or out of region long distance calls. This type of service billing structure has begun to disappear. Today, customers make on demand calls that are global in nature. A person in the U.S. can call a number with the correct country code and have it ring in nearly any nation-state. A person in the U.K. could call a U.S. number and have it ring in Beijing. The changing nature of telephony is a reflection of the beginning of a convergence of geographic markets through technology innovation.

As a global community we are consumers of content that is delivered by a variety of service mechanisms that historically were the domain of service providers. End-users place phone calls, access web pages, transmit data and demand video, music, entertainment content and real time data streams such as sports and news. In the post Return Stage of the ITO Revolution, the companies that vie for market share must address the convergence of four forces that are affecting the delivery of content:

- Consumers and business will demand ubiquitous access via many options, but the requirement will be for increasingly faster connections with broader capacities delivered via wireline (e.g. fiber, bonded copper, other) or wireless (WiMAX, EVDO, OFDM, other).

- The ability for service provides to differentiation services will decline – adversely affecting the ability of companies to derive high margins from bandwidth (i.e. rate plan) and service (i.e. amount of plan used) only business models.

- The end-user, whether a consumer or a business, will be buying on-demand content and services which will come in many forms from many providers on global geographic scale.

- Providers of original content have the ability to bypass traditional distribution mechanisms such as wireline, mobile, and cable service providers. Providers of original content and real time content such as sports and news are already exploring the option to create their own distribution networks via the internet, realizing that they can shorten the chain of commerce and keep more margin dollars within their business model. The pull economic model provided by the transaction capabilities of the internet enables content providers to expand the reach of their brand by providing more methods of access.

Over time, consumers and businesses will have many choices to access the networks that provide services and content – but this is not the real convergence that is going to happen. The real convergence that is going to occur will be far more expansive than the limited triple play (i.e. voice, video, and internet) or quad play (i.e. voice, video, and internet, wireless) that has been the rage in 2003, 2004, and 2005. The convergence that will drive the next revolution is that every electronic device in the world will become addressable. This will bring a massive amount of new devices onto global networks that will increase the infrastructure investment requirements. Real network convergence happens when access becomes ubiquitous. Network connectivity accelerates change, volatility, and disruption. These three elements will create opportunity for innovation and quite possibly lay the foundation for the next great revolution. Before the next revolution, the future of the ITO markets lies in creation of real convergence.

The seeds laid by the ITO Revolution are changing the economic ecosystem and this will have a profound affect on global social and political structures. This essay began with the question of whether there was linkage between technology markets, financial markets, political structures, and social currents. It is clear that the chain of commerce that has been a mainstay during the last millennium is changing. The emergence of a pull economic model will disrupt economic order and change the competitive nature of many markets the world over. For many years to come the ITO markets will be hard at work building a new network infrastructure with access to content unimagined. The complexities of computing power will become embedded in the diverse geographic intricacies of the global telecom infrastructure. This might appear as a simple task, but the past thirty years has left a diverse legacy infrastructure that is often regionally specific to the ruling nation-state. Integrating computing power with the telecom infrastructure is not a simple problem. Industry pundits will probably describe this as the second internet revolution or a renaissance for the telecom industry. In reality, it is the natural course of events according to Perez [see *Essay Two, Chapter Nine*]. *"In today's global marketplace, mega-institutions face few external limits on their size and profitability: for instance, Citigroup – the world's largest financial institution, with $250 billion in market value and nearly 300,000 employees – holds only 5 percent of the global financial-services market. Straightforward projections, based on the experience of the past 20 years, indicate that in 2015, 350 companies would be larger than the smallest company on the list of today's 150 biggest corporations. The largest of them would approach $700 billion in market capitalization and earn $40 billion or more a year,"* [see, *Strategy in an Era of Global Giants*, McKinsey Quarterly, Lowell L. Bryan and Michele Zanini, October 2005, page 47-28]. There are several driving factors that are part of our future and dawn of real convergence.

Global Market Integration

There is a stigma that the word globalization carries for many people. For some it means inexpensive products made by people in a foreign land who are paid a wage that workers in the America could not live on. For farmers in Europe it means food imports and the end to government subsidies. For others, globalization means outsourcing and call centers in India. Aside from definition or perception, the reality of globalization is upon us and the internet is a median by which globalization travels. In mid-2005, John Chambers, CEO of Cisco Systems remarked that low-cost, off shore suppliers of networking products will have success. He said, *"We could literally have our competitors give away the products and have a lower cost of ownership than our peers have, and that's before you take into consideration investment protection, flexibility, business partnership, the revenue we can bring to them."* The comment by Chambers reveals the strategy that Cisco will use against foreign equipment developers who compete on cost. That strategy involves market share. Cisco has a significant position or is the market share leader in the nearly every major geographic territory for their products. It is possible for Cisco to leverage their market share to drive final decision making by end-users to entail more than a simple cost analysis. Cisco wants to compete against low-cost suppliers using a strategy that involves innovation and a comparative economic analysis of the entire business case.

When market share becomes static, the large companies that control market share drive purchase decisions that are based on control their of market share. Cisco controls an enormous amount of network market share through their deployed systems. They do not have a perfect control plane across all of their products, but the comment by Chambers reveals that this is where Cisco can provide innovation and market leadership. If Cisco can develop tighter integration across their product line and deliver this innovation to the market, they will control existing market share, thus offsetting competitors based on cost and have the ability to capture new market share.

Globalization will force U.S. based companies to leverage the competitive advantages of the emerging pull economic model. The destruction of the push model and the emergence of the pull economic model should not be discerning to U.S. companies. It was the American innovation that built the majority of the foundation for the new economy based on pull and leveraging the internet. America is born from revolution and her industries and businesses are no different. Globalization is will force U.S. companies to solve complex problems. Companies wanting to be successful will be forced to innovate faster, solve increasingly complex problems, and match and exceed the capabilities of strong competitive companies from all global markets. These are strengths of American culture, society, and business. Failure is an acceptable learning mechanism in the U.S. Failure in pursuit of success coupled with rapid assessment and creative destruction are inherent cultural capabilities of American business. Globalization is a product of America and American companies will be forced to succeed in the environment of their creation.

Computing and Network Integration

The evolution of computers from mainframes to minis to the personal computer, share a common characteristic in that they are islands of isolated computing power. Networking computers from the early days of SNA through the corporate LAN, into the WAN, through the evolution of the client/server model and the proliferation of internet primarily was concerned about two driving forces: obtaining connectivity and improving connectivity. Almost all of the challenges identified with the network and solved through innovation over the past thirty years were about obtaining connectivity and improving connectivity speed and capacity. The computing application challenges caused by the network were solved by building better routers, faster switches, increasing fiber capacity, and building more access points (e.g. IP-VPN, broadband, WiFi, wireless, etc). There was a near universal belief that an all optically based network would develop in which every human would have a fiber optic cable to their house, place of work, and coffee shop in between. Equally committed are the wireless visionaries who believe that all networking connectivity goes wireless as witnessed by WinStar, Teligent, and Terabeam. These conclusions may in fact be true in time – but they assume that the ITO Revolution was a short transition event from the old methods to a new panacea built on new technologies. We have concluded that social habits are difficult to change and technology waves are long duration events. It is appropriate to think of the ITO Revolution in a time line on the scale of a Kondratieff cycle (i.e. 50-60 years starting from 1971). The truth is the ITO Revolution was a proof for many technical and business concepts. The next evolution of the ITO Revolution will be expanding the infrastructure, solving complex problems, and ensuring the pull economic model works. It is impossible to ignore the vast amount of legacy infrastructure that did not get upgraded during the ITO Revolution. If it required $300 billion to fix the date sequence for Y2K readiness in the legacy computing and network infrastructure, it is going to require hundreds of billions more to upgrade the infrastructure and billions more to realize the dreams for the computing and network infrastructure. In simple terms, there is a vast amount of work to do and many complex problems to be solved.

In mid 2005, 60% of all computer data backup and disaster recovery storage is replicated and stored on tape. In a time when computer users can purchase 4 gigabytes of storage capacity on USB drive for $500, the world is still storing vast amounts of data on the medium of tape. Predictions are that advancements in storage will shortly lead to the ability to store vast amounts of content on portable drives and the cost of such systems will be low. This is a wonderful advancement that will affect all technology based businesses, but what about all the systems still using tape? Tape backup and data storage via tape has been a mainstay of the computing industry since the 1970s. This small example highlights the macro level challenges that need to be solved. The ITO Revolution was wonderful for extending the infrastructure of the network, but it was not an all inclusive panacea. The all optical network did not develop and if it did, it probably would have driven bandwidth prices to a zero margin business, which would have altered the market ecosystem. Challenges still exist in the network and within the computing domain. From a macro perspective, the most prominent description of the challenge is the fusion between computing power minus the I/O bus and the network. The network becomes more than just about connectivity; it will become an integral component of the computer architecture. The network will become the I/O bus of the computer and the internet the control plane of metadata. Computing power and the network will become fused and in this evolution, many interesting and challenging problems must be solved.

From a broad perspective, the '80s were all about computing. The decade opened with the mainframe, observed an explosion in mid-range computers, and witnessed the dawn of the personal computer. The '90s were all about the network. The first five years of the decade of the '90s was about networking the enterprise and the evolution to the client/server network from the mainframe model. The last five years of the decade was about the internet and the service provider network. Now that the ITO markets have settled from the upheaval of revolution, the focus is again shifting from the network to the deployment of computing power. The future evolution will be that computing power will evolve from isolated pockets that are networked – to a distributed, integrated component of the network. That is the real difference. Computing power is becoming distributed across the network. Enhancing the infrastructure in order to achieve real productivity gains, involves more than connectivity. It involves deploying computing power from deep pockets, reached through connectivity conduits; to a global distribution of computing power that is synchronized. This is how Google is attacking Microsoft. This is how IBM sees the evolution of the computing power contained in the mainframe.

Microsoft has a lock on the desktop computer operating system (OS) and productivity application market. There are other suppliers for a PC operating system, but the superior position of Microsoft in the PC market for the operating system and productivity applications is unquestioned. Linux has made substantial inroads, but it does not command the majority market share nor does it have the ability to enact and enforce market barriers. Google looks at their strength in information location and information quality and realizes that if a system of distributed computers know where information and applications reside across the full scope of the network (i.e. internet), then there is little need for application awareness at the desktop computing level. The personal computer needs a complex operating system because the operating system of a PC needs to do more than just run the computer. It needs to know how to process applications that know where content and data are located within the personal computer. If the network capacity and network awareness is in place, it is clearly possible to view the operating system of the future as the internet that enables a distribution of computing power. The internet then connects the many computing systems together. Applications become services that reside in the network. Systems (i.e. computers) eventually become appliances and value is created by content at the point at which content is transmitted to the appliance. The transmission of content will occur over many types of broadband internet connections. Personal and business data (i.e. content) does not need to be stored on the personal computer. It becomes part of the network as Ester Dyson envisioned. Content is structured as metadata and computing power will be deployed to have awareness of metadata with version control and access rights. Economic transactions will be completed by gaining access to content via the internet.

Even today there are many internet users who use email applications that reside in the network. Any computer or hand held device in the world with internet access can connect to the email application. If this works for email, it can most certainly be made to work for productivity applications, games, and all forms of content. The future of the network and the computer will have profound affects on the winners of the ITO Revolution. If applications and information can exist in an integrated computing/network model in which service cost is marginalized by many types of service providers and technology, it creates an interesting question. How will capital be raised to maintain, expand, and upgrade the network infrastructure? The changes are already occurring around us. It is quite possible that these changes are going to lead to a restructuring of the regulations that govern the telecommunications industry of the United States.

At a level above the distributed and cataloged global information base called the internet, there is a higher order challenge. That challenge is deploying real computing power into the network. Currently, computing power is deployed in pockets. When connectivity is lost to these pockets, productivity declines. Network wide viruses affect all the computing power in the network as access is restricted to contain the outbreak. If computing power was integrated into the network, it would enable a deeper extension of the computing power into the legacy technology base as well as an ability to share transaction loads, isolate viruses, network disruptions, and provide real time, adaptive data mirroring, and backup. The internet is the basis for the emergence of pull economic model, and rising productivity drives economic development, it is therefore a reasonable assumption that a long period of substantial investment is required in completing and perfecting the infrastructure of the new economy, which is the internet. The potential for productivity gains of geographically dispersed computing systems that can utilize the legacy telecom infrastructure is enormous. This is the great challenge that is before the large and small companies of the ITO markets. Forces are converging that will drive massive, long-term changes to the ITO markets. These changes occur over long periods of time – not weeks.

The first prominent change is content. Content is produced by every application that transmits information to our phone, television, computer, PDA, or electronic device in the future. Content is applications. Applications provide services. Users access content via applications to complete an economic transaction, thus creating value. All content must become addressable and accessible in real time on a 7x24 basis. This will produce transactions. Transactions drive computing power and network capacity. Computing power and increased transactions will force processors to get faster and in turn it will compel service providers to increase the capacity and the speed of the network. Accurateness and access to content will become the core competency that will separate the extremists from the old regimes. This is why Google is the first company to have a real opportunity to become a major competitor of equal strength to Microsoft. From their roots, Google specialized in accurateness, relevancy, and access to information. Microsoft's position of strength came from their dominance of the desktop operating system in which they had the advantage of accurateness, relevancy, and access to information and applications that reside on the personal computer; which was the core element of the dispute between the government and Microsoft. Prior to the ITO Revolution, applications resided on the PC and in the client/server model information was located in a closed network model. This provided Microsoft an inherent competitive advantage. If applications can now reside outside of the network in the form of services, a significant competitive advantage for Microsoft has been overcome. The Microsoft business plan to destroy Netscape was simple. Microsoft gave their internet browser away for free. Netscape did not have a core position of strength within the market, or an innovative edge that was defensible against Microsoft. Google is different from Netscape. Time will tell, but if Google can bridge the gap from what was easy (e.g. cataloging information) to what is difficult (e.g. deploying computing power into the network), they will be the next Microsoft.

Intel, Microsoft, and Cisco Systems share a common technologic concept that can be attributed to their success and ability to create value. All three companies created what can be termed a control plane and were successful in convincing customers to purchase and use their control plane. Intel's control plane was provided on a semi-conductor chip, Microsoft provided the control plane for the personal computer, and Cisco provided the control plane for the client/server network which became the internet. Value is created by controlling market share. Innovating and bringing to market a control plane that is accepted by end-users creates value. The emergence of a pull economic model based on the internet presents a threat to the market that Microsoft and Cisco command through the control planes found in their products. If the internet drives the homogenization of networking technology, then Cisco's innovative advantage will decline over time as will their product margins. If Cisco can continue to find innovative advantages by a tighter coupling of their products, they will force new competitors from global markets onto steep intellectual learning curves.

The ITO Revolution proved that many things were easy and that many things were difficult. It was easy to extend the network and computing infrastructure; it required money and labor, but it was not an overly challenging intellectual problem. An argument can be made that this infrastructure problem was solved so well that it has created pockets of deep network capacity reserves that can be exploited over a long period of time. More work needs to be done on the network infrastructure, but it is a function of financial capital – not the inventing of something new. The difficult part of the infrastructure problem is making it transparent and ubiquitous. No service provider or private enterprise network exists built on a common technology base that seamlessly provides an easily reconfigurable and manageable infrastructure. The diverse nature of the network infrastructure is an impediment to transactions and access to content that must occur in real time. The global computing and network infrastructure must become adaptive and self-defending. Enron's idea of an intelligent, adaptive network that scaled capacity is the future for the internet. Networks and the computing infrastructure attached to the network must become self-defending. The internet cannot be disabled because a fifteen year-old in far away land built a virus and attached to an email. To achieve this goal, the network and the computing infrastructure must become integrated in a form that enables adaptive coupling and decoupling of functions and systems.

Computing transactions must be carried seamlessly across systems and sub network boundaries. Networks need to enable collaboration to improve productivity. Collaboration assumes that the fusion of computing power and the network will enable real-time processing of information to empower the ability of the network to prioritize services (i.e. applications). The network will use dynamic analytics to adapt to information change and enable the provisioning of services as users demand access to content. The driving force for the ITO revolution for the foreseeable future will be making the computing and network infrastructure work better to enable the transition to a pull economic model. The current state of the computer/network model does not adequately support real-time applications as services. Email is not a real-time application that enhances productivity. Applications that enhance productivity and drive economic value are an order of magnitude more complex and taxing on the internet than email and web browsing.

As new and advanced capabilities evolve in the network, it will change how the network is used and how the world will rely on the fusion of computing and network power. It will also mean that service providers will have a different set of requirements and market conditions from which to build a business. In the past, service providers secured market share by being the only provider of service or the lower cost provider in a minimally competitive market. Cable franchises by definition have a non-competitive right to offer a television service. Even today, there are major markets in the U.S. with limited competitive service providers for telephony, television, and broadband services. As the evolution of the ITO markets move forward, service providers will be forced to address how they offer services to customers. Being the seller of the lowest cost service is not a strategy that generates high margins that empower investment in the network infrastructure. Commanding the majority market share and generating minimal profit margins is not a business plan that supports innovation and creativity. As competitors exist outside of the network, the winning service providers who own the network will be the ones that offer solutions that leverage the infrastructure to provide:

- Enhanced, ubiquitous mobility and access to content in the network
- Uncompromising security that protects customers, intellectual property, and the network
- Focus on cost as a function of value that delivers measurable benefits
- Empowerment of technology from showcases to network wide applications that improves productivity
- Evolvement from islands of implementation to true global networks (i.e Global Grid)
- Evolvement from products to services that are on demand – purchased in increments that are specialized content

Innovation versus Commoditization

Globally we are becoming an on demand society and the technology that supports and promotes our habit for on demand is our future. We are evolving to a harmonized network that provides for a converged set of on demand content and services. Service differentiation will be challenging in competitive markets in which the buying decision is based on price or the value proposition from the supplier is based on cost. This is the evolution of the market structure nearly ten years after the passage of the Telecom Act of 1996. Market share is nearly as concentrated as it was in early 1996; the cost for services has declined to the point that few service providers can finance the upgrade of the telecom infrastructure in order to offer a broad and rich range of new services. If we overlay a qualitative measurement of a market bearing price level and profitable price level, it reveals the effect of deregulation of the U.S. telecom services market and investment in concentrated segments of the network has created an unhealthy market structure. If we assume that services can exist outside of the network infrastructure and service differentiation within the market structure is based on price, then there is no reason to believe that an increase of profits is imminent unless there are fewer competitors.

Service providers have been marginalized by the market structure created by the Telecom Act of 1996. The current state of the telecom services market in the U.S. is a directionless market. The majority of market share is concentrated within a few service providers spread across the service silos of telephony, mobile, data and broadcast (i.e. cable and satellite) that are increasingly overlapping into a single market. The increase in voice and data revenues through infrastructure build-out, coupled with the inability to create value through service differentiation and the pace of technology evolution has created a market, in which revenue flow is still occurring, but the costs to secure market share have risen and profits have been minimized. As such, the current structure of the technology ecosystem is unhealthy. Profits cannot be sufficiently generated by service providers and passed through the ecosystem to the network equipment providers and onto the component suppliers to sustain innovation and infrastructure build-out.

Network wide investment and upgrades are required. Few, if any, service provider emerged from the ITO Revolution with a state of the art network that provided for productivity gains and cost efficiencies. This is a result of the frenzied pace of the Perigee stage of the ITO Revolution wherein accelerated development cycles, new startup companies, and the merger and acquisition turmoil left few companies with efficient infrastructures. As such, the large global service providers are realizing they will need to spend billions of dollars fixing their infrastructures. In 2004, British Telecom announced an approximate spend of $15 billion over a multi year period to upgrade their network infrastructure. Three hundred vendors attended the opening supplier conference – nine were selected as winners. *"Some other operators have decided to hunker down, cut back on investments, and wait to see what happens... It's a doomed strategy. Those that sit back and wait will be relegated to commodity players,"* [see, Paul Reynolds, CEO of BT Wholesale, March 2004]. BT's investment in transforming their network infrastructure is a harbinger of the future. BT was the first major PTT to be privatized in the 1980s and post the Apogee stage (i.e. turning point) of the ITO Revolution; it is the first to publicly commit massive funds to building a new network infrastructure. It is also important to note that BT's commitment to the 21st Century (i.e. 21C) program required an additional commitment to creating a viably competitive telecom services market in the UK. As part of the 21C program, BT committed to creating a separate business entity called Access Services, staffed with 30,000 people who will be responsible for the operation and development of local access networks. This business unit will be required *"...through a set of formal rules on governance and separation, to support all providers' retail activities (including those of BT Retail) on a precisely equivalent basis."* BT's willingness to commit massive CAPEX to solve their network problems, coupled with a regulatory commitment, is further evidence as to the deep and complex problems that need to be solved in the telecom services infrastructure and market structure. The U.S. market will need to address the same problems.

Revolutionary cycles or technology waves as Perez defined them are the product of technology innovation as a result of complex problem solving. The ITO Revolution did not solve all the problems with the internet, telecom, and optical markets. It can be aptly argued that the ITO Revolution was a global proof for the concepts that were the drivers for the massive and speculative investments that were a highly public feature of the ITO Revolution. As the ITO Revolution emerged into the Return stage, it was apparent to many of the survivors that after the highs and lows of great distance, we had arrived at market that appeared very much like the market when the revolution started. The telecom structure of the U.S. market did not look dramatically different from ten years earlier. Many of the problems regarding application efficiency over the internet existed prior to the internet when companies were building private wide area networks. The availability of the network connectivity options and the high cost of high-speed connectivity options look similar to the problems of ten years ago. The only real difference is that the speeds are faster and capacities increased. A high-speed OC-192 circuit is expensive today as was an OC-3 circuit ten years ago. Fiber is concentrated in pockets, but it is not universally available. There are a great many difficult challenges to be solved in the ITO markets. The real outcome of the ITO Revolution was the realization of what remains to be done, what is possible, and the complexity of the vast amount of work that remains. This leads to the inevitable conclusion that the ITO markets have a long and healthy life-span ahead for those companies that apply themselves to solving the difficult challenges. These challenges are both technical and regulatory.

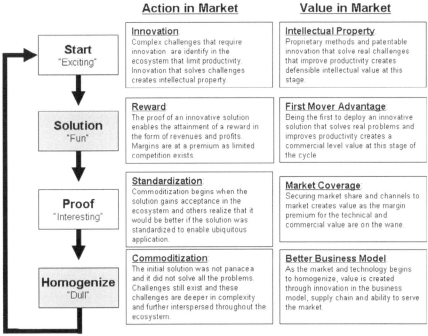

Figure 54: Innovation Value Life Cycle
Source: *Extrapolated and expanded from a model developed by Larry Samberg*

The above chart reflects a model for understanding how innovation and commoditization interplay in the problem solving life-cycle of technology. The forces of innovation and commoditization are opposing forces. The pull of these two forces dictate when and where value is created. In the beginning of the cycle a problem is identified and solution is created. This is the point at which innovation occurs. Innovation leads to intellectual property value via patents, which then leads to the creation of intellectual capital. The process of creating a solution is usually the most exciting part of the process. When innovation provides a solution that solves a business need, the next step is deployment. When a technology company has a first mover advantage in the market with an innovative, proprietary solution that solves a problem and this solution is accepted, value is created and rewards are achieved. Two great examples from the ITO Revolution for this phase of the cycle are US Robotics and Cisco Systems.

US Robotics was the first to market with a 56k modem – even though US Robotics did not implement the industry standard upon which a consortium of allied modem manufactures were collaborating. USR solved the complex 56k chip problem first, beat the consortium to the market, and received a substantial reward from market for their solution. When the other suppliers brought their 56k modems to the market – they realized they had lost because US Robotics had acquired a defensible market share and created a brand around their 56k modem product. Cisco Systems was the first company to bring to market a robust adaptation of a routing protocol called IRGP. IGRP was an enhanced version of the RIP 1 routing protocol with a number of proprietary enhancements that solved real problems that limited the scalability of RIP 1. IGRP provided Cisco with a significant innovative advantage that they used to capture market share. In time, the other router companies positioned IGRP as proprietary and pushed for standardization of routing protocols which led with RIP 2, OSPF, and a host of other standards. This is the third phase of the innovation cycle. When a technology company innovates, competitors will seize the technology to copy it or standardize it in the name of interoperability. Interoperability is a code word for declining margins and a reduced competitive advantage through innovation in the market. At this point in the innovation cycle value is created – not from technical innovation, but rather from business innovation within the chain of commerce.

In the last step of the innovation cycle two conclusions are realized. The first is that the mass deployment of commoditized technology is really the work of companies that innovate within the supply chain and excel in cost leadership and operating efficiency. Signs of this stage include actions such as outsourcing, off-shore development, and business downsizing. It is also at this point in the innovation cycle that the innovators realize that all challenges have not been solved. The original innovation did solve a problem or set of problems, but upon closer inspection the deployment of the innovative technology has revealed a deeper set of challenges to be solved. These challenges are deeper in complexity and usually further interspersed. The more times technology vertical markets move through the innovation cycle, the more complex and larger in scope the problems become. This is the fundamental reason why the ITO markets have a long, sustainable future ahead of them. The problems are not solved. Everything does not work and only now are the revolutionaries and the intellectuals of the ITO markets realizing the complexity of the challenges that lay ahead. This is why BT is willing to spend billions of dollars fixing their network. This is also way regulatory bodies in the UK demanded from BT concessions to ensure that a competitive market structure was created. These two developments are not wonderful endorsements of the ITO Revolution – but rather an admission that there is a vast amount of work to done.

Another perspective of the innovation cycle is to identify where and how value is created at each stage. For the venture capitalists and private equity people who consider themselves revolutionaries and intellectuals – investments in the ITO markets can still yield substantial value and drive an overall healthy ecosystem. At each stage of the innovation cycle, companies need to realize how value is created and quantified.

Conclusion

The telecom industry and the adjacent technology markets which created the market ecosystem have changed significantly post the market correction and entrance into the Decline stage (i.e. 2001) of the ITO Revolution. Four years after the market correction began the U.S. market structure for telecom, and technology has returned to a period of normalized investment in networking, computer and technology infrastructure. The current levels of investment are significantly less than the five years after the Telecom Act of 1996 – but there is sustained investment occurring at historical, normalized rates of growth. This is the difference between the speculative days of the ITO Revolution and the historical growth metrics of the technology related industries. Globally, telecom and technology investment continues to rise as emerging markets add networking infrastructure and new markets such as nation-states that emerged from the Warsaw Pact, and the former Soviet Union began a complete upgrade of their network and computing infrastructure.

The market direction post the ITO Revolution suggests that a far-reaching reordering of the telecom and technology markets is underway. The U.S. technology market is no longer the single largest consumer of technology and U.S. centric technology companies must be acutely aware of major shift in the market dynamics of the technology industry. Technology companies that have long relied on intellectual capital as a competitive advantage are now facing a world in which that very advantage has been minimized and the challenges to be a global supplier of technology have become business centric as opposed to technology centric. In the past, companies could rely on value creation through the innovative creation of intellectual property and commercialization of intellectual property into products and solutions. The relentless drive for technology standards and interoperability has a long term detrimental affect on the companies that create value through innovation. If the value of innovation is marginalized through standardization – the new market structure then rewards companies that derive a competitive advantage from a better operating model opposed to better intellectual capital. The choice that companies must face is to solve more difficult problems or build a better business model – doing both is typically out of the reach of most companies.

The challenge for technology companies is not as simple as developing a technical advantage and then capitalizing on this advantage in the market. The new challenges facing technology companies are far more complex. Building an efficient technology company that is capable of sustained, profitable growth as a global technology supplier requires an understanding of market forces as well as the adoption of a business model that aligns internal structures that leverage competitive advantages and a pull economic business model. The alternative to this strategy is to fall victim to the changing global market for technology companies and the new competitive forces that are emerging in major global markets beyond the U.S. market. In the past it was sufficient for U.S. based technology companies to be strong in their home market and look to international markets for supplemental growth. Globalization and the size of emerging markets in Eastern Europe and the Asia-Pacific regions are equal to or greater than the U.S. market. It is quite plausible to theorize that these markets will eventually assume the mantle of leadership as the primary driver of technology standards as their consumption of technology eclipses the rate of U.S. technology consumption. Global markets and the competitive forces emerging from strong international markets is why there must be linkage between the foreign policy of the U.S. and the objectives of our commercial industries. The economic pressures emerging from globalization and the foreign policies of the U.S. are not mutually exclusive.

Telecom, networking and technology investment are not declining. The crash of the technology bubble was product of unrealized expectations – rather than an incorrect business supposition. The sudden decline of the technology industry and the global recession within the technology industry that followed, led intellectuals who once extolled the ITO Revolution to declare the revolution over and a failure. Once upon a time, predications of new economy and a global revolution based on digital technology and optics reined upon the world – the crash of the technology industry brought forth the naysayers and pundits of disillusionment with equal vigor. The technology industries are not in the twilight of their life as was the transatlantic passenger ship business at the dawn of the commercial jet aviation. The global market for telecom and technology has emerged from an extended turning point that was the transition between technology and telecom's first epoch (1971 to 2001) and embarking on its new epoch that will last another thirty years. Carlota Perez describes this next period as time of institutional recomposition. It is the emergence of the second golden era for telecom and technology post the market correction (i.e. turning point). It is an era of big companies that have the size, scope, and reach to be a global suppliers and leaders. Derived from the G3 Market Model and Perez's model, we are entering the market structure that will in time lead to the formation of old regimes. There are complex problems that need to be solved in the market of technology infrastructure. The solution to these problems will emerge in the form of innovation. Companies that provide innovative solutions to complex problems will find a sustainable business model. The difference is that innovation may become specific to markets in India and China and then exported to the U.S. market – rather than the inverse which was the de facto standard from the past thirty years. This is the effect of globalization. The new global market structure for technology is not without significant challenges and the leading technology companies must respond to a market structure that is unfamiliar for the technology and telecom business – but not unfamiliar for U.S. companies. There is a historical record to review for U.S. companies facing commoditization of networking and computer technology. This is the record of the rise of the U.S. consumer electronics industry, its decline, and reemergence in recent years as an offspring of innovation.

If the technology markets evolve in the same manner as the consumer electronics market, it does not mean that U.S. based suppliers will withdraw from the market. It means U.S. based technology suppliers will be forced to adopt a more aggressive business model and leverage their strengths. One of the pillars of strength of the U.S. business model is the ability of U.S. corporations to solve complex problems. As a society, the U.S. has always had an affinity for complex problems such as democracy, the Bill of Rights, the Manhattan Project, and the Apollo Program to name a few. There has been a closing of the intellectual gap that separated U.S. based technology suppliers from their global rivals in developing markets. As such, U.S. based companies will need to focus on the aspects of their business that they do well, which are innovation and software. Software for computers and systems is an arbitrary, complex, virtual creation. Who would have thought five, ten, twenty years ago that companies such as Apple, Eastman Kodak, and palmOne would be consider consumer electronic leaders? Today, these companies are leaders in digital music players, digital cameras, and digital PDAs. Sony and Panasonic are not the innovative leaders in these product verticals. The answer lies in the software and innovation. The complexity of the software required to build these machines has risen significantly, while the hardware and manufacturing barriers have remained low. To be successful in the consumer electronics market requires the rapid creation of complex software that makes the new age of consumer electronic products easy to use. U.S. companies have leveraged their software development skills to open an intellectual gap over their foreign rivals, while incorporating the same development cycles and manufacturing processes which their foreign rivals used to create value in the last stage of the innovation cycle.

There has been an acute global market correction in regard to the price of technology. To understand the market correction and the affect it has had on market price points is not as simple as supply and demand. The easy analysis is to believe that the price of optical systems has fallen because there were too many suppliers. The price of bandwidth has fallen because there is a fiber glut. Oversupply is the conventional wisdom. In some cases there is a fiber glut in specific locations, but there is still a significant and reoccurring need to deploy optical systems. The fiber and physical copper plant used to network end-users does not provide universal service. Fiber does not reach all end-users in the U.S. market and in many metro areas the copper infrastructure is more than thirty years old. The market altering event that has occurred is in relation to the intellectual capital required to develop and build networking technology. To understand the decline in price, we should look to the past to understand the future market structure for telecom and technology companies.

For the past thirty to forty years, Japan has ruled the consumer electronics industry. This was an industry that was once led by U.S. companies. The emergence of Japanese suppliers, who mastered the art of engineering, manufacturing, and product life-cycle management, forced their competitors from the market because they were able to (a) engineer products faster and (b) manufacture at lower cost than any of their rivals. Companies such as Sony and Panasonic were able to develop products for the market inside of their rivals O-O-D-A loop. They changed the structure of the market and dramatically affected the business model required to be successful in the consumer electronics market. Companies that could not create a business model that engineered faster, manufactured cheaper, and achieved profitability within that market structure, were resigned to failure. The same transformation is occurring within the networking and technology markets. In the global drive to create international standards for technology and networking, the result of standardization is that the innovative barrier to entering technology markets is being removed. If there is a technical standard, the leading suppliers have the best business model and the product differentiation is minimized. In the networking industry there are two rules that govern technical standards. The first rule is the efforts to standardize technology and interoperability by the various international standards organizations does achieve interoperability – but it also homogenizes technology. The second rule is the rule of the Cisco.

The size and dominance of Cisco Systems as a supplier of networking technology is unquestioned, but their position does not insulate Cisco from being vulnerable to attack by new suppliers. The business plan to compete against Cisco would be to build competitive products based on the Cisco standard and do so at lower cost points. Create a company that matches Cisco's products feature for feature with the same look and feel and build these products faster and cheaper than Cisco. Compete on price using a more efficient business model. This is how companies such as Hitachi competed against IBM mainframes in the 1970s and this is how technology companies will compete against Cisco in the new millennium. Software will be written in India, hardware will be designed in China, manufacturing will be located in Korea, and products that are close to equal or equal to Cisco's products will be created at a fraction of the cost. The net result could be the same for the technology and networking industry as it was for the consumer electronics industry. Throughout the global market for technology companies, cost of equipment has become the governing decision making metric. *"Cost leadership is definitely a driver. Using Huawei's routers helps to simplify deployment rules and operations. They use the same management software across the whole Quidway range, and that helps to simplify network configuration,"* [see John Baldwin, Director Managed Data Services, COLT, March 2004]. When product price rules the market, there has been a migration away from innovation and focus on cost and efficiency. This does not mean that U.S. companies cannot compete in this market structure. Clearly Dell and Wal-Mart demonstrate that U.S. companies can execute and be global leaders in the last stage of the innovation cycle. The challenge for U.S. based technology companies is that this is not where their typical strengths are concentrated. To offset the drive to commoditize technology and move the market drivers to advantages of off-shore companies (i.e cost, manufacturing, supply chain), U.S. technology companies must return to their roots. Solving complex problems through creative innovation is how U.S. companies will respond to global challenges. *"Startups and gazelles exert competitive pressure on large companies. We all benefit. Example: For a decade now America's large telcos have yawned and dithered on supplying high-speed data lines to homes. It sickens one to learn that South Korea has more than 70% home penetration while we have a pathetic 15%. Worse, South Korea's fiber lines operate at much faster than our typical DSL and cable connections. In Seoul you can watch a soccer match on the Internet and catch every bead of goalie sweat,"* [see Rich Karlgaard, *Why we Need Startups*, Forbes, July 21, 2003].

On April 23, 1910 President Theodore Roosevelt addressed the University of Paris at the Sorbonne. Roosevelt's words on that day have not been long remember nor are they often quoted – but his words should be remembered and they should be read by all those who plot revolutions. Revolutions in business and technology are not evil. The revolutionaries who started a thousand dotcom companies and failed do not deserve our scorn, they desire our admiration. If one's intentions are noble, then one cannot fault effort – only the lack of effort. Roosevelt's words in Paris eloquently framed the human spirit to endure and fail and endure again. When the conditions for revolution converge again, the revolutionaries, the daring, the dreamers, will step forward to champion the banner of change. On that day in the month of April, 1910, President Roosevelt spoke the anthem for those who dare to attempt change. He said, "*It is not the critic who counts; not the man who points out how the strong man stumbles, or where the doer of deeds could have done them better. The credit belongs to the man who is actually in the arena, who's face is marred by dust and sweat and blood; who strives valiantly; who errs, and comes short again and again, because there is no effort without error and shortcoming; but who does actually strive to do the deeds; who knows the great enthusiasms, the great devotions; who spends himself in a worthy cause; who at the best knows in the end triumph of high achievement, and who at worst, if he fails, at least fails while daring greatly, so that his place shall never be with those cold and timid souls who know neither victory nor defeat.*"

Roosevelt continued in his speech to expose the virtues of leadership and democracy that is well intended and noble in nature. The leadership of a nation, a people, or a company that is drawn from a nation and a people must be considerate of the global community and the role that the policies, especially the foreign policy, of a nation-state play in the community of nation-states. "*The leaders of thought and of action grope their way forward to a new life, realizing, sometimes dimly, sometimes clear-sightedly, that the life of material gain, whether for a nation or an individual, is of value only as a foundation, only as there is added to it the uplift that comes from devotion to loftier ideals. The new life thus sought can in part be developed afresh from what is roundabout in the New World; but it can developed in full only by freely drawing upon the treasure-houses of the Old World, upon the treasures stored in the ancient abodes of wisdom and learning, such as this is where I speak to-day. It is a mistake for any nation to merely copy another; but it is even a greater mistake, it is a proof of weakness in any nation, not to be anxious to learn from one another and willing and able to adapt that learning to the new national conditions and make it fruitful and productive therein…Today I shall speak to you on the subject of individual citizenship, the one subject of vital importance to you, my hearers, and to me and my countrymen, because you and we a great citizens of great democratic republics. A democratic republic such as ours - an effort to realize its full sense government by, of, and for the people - represents the most gigantic of all possible social experiments, the one fraught with great responsibilities alike for good and evil. The success or republics like yours and like ours means the glory, and our failure of despair, of mankind; and for you and for us the question of the quality of the individual citizen is supreme…The average citizen must be a good citizen if our republics are to succeed. The stream will not permanently rise higher than the main source; and the main source of national power and national greatness is found in the average citizenship of the nation. Therefore it behooves us to do our best to see that the standard of the average citizen is kept high; and the average cannot be kept high unless the standard of the leaders is very much higher…It is well if a large proportion of the leaders in any republic, in any democracy, are, as a matter of course, drawn from the classes represented in this audience to-day; but only provided that those classes possess the gifts of sympathy with plain people and of devotion to great ideals. You and those like you have received special advantages; you have all of you had the opportunity for mental training; many of you have had leisure; most of you have had a chance for enjoyment of life far greater than comes to the majority of your fellows. To you and your kind much has been given, and from you much should be expected. Yet there are certain failings against which it is especially incumbent that both men of trained and cultivated intellect, and men of inherited wealth and position should especially guard themselves, because to these failings they are especially liable; and if yielded to, their- your- chances of useful service are at an end. Let the man of learning, the man of lettered leisure, beware of that queer and cheap temptation to pose to himself and to others as a cynic, as the man who has outgrown emotions and beliefs, the man to whom good and evil are as one. The poorest way to face life is to face it with a sneer. There are many men who feel a kind of twister pride in cynicism; there are many who confine themselves to criticism of the way others do what they themselves dare not even attempt. There is no more unhealthy being, no man less worthy of respect, than he who either really holds, or feigns to hold, an attitude of sneering disbelief toward all that is great and lofty, whether in achievement or in that noble effort which, even if it fails, comes to second achievement. A cynical habit of thought and speech, a readiness to criticise work which the critic himself never tries to perform, an intellectual aloofness which will not accept contact with life's realities - all these are marks, not as the possessor would fain to think, of superiority but of weakness. They mark the men unfit to bear their part painfully in the stern strife of living, who seek, in the affection of contempt for the achievements of others, to hide from others and from themselves in their own weakness. The rôle is easy; there is none easier, save only the rôle of the man who sneers alike at both criticism and performance."*

A homogenized world composed of neither victors nor losers is a terrible place to be. It would be a world without passion, without fun, without drive, and leaves us in an emotional state. Revolutions are emotional events. The human condition is capable of extraordinary creation when it is passionate. Revolutionaries and intellectuals who dare attempt change are products of a passionate belief held close and dear.

The U.S. based technology companies and the financial community that supports these companies have a lot of work before them. The time for sorrow and sympathy over the collapse of the ITO Revolution is over. U.S. companies need to stand up and seek the driver of change. Change is coming every day to their markets throughout the global community. In April 2005 I traveled to Beijing to look at a technology company that was partially funded by a U.S. based, global private equity firm. What I found was 700 development engineers building a clone of every Cisco product. They did not need market research. They did not need marketing. All they needed to do was look at the

Cisco product catalog and copy every product in the Cisco router and switch portfolio and some other products in the access and wireless portfolio. This company matched every feature within six months of Cisco adding a feature and claimed they were half the cost of Cisco products. Their loaded cost per engineer was $25,000 per year. They paid an excellent wage for the Chinese market and they offered stock options and lunch everyday for $1 per employee and claimed they were making a small profit on the lunch service they provided to their employees. What the company was missing was true innovation that could produce sustainable IPR. They were not advancing the technology of networking beyond what Cisco had, they were fast followers attempting to secure market share through a better, lower cost business model.

U.S. based technology companies cannot compete with the cost and efficiently of the business model I witnessed in China – but this does not mean U.S. technology companies cannot be successful. Returning to a focus on innovation and solving complex problems is the road to global dominance for U.S. technology companies. There are complex problems to be solved. The networks do not work well enough. Computing power has not been deployed and integrated into the network. The vast land of legacy infrastructure that has been deployed over the last thirty years needs to be refreshed and improved. No other nation-state can match our investment in research, and development. No other nation-state has an infrastructure built upon access to capital, to education, to research and business acumen that rewards innovation. The global economy will continue to grow and this growth will create never before competitive forces and market drivers from nation-states that in the past were followers, not leaders, but one constant will remain true; if companies produce innovative solutions to complex problems, these will lead to value creation and perhaps launch the next great revolutionary cycle. The cycle of innovation and entrepreneurial investments place U.S. companies on a steeper learning curve. We must learn to optimize and improve the advantages that this market structure provides and the answers may not be found in the U.S. market first. *"The strength of the American economy over the next twenty years depends largely on our ability to keep our productivity growing. And productivity grows when a large set of novel technologies changes business practices and creates new industries,"* [see W. Brian Arthur, *Why Tech is Still the Future*, Fortune, November 24, 2003]. Our leaders and our government must realize that the foreign policy of the United States must be formed in conjunction with our economic polices. This is not a plea for protectionist legislation – but rather an opinion that democracy is best promoted through good practices and global thought leadership. There is a time for war, but the policies of war must be subservient to the citizens of the nation-state and the promotion of a high-order of ideals, values, and objectives for the nation-state. The global revolution can be won by providing economic determination and the spirit of hope in the individual that that in the end, they or their children will be better off than when they started. This is called a democracy.

- Boston Massachusetts, April 2006

CHARTS AND MODELS

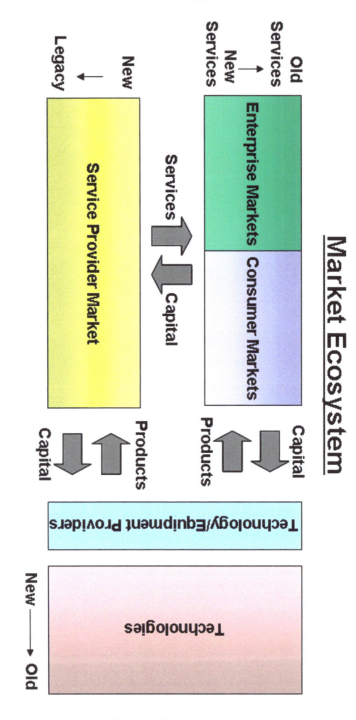

Chart 1: Market Ecosystem

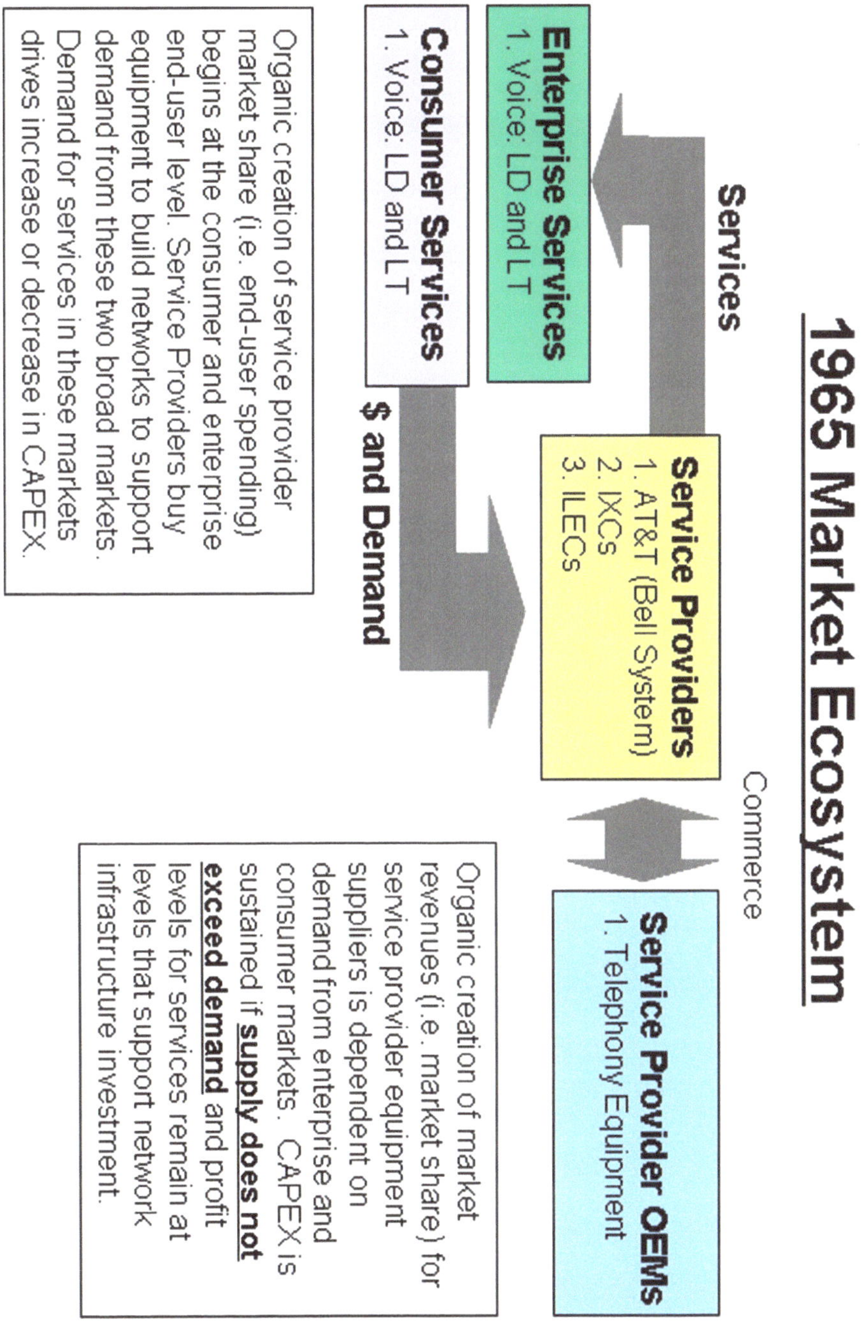

1965 Market Ecosystem

Services

Enterprise Services
1. Voice: LD and LT

Consumer Services
1. Voice: LD and LT

$ and Demand

Organic creation of service provider market share (i.e. end-user spending) begins at the consumer and enterprise end-user level. Service Providers buy equipment to build networks to support demand from these two broad markets. Demand for services in these markets drives increase or decrease in CAPEX.

Commerce

Service Providers
1. AT&T (Bell System)
2. IXCs
3. ILECs

Service Provider OEMs
1. Telephony Equipment

Organic creation of market revenues (i.e. market share) for service provider equipment suppliers is dependent on demand from enterprise and consumer markets. CAPEX is sustained if **supply does not exceed demand** and profit levels for services remain at levels that support network infrastructure investment.

Chart 2: 1965 Market Ecosystem

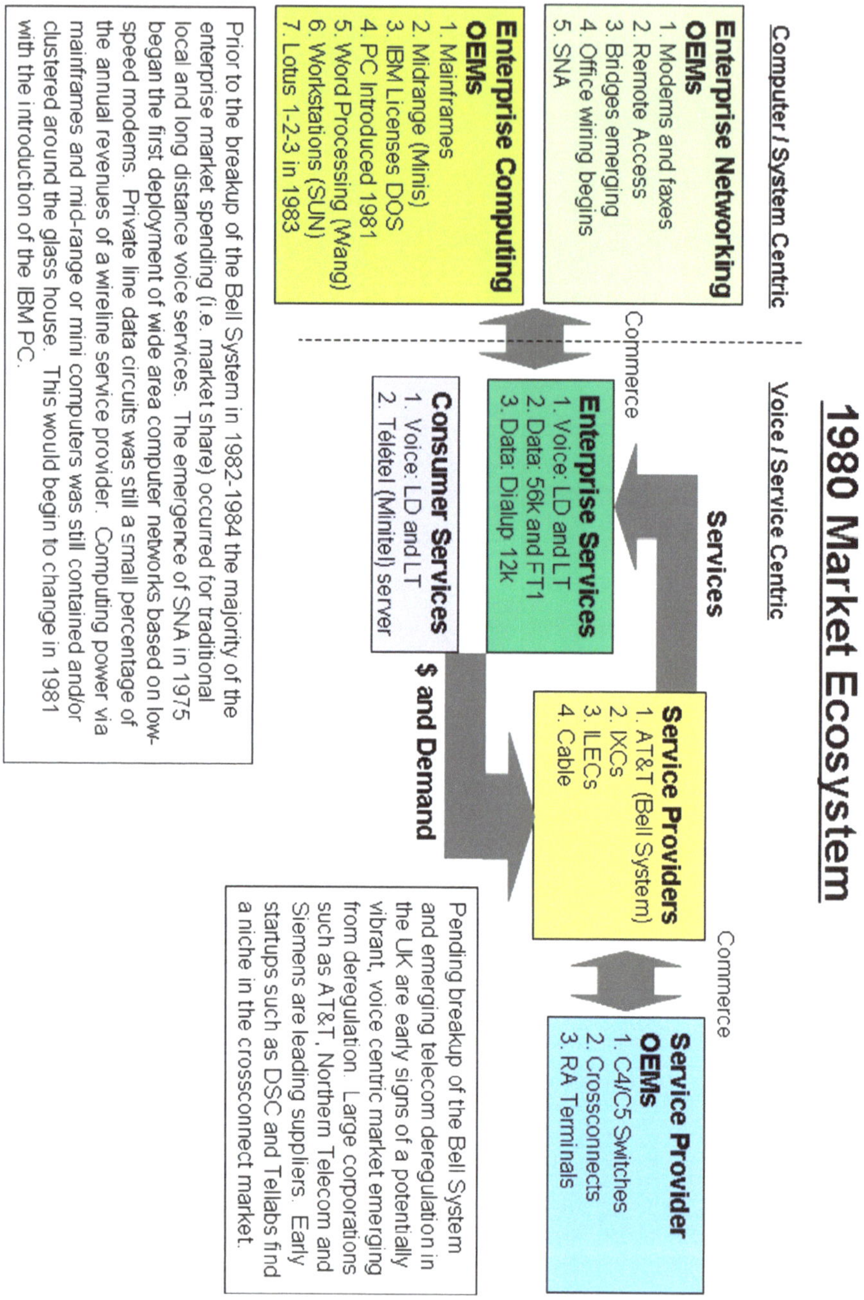

1980 Market Ecosystem

Computer / System Centric | Voice / Service Centric

Enterprise Networking OEMs
1. Modems and faxes
2. Remote Access
3. Bridges emerging
4. Office wiring begins
5. SNA

Enterprise Computing OEMs
1. Mainframes
2. Midrange (Minis)
3. IBM Licenses DOS
4. PC Introduced 1981
5. Word Processing (Wang)
6. Workstations (SUN)
7. Lotus 1-2-3 in 1983

Prior to the breakup of the Bell System in 1982-1984 the majority of the enterprise market spending (i.e. market share) occurred for traditional local and long distance voice services. The emergence of SNA in 1975 began the first deployment of wide area computer networks based on low-speed modems. Private line data circuits was still a small percentage of the annual revenues of a wireline service provider. Computing power via mainframes and mid-range or mini computers was still contained and/or clustered around the glass house. This would begin to change in 1981 with the introduction of the IBM PC.

Commerce

Enterprise Services
1. Voice: LD and LT
2. Data: 56k and FT1
3. Data: Dialup 12k

Consumer Services
1. Voice: LD and LT
2. Télétel (Minitel) server

Services

Service Providers
1. AT&T (Bell System)
2. IXCs
3. ILECs
4. Cable

$ and Demand

Commerce

Service Provider OEMs
1. C4/C5 Switches
2. Crossconnects
3. RA Terminals

Pending breakup of the Bell System and emerging telecom deregulation in the UK are early signs of a potentially vibrant, voice centric market emerging from deregulation. Large corporations such as AT&T, Northern Telecom and Siemens are leading suppliers. Early startups such as DSC and Tellabs find a niche in the crossconnect market.

Chart 3: 1980 Market Ecosystem

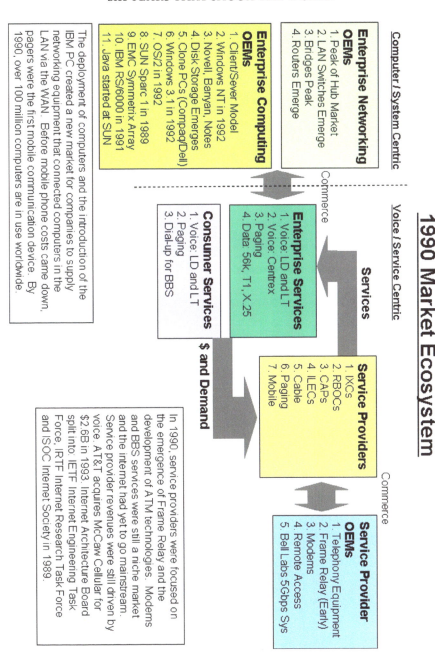

1990 Market Ecosystem

Computer / System Centric

Enterprise Networking OEMs
1. Peak of Hub Market
2. LAN Switches Emerge
3. Bridges Peak
4. Routers Emerge

Enterprise Computing OEMs
1. Client/Sever Model
2. Windows NT in 1992
3. Novell, Banyan, Notes
4. Disk Storage Emerges
5. Clone PCs (Compaq/Dell)
6. Windows 3.1 in 1992
7. OS/2 in 1992
8. SUN Sparc 1 in 1989
9. EMC Symmetrix Array
10. IBM RS/6000 in 1991
11. Java started at SUN

The deployment of computers and the introduction of the IBM PC created a new market for companies to supply networking equipment that connected computers in the LAN via the WAN. Before mobile phone costs came down, pagers were the first mobile communication device. By 1990, over 100 million computers are in use worldwide.

Voice / Service Centric

Commerce

Services

Enterprise Services
1. Voice: LD and LT
2. Voice: Centrex
3. Paging
4. Data: 56k, T1, X.25

Consumer Services
1. Voice: LD and LT
2. Paging
3. Dial-up for BBS

$ and Demand

Service Providers
1. IXCs
2. RBOCs
3. CAPs
4. ILECs
5. Cable
6. Paging
7. Mobile

Commerce

In 1990, service providers were focused on the emergence of Frame Relay and the development of ATM technologies. Modems and BBS services were still a niche market and the internet had yet to go mainstream. Service provider revenues were still driven by voice. AT&T acquires McCaw Cellular for $2.6B in 1993. Internet Architecture Board split into: IETF Internet Engineering Task Force, IRTF Internet Research Task Force and ISOC Internet Society in 1989.

Service Provider OEMs
1. Telephony Equipment
2. Frame Relay (Early)
3. Modems
4. Remote Access
5. Bell Labs 5Gbps Sys

Chart 4: 1990 Market Ecosystem

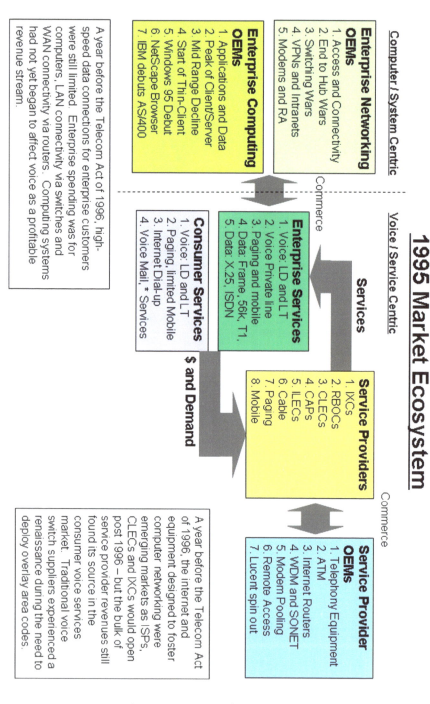

Chart 5: 1995 Market Ecosystem

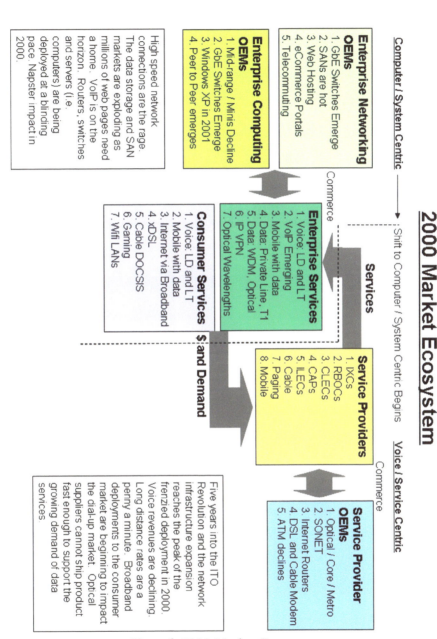

2000 Market Ecosystem

Computer / System Centric ⟶ Shift to Computer / System Centric Begins   Voice / Service Centric

Commerce

Commerce

Services

$ and Demand

Enterprise Networking OEMs
1. GbE Switches Emerge
2. SANs are hot
3. Web Hosting
4. eCommerce Portals
5. Telecommuting

Enterprise Computing OEMs
1. Mid-range / Minis Decline
2. GbE Switches Emerge
3. Windows XP in 2001
4. Peer to Peer emerges

High speed network connections are the rage. The data storage and SAN markets are exploding as millions of web pages need a home. VoIP is on the horizon. Routers, switches and servers (i.e. computers) are being deployed at a blinding pace. Napster impact in 2000.

Enterprise Services
1. Voice: LD and LT
2. VoIP Emerging
3. Mobile with data
4. Data Private Line, T1
5. Data: WDM, Optical
6. IP VPN
7. Optical Wavelengths

Consumer Services
1. Voice: LD and LT
2. Mobile with data
3. Internet via Broadband
4. xDSL
5. Cable DOCSIS
6. Gaming
7. Wifi LANs

Service Providers
1. IXCs
2. RBOCs
3. CLECs
4. CAPs
5. ILECs
6. Cable
7. Paging
8. Mobile

Service Provider OEMs
1. Optical / Core / Metro
2. SONET
3. Internet Routers
4. DSL and Cable Modem
5. ATM declines

Five years into the ITO Revolution and the network infrastructure expansion reaches the peak of the frenzied deployment in 2000. Voice revenues are declining. Long distance rates are a penny a minute. Broadband deployments to the consumer market are beginning to impact the dial-up market. Optical suppliers cannot ship product fast enough to support the growing demand of data services.

Chart 6: 2000 Market Ecosystem

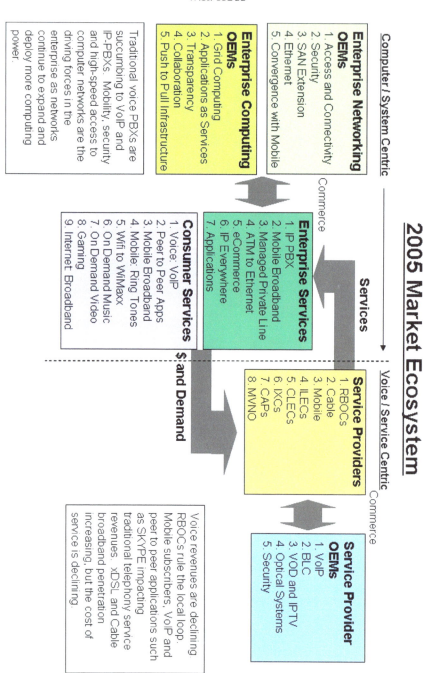

Chart 7: 2005 Market Ecosystem

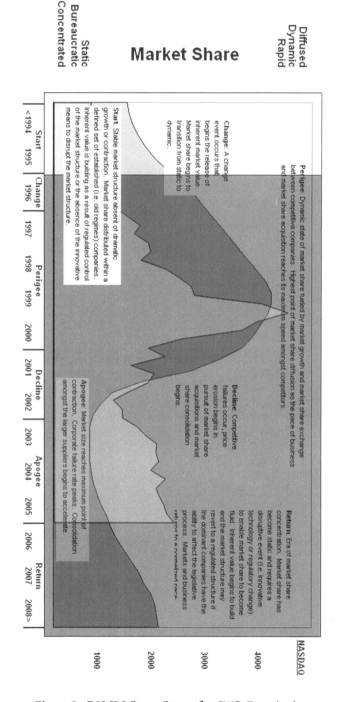

Chart 8: G3MM Start Stage for ITO Revolution

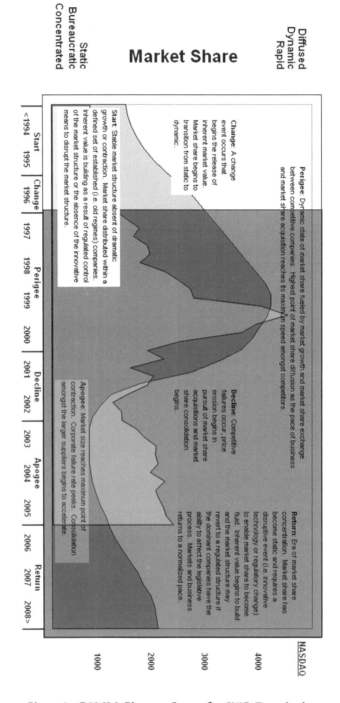

Chart 9: G3MM Change Stage for ITO Revolution

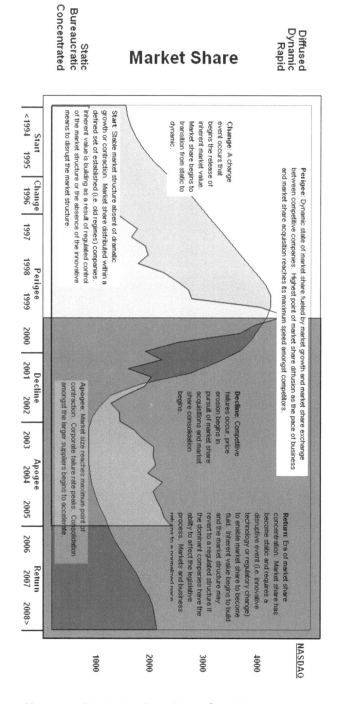

Chart 10: G3MM Perigee Stage for ITO Revolution

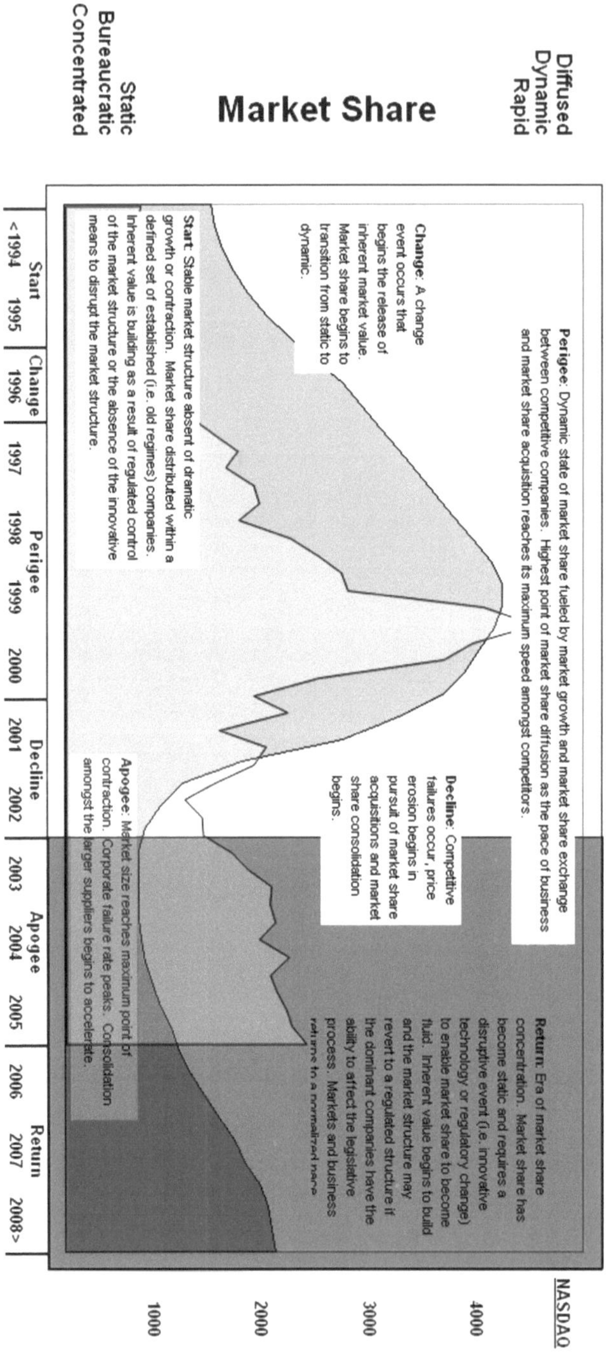

Market Share

Diffused
Dynamic
Rapid

Static
Bureaucratic
Concentrated

Perigee: Dynamic state of market share fueled by market growth and market share exchange between competitive companies. Highest point of market share diffusion as the pace of business and market share acquisition reaches its maximum speed amongst competitors.

Change: A change event occurs that begins the release of inherent market value. Market share begins to transition from static to dynamic.

Start: Stable market structure absent of dramatic growth or contraction. Market share distributed within a defined set of established (i.e. old regimes) companies. Inherent value is building as a result of regulated control of the market structure or the absence of the innovative means to disrupt the market structure.

Decline: Competitive failures occur, price erosion begins in pursuit of market share acquisitions and market share consolidation begins.

Apogee: Market size reaches maximum point of contraction. Corporate failure rate peaks. Consolidation amongst the larger suppliers begins to accelerate.

Return: Era of market share concentration. Market share has become static and requires a disruptive event (i.e. innovative technology or regulatory change) to enable market share to become fluid. Inherent value begins to build and the market structure may revert to a regulated structure if the dominant companies have the ability to affect the legislative process. Markets and business returns to a normalized pace.

Start			Change				Perigee				Decline			Apogee				Return	
<1994	1995	1996	1997	1998	1999	2000	2001	2002	2003	2004	2005	2006	2007	2008>

NASDAQ

1000   2000   3000   4000

Chart 11: G3MM Decline Stage for ITO Revolution

374

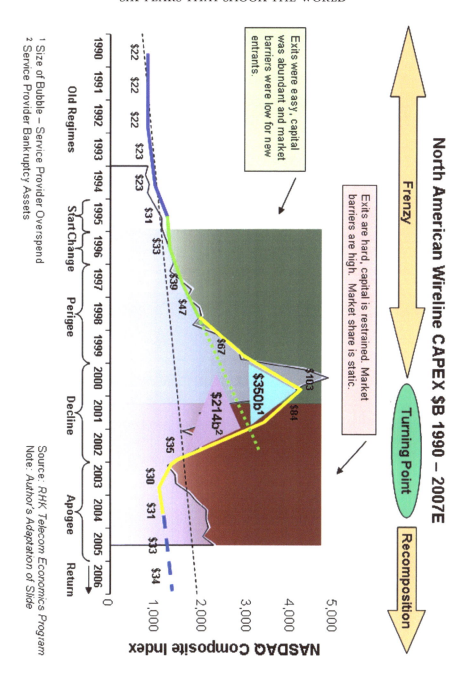

Chart 12: North American Service Provider CAPEX Model

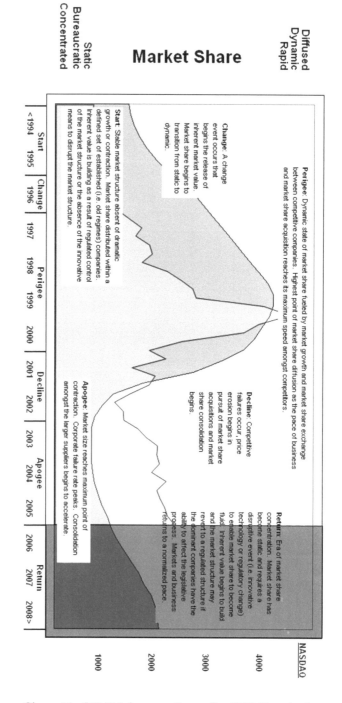

Chart 13: G3MM Apogee Stage for ITO Revolution

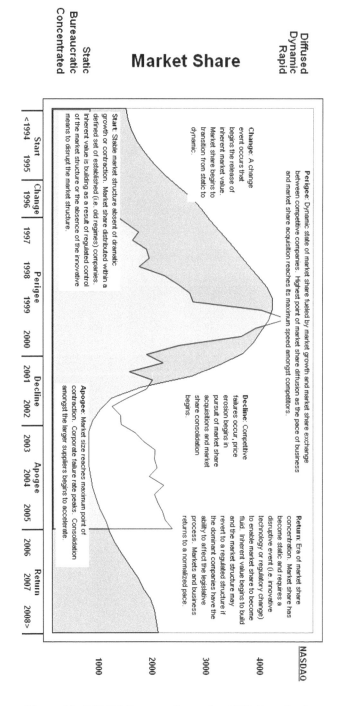

Market Share

Diffused
Dynamic
Rapid

Static
Bureaucratic
Concentrated

Perigee: Dynamic state of market share fueled by market growth and market share exchange between competitive companies. Highest point of market share diffusion as the pace of business and market share acquisition reaches its maximum speed amongst competitors.

Change: A change event occurs that begins the release of inherent market value. Market share begins to transition from static to dynamic.

Start: Stable market structure absent of dramatic growth or contraction. Market share distributed within a defined set of established (i.e. old regimes) companies. Inherent value is building as a result of regulated control of the market structure or the absence of the innovative means to disrupt the market structure.

Decline: Competitive failures occur, price erosion begins in pursuit of market share acquisitions and market share consolidation begins.

Return: Era of market share concentration. Market share has become static and requires a disruptive event (i.e. innovative technology or regulatory change) to enable market share to become fluid. Inherent value begins to build and the market structure may revert to a regulated structure if the dominant companies have the ability to affect the legislative process. Markets and business returns to a normalized pace.

Apogee: Market size reaches maximum point of contraction. Corporate failure rate peaks. Consolidation amongst the larger suppliers begins to accelerate.

Start		Change		Perigee			Decline			Apogee			Return	
<1994	1995	1996	1997	1998	1999	2000	2001	2002	2003	2004	2005	2006	2007	2008>

NASDAQ

4000

3000

2000

1000

Chart 14: G3MM Return Stage for ITO Revolution

	Start 1995	Change 1996	1997	Perigee 1998	1999	2000	Decline 2001	2002	2003	Apogee 2004	2005	Return 2006
Tier 1 >$2B Quarters	ALA, LU, ERICY, NT	LU, ALA, ERICY, NT	LU, ALA, ERICY, NT	LU, ALA, ERICY, NT, CSCO	LU, ERICY, ALA, NT, CSCO	LU, ERICY, ALA, NT, CSCO, MOT	ALA, CSCO, ERICY, LU, NT, MOT, NOK	CSCO, ALA, ERICY, LU, NT, NOK, MOT	CSCO, ERICY, ALA, NT, LU, UTSI, ZTE, NOK, MOT, AV	CSCO, ERICY, ALA, NT, LU, NOK, MOT, AV, ZTE, UTSI	CSCO, ERICY, ALA, NT, MOT, LU, NOK, AV, UTSI, ZTE	CSCO, ALA (LU), ERICY, NT, MOT, NOK (SIE), AV, UTSI, ZTE
Tier 2 $300-$1.5B Quarters	NOK, MOT, CSCO, COMS, BAY, NN	CSCO, COMS, NOK, MOT, BAY, NN, CS	CSCO, MOT, COMS, NOK, BAY, NN, CS, TLAB, ASND	MOT, NOK, COMS, TLAB, ADCT, ASND, CS	MOT, COMS, TLAB, ADCT, NN, CS, CIEN, ADTN	COMS, TLAB, ADCT, CS, JNPR, ADTN, EXTR, SCMR	AV, ADCT, TLAB, COMS, CIEN, JNPR, CS/ETS, UTSI, EXTR, ECIL, ADTN, FDRY, AFCI	ZTE, AV, TLAB, COMS, UTSI, ADCT, CIEN, JNPR, CS/ETS, EXTR, ECIL, ADTN, FDRY, AFCI	TLAB, ADCT, COMS, JNPR, ECIL, CS/ETS, ADTN, FDRY, EXTR, AFCI	JNPR, TLAB, ADCT, COMS, ECIL, CS/ETS, FDRY, EXTR, CIEN	JNPR, TLAB, ADCT, COMS, ECIL, CIEN, ADTN, FDRY, EXTR	JNPR, TLAB, ADCT, COMS, ECIL, CIEN, ADTN, FDRY, EXTR, ZHNE
Tier 3 $75-$275M Quarters	CS, TLAB, ADCT, NWK, FORE, ADTN, ASND, CASC, AFCI, XYLN	TLAB, ADCT, ASND, FORE, CASC, NWK, ADTN, AFCI, XYLN, CIEN	CIEN, FORE, NWK, AFCI, ADTN, XYLN, ATON, ADVA, RBAK	FORE, CIEN, XYLN, AFCI, NWK, ADTN, ATON, FDRY, ADVA, RBAK, JNPR, ARPT	AFCI, NWK, UTSI, EXTR, FDRY, JNPR, RBAK, SCMR, ATON, ONIS, ADVA, AVCI, ARPT	AFCI, FDRY, UTSI, RBAK, NWK, ADVA, RSTN, ONIS, CORV, AVCI, ZHNE	RBAK, ONIS, RSTN, CORV, SCMR, NWK, ZHNE, TELM, ADVA, AVCI	RBAK, CIEN, NWK, ZHNE, ADVA, RSTN, TELM, AVCI, SCMR, CORV	CIEN, NWK, RBAK, ADVA, ZHNE, RSTN, AVCI, SCMR, CORV, TELM	ADVA, NWK, RBAK, ZHNE, SCMR, AVCI	ADVA, RBAK, ZHNE, SCMR, NWK, AVCI	RBAK, ADVA, SCMR, NWK, AVCI
Tier 4 <$75M Quarters	AFCI, XYLN	XYLN, CIEN	ADVA, RBAK									
M&A			ASND/CASC	ALA/NN, ALA/XYLN, NT/BAY, ALA/DSC, MRCI/FORE	LU/ASND	ALA/INN, NT/ATON, CSCO/ARPT		CIEN/ONIS	ZHNE/TELM	TLAB/AFCI	LBO-CS/ETS, MRCI/ERCY	ALA/LU, TLAB/ECIL, NOK-SIE JV
Tier 1	78.52%	76.59%	72.63%	85.06%	84.96%	85.84%	85.49%	71.48%	72.32%	78.83%	78.35%	79.16%
Tier 2	16.94%	19.81%	25.79%	13.14%	12.99%	11.27%	9.39%	21.44%	21.04%	17.01%	17.50%	17.47%
Tier 3	3.36%	3.08%	0.98%	1.28%	1.12%	2.48%	4.13%	6.12%	5.70%	3.66%	3.59%	2.70%
Tier 4	1.18%	0.53%	0.60%	0.52%	0.91%	0.41%	0.99%	0.96%	0.93%	0.50%	0.56%	0.67%

Chart 15: Annual Revenue for Public OEMs

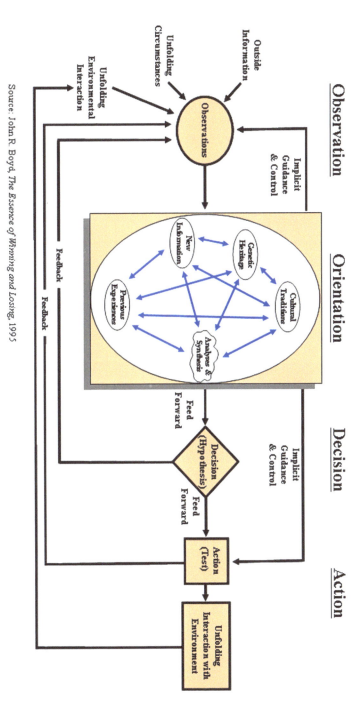

Source: John R. Boyd, *The Essence of Winning and Losing*, 1995

Chart 16: O-O-D-A Loop

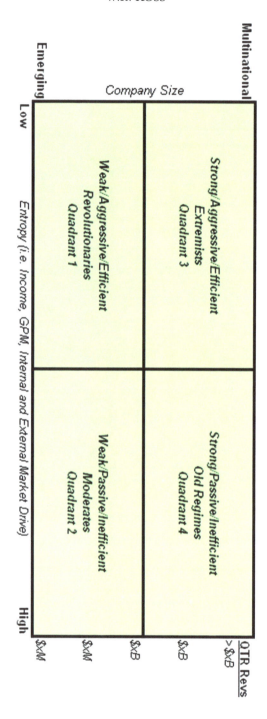

Chart 17: Entropy Base Model (EBM)

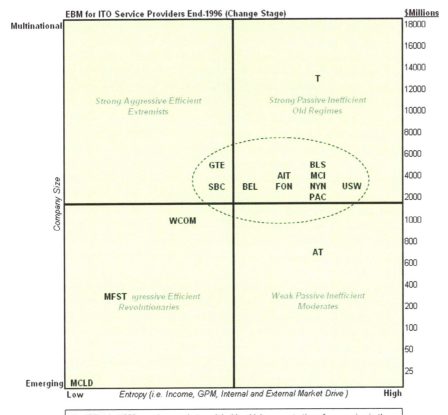

Chart 18: EBM for Service Providers, Change Stage

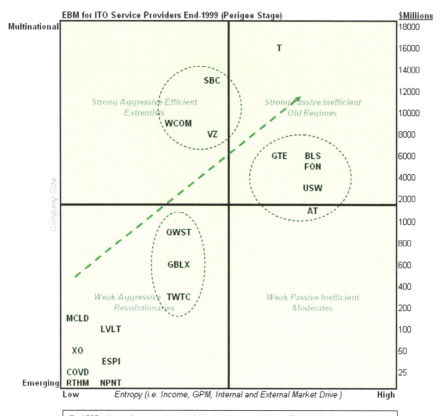

By 1999 a host of new service providers had become visible. The midlevel concentration seen in the first phase has broken apart with some companies using M&A to gain market share. AT&T (T) continues to set the pace as the largest service provider.

Chart 19: EBM for Service Providers, Perigee Stage

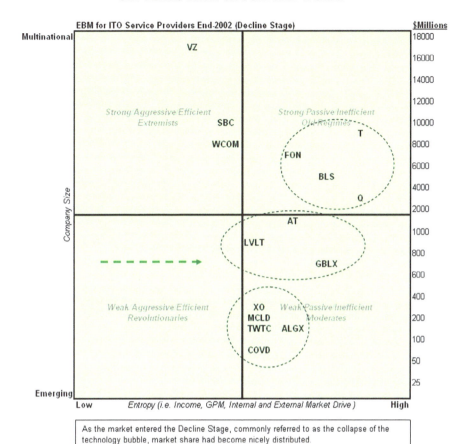

Chart 20: EBM for Service Providers, Decline Stage

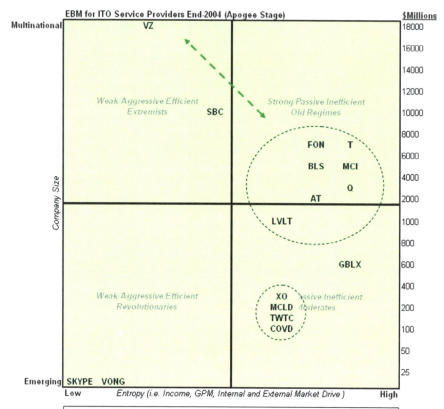

Chart 21: EBM for Service Providers, Apogee Stage

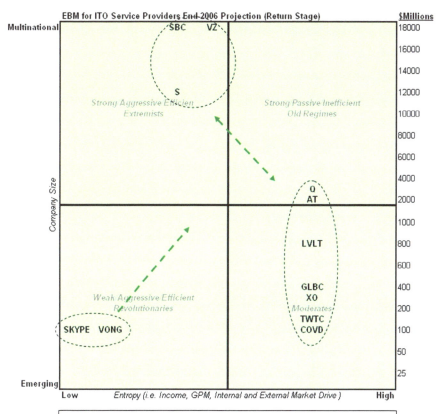

Chart 22: **EBM for Service Providers, Return Stage**

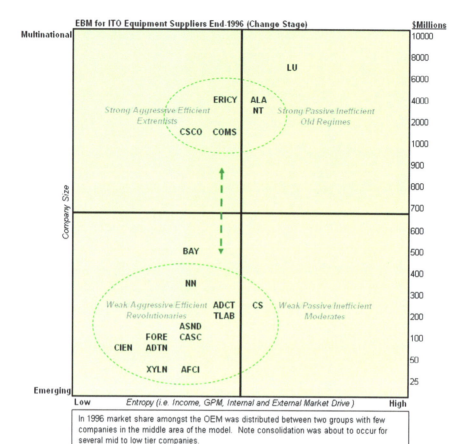

EBM for ITO Equipment Suppliers End-1996 (Change Stage)

In 1996 market share amongst the OEM was distributed between two groups with few companies in the middle area of the model. Note consolidation was about to occur for several mid to low tier companies.

Chart 23: EBM for Equipment Suppliers, Change Stage

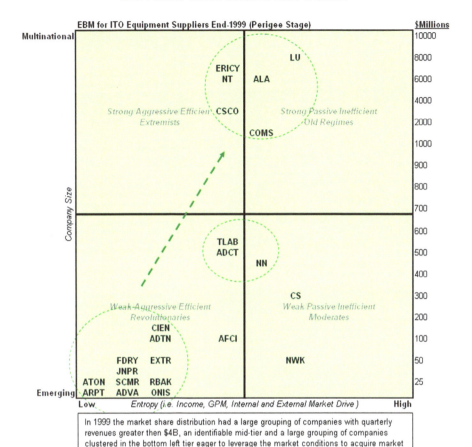

In 1999 the market share distribution had a large grouping of companies with quarterly revenues greater then $4B, an identifiable mid-tier and a large grouping of companies clustered in the bottom left tier eager to leverage the market conditions to acquire market share.

Chart 24: EBM for Equipment Suppliers, Perigee Stage

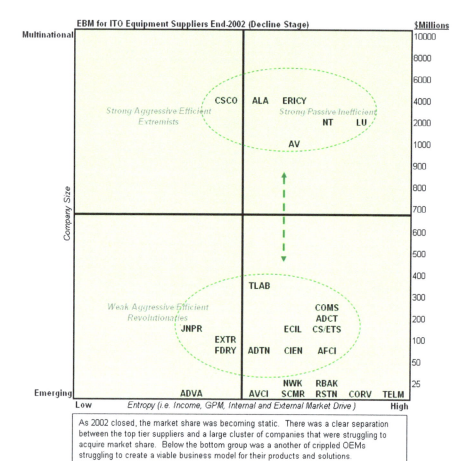

Chart 25: EBM for Equipment Suppliers, Decline Stage

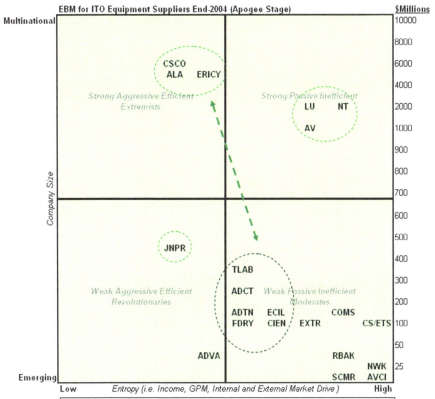

Chart 26: EBM for Equipment Suppliers, Apogee Stage

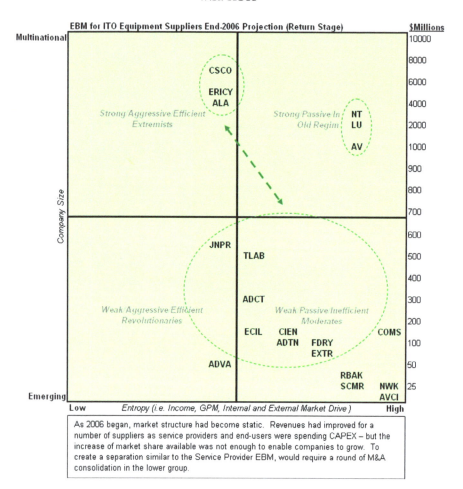

Chart 27: EBM for Equipment Suppliers, Return Stage

ABOUT THE AUTHOR

William R. Koss lives with his family in the Boston area. He has worked for CrossComm, Stratus, Sonoma Systems, Internet Photonics and Ciena in his fifteen year career in the technology and networking industry. He presently consults, writes and speaks for technology companies, private equity, and investment firms. He can be reached via email at wrkoss@gmail.com.

www.ingramcontent.com/pod-product-compliance
Lightning Source LLC
Chambersburg PA
CBHW041140050326
40689CB00001B/431